Hoodwinked

Other books by John Prados

Inside the Pentagon Papers (ed., with Margaret Pratt Porter)
The White House Tapes: Eavesdropping on the President (ed.)
Lost Crusader: The Secret Wars of CIA Director William Colby
Operation Vulture
America Confronts Terrorism (ed.)
The Blood Road: The Ho Chi Minh Trail and the Vietnam War
President's Secret Wars: CIA and Pentagon Covert Operations from World War II
    Through the Persian Gulf
Combined Fleet Decoded: The Secret History of U.S. Intelligence and the Japanese
    Navy in World War II
The Hidden History of the Vietnam War
Valley of Decision: The Siege of Khe Sanh (with Ray W. Stubbe)
Keepers of the Keys: A History of the National Security Council from Truman to Bush
Pentagon Games
The Soviet Estimate: U.S. Intelligence and Soviet Strategic Forces
The Sky Would Fall: The Secret U.S. Bombing Mission to Vietnam, 1954

Hoodwinked

The Documents That Reveal
How Bush Sold Us a War

———◆———

JOHN PRADOS

THE NEW PRESS

NEW YORK
LONDON

Published in the United States by The New Press, New York, 2004
Distributed by W. W. Norton & Company, Inc., New York

ISBN 1–56584–902–7 (pbk.)
ISBN 1–56584–931–0 (hc.)
CIP data available

The New Press was established in 1990 as a not-for-profit alternative to the large, commercial
publishing houses currently dominating the book publishing industry. The New Press operates
in the public interest rather than for private gain, and is committed to publishing, in
innovative ways, works of educational, cultural, and community value that are often deemed
insufficiently profitable.

The New Press
38 Greene Street, 4th floor
New York, NY 10013
www.thenewpress.com

In the United Kingdom:
6 Salem Road
London W2 4BU

Composition by Westchester Book Group

Printed in Canada

2 4 6 8 10 9 7 5 3 1

For a return to first principles

Beware that you do not lose the substance
By grasping
At the Shadow

Aesop

You load sixteen tons, what do you get?
Another day older and deeper in debt
Saint Peter don't you call me 'cause I can't go
I owe my soul to the company store

Tennessee Ernie Ford

Contents

Introduction

The day Saddam Hussein was captured in December of 2003, the *New York Times* editorialized: "Though the Hussein regime ended with the fall of Baghdad on April 9, many frustrating puzzles remain. These include the question of what happened to Iraq's unconventional weapons programs in recent years. Thanks to the Bush administration's mammoth propaganda campaign prior to the war, most Americans believe U.S. intelligence reports had already answered that question: Saddam Hussein's unconventional weapons program was alive and well, constituting a real and present threat to the United States and others as recently as April 2003. It is the fear inspired by this belief that George Bush and his colleagues played on in their efforts to win popular support for an unprovoked war.

What the intelligence record shows, however, is that contrary to the reports it put out, most of what the Bush administration knew indicated that Iraqi weapons programs were either nascent, moribund, or non-existent—exactly the opposite of the President's repeated message to Americans.

This book is an attempt to compile and share with the American public for the first time the actual intelligence available to the Bush administration as it made its case for war. It then aims to show how this information was consistently distorted, manipulated, and ignored, as the president, vice president, secretaries of defense and state, and others, sought to persuade the country that the facts about Iraq were other than what the intelligence indicated. The tale involves national leadership; manipulation of politics, diplomacy, and intelligence; and subornation of the best instincts of a generous people in service of a particular enterprise under false pretenses—a story with tremendous implications for America in the twenty-first century.

This book contains documents from the White House, Central Intelligence Agency, and State Department. Juxtaposed with these transcripts of speeches and statements made by members of the administration to Congress, to the UN, and to the nation at large, is evidence based on intelligence documents, some of which were originally classified, but all of which are now available, and other sources. Comparison of these two sets of primary source materials offers a case study in government dishonesty, which begs the question of why? Reconstructing the planning and preparations for war, and placing them in the context of evolving political and diplomatic opposition, makes clear that the succession of charges the Bush administration leveled against Iraq were offensive rather than defensive tactics: they were designed to create the conditions President Bush hoped would justify a war. This effort involved deception of the American people, and, as this account shows, that deception was systematic and carried out purposefully.

Critics have offered several explanations for the Bush administration's unswerving commitment to waging war on Saddam Hussein. These range from George W. Bush's personal desire to avenge Saddam Hussein's assassination plot against Bush's father in 1993, to "it's the oil, stupid," to other more complicated theories involving long-term strategies for affecting the balance of power in the Middle East. The jury is still out on the real reasons for war, and conclusions will have to await the emergence of the authoritative record of the Bush presidency. It is already clear, however, that Bush's postwar plans pale in comparison to his arrangements to make the war happen.

While it remains difficult to assign the motive for conflict, the evidence presented here shows conclusively that George W. Bush's devotion to attacking Saddam Hussein had little to do with the reasons given to the American public. The argument that Hussein's Iraq presented a threat on weapons of mass destruction has been described by a member of the administration, Undersecretary of Defense Paul D. Wolfowitz, as an excuse: "We settled on one issue, weapons of mass destruction, because it was the one reason everyone could agree on." Charges of chemical and biological weapons, viewed in light of U.S. intelligence reports, seem clearly to have been trumped up. The idea that Iraq possessed a single weapon that was an actual threat to the United States is shown to be entirely disputable, making the fact that the Bush administration implied a real threat to Americans that much more egregious.

Most Americans had no way of knowing what the Bush administration was privy to in the way of intelligence about Iraq, or of decoding the jargon and technical terms being tossed around so freely. It was also difficult to see the forest for the trees, because Bush's charges against Iraq swept past in a fierce torrent of daily sallies, with objections swept away by the rush of developments. Even today, most Americans fail to understand the degree to which the hoodwinking of America was systematically planned within the White House and carried out throughout the administration. This book aims to supply and decode the relevant documents, giving Americans the tools to make their own judgment.

This book comprises several different elements: An overarching narrative plotting the trajectory of the march up to and through the war; reprints of the key primary source documents—intelligence white papers, speeches, letters, fact sheets, and a key briefing to the United Nations Security Council—generated by the Bush administration both to inform policy and to influence domestic and international opinion; numbered annotations to the documents, designed to show where public statements diverge from other information; and a series of longer analyses of the four most contentious issues in the selling of the war on Iraq: the Iraqi nuclear program and the associated question of Iraq's reasons for importing certain aluminum tubes, unmanned aerial vehicles, alleged Iraqi uranium purchases from Niger, and the question of Saddam Hussein's ties to Al Qaeda and 9/11.

President Bush decided on war early, and that process is laid out in the initial chapter, as well as the rising tide of objection to the president's plan. Bush and his cohorts realized they needed to sell the war and settled on a tale of the Iraqi threat as the most suitable means to do so. That is the focus of the second chapter, which includes Bush's drive to secure a congressional resolution authorizing him to use force against Iraq. The exigencies of convincing Congress to vote that resolution ultimately required the Bush administration to produce an authoritative statement of Saddam's threat—what we term the CIA white paper—that appears as a document in that section. Two sets of charges raised by the white paper, about Iraqi nuclear weapons and about Baghdad's unmanned aerial vehicles, are dealt with in detail within that chapter.

President Bush may have thought he was out of the woods after making his charges about Saddam and then having them backed up by the Central Intelligence Agency, but Congress raised more questions. There were discrepancies between claims in Bush's speeches, Secretary of Defense Donald Rumsfeld's testimony, and the written and oral presentations of the Central Intelligence Agency's view of Iraq. When these issues were raised, CIA director George Tenet sought to settle them by means of a letter to the chairman of the Senate intelligence committee. That embroidery on the original setup is explored in chapter three, where Tenet's letter appears as a document.

Bush sought to cap the political debate with more public assertions of the threat from Saddam, highlighted by a speech he gave in Cincinnati to the Veterans of Foreign Wars. The Cincinnati speech appears as a document in chapter four.

How Bush achieved the congressional resolution he wanted, and then moved on to the international stage, is at the heart of chapter five. The problem for Bush would be transformed by Saddam Hussein's agreement to the international weapons inspections Bush had been calling for, all before the United States was actually ready to launch a war, and while a growing body of public opinion, both domestic and international, began to pay closer attention to Bush's maneuvers. This chapter details how it became central to the Bush enterprise to avoid any judgment that Iraq had complied with UN disarmament provisions. The chapter includes both the CIA/State Department Fact Sheet put out to discredit Iraqi disarmament reports and the relevant portion of President Bush's 2003 State of the Union address. Those documents also make serious allegations that Saddam Hussein was attempting to purchase uranium ore in Africa, so this matter is discussed in detail following the State of the Union text.

As Bush positioned military forces for the actual invasion of Iraq, it became necessary to secure a final approval from the UN in accordance with the resolution that had been passed in the fall of 2002. That required a marathon attempt to convince the world, or at least enough Security Council members to pass a fresh UN resolution, of the threat from Saddam. Secretary of State Colin Powell made that his aim in a briefing he gave at the UN in February 2003, a transcript of which appears in chapter six. In the briefing, Powell made a determined effort to link Saddam Hussein to terrorism, especially the bin Laden organization Al Qaeda, a subject also explored in detail in this chapter.

The United States, with a narrow coalition of a few other countries, finally launched the war in the spring of 2003. Suddenly the United States itself held the responsibility for finding the weapons of mass destruction that George Bush and his cohorts had been talking about for so long. The Bush administration's inability to find those weapons, its endeavors to get people to think it had found them, associated attempts to discredit critics, and finally the disintegration of the case against Saddam, are the primary focus of chapter seven. Three documents appear in this chapter—a Central Intelligence Agency/Defense Intelligence Agency paper on captured Iraqi vans alleged to be mobile biological weapons laboratories, a Pentagon press conference explaining its private intelligence unit, which influenced the CIA, and a speech by Vice President Cheney defending the Bush administration intelligence on Iraq after the fact.

The final chapter offers an analysis of the meaning of what happened here, and of the administration's complicity in the hoodwinking of America.

This book is a journey of discovery. The deception emerges gradually as the narrative proceeds. The work can be used several ways. Readers who wish to keep to the narrative can skip the annotated documents and sections of detailed analysis. Observers who wish to see how Bush administration pronouncements distorted aspects of Iraqi activity can look at the documents and their annotations. Those interested in the specific subjects in dispute can proceed directly to the detailed sections of analysis. In short, the book is arranged in a sort of building-block format. The blocks are in places where they are central to the story and thus most readily appreciated.

I am a national security analyst, an observer of the United States intelligence community for more than two decades, and an observer of military affairs since the Vietnam War. I am not given to conspiracy theories, but I watched the unfolding debate over a war with Iraq with growing unease, and a feeling that the Iraqi threat was being exaggerated. My unease turned to horror as I looked into these questions and saw how skewed was the data, then how President Bush remained impervious to all objections to his course of action, unmoved as his charges about Iraq were one by one called into question. I held no love for Saddam Hussein, then or now, but I do feel strongly about the larger question of intervention in the internal affairs of sovereign nations, and, about an American president's use of charges about weapons of mass destruction to create public hysteria.

Every American, and everyone with a stake in the world of the twenty-first century, needs to be concerned about what happened in the run up to the Iraq war, during which the Bush administration attempted to set new precedents for international security, with implications for war and peace, national sovereignty, unilateral action, and war powers in the American constitutional system. The way the Bush administration marshaled evidence, its treatment of intelligence material, its use of intelligence for essentially political purposes, its strategic leaks of intelligence to bolster the demand for war, and its methods of dealing with those who would not countenance such practices, all bear deep scrutiny. Our purpose here is to lay the foundation for such a public examination, which President Bush and his officials have systematically avoided. The postwar morass in Iraq serves as further reminder that intervention is much easier than extrication and that outcomes are not the same thing as consequences. The Iraq war and its antecedents bear grave implications for us all.

JOHN PRADOS
Washington, DC
February 2004

Sources and Acknowledgments

I have used no secret information in producing the critiques here. The main sources for this book are public documents from the Bush and earlier administrations, including a wide variety of materials from the White House, Central Intelligence Agency, Department of Defense and State Department, as well as declassified documents, particularly CIA documents on the Gulf war and on Iraq from the 1980s and 1990s. An important additional element of evidence has been the material brought out by the investigations of Iraq intelligence that have taken place in Great Britain and Australia. Various public policy think tanks and groups have issued studies with important bearing on the Bush administration's claims about Iraq. A wide array of press accounts and some interviews complete the sources.

I wish to acknowledge in particular Steven Aftergood and the Federation of American Scientists, whose tireless work to keep secrecy issues at the forefront of political discourse has had a beneficial impact on government departments and agencies keeping their records open to access. Steven also helped me directly in finding a couple of documents. Those who maintain the Web sites of the White House, Central Intelligence Agency, Department of State, Department of Defense, Senate Select Committee on Intelligence, and House Permanent Select Committee on Intelligence also deserve thanks. The helpful staffs of the libraries at George Washington University, Columbia University, the Martin Luther King Jr. Library of the District of Columbia, and Wharton Regional Library of Montgomery County, Maryland, have graciously given advice and help. Ms. Diane Wachtell of The New Press deserves thanks for her huge efforts to edit and shape the manuscript. Mr. Andrew Hudak of Westchester Book Group guided the book from the manuscript to the bound book stage. Ms. Ellen Pinzur also read the manuscript, provided a preliminary edit, and assisted in preparing the manuscript at a critical moment. I am greatly indebted to her for that tremendous effort. The views expressed here and such errors as persist in the book are entirely my own.

Hoodwinked

1

George Bush's Problem

On Sunday, August 4, 2002, the morning television brought into American living rooms Brent Scowcroft, a Republican national security expert who chaired the President's Foreign Intelligence Board for President George W. Bush. Scowcroft's message that day would not be what his president wanted to hear. He warned against a U.S. invasion of Iraq. Though prepared to acknowledge that Iraqi leader Saddam Hussein held ambitions of dominating the Middle East, Scowcroft asserted, "This is not a man who will risk everything on a roll of the dice." Conversely, for America, Scowcroft warned that mounting an invasion "could turn the whole region into a cauldron and, thus, destroy the war on terrorism." Doubts regarding whether Iraq possessed weapons of mass destruction, the general advised, should be resolved through inspections conducted by the United Nations.

Until that August day, the White House project to overthrow the ruler of Iraq had seemed perfectly straightforward to its architects. The daring thing, the sheer audacity of the plan, conjured beyond the view of the American people, would be to unleash an aggressive war at whatever level of violence seemed necessary to secure the goal of an Iraq free of Saddam Hussein, and without recourse to the declaration of war required by the Constitution of the United States. And by August 2002 the violence deemed necessary had become considerable indeed—mere political action fell far short in the view of those who crafted this scheme, while covert operations waged by the Central Intelligence Agency (CIA) and its cohorts also appeared insufficient for success. The anti-Saddam enterprise had come to center upon a full-scale invasion by the United States, with its own forces and anyone Washington could enlist in the cause, the "coalition of the willing" in the rather odd phrase ultimately used to describe this tiny grouping. By August the military planning was well along, the required accumulation of forces foreseen if not yet carried out, and the necessary diplomatic contacts long underway.

Difficulties with the anti-Saddam project were construed in the Oval Office as minor and technical. There was a notable lack of international enthusiasm at the prospect of this war—about which more presently—but structured properly an invasion could be carried out with minimal dependence on foreign allies. The American military had difficulties of their own, in assembling sufficient quantities of weapons and munitions and in conducting the buildup of forces in the eventual theater of war—all technical difficulties. The only real danger lay in a shift in American public opinion. So far the Iraq project had proceeded almost below the radar of the public. There had been a certain amount of comment, to be sure, but the columnists and talking heads could be dismissed as pundits, opponents on the left trashed as somehow unpatriotic, and experts making technical objections mollified by cosmetic concessions. All that changed with Brent Scowcroft's Sunday morning television appearance.

This man was not a man to be trifled with. A retired Air Force general with twenty-five years of service, Brent Scowcroft had been around presidents since Richard Nixon, for whom he headed White House military operations. The only man to have served two presidents (Gerald R. Ford and George H.W. Bush) as national security adviser, *and* the only person to have held the deputy security adviser job under two presidents (Nixon and Ford), Scowcroft had been an important member of George W. Bush's foreign policy brain trust during the 2000 campaign and had headed the transition team that smoothed the new president's way into office. Key Bush administration officials, from Vice President Richard B. Cheney to Defense Secretary Donald H. Rumsfeld, had worked alongside Scowcroft in the Ford White House. Secretary of State Colin L. Powell had labored with Scowcroft in the first Bush administration. The current national security adviser, Condoleezza Rice, is a Scowcroft protégé. All knew Scowcroft as a supremely level-headed individual not afraid to speak his mind. When General Scowcroft warned of a cauldron if the United States invaded Iraq, that was a serious statement. It changed the White House calculation on the degree to which a war with Iraq would have to be sold to the American people.

For months Americans had heard suggestive claims about Iraqi weapons of mass destruction and the Bush administration's desire to dispense with the Saddam regime, but before the Scowcroft television appearance nothing had ignited much real public debate. Suddenly in August came an outpouring. General Scowcroft reinforced his initial statements with an op-ed piece in the *New York Times*. He was followed by others, including two colleagues, Bush (I) administration secretaries of state James W. Baker III, and Lawrence S. Eagleburger, experienced diplomats like Richard C. Holbrooke, and many politicians, even Texan Dick Armey, a Bush associate from gubernatorial days and the powerful Republican whip in the House of Representatives. Members of the public increasingly weighed in, elevating the entire Iraq issue far above the level of a spat between elite policymakers. Congress had held some preliminary hearings on Iraq policy, but it now began scheduling more serious inquiries. The opinion polls President Bush professes not to use began to flicker, bringing an instant response from the White House, which orchestrated its own campaign of encouraging notables who favored action. Suddenly the Bush administration could see many months of its work on the Iraq plan threatened in a very real way. Its response was to craft a scheme to convince America and the world that war with Iraq was necessary and urgent, a scheme, unfortunately, that required patently untrue public statements and egregious manipulations of intelligence, as the documents in this book will demonstrate.

Iraq on the Installment Plan

Before Bush's Iraq project became so controversial, the administration's policy toward Iraq had evolved effortlessly from equanimity to hostility. During
the presidential transition from the Clinton administration to that of George
W. Bush, outgoing national security adviser Sandy Berger told his successor,
Condoleezza Rice, that terrorism had risen to become the most important
problem the new leadership would face. Not Saddam Hussein but Osama
bin Laden was the threat. We do not yet have an account of how Rice
responded, but it is a fact that a Bush administration policy directive on
terrorism languished for months, being finalized only in the late summer of
2001 and reaching the president's desk just the day before September 11.
This torpid progression contrasts sharply with Bush's change on Iraq policy,
which turned on a dime after the September 11 attacks.

Ten days before his inauguration as president, George W. Bush had
gone to the Pentagon for a global military briefing by the Joint Chiefs of
Staff. Fully half the seventy-five-minute-long meeting was taken up with talk
of Iraq. Mainly the military emphasized the capabilities it had in the Middle
East and its ability to move forces where needed, when needed. There was
also talk of terrorism, and the Chiefs objected to keeping forces on call, as
President Bill Clinton had obliged them to do, to mount an instant attack on
bin Laden in Afghanistan.

Bush's former Secretary of the Treasury, Paul H. O'Neill, in the biogra-
phy *The Price of Loyalty* by Ron Suskind, recounts that at the very first National
Security Council (NSC) meeting held by the new administration, Iraq was discussed in the context of getting rid of Saddam Hussein. O'Neill recalled the
tone at the NSC as being focused on finding a way to make it happen. O'Neill's
files used by Suskind included documents that predated the September 11 attacks and bore titles like "Plan for Post-Saddam Iraq," that discussed peacekeeping forces and war crimes trials, and "Foreign Suitors for Iraqi Oilfield
Contracts." At the NSC George Bush seemed disengaged, so much so that
O'Neill likened him to "a blind man in a room full of deaf people." That left
the playing field to subordinates with agendas, of whom there were many.

The Bush administration mainly followed a course away from, not toward, military action. Though the United States had concerns about the possibility that Iraq possessed weapons of mass destruction, concerns that had existed since United Nations inspectors were expelled from Iraq in 1998, Bush's public stance would be that any dangers had been adequately taken into account. Secretary of State Colin Powell, speaking to reporters in February 2001 after meeting with Egyptian foreign minister Amre Moussa, argued that UN economic sanctions had worked: Saddam "has not developed any significant capability with respect to weapons of mass destruction. He is unable to project conventional power against his neighbors." Powell, another former general, who had been chairman of the Joint Chiefs of Staff during the Gulf War, was in accord with Vice President Richard Cheney, secretary of defense at the time of the Gulf War. Asked about the UN weapons inspections in a March 2001 interview, Cheney had said, "It may not be as crucial if you've got other measures [i.e., sanctions and import controls] in place and you've got a [system] that people are willing to support."

Cheney's comment is significant because by this time it had become difficult to preserve the sanctions system, *any* sanctions system. Powell's defense of sanctions had been merely rhetorical. The existing system was in extremis. Arab nations were unhappy at this treatment of a brother country. European countries with major export interests in Iraq, principally Russia, Germany, and France, were increasingly reluctant in their support. Several nations had symbolically defied the prohibition against commercial aircraft flying into Baghdad. Iraqi oil was being smuggled through Turkey, Syria, and Jordan (Great Britain estimated the leakage at a billion and a half dollars a year). Iraqi people lacked vital medicines, jobs, and consumer goods as the result of sanctions. Public health indices such as live-birth and survival-to-age-one ratios were down from 1990 levels. Iraq fed the UN Security Council a steady stream of complaints against the system, as well as appeals for special dispensations to export amounts of oil to finance medical supplies and other necessities. Cheney's allusion to people (i.e., countries) willing to support sanctions constituted an admission the system needed fixing anyway.

Colin Powell's answer, smart sanctions, was a formula intended to aim the economic sanctions more directly at Iraqi military corporations and governmental entities. Smart sanctions faced opposition from the beginning, even before the proposal went to the United Nations. Other Bush people saw an alternative: overthrow Saddam Hussein. Agitation for an overthrow had begun in 1992, when Bush's father was president and Brent Scowcroft the national security adviser. The push continued through the Clinton administration. Both presidents supported CIA operations (that failed) aimed at fomenting rebellions or coups to oust Saddam. In 1998 an open letter to President Clinton from many of the same individuals who became Bush administration officials insisted the United States get rid of Saddam by supporting Iraqi exile groups, advocacy that was continued into the new millennium by the lobby group Project for a New American Century. PNAC became a center for muscular, so-called neo-conservative views, and a wellspring for the Bush (II) administration.

Much wind and quite a lot of paper has been devoted to the neoconservatives, their ideological bent and their agenda for George W. Bush; the point necessary here is that PNAC's agenda included overthrowing Saddam. Central figures among the PNAC ideologues advised the Bush presidential campaign and went on to hold posts in the new administration, including I. Lewis Libby, chief of staff to the vice president; Paul R. Wolfowitz, deputy secretary of defense; Douglas Feith, an assistant; Richard N. Perle, chairman of the Defense Policy Board, which advises the Pentagon; Zalmay Khalilzad in the Bush White House; James R. Woolsey, former CIA director; John Bolton at the State Department; and others. Fellow travelers included among their numbers Secretary of Defense Donald Rumsfeld and Undersecretary of State Richard L. Armitage.

The neo-conservatives were not happy with smart sanctions. Before the Senate Foreign Relations Committee in March 2001, Richard Perle declared that "the changes that are being talked about will be no more effective than what we've had in the past." At his confirmation hearing before the Senate Armed Services Committee, Paul Wolfowitz remarked that if there were a "real option" to overthrow Hussein, "I would certainly think it was worthwhile."

Bush permitted Powell to forge ahead with the smart sanctions diplomacy, but he ordered a series of policy reviews. Several separate groups were assigned to make the best cases for each option, including sanctions schemes. One review group studied the neo-conservative preference: "regime change" in Iraq. While the policy reviews continued, however, Colin Powell lost the game diplomatically. The member states on the UN Security Council showed little inclination to approve a fresh sanctions scheme, forcing the United States into a posture of lobbying to build support. Progress, never better than glacial, slowed even more through the late summer of 2001. Then came September 11.

Although the Muslim fundamentalists who crashed their hijacked airliners into the World Trade Center and the Pentagon never imagined that they were setting the stage for a war on Iraq, that is what happened. The United States actually did Osama bin Laden's bidding by carrying out a war against the government of Iraq, Baghdad did no good for itself with its initial reactions to the September 11 tragedy, which were to praise the militants who had perpetrated the atrocity. In the immense confusion immediately following the attacks, this raised suspicions about Iraq among some Americans. Especially among the ranks of neo-conservatives, many were convinced that Saddam, not Al Qaeda, was behind the bombing.

At the very first Bush administration national security meeting after the attacks, Donald Rumsfeld raised the issue of going after Iraq, arguing that would be a broader response than simply fighting Al Qaeda. A few days later President Bush convened a larger group of advisers at his retreat at Camp David. There Paul Wolfowitz joined in the demand for attacking Iraq. In between sessions of the meeting, Bush made sympathetic comments to Wolfowitz, but for the moment both he and Richard Cheney opposed the move. President Bush did not reject the Iraq option, he simply felt the time was not right. In any case, by September 2001, smart sanctions were dead, and Pentagon leaders were solidly backing the option for waging an aggressive war on Iraq.

In reconstructing the time line for the preparation of this war it appears that in either late December 2001 or early 2002, George W. Bush issued a series of orders with profound implications. One was a "memorandum of notification," the formal term for the presidential findings that are required to authorize a CIA covert operation, in this case against Saddam. The second order went to the Department of Defense, instructing the Pentagon to initiate planning for an invasion of Iraq. According to former Central Command (CENTCOM) intelligence chief Major General John F. Kimmons, an initial concept for an Iraq operation was first aired outside CENTCOM in December 2001. Opposition within government to the Iraq plan after this point amounted to little more than a rearguard action, objecting that munitions were insufficient, forces still inadequate, or diplomatic alternatives yet to be tried.

At the level visible to the public, President Bush prepared a State of the Union speech casting Iraq as one of three rogue nations constituting an "Axis of Evil," conveniently painting black hats on the Iraqi leadership he wished to depose.

About this time, senior officials at the White House in the Principals Committee, a rump National Security Council (NSC) meeting without the president, gave failing grades to the policy of containment of Iraq. They advised that active measures be taken to get rid of Saddam Hussein. The term "regime change" got a boost in public discourse on February 6, when Secretary Powell told a congressional committee that Bush was exploring "a full range of options" on Iraq and that "regime change" was "something the United States might have to do alone." Reports suggest that initial CIA and Pentagon plans against Saddam reached the White House around mid-February, but in any case it was Powell, on February 12, who testified in Congress that "with respect to Iraq, it has long been . . . a policy of the United States government that regime change would be in the best interests of the region, in the best interests of the Iraqi people, and we are looking at a variety of options that would bring that about." Reporters soon got a chance to question President Bush about that statement. "I will reserve whatever options I have," Bush replied. "I'll keep them close to my vest."

The role of Richard B. Cheney remains hidden but is central to the entire Iraq war. Cheney's complacency about sanctions in the administra-

tion's early months and his opposition to moving against Iraq in the immediate aftermath of September 11 stand in vivid contrast to the fierce advocacy
we shall see as this account proceeds. Prior to 9/11 the vice-president, a
former chief executive of Halliburton Corporation, a company with major
oil interests, chaired a commission reviewing energy policy. Records released
two years later as a result of a lawsuit show the commission possessed maps
of Iraqi oil installations, plus a document listing foreign oil projects in the
country, implying some U.S. interest in Iraqi oil. There was talk on the
energy panel of relaxing the Iraq sanctions as a way to increase supplies of
energy for the United States, but nothing ever came of that, and Cheney
certainly aligned himself with the alarmist rhetoric of the neo-cons and their
Pentagon water carriers. Cheney's earlier position on Iraq sanctions and his
initial relaxed rhetoric may have been tactical maneuvers in a larger debate
within the administration, the same one that brought Colin Powell from his
opposition to effective support for the Iraq war option.

In mid-February 2002, as the Bush administration began stoking up its
comments on regime change for Baghdad, Vice President Cheney was selected to execute the first major diplomatic initiative of the anti-Iraq campaign,
a visit to nearly every nation in the Middle East and Persian Gulf region
whose help would be needed to mount an invasion of Iraq. Almost all of
them rejected the idea. The vice-president kicked off his diplomatic journey
with a speech on February 19 at El Toro Marine air base in California, in
which Cheney insisted that Iraq harbored terrorists and that the United States
would never allow "terror states" or their "terrorist allies" to threaten with
weapons of mass destruction.

While the public remained largely oblivious, actual preparations for war
began with the Cheney tour. Military planning for an attack on Iraq was the
province of Central Command (CENTCOM), headquartered at MacDill Air
Force Base in Tampa, Florida. Headed by General Tommy R. Franks, the
command was responsible to the Chairman of the Joint Chiefs of Staff for
the plan, and the chairman, in turn, answered to Defense Secretary Rumsfeld
and President Bush. Franks, already carrying on a war in Afghanistan against
guerrillas of the former Taliban government, had a heavy burden. In Af-

ghanistan a very small American force had succeeded in ousting the Taliban rulers, but most of the Al Qaeda terrorists had gotten away. In no mood for a repeat, Franks rejected any notion of using a similar tiny force for Iraq, and also guffawed when military men on the National Security Council staff suggested a covert operations plan akin to the Bay of Pigs, the disasterous 1961 CIA paramilitary invasion of Cuba. General Franks wanted a powerful invasion force—the military liked to use the word "robust"—that could enter Iraq, sweep away all resistance, then occupy the country.

Don Rumsfeld saw the Franks plan as a relic of a past era. "Rummy," as the secretary of defense was nicknamed, had dedicated himself to a trans-formation of the U.S. military, bringing it into the twenty-first century with even more sophisticated technology. The Afghan style of operations, lithe, agile, highly flexible, seemed the very template for modern warfare. Rumsfeld wanted a smaller-scale invasion. Caught in the middle was General Richard B. Myers, the Air Force officer who was chairman of the Joint Chiefs. Known as a team player, Myers had headed the U.S. Space Command before coming back to the Pentagon. Through piloting fighter-bombers in the Vietnam war, he had participated in the most technically advanced part of the effort, the pinball wizardry of the attack on the Ho Chi Minh Trail. Myers and Rums-feld were of like mind in pressuring CENTCOM to come up with a more economical Iraq plan.

The frenzy of military planning peaked in the early months of 2002. When reporter Bob Woodward encountered Rumsfeld in a Pentagon hall-way on March 19, while Cheney was in the middle of his journey to the east, Woodward found the defense secretary ebullient. Rumsfeld bragged about "the war you don't see," likely a reference to the advanced stage of the Iraq planning and the fact that the U.S. government, through the Cheney trip, was already moving pieces on the board to make an invasion workable. In May, the Joint Chiefs of Staff carried out a series of war games called "Prominent Hammer," intended to show whether the U.S. military could conduct a war with Iraq while simultaneously meeting its other global com-mitments. Indications are that President Bush received his first presentation of the CENTCOM plan in the late spring. Rumsfeld, neo-conservatives on his staff, and members of the National Security Council staff at the White House criticized the concept as too conventional, requiring an overly large force. General Franks was sent back to the drawing board. Franks briefed a revised plan to a White House meeting on June 19. CENTCOM continued responding to demands for increased flexibility by adding features like attacks against Iraqi forces to come out of the west (Jordan) and the north (Turkey). General Franks visited Jordan in late June, and Deputy Defense Secretary Paul Wolfowitz went to Turkey during July.

Thus military plans were in place from the early summer of 2002. They would be adjusted later when Turkey and Jordan refused permission for the United States to mount operations from those lands, but the notion of an invasion had gone from concept to practicality. The resulting strategy was a compromise. Franks made his plan more flexible, Rumsfeld gave up the idea he could proceed on the Afghan model. General Myers and the Joint Chiefs of Staff labored to eliminate misconceptions in Rumsfeld's office and won points for CENTCOM.

Early leaks about the military plans, almost certainly provoked by the subterranean struggle over the shape of the invasion, brought the public its first real inkling that George Bush was serious about attacking Iraq. Congress held some early hearings. At the end of July, giving up his highest technology vision, Rumsfeld testified before Congress that airpower alone could not defeat Iraq. The actual invasion force would number about 140,000 troops on the ground, among a total force of perhaps 230,000. Reports of this testimony were what motivated Brent Scowcroft and others to speak out as they did.

While military preparations began, diplomacy lagged. Russia went on record opposing any military option as early as December 2001. UN Secretary General Kofi Annan rejected this project that same month, in his speech in Oslo accepting the Nobel Peace Prize. France and Germany publicly denounced war only a couple of months later. European Union officials, including both its foreign affairs and defense ministers, spoke out against war in early 2002. When Vice President Cheney made his March 2002 visit to Europe and the Middle East, almost the only ears friendly to his message were those in London, Tel Aviv, Qatar, and aboard a U.S. aircraft carrier in the Persian Gulf. Leaders in Egypt, Jordan, Saudi Arabia, Turkey, and European countries not only opposed the option but warned the United States against it.

The administration's only major foreign ally would be the United Kingdom. George Bush met Tony Blair, the British prime minister, repeatedly throughout the period. In his excess of enthusiasm after one of these reunions, Bush revealed his objective clearly: "I explained to the prime minister that the policy of my government is the removal of Saddam." Lack of international support made that goal difficult to reach, however, and in May President Bush traveled to Europe himself to recruit backers. The ploy hardly worked. Major allies France and Germany did not budge an inch. The former Russian satellite states of Eastern Europe, possessed of minimal capabilities and excited to be taken seriously by the United States at all, were the only states to respond to the American appeal. Invidious comparisons U.S. officials would later make contrasting the (powerful) "Old Europe" with puny "New Europe" had their origins here. Rumania would eventually permit the Americans to use its air bases and the Czech Republic left in place a small chemical decontamination contingent it had long had stationed in Kuwait. That would be the sum total of the helpers George Bush recruited from Eastern Europe for his Iraq war.

A reporter surveying the views on Iraq of the member states on the UN Security Council in May 2002 could write (correctly, except for somehow leaving out the British): "The United States is alone among the fifteen Security Council members in leaning toward a military route."

The continued opposition of other countries combined with the stridency of Bush administration rhetoric woke up Americans to the president's Iraqi enterprise. That returns us to August 2002. The fat was in the fire. The rise of public criticism signaled George Bush that an invasion of Iraq needed more than military and diplomatic preparations; it would have to be sold to the American people and to the world.

George Bush's Wurlitzer

On August 5, while the newspapers reported Scowcroft's comments on Iraq, the White House became the setting for a full-scale briefing of the CENT-COM war plan. General Franks presented concepts like early attack on Baghdad and key Iraqi command centers, and satisfied Rumsfeld with a relatively small total force package. That afternoon, when other officials left, Colin Powell stayed behind to speak to the president. Condoleezza Rice sat in on the discussion, which went on into the evening, through dinner, and finally moved to the White House residence that night. Powell advised against unilateral U.S. action, arguing such a course would hurt America in the Arab world, and would affect the cost to the United States of a postwar occupation of Iraq. Powell did not insist that Bush give up his dream of regime change but instead tried to shape the president's approach.

Bush was receptive to Powell's arguments. The next day at a high school in Mississippi, Bush gave a speech in which he thundered, "We owe it to our children to deal with these threats," including even by military means, then went on to say he would be "patient and deliberate" and would consult Congress and America's allies. The White House information machine, very good at keeping people "on message," put out the word that no decisions had been made about war. Three days later, on August 9, however, the Bush administration suddenly shifted gears, making the case that war with Iraq was necessary and justified. Secretary Rumsfeld told the public that the containment of Saddam Hussein had not worked, implying that force had to be the next alternative. The selling of the war had begun.

White House political aides would later tell the press that August is no time to create a sales campaign, insisting that what was said about Iraq had long been planned. But the record shows that only as far along in the process as August 2002 did the Bush people gear up for a public relations blitz. During that month, Bush Chief of Staff Andrew H. Card Jr. set up a special unit, the White House Information Group (WHIG), to ensure that elements throughout the executive office were working the Iraq issue. WHIG was considered so important that it rated the supersecret Situation Room for its weekly meetings and was chaired by the president's political guru Karl Rove. A high-powered group, composed of senior people and top staffers in their departments, WHIG's members included national security adviser Condoleezza Rice and her deputy, Stephen J. Hadley, representing the National Security Council (NSC) staff. Two key people from Vice President Cheney's entourage, staff chief I. Lewis Libby and communications director Mary Matalin, ensured top-level input from the vice-president. From Bush's own communications staff were its chief, Karen Hughes, plus James R. Wilkinson. The president's chief congressional lobbyist, Nicolas E. Calio, was another member. There could be no doubt the assignment given to the WHIG had the highest presidential priority.

At the Pentagon, Secretary Rumsfeld ordered the establishment of a parallel information unit on Iraq, created around the middle of August. The State Department took similar action. With no actual crisis concerning Iraq at hand, these entities were intended to work in tandem with WHIG stoking up public concern regarding Saddam Hussein and his country.

Also on the front line was George Bush's press secretary, Ari Fleischer. Under Fleischer, a brash forty-one-year-old fellow whose entire career had been as a spokesperson or a Republican political operative, the White House press operation had become more tightly wound than ever. Fleischer gave daily noontime press briefings that were televised, and early morning "gaggles" where no cameras were allowed, plus additional briefings as required. Journalists on the White House beat complained they could learn little from Fleischer or his deputy, Scott McClellan, that the White House was not itself promoting. More often than not, the spokespersons responded to reporters' questions on other matters by referring them to government agencies, a change from the practice of previous administrations. The system enabled President Bush, his NSC staff, and WHIG to carefully select and coordinate the charges that would be made about Iraq as well as their responses to the developing story.

The final element of the Wurlitzer was the Bush speechwriting staff, headed by Michael J. Gerson, who in the summer of 2002 received a promotion to assistant to the president and a move from the Eisenhower Executive Office Building to the West Wing—a token of the increased importance of the speechwriting unit. The staff included eight full-time speechwriters with good access to the chief executive. Gerson often sat in on meetings in the White House Situation Room to absorb the tenor of discussions he could then use to set rhythm in Bush's public addresses. Bush had become comfortable with Gerson, chief speechwriter in his presidential campaign, who had previous experience in the unsuccessful presidential runs of Jack Kemp and Robert J. Dole. Gerson strove to fashion language outlining clear and blunt alternatives, while invoking the symbolism of faith.

George Bush prided himself on a disciplined cadre of officials who presented a single message to the public. Bush set the tone, the White House Information Group supplied key points and furnished supplementary factual papers, White House press spokespersons and speechwriters gave the message idiom, and the departments and agencies repeated and broadened the message. This information Wurlitzer became the key mechanism in Bush's campaign to sell the Iraq war.

*   *   *

Regime change as a concept has a hard edge. Overthrowing governments at a whim is something imperialist powers do. Effecting such change by invasion, by aggressive war, is a further step across the line. For an enlightened America to do this in the twenty-first century seemed a stretch. These aspects complicated the selling of the war. The issues were put quite directly by Henry A. Kissinger in an article published about a week after Brent Scowcroft's comments crystallized an Iraq debate. In a syndicated column Kissinger wrote: "Regime change as a goal for military intervention challenges the international system established by the 1648 Treaty of Westphalia, which, after the carnage of the religious wars, established the principle of nonintervention in the domestic affairs of other states. And the notion of justified preemption runs counter to modern international law, which sanctions use of force in self-defense only against actual, not potential, threats."

A foreign affairs commentator, former national security adviser and secretary of state in the Nixon and Ford administrations, Henry Kissinger had

close ties to the Bush administration as a member of the Defense Policy
Board. Kissinger was in a position both to know the inner thinking of officials
and articulate public arguments to win support for Bush policies. As such,
Kissinger's writings furnish an ideal mirror in which to view this progression.
A controversial figure, who worked alongside Brent Scowcroft in government, Kissinger has a good sense of the enigmas of policy, though his solu-
tions are frequently less perceptive than his outlines of the problems they are
meant to solve. Kissinger's columns during the first part of 2002 reflect the
evolution of George Bush's strategy during that time.

In mid-January 2002 Henry Kissinger published a piece arguing for an
attack on Iraq. Looking ahead to "Phase II" of the war on terror, Kissinger
worried that cutting back on military pressure would yield diplomatic stale-
mate. "Anti-terrorism policy is empty if it is not backed by the threat of
force," went his analysis, but the campaign for Afghanistan was already over.
What to do? Kissinger scoffed at possible options in Yemen or Somalia—"the
United States will have to decide whether action against them is strategically
productive." He preferred an attack on Iraq. *That* was the "greatest opportunity," a chance to change regional dynamics in the Middle East.

Kissinger accurately projected the diplomatic obstacles to the Iraq invasion. In the January think piece he anticipated that use of force in a self-
described (by the United States) second phase of the war on terror would
separate the nations willing "to pursue an implacable strategy" from those
cooperating merely to have a say in U.S. actions. By March, Kissinger was
acknowledging that there was no agreement among the international community on the danger, and even some who perceived the Bush administration
"as if it were a revolutionary government in danger of veering out of control."

Kissinger's August column, the one in which he began with the Treaty
of Westphalia, contained an ominous warning on the failure to secure global
cooperation: "Any other attitude gradually will isolate and exhaust us."

A longtime observer of the globe, Henry Kissinger included comments
on how nations would line up on the war: European allies would lend support "only grudgingly, if at all," Middle Eastern states would split. Therein
lies the reason Kissinger saw a need for Bush to seek cooperation on the

policy. But there was no turning back: if the invasion of Afghanistan, Kissinger wrote, "remains the principal move in the war against terrorism, it [the war] runs the risk of petering out into an intelligence operation."

Henry's prescription? "The objective of regime change should be subordinated in American declaratory policy to the need to eliminate weapons of mass destruction from Iraq as required by the UN resolutions." Kissinger argued that the ambiguity Bush had depended upon to shield his preparations had reached the point that it invited leaks, congressional inquiries, and allied pressures; the time had come to abandon that approach and shift to a hearts and minds campaign: "The administration should be prepared to undertake a national debate."

President Bush did most of these things in the weeks that followed. His rhetoric followed closely from Kissinger's prescription. But George W. Bush, unable to tolerate a true Great Debate over an issue of war, or perhaps fearful of losing a debate argued on the merits, resorted to doctoring the information made available to the American people. As a result the national dialogue over war with Iraq was a pseudo-debate, not a real one—a hoodwinking. The next chapters and the documents they analyze show exactly how and where Bush's deceptions occurred; how they were necessitated, in his view, by the timetables established in his plans; the lack of international support; the wavering of public support as measured in opinion polls; and the rise of a vocal domestic and global opposition. President Bush and his cohorts crafted a litany of largely baseless charges about Iraq, then repeated, escalated, and rearranged those charges in places and times calculated to contribute to their goal of opening the way to an unprovoked war.

2

The Setup

George W. Bush likes his summer vacations. The high summer heat at
his ranch in Crawford, Texas, draws the president almost irresistibly.
Bush would spend weeks on the Texas ranch, taking time out only for
speech-making or political fund-raising forays. Some complained Bush spent
too much time on the prairie, but Americans elect their president and, having
done that, pretty much take presidential style in stride. For Bush on the Iraq
issue, however, the summer sojourn may initially have appeared as an advantage. Getting out of Washington lowered visibility, encouraged Americans
to think nothing much would happen until the president returned to the
White House, and got a lot of the press corps to relax as well, easing the
pressure on the administration. Drawn reluctantly into a public debate on
Iraq by the swell of doubts in August, Bush had an opportunity to craft his
response without seeming to be engaged. The president, it was reported sug-
gestively, had taken for summer reading *Supreme Command*, a book about the
heroics of national leaders in World War II by conservative historian Eliot
Cohen.

Having President Bush out of Washington did not mean business could
not be done. On Wednesday, August 14, the Principals Committee of the
National Security Council gathered at the White House to discuss the creation of a coalition to fight Iraq. Condoleezza Rice chaired the meeting, which

included Vice President Cheney, secretaries Powell and Rumsfeld, and CIA Director George Tenet. According to journalist Bob Woodward, who has provided the only account of these proceedings available so far, Colin Powell advised President Bush to unveil his appeal for coalition partners at the annual opening of the UN General Assembly in September, an event attended by many world leaders and a ready recruiting ground. Dick Cheney advised that the speech should advance the claim that if the United Nations did nothing about Iraq it would be seen as a powerless institution. Condi Rice agreed with both propositions. All present supposedly agreed that President Bush should *not* go so far as to use his remarks to call for a United Nations resolution authorizing war with Iraq.

While within the White House the Bush people worked to put together their strategy, in public they were already making efforts to pump up the perception that action on Iraq was urgent and necessary. Vice President Cheney had already given one speech on Iraq in early August. National Security Adviser Rice told British television reporters on August 15, "We certainly do not have the option of doing nothing," a bid to paint the Iraq matter in the vivid hues of crisis urgency.

The next day there was a National Security Council meeting by teleconference, with President Bush participating from Crawford. Bush asked each of his advisers what they thought about a coalition appeal made at the U.N.; all were in favor. At some point in this process, possibly in mid-August, the decision was made to focus on allegations that Iraq possessed weapons of mass destruction, and was in league with Al Qaeda terrorists, as the primary bases for U.S. demands that action be taken against Baghdad. It does not seem coincidental that shortly after these mid-August meetings various Bush officials began as if with one voice to push home the same charges about Saddam Hussein, in the classic style of the Bush Wurlitzer.

President Bush and his cohorts took every opportunity to hammer away at the Iraq issue. On August 21, Dick Cheney, Don Rumsfeld, and Condi Rice went to Crawford with Joint Chiefs of Staff Chairman General Myers and other Pentagon officials involved with ballistic missile defense issues. Their meeting with Bush would be billed as being about military procurement. Bush emerged and told reporters that Iraq had not come up in the (formal) morning meeting. Nevertheless the president went on to say that "regime change is in the interests of the world," and he would consider all options and "all technologies," but that he was a patient man who would consult with Congress and U.S. allies. "We take all threats seriously and we continue to consult with our friends and allies," President Bush declared. When reporters queried Donald Rumsfeld, who stood at Bush's side, why so few U.S. allies had offered to participate in a war with Iraq, the defense secretary snapped back, "The president has not asked them to."

Secretary Rumsfeld went directly from Crawford to Fort Hood, where he issued a warning that if Russia continued its economic ties with Iraq it would be branding itself a friend of terrorist states. During questions from the troops afterward, a young soldier from Chicago, Rumsfeld's home town, asked whether war with Iraq would affect U.S. relations with Russia. Rumsfeld replied, "The president has made no such decision that we should go into a war with Iraq." A week later at Camp Pendleton, Rumsfeld told another military audience that unilateralism—sole U.S. action against Saddam—"at the onset may seem lonesome" but would pay off for the United States.

Vice President Cheney elevated the Iraq debate to a new intensity on August 27. Speaking in Nashville before the Veterans of Foreign Wars convention, Cheney thundered, "We now know that Saddam has resumed his efforts to acquire nuclear weapons." Conceding that "intelligence is an uncertain business, even in the best of circumstances," the vice-president nevertheless proclaimed, "Many of us are convinced that Saddam will acquire nuclear weapons fairly soon." Invoking Pearl Harbor, Cheney reiterated a theme he had used a couple of weeks before in California—that sending weapons inspectors into Iraq would not solve the alleged problem of Iraqi weapons of mass destruction. Cheney worked up to his climax: "Deliverable weapons of mass destruction in the hands of a terror network or a murderous dictator or the two working together constitutes as grave a threat as can be imagined. The risks of inaction are far greater than the risks of action." Cheney's caveat, that intelligence is an uncertain business, surely intended to excuse the horrors he then dangled before this audience, was tried by the claims the vice president then made. He also dangled opportunity before the audience: "Regime change in Iraq would bring about a number of benefits for the region." This last, a central element in neo-conservative beliefs about Iraq, amounted to the assertion that military victory in Iraq would lead to the end of the Israeli-Palestinian *intifada*, a pure speculation.

Saudi Arabia several times during the spring of 2002 warned the United States against its Iraqi adventure, and refused to permit the United States to use its air bases in a war. Secretary Rumsfeld failed on a visit to the Persian Gulf in June to move the Saudis off their opposition. The day after Cheney's speech in Nashville, President Bush had the Saudi ambassador visit Crawford for another try at persuasion. Personally sympathetic, Prince Bandar al Faisal, the ambassador, had to warn the president not to expect much to come from his latest initiative.

The Saudi rejection only added to the rising chorus of concern expressed among the public. Senate hearings at the end of July and beginning of August had been more grist for the mill. Bush's own acolytes built the fires higher. Already in early August, the *New York Times* had editorialized that it was "A TIME FOR CANDOR ON IRAQ" from the Bush administration. Yet this concern was no made-up perception flowing from a media feeding frenzy. No less a figure than British Prime Minister Tony Blair, an acute political observer as well as Bush's staunchest ally, told an official inquiry in 2003: "Throughout the August break last year literally every day there were stories appearing saying we were about to go and invade Iraq. Military action had been decided upon." In their press appearance at Crawford, President Bush and Secretary Rumsfeld themselves had come up with words like "churning" and "frenzy" to describe the public concern. The fear that war had already been decided upon drove a rapidly growing and increasingly visible public opposition. They wanted to suggest the public's worries were exaggerated.

Despite Henry Kissinger's advice, Bush was not ready to abandon the rhetoric of ambiguity. Admitting an Iraq war was on, in Bush's view, could lead to a political firestorm. Instead he responded in two ways. First, by declaring that the administration would consult with Congress and America's allies, Bush sought to lessen fears that his administration was, in Kissinger's phrase, a revolutionary government out of control. At the same time, by collecting and massaging intelligence on Iraq, Bush began to orchestrate the hoodwinking of America.

Toward the end of August Tony Blair and George Bush had a telephone conversation. Bush remained at Crawford. He arranged for Blair to visit the United States early in September. They would hold meetings at the presidential retreat at Camp David. Blair's testimony, under oath in an official British judicial proceeding, was: "We decided: look, we really had to confront this issue, devise our strategy and get on with it." Theirs was an information strategy. Prime Minister Blair ordered British intelligence authorities to produce a white paper on the threat from Iraq, and announced a few days before his departure for the United States that such a document would be released by the government. In fact, a senior intelligence official brought Blair an early draft of the British Iraq report during that trip.

The American side of this story is more complex. President Bush approved the essential marching orders, the goals, objectives, and strategy for a war on Iraq in a directive on August 29. This made the strategy of persuasion he had agreed with Tony Blair all the more urgent. A strategic communications task force under Bush's White House Information Group planned themes that would be the message all Bush administration officials were expected to convey. The group also had a key role in planning speeches, and it commissioned a series of white papers. Very early on, the WHIG seized upon nuclear weapons as a primary vehicle for advancing the argument that Iraq posed a clear and present national security danger, capitalizing on the public's visceral fear of things nuclear. The information group's initial effort to use this issue came in the form of a paper titled "A Grave and Gathering Danger: Saddam Hussein's Quest for Nuclear Weapons." For source material Jim Wilkinson of WHIG gathered a yard-high stack of intelligence reports, academic papers, and press articles. Written by Will Tobey and Susan Cook, supervised by NSC staff director for counterproliferation Robert G. Joseph, the paper went through at least five drafts before being abandoned. According to a remarkable report by journalists Barton Gellman and Walter Pincus, speechwriter Wilkinson admitted that Condi Rice and Bob Joseph shot down the paper because it was "not strong enough."

White House spokespersons, asked about the report, dismissed it as irrelevant since the document was never published. In fact, the entire WHIG enterprise is *highly* relevant because it shows that the stream of exaggerations, half-truths, and outright lies purveyed to Americans over the next months were not by accident or misunderstanding but were elements in a purposeful political program.

Meanwhile, George W. Bush's focus remained on organizing action, first in the domestic arena, next in concert with the British, finally in creating some larger coalition against Iraq. These tasks required both diplomacy and persuasion. The day before Tony Blair's arrival at Camp David there was another go-round among Bush's top people. Bush had lunched with Colin Powell and Condi Rice and affirmed his desire to get UN weapons inspectors into Iraq. At a meeting of the Principals Committee on September 6, however, there was heated debate. Bob Woodward describes Cheney as "beyond hell-bent" to act against Iraq. Cheney and Rumsfeld continued to oppose any effort to seek a UN resolution. But Colin Powell had convinced the president to at least sound out the permanent member states represented on the UN Security Council. That night Bush spoke with the leaders of France, Russia, and China, consultations that apparently confirmed Powell's assertions that obtaining a UN resolution would be the wisest course, and that the price for international harmony was a resolution focused on a new UN inspection system to divest Iraq of any remaining strategic weapons. Just before Blair arrived the next morning, President Bush held a further meeting of his national security team, including several members of the WHIG. Present were Cheney, Rice, Stephen Hadley, Rumsfeld, Powell, George Tenet, and Chief of Staff Andrew Card. Bush gave final instructions for drafting of the speech he planned to give at the UN General Assembly session of September 12. Michael Gerson would be the drafter. Rumsfeld, Powell, and Tenet left for Washington on the helicopter that brought Tony Blair to Camp David.

Building up for the UN speech, a succession of administration offerings to the media put a harsh light on Iraq. On September 6 the press described a "new" report from the International Atomic Energy Agency (IAEA), the UN arm responsible for monitoring the worldwide use of fissionable nuclear materials, that indicated satellite photos showed hundreds of buildings being repaired or constructed at Iraqi industrial sites, including several nuclear sites. The unpublished WHIG paper on Iraqi nuclear developments actually quoted part of a sentence from a newsmagazine interview with IAEA chief Hans Blix that mentioned the construction, without reference to the remainder of the sentence showing IAEA had no indication the construction activity had anything to do with nuclear weapons. Indeed when the new report first appeared in the press the IAEA took pains to debunk it. Agency spokeswoman Melissa Fleming, even as President Bush met with his advisers at Camp David, called in reporters to note that the alleged "new" report had originally been put out by the agency in July to complete snores from the press. "Construction of a building is one thing. Restarting a nuclear program is another," Fleming declared. "We have a lot of commercial satellite imagery that there has been construction at sites that were formerly nuclear. But what that means we don't know."

International agency denials had no impact on President Bush who, upon emerging with Tony Blair from their meeting, referred to the "new" IAEA report, then, after citing data from IAEA announcements in 1998 and 1995, said, "I don't know what more evidence we need." Tony Blair said that the international community ought to form a coalition against Saddam Hussein. Bush also came back to his bottom line: "It's the stated policy of this government to have regime change. And it hasn't changed. And we'll use all tools at our disposal to do so."

The next strategic leak, which came from Washington the same day, consisted of the claim that over fourteen months Iraq had sought to buy thousands of aluminum tubes for gas centrifuges necessary to enrich uranium to the level of purity necessary to construct a nuclear weapon. Unlike the July 2002 leaks about invasion plans, which would promptly be investigated by the Pentagon's detective unit, the aluminum tube leak was confirmed by two senior administration officials. Richard Cheney reiterated the charge that Iraq sought the tubes for nuclear weapons on NBC's *Meet the Press*. Condo-

leezza Rice, appearing on a noontime talk show on Cable News Network
(CNN) on September 8, not only referred to the aluminum tubes but invoked
the nuclear genie: "There will always be some uncertainty about how quickly
he [Saddam Hussein] can acquire nuclear weapons, but we don't want the
smoking gun to be a mushroom cloud."

Inside the administration Cheney and Rumsfeld continued to fight a
rearguard action against seeking any UN resolution. Secretary of State Powell, in reviewing the twenty-first draft of the Bush speech on September 10,
the day before the president's departure for New York, discovered that all
reference to a resolution had disappeared from the prepared text. As late as
September 11, Vice President Cheney argued against seeking a resolution
based on the loss of prestige Bush would suffer if he failed to secure one.
Bush made his final decision that night when already in New York for the
9/11 anniversary.

President Bush did ask for a resolution when he spoke at the United
Nations. In that speech on September 12 George Bush told the General
Assembly that "our principles and our security are challenged today by outlaw groups and regimes." Without mentioning Al Qaeda, Bush then cut
straight to Iraq. This nation, Bush intoned, was "exactly the kind of aggressive threat the United Nations was born to confront." The president recited
the history of the UN weapons inspections in Iraq through the 1990s, which
he pitched as a trail of Saddam breaking promises to abide by successive UN
resolutions. After that came the setup, George Bush's depiction of the Iraqi
threat: Iraq possessed all the infrastructure, designs, and plans it needed for
building nuclear weapons. Bush himself then made the aluminum tubes
charge, referring to "several attempts to buy high-strength aluminum tubes
used to enrich uranium." If Saddam got the fissile material, Bush stated flatly,
he "would be able to build a nuclear weapon within a year." And, the president of the United States continued, "Iraq also possesses a force of SCUD-
type missiles," was working on even longer-range missiles, and "can inflict
mass death throughout the region." As Bush summarized, "Saddam Hussein's
regime is a grave and gathering danger." The lead drafter of this UN address,

speechwriter Michael Gerson, saw it as creating an impression of inevitability justified by evidence.

The "conduct" of the Iraqi government, President Bush declared, "is a threat to the authority of the United Nations, and a threat to peace." The president promised to work with the Security Council for "the necessary resolutions." Yet before launching into his peroration Bush put his real point: "The purposes of the United States should not be doubted . . . our action will be unavoidable. And a regime that has lost its legitimacy will also lose its power."

One day after Bush's UN speech, the WHIG unit in Bush's White House put out its first public paper, a piece on Iraqi deception and denial practices called "A Decade of Deception and Defiance."

Iraq was hardly blind to her growing peril. During the summer Baghdad offered to let UN weapons inspectors return and resume the disarmament process that had lain fallow since 1998. For some weeks before the Bush UN speech, Baghdad and the United Nations conducted on again–off again talks about conditions under which the inspectors might work. Saddam Hussein's government had played cagey, grudgingly making concessions, at times stopping the negotiations or going back on points already covered. As the drumbeat of Bush rhetoric about regime change continued, Baghdad's reluctance seemed to disappear. Iraqis still wanted the end of sanctions against their country. The Bush speech, with its call to rally against Saddam, crystallized Iraqi realization that new UN inspections were impossible to resist. On September 17, the Iraqi government announced it would readmit UN inspectors without conditions. Not willing to rubber-stamp Baghdad's claims to have disarmed, the International Atomic Energy Agency (IAEA) and a new authority, the United Nations Monitoring, Inspection, and Verification Commission (UNMOVIC), spent more weeks with the Iraqis carefully hashing out a set of procedures to prevent the kind of obstruction and denial that had blocked inspectors in the 1990s. In parallel with these arrangements the UN Security Council began to craft a fresh resolution to govern the new inspection system.

Had President Bush stopped here, assuming a stance of support for IAEA and UNMOVIC inspections, this story could have had a happy ending. The Iraq crisis could have ended in full disarmament, not war, and the outcome would have been accounted an American diplomatic triumph. Though there would probably have been bruised feelings among nations hurt by Washington's strong-arm diplomatic tactics over the spring and summer of 2002, Bush would have emerged with a mantle of glowing achievement. There were people telling Bush that is what he ought to do. Australian Prime Minister John Howard, for one, met with George Bush just before the president's UN speech and put to him the view that the best way to deal with Saddam was to work through the United Nations.

Bush chose instead to incite picture of the world with a clear and present danger from Iraq: nuclear weapons within a year plus a long-range missile force, yielding capacity for mass destruction throughout the region. Bush attributed activity ("conduct") to the Iraqis, something that could be established by investigation. That investigation would occur, and it would yield quite a different picture. As we shall see, none of the elements in Bush's picture was accurate.

Rumsfeld's Rehearsal

On September 19 President Bush asked Congress for a resolution authorizing the use of such force as deemed necessary in the Iraqi situation. In an effort to substantiate Bush's request and still public doubts, Secretary of Defense Donald H. Rumsfeld appeared that day before the Senate Armed Services Committee. Rumsfeld's testimony, argumentative to a fault, started with over two dozen "facts" about Saddam's Iraq. The "facts" were intended to paint Baghdad as a major menace and ranged from charges that Iraq had praised the September 11 attacks, to ones that Saddam had repressed the Iraqi people, leading up to the "fact"—actually a mere article of faith—that "his regime is determined to acquire the means to strike the U.S., its friends and allies with weapons of mass destruction."

Bush administration allegations regarding Iraqi weapons were presented as facts in secretary Rumsfeld's testimony. Rumsfeld would become a point man for surfacing claims of Iraq's weapons and power. As early as July 30, he had made the first mention of alleged Iraqi mobile laboratories designed to produce biological weapons. In the September testimony that claim was not repeated, but the secretary of defense evoked many others. These included charges (each made into a separate "fact" in a list) that Saddam's regime had "amassed large, clandestine stockpiles" of biological weapons, of chemical weapons, "dozens" of ballistic missiles (skirting the objection that Iraq's missiles were limited by short, battlefield-type ranges with the statement that Iraq "is working to extend their ranges"), and pilotless aircraft "as a means of delivering chemical and biological weapons." As for nuclear weapons, Saddam allegedly had "designs for at least two different nuclear devices," a ready infrastructure, and all necessary scientists, engineers, and technicians in place, so that "Very likely all they need to complete a weapon is fissile material—and they are, at this moment, seeking that material—both from foreign sources and the capability to produce it indigenously." This last statement included September's new charge: that Iraq was currently seeking nuclear material abroad, a reference to claims that would be shown to be forgeries, about which much more will be heard later.

Later in his testimony, Secretary Rumsfeld demonstrated that he was "on message" for the White House Information Group: in a series of questions Rumsfeld posed rhetorically and then answered, he rejected the need for a "smoking gun" in evidence that Iraq constituted a present danger, not quite resorting to the "mushroom cloud" imagery that Cheney and Rice had used little more than a week before, but essentially alluding to it. Rumsfeld went on to declare, "I suggest that any who insist on perfect evidence are back in the twentieth century."

Another of Rumsfeld's rhetorical questions attempted to refute analysts who said that the Iraqi threat was not imminent, that Baghdad needed five to seven years to create a nuclear weapon. Conceding the answer to this question was not knowable, Rumsfeld changed the subject: "Those who raise questions about the nuclear threat need to focus on the immediate threat from biological weapons." In fact, key U.S. intelligence assessments continued to project Iraq as years short of a nuclear capability (the interval being almost precisely the same), while there was no consensus among American and British intelligence analysts on whether, in fact, Iraq had *any* current inventory of biological weapons.

Further on in his testimony, the secretary of defense disputed whether new UN weapons inspections could be effective. He discounted Iraq's agreement to a new disarmament mission. Rumsfeld's view: "If failure to comply with WMD inspections is a *casus belli*, the UN already has it." (Of course, unknown to his listeners, Rumsfeld was the same man who, within Bush's inner council, insistently rejected a UN, as opposed to a U.S., war.) In this testimony Rumsfeld also responded to the argument that there was no international consensus on a need to attack Iraq with Polyannaish aplomb, and another misuse of the word "fact." Rumsfeld said, "The fact is there are a number of countries that want Saddam Hussein gone. Some are reluctant to say [so] publicly yet." He alluded to the large number of states concerned about terrorism—at another point he misleadingly equated attacking Iraq with attacking terrorists—to suggest that a coalition would respond to U.S. leadership and fall into place on Iraq. As to the argument that overthrowing Saddam Hussein ought to be a last resort, not a first one, Rumsfeld opined, "I would respond that for more than a decade now, the international community has tried every other step." Rumsfeld's words were not about disarming Iraq; they were the testimony of a man who wanted war.

To the question of why Saddam *had* to be overthrown, Rumsfeld began his reply by saying, "The President has not made that decision." This afforded the public some reassurance, but it was false testimony, belying Bush's decision of August 29. Knowingly providing false testimony to the Congress, even when not under oath, is a crime under U.S. law.

There was also the matter of international law. The UN charter, which forms part of U.S. law under appropriate treaty statutes, enshrines the promise not to interfere in the internal affairs of other nations (and imposing "regime change" in Iraq was an obvious interference), and recognizes the legitimacy of war only for self-defense. Secretary Rumsfeld raised and rejected the question of whether a U.S. attack would violate international law by flatly declaring, "That is untrue." Rumsfeld evoked a right of "anticipatory self-defense" (also referred to by the Bush administration during these months as "preemptive self-defense") in a highly artificial way. Self-defense applies solely against an attack that is already in progress. To attack someone because, in some unspecified future, they *could* (there was, and still remains, no information on any *actual* Iraqi *intention* to attack the United States) mount some attack is not self-defense, anticipatory or otherwise. It is simply aggression. That the Bush administration adduced this legal mumbo jumbo only furnishes evidence that the U.S. attack was premeditated.

One of Rumsfeld's "facts" concerned the allegations that Iraq had links to terrorists. The secretary of defense characterized as an "opinion" the view that "there is scant evidence of Iraq's ties to terrorists," and later characterized that opinion as "not correct." Shortly thereafter he asserted, "We know that Al Qaeda is operating in Iraq today." In addition, Rumsfeld cited "a number of contacts" between Saddam's government and Al Qaeda over the years. To bolster his claim, the secretary of defense also referred to the presence in Baghdad of Abu Nidal, a Palestinian terrorist who had been inactive for many years, and insisted that *no* link between Saddam and the September 11 attacks was necessary to make the case for regime change in Iraq. Every one of these assertions was questionable. The evidence will be discussed in detail in the analysis of Secretary Powell's Security Council speech of February 2003, below.

Defense Secretary Donald Rumsfeld's September 19, 2002, testimony in Congress rehearsed every one of the key elements of the Bush administration's justification for war with Iraq. It is a measure of the controversial nature of the case for war that the senators did not swallow the Rumsfeld testimony, but rather questioned him. Members of the Senate Select Committee on Intelligence, who had access to the latest CIA analyses, had been wondering why they could not find an authoritative current estimate on the Iraqi question. With Congress being asked to approve the use of force against Saddam, the lack was particularly glaring.

Ten days before Secretary Rumsfeld's Capitol Hill appearance, the Il-

linois Democratic Senator, Richard Durbin, pointed out that the actual views
of the U.S. intelligence community were not being given attention either in
Congress or by the White House. Durbin's complaint added to a chorus of
doubts raised by the public and in the media. The answer to all doubt, in
the Bush administration, would be to wave a supposed Iraqi menace. On
September 24, Tony Blair's government issued its own dossier on the Iraqi
threat. Among its disturbing allegations was that Saddam Hussein could order an attack with biological or chemical weapons that could be carried out
within as few as forty-five minutes. The claim, later shown to be highly
misleading by investigations in the United Kingdom, was one Bush seized
upon. He used it twice, in a "Global Message" from the Rose Garden on
September 26 and in a radio speech two days later, in which he also declared
"there are Al Qaeda terrorists inside Iraq," more statements long on assertions of menace but short on fact.

The National Intelligence Estimate and the CIA White Paper

Representative of public clamor at this moment was a *New York Times* editorial, "SHARING THE EVIDENCE ON IRAQ," that appeared on August
21. The *Times* referred specifically to how the Bush administration had
"floated" a succession of charges about Iraq—that Saddam was linked to international terrorism, that it was a member of a global "Axis of Evil," and
that Baghdad was attempting to develop nuclear weapons. "Few firm facts
have been offered in support of any of these claims," the newspaper declared,
"but there have been frequent allusions to secret intelligence information that
officials are unwilling to make public." Serious public deliberations on war
and peace could not proceed in the absence of information the *Times* editorialized.

Consultation with Congress brought the administration into further contact with these views. Demands for more specific data resulted in a top-secret
briefing for the four most senior members of Congress on September 5 by

CIA Director George Tenet. White House concern was evident in the fact that Vice President Richard Cheney attended as well, and both Cheney and Tenet joined Secretary Rumsfeld the next morning when a larger group of twenty-five senators were given a breakfast briefing on weapons proliferation issues. There were private briefings as well, such as of friendly Democratic leader Richard Gephardt by Tenet on September 13 and Robert Menendez (D-NJ) by Condi Rice and Tenet that same week. But there was a clear effort to stifle any flow of information to the public—members of Congress who attended briefings were asked to sign special secrecy agreements. Republican Senator John McCain stomped out of one such briefing when, after all the hoopla, he found Donald Rumsfeld saying nothing more than what was in the media.

The Senate Intelligence Committee had clear standing in this area. Florida Democrat Bob Graham, its chairman, had asked for an intelligence estimate on Iraq on July 22 and got a twenty-five-page CIA analysis reportedly noting the inconclusiveness of claims on Iraqi nuclear weapons and links to Al Qaeda terrorists. The document was oddly anonymous, arriving with no cover sheet or letterhead. Another report, a Defense Intelligence Agency paper in early September, "reflected the same cautious assessments," according to John B. Judis and Spencer Ackerman, writing in *The New Republic*. Richard J. Durbin seized on the reports to urge that the intelligence community's reporting be given greater attention by both Congress and the Executive. Consequently Graham, on September 11, wrote to Director George Tenet insisting that a National Intelligence Estimate be done on Iraq.

Until August the Bush administration had assumed it could launch a preemptive war against Iraq without qualms about public opinion. Even then the White House still supposed that a war could be conducted without formal authorization, on the authority of the president as commander-in-chief, and under the congressional resolution hastily passed after the 9/11 attacks. That notion evaporated in the first days of September. While it seemed desirable in the White House to avoid any declaration of war or congressional authorizing resolution, political soundings confirmed that would be a dangerous path to take. Once it became clear to Bush that the road to war would have to comply with a legislative process, political concerns assumed tremendous importance.

The highest form of intelligence report in the United States is called the National Intelligence Estimate (NIE). In the American intelligence system there is a highly formalized procedure for creating the national estimates and their more crisis-oriented brethren, the Special National Intelligence Estimates (SNIEs). The motivation for a national estimate can come from several sources. There are NIEs that are regularly done to assess particular countries or situations. During the Cold War years, for example, a series of national estimates were done every year on the Soviet Union. In addition, the Director of Central Intelligence can order up an estimate, either on his own account or as proposed by the National Intelligence Council, the unit that creates the estimates. The White House can request NIEs, and so can Congress, as happened with the Iraq NIE of September 2002.

Director George Tenet held a very precarious position when the Congress asked for an Iraq estimate. Tenet was being forced to play a delicate multisided game, rather like a multiboard chess match, caught between his own analysts at the CIA, analysts throughout the rest of the intelligence community, the Congress, and the White House. Director Tenet had been pulled directly into the Iraqi political fray by Vice President Cheney, who breathed down the CIA director's neck when Tenet first briefed the top congressional leaders at the beginning of September. Cheney continued to ride close herd over the CIA, going out to agency headquarters at Langley, Virginia several times during the months before the war. Other times the vice president sent his staff chief and national security assistant I. Lewis Libby. In the wake of the Iraq war, Cheney's office has denied that any of this attention had a chilling effect on CIA analysis, but it could hardly be otherwise. This kind of interference from the executive branch is extremely unusual; vice presidents almost never go out to the CIA except for morale purposes or ceremonial occasions. Nixon, Ford, Carter, Bush (I), and Clinton had each been to the CIA once, Reagan twice perhaps, never for a working visit, their vice presidents never at all. Rather, the CIA's briefers go to them.

One former CIA officer, who worked as a White House briefer during the
1980s, recalls that in his time on this job the vice president never once came
to Langley. For most of that time the vice president had been George W.
Bush's father, who had had *special* interest in intelligence, having once been
CIA director himself.

George J. Tenet was close to the current president, of course, and had
no wish to disappoint either Bush or Cheney. Tenet had achieved the unusual distinction of surviving from one administration to the next, even a
presidency of one political party to the other. Only two of Tenet's predeces-
sors held that distinction (Allen W. Dulles and Richard M. Helms), and
Tenet was quickly coming to the moment he would have held the director's
job longer than Helms. But there was a problem: September 11, or more
specifically, the charges swirling through Washington that the ability of Al
Qaeda to pull off the 9/11 attacks resulted from a massive intelligence failure.
Through the summer of 2002 a joint investigation by the Senate and House
intelligence committees was looking at the 9/11 charges and a number of
powerful people were out looking for George Tenet's head. Tenet had already testified once about September 11, his subordinates were being given
the third degree, and he was fighting a losing battle to avoid public hearings
that would grill Tenet himself and other CIA officers. Clearly, George Tenet
would be obliged to take responsibility for the CIA's failures on 9/11, making
the director especially dependent upon President Bush, who would be pressured to demand the CIA director's resignation.

The truth is that the White House *did not want a national estimate about
Iraq.* There were plenty of uncertainties in the intelligence, and crafting an
NIE would serve only to reveal them to congressional eyes, including those
of Bush's opponents. And that was the best case. A less good case would be
a national estimate demonstrating how little hard data lay behind the administration's extravagant claims for Iraqi military power. The *worst* case resided
in the possibility the NIE would authoritatively refute the assertions being
made by the president, vice president, secretary of defense, and others.

Still, as a practical matter, Director Tenet had little choice. With the
United States considering war, failure to produce such a paper, particularly

in the context of the 9/11 intelligence debacle, would have left the director in an untenable position. Responding to the congressional request also helped Tenet curry favor on the Hill. Bush and Cheney understood. Nevertheless, yet another first of the Iraq war is that it is the first time in U.S. history that the legislative branch of government, not the executive, provided the impetus for such high-level intelligence analysis as the subject received. The dynamics of this situation do much to explain the "fact"—later claimed by chief of staff to the president Andrew Card and other White House spokespersons—that Condoleezza Rice, the *national security adviser,* never read the footnotes in the NIE.

Once a determination was made to proceed with a national estimate on Iraqi weapons of mass destruction, the CIA director had to contend with considerations of access to information and undue influence as well. With the departure of UN weapons inspectors in 1998, American intelligence lost its main source of on-the-ground data from Iraq. Director Tenet had had his top collection official review the community's ability to gather intelligence on various Iraqi subjects in 1998 and weapons of mass destruction were a leading intelligence collection requirement. Though the CIA insists advances in collection resulted from this review, the capabilities of machine spies remain inherently limited.

The formal process in the U.S. intelligence community is that the National Intelligence Council (NIC) receives a set of criteria (called "terms of reference") for the report. The NIC is a panel composed of a number of national intelligence officers (NIOs), each of whom covers a given area or function. Once the appropriate NIO is assigned to compile the national estimate, the terms of reference are circulated to all the agencies that comprise the U.S. intelligence community, and each of these is asked for its contribution to the NIE. A "contribution" is a specific paper and represents the considered view, or intelligence position, of the concerned agency. The job of the NIO is to boil the contributions down into a draft national estimate. He is partly an analyst and partly a manager. The NIO does have some help—the NIC has an analytic group that supplies a pool of skilled analysts who can supplement the NIO and his assistant. In addition, the NIO can call on resources anywhere in the community, for example, tasking a specific expert to provide a paper in his field.

Once a draft national estimate is finalized, it is reviewed by the National Intelligence Council. The draft then goes up to the top level of the community, the National Foreign Intelligence Board, on which sit the directors of all the agencies. These directors have already furnished the NIC with their departmental contributions to the estimate and are interested to see that the intelligence positions of their agencies are represented in the national estimate. Members of the board can concur in the National Intelligence Estimate (NIE), can allow themselves to be convinced by the evidence, or they can disagree. A disagreement is formally recorded in the NIE in a "footnote," which states what agency is dissenting to what specific statement, and provides alternate language for that part of the national estimate. Over the years these dissents have sometimes been printed at the bottom of the page, sometimes gathered at the back of the paper, and sometimes printed in a parallel column of text on the margin of the page, but to dissent has always been termed "taking a footnote." Ultimately the National Intelligence Council works for the Director of Central Intelligence (DCI) and the NIE is the director's paper. Some DCIs have sent back national estimates for redrafting, some have kept hands off the process, a few have taken footnotes themselves when they disagree. With some notable exceptions, George Tenet has largely avoided interfering with the national estimates.

The National Intelligence Council itself has recently put more emphasis on general global developments and even longer-range studies in place of NIEs on single countries and their policies. The NIC has studied the impact of AIDS on populations and national armies, worldwide development of ballistic missiles through 2015, global trends through that same year, to cite a few examples. The last-known national estimate projecting Iraq was several years old (George Tenet has referred to a 1999 report, but the reference may have been to a global NIE on weapons of mass destruction). There had been estimates in 1989, prior to the first Gulf War, in 1992 in its wake, 1994, and the 1999 report already noted, but there has also been a tendency to have many of these reports written by functional analysis centers like CIA's Nonproliferation Center or its Counterterrorism Center. It is an open question whether some of the old estimative skills have not become rusty over the past few years.

Another factor George Tenet had to deal with in the making of the Iraq national estimate was more structural. Years ago the NIC replaced an older system under which the collective group, not a single NIO, was responsible for the estimate, and they were supported by a larger office that provided necessary analysts to help with the drafting. With corporate responsibility came a measure of built-in integrity. The NIO system in place now is inherently more susceptible to influence. With a single individual as the focal point for drafting, his opinions become hugely important. Outsiders wanting to affect the process also have a ready target for their attempts at influence. At the level of NIC review, since the NIOs hold portfolios, the other council members are not expert in the field of the national estimate drafter and may be loath to object when something in the paper seems out of kilter. At the level of National Foreign Intelligence Board review, agency positions are driven largely by bureaucratic interests, though, as we shall see, something unusual happened with the national estimate on Iraq.

Chairman of the National Intelligence Council when the Iraq NIE was proposed in September 2002 was John L. Helgerson, who had so much on his plate after 9/11 that his vice-chairman effectively led the Council. Stuart A. Cohen, the vice-chairman, had been on the NIC since 1998, at first in charge of its analytical group. Cohen had been a special assistant to Bill Casey in the Reagan years. He had held jobs on both the analytical and operations sides of the agency, and was a plank-holder in the formation of both the Counterintelligence Center and the Weapons Intelligence, Nonproliferation, and Arms Control Center (WINPAC), of which he had been the first director.

There was a choice to make on the National Intelligence Council when it came to assigning an NIE on Iraq. That country, after all, is of the Middle East, and the Council has an NIO specialized in Middle Eastern issues. The estimate would revolve around a lot of advanced military hardware, though, and there was an NIO for strategic weapons. The Council also had an NIO for science and technology. Paul R. Pillar, the NIO for the Near East and South Asia, held relatively sophisticated views on the new age of terrorism, and had had military experience in Vietnam. He had previously served the NIC and the CIA, twenty-five years of experience in all. Pillar's forte was regional expertise, certainly critical in the case of Saddam Hussein. The NIO on science and technology, Lawrence K. Gershwin, was a bit of an oddity at the CIA. Gershwin had spent his entire agency career as a senior person, an NIO, and probably had been an NIO longer than anyone in the history of the Council, with medals to prove it. Those who arrive from the outside as Gershwin did usually leave after a few years. Gershwin was a dedicated techie, and though he had been involved in some of the CIA's more serious overestimates of Soviet nuclear forces, he was considered the agency's best expert on deception techniques, a clear factor in the Iraq estimate.

The other obvious possibility was Robert D. Walpole. Originally a photo interpreter, Walpole joined intelligence about the same time as Pillar, but moved between the CIA and the State Department's Bureau of Intelligence and Research (INR), with a break during the first Bush administration, when Walpole managed arms control policy as a deputy assistant secretary of state. He had returned to the CIA in 1992 as deputy director of WINPAC, and took over the agency's response to inquiries on Gulf War illness, an issue on which Walpole is still the CIA focal point even though he has been the NIO for strategic and nuclear programs since 1998. Walpole had received the CIA's Distinguished Intelligence Medal for his work on Gulf War illnesses. He was well versed on proliferation issues, held the strategic forces portfolio, and had some area experience as well.

Vice-Chairman Cohen of the National Intelligence Council could have selected any of the NIOs for this job. Though the portfolio most straightforwardly belonged to Bob Walpole, Gershwin had a good claim as the deception expert and knew plenty about chemical and biological weapons and nuclear ones too. Paul Pillar had the regional portfolio. Cohen chose Walpole to do the national estimate on weapons of mass destruction. The agency reportedly started an estimate on Iraqi conventional capabilities at the same time, and that would have gone to Pillar.

A colorful character in some respects, in college Walpole had combined interior design with his study of international relations. His visual acuity helped him later as an imagery analyst, and his tactile sense made him a motorcyclist. A Mormon—not all that unusual at CIA—Walpole had attained the rank of bishop, making him the bishop on a motorcycle who happened to be one of the dozen or so top analytic authorities in U.S. intelligence.

Walpole had had a sterling reputation with the Bureau of Intelligence and Research at State in the 1980s. Colleagues recall him as quite critical of CIA on some of its extravagant claims about Soviet weaponry. Yet some of his most recent efforts have been more suspect. In 1995 Intelligence had done an NIE on foreign ballistic missiles that projected little threat and undercut proponents of ballistic missile defense for the United States. A blue-ribbon panel created by Congress to study missile defenses, headed by then-private citizen Donald H. Rumsfeld, was highly critical of the missile NIE and included an extensive critique of Intelligence as a side report to its findings. When U.S. Intelligence responded by ordering up a fresh national estimate in 1999, Walpole had become the NIO for strategic forces, in charge of the estimate and worried that Congress would denounce an NIE perceived little threat. But there was little evidence that challenged the conclusions reached in 1995. Even the recent launch of a North Korean missile to an intermediate range was merely a new instance of nations developing medium-range systems, none of which was capable of reaching the United States. In addition the U.S. standard for measuring threat used a concept known as "initial operational capability," which meant a foreign nation not only had to develop a technology but had to field it in significant numbers (in Cold War days, ten operational missiles, for example). That standard further postponed potential threats to the United States. For the 1999 NIE Walpole reportedly devised a new standard, "initial threat availability," which permitted a judgment of threat as soon as a missile had been flight-tested. The 1999 NIE thus projected a nearer-term threat that might require U.S. missile defenses.

This leads to suspicion that prevailing political winds might be influencing Walpole's judgments as an intelligence officer.

The process of creating the Iraq NIE remains opaque at this writing. Unlike Great Britain, where there have been both judicial investigations and a parliamentary inquiry into the drafting of the British intelligence pamphlet that paralleled the CIA's product, the U.S. government has made public almost nothing about the intelligence reporting on Iraq. There *have been* reviews on this side of the Atlantic, including one by a special group of former CIA officers brought back from retirement by Director George Tenet, another by the CIA inspector general, one by the House Permanent Select Committee on Intelligence, one by the Senate Intelligence and Armed Services Committee, and one, within the White House, by the President's Foreign Intelligence Advisory Board (headed by Brent Scowcroft). None of their reports has been made public. Scowcroft told a CIA-sponsored conference in September 2003, "The bulk of opinion now is that the intelligence books were cooked." The head of Tenet's review board, former senior CIA officer Richard J. Kerr, defended the sourcing on the CIA estimates at a press conference. Proposals in both the Senate and House of Representatives for a public commission to investigate the intelligence reporting on Iraq have been resisted by the Bush administration and its allies in Congress.

A few points can be made from outside this process. First, the NIE was a rush job. Only a couple of weeks passed between the CIA's agreement to proceed with an NIE and the date in October 2002 when the estimate was available for congressmen to read on Capitol Hill. One source reports that Tenet's original guidance was to complete the estimate within ten days. That included time for the agency contributions, a draft written by the National Intelligence Council, time for NIC review of the draft, then formal coordination of the estimate by the National Foreign Intelligence Board (NFIB), and finally for the printing and distribution of the final product.

We also know that the Iraq NIE, red hot in terms of its political sensitivity, could only be as immune to outside influences as George Tenet chose to make it. Resilience in the face of political pressure is not a strong point of the NIC. The NIC forms part of the director's office and works directly for him. George Tenet was vulnerable within the Bush administration. It would have taken just one demand from, say, Richard Cheney, for a briefing from the national intelligence officer responsible for this NIE to make abundantly clear the importance of this document to the White House and suggest to intelligence analysts they ought to engage in a little creative writing. This kind of pressure is far from unknown in intelligence; there is even a term of art for it: an analyst may have to write in a "directed position." In the House of Representatives Dennis J. Kucinich (D-OH) offered an amendment to the intelligence appropriations bill for the 2004 fiscal year that would have required an audit of all telephone and electronic communications between the vice president's office and the CIA on the subject of Iraqi weapons of mass destruction. This initiative was defeated on June 25, 2003.

Owing to the secrecy of the process, we have no evidence at this point that Vice President Cheney or anyone else exerted influence on the conclusions in the CIA's Iraq NIE. We do, however, have the extremely suggestive example of the British case. Prime Minister Tony Blair had agreed with Bush to move forward on action against Iraq, and announced that a report—which the British called a "dossier"—would be made public. The document, duly made public on September 24, 2002, was titled "Iraq's Weapons of Mass Destruction: The Assessment of the British Government." Soon after its release the press reported that elements within British intelligence thought the report went too far in its claims abut Saddam's weapons. After more such reports, the British Parliament initiated a formal inquiry in early 2003. After David Kelly, a weapons scientist who testified before that inquiry, committed suicide in June 2003, a judicial investigation of the suicide went back over the entire process of the drafting of the dossier, compelling testimony from Tony Blair, senior cabinet and intelligence officials, the intelligence officers who had drafted the dossier, other defense and intelligence managers, and many more persons. There was also a separate parliamentary inquiry by the committee that oversees the British intelligence community directly into the quality of their intelligence reporting.

The British judicial investigation, based on documentary evidence declassified for the purpose, gathered sworn testimony. There is no reason to suppose that the picture built here of the drafting of the British Iraq dossier is anything other than accurate. That picture shows that the officer assigned to write the dossier, John Scarlett, chairman of the Joint Intelligence Committee (the British equivalent to the NIC), was subjected to intense pressures designed to guide him into producing a document that would have the exact effect intended. Over a period of several weeks Blair's cabinet staff worked over three drafts of the report. Blair himself read two of the drafts; there were a good half-dozen meetings, attended by senior Blair aides, giving marching orders for the paper, then reading through the successive drafts. Cabinet staffs, defense intelligence staffs, and Scarlett himself penned over a dozen memoranda or e-mails regarding presentation of facts in the dossier and half that many more on substantive issues. Blair's top communications aide, Alastair Campbell, insisted throughout, to both parliamentary and judicial investigators, that his interventions in the process had been purely giving advice to Scarlett on presentation of the material, but his memoranda to Scarlett show otherwise. To cite just a few examples, Campbell asked Scarlett to change the claim that Iraq had "sought" uranium in Africa and make the paper say Saddam had "secured" that uranium. Similarly, Campbell wanted to shape Scarlett's description of the Iraqi nuclear program. The constant drive would be to make the document stronger. A foreword issued over Blair's own signature was rewritten at least five times, including once by John Scarlett. Memoranda from British intelligence expressing concern regarding claims made at points in the paper were met by finding language to paper over differences. In short, the British intelligence white paper was shepherded to publication very carefully by the Blair government.

An independent review of the intelligence reports by the Intelligence and Security Committee of the House of Commons concluded that the Blair government had not exerted undue influence on the British estimates, but criticized the reports themselves. On the dossier's claim that Saddam was producing chemical and biological weapons, the parliamentary inquiry concluded that John Scarlett's group "did not know what had been produced and in what quantities" and therefore ought to have highlighted its lack of certainty in the published report. The most likely use of such weapons as did exist, which would be on the battlefield against opposing forces, should also have been stated explicitly, the inquiry concluded. The claim that Saddam's weapons could be made ready for use in forty-five minutes' time, the committee decided, was "arresting detail" and obligated Scarlett and the report drafters to handle it carefully. The report they crafted did not say the claim applied only to battlefield use, and only to the movement of chemical and biological munitions to firing points. As the inquiry concluded, "The omission of the context and assessment allowed speculation as to exact meaning."

The British example begs the question: given Bush's desire to move against Iraq, the known political sensitivity of the issue, and the administration's own desire to *avoid* certain judgments in an intelligence report on Saddam Hussein's weapons, did the Bush White House in fact keep its hands off the process of crafting the American national intelligence estimate? At a minimum, resolving doubts about the NIE in such a way as to restore public confidence requires some investigation along the lines of the one in Britain.

It remains impossible at this writing to analyze the NIE directly. The document still remains secret except for its "key judgments" section, which was subsequently declassified and is discussed in detail below. A distilled version of the CIA's classified NIE, however, was issued in the form of a public commentary, or "white paper," which is available here. The white paper shows indications of many of the identical techniques used to massage the threat in the British report. Claims without context, partial information, efforts to obscure key objections to the secret report—all are present in the white paper. Given the short time available to prepare the paper, and the similarly short time for the NIE, it is an open question whether the same person was responsible for both documents. Stuart Cohen may well have adopted a sort of parallel process in preparing the CIA white paper. If so, my speculation would be that Lawrence Gershwin drafted it.

Journalists John B. Judis and Spencer Ackerman, in one of the best early treatments of the selling of the Iraq war, note the existence of a mid-September CIA paper "that highlighted the Bush administration's claims and consigned skepticism to footnotes. According to one congressional staffer who read the document, ... 'they didn't do analysis. What they did was they amassed everything they could that said anything bad about Iraq and put it into a document.' " This statement may be a reference to the differences between the NIE and the white paper the agency eventually delivered to Congress. These differences will be illustrated in detail below.

Former CIA deputy director Richard J. Kerr's later review of the intelligence reports, conducted for Director Tenet, speaks to the manipulation of intelligence, but only vaguely. Kerr's panel's preliminary report, delivered in July 2003, studied only whether the documents were solidly grounded in the intelligence available to the community, and found that they were. There was "a base of hard evidence growing out of the lead-up to the first war, the first war itself, and then the inspections process," and the United States drew on that. But after 1998, when the UN inspectors left, "There were pieces of new information, but not a lot of hard information." The result was fragmentary and inconclusive. It was therefore inevitable, as Kerr told journalists, that the prewar reports had contained some caveats and disagreements over data, particularly on the Iraqi nuclear program and on the extent of ties between Saddam and Al Qaeda. A Pentagon official quoted in the same story proved more direct: "We were reduced to dead reckoning. We had to go back to our last fixed position, what we knew in '98, and plot a course from there." As for political pressure on the analysts, Kerr told the *Los Angeles Times*, "There probably was pressure. There always is pressure. But the primary conclusions didn't change."

The NIE came in at ninety pages and was approved in late September 2002. In the course of the furor over misleading intelligence that followed the war, the key judgments section of the NIE was declassified on July 18, 2003, and portions of the estimate have been described in official statements from the CIA director on July 11 and August 11, 2003. This material offers points of comparison between the NIE and the CIA white paper on Iraqi weapons, which in turn yield insights about how information was recast for broader consumption.

We know from the evidence available that the intelligence community did not hold a unified view of the Iraqi threat characterized in the national intelligence estimate. Several agencies took footnotes in the estimate, dissenting from the views of the NIE. These include the State Department's Bureau of Intelligence and Research (INR), which dissented on the projection of the Iraqi nuclear weapons program and on the allegation that certain aluminum tubes detected among Iraq's imports were intended to create machinery for uranium enrichment for nuclear weapons. The Department of Energy (DOE) joined in the INR dissent on the aluminum tube issue. There are reports that the DOE objections would have been even stronger save for the fact that the DOE's representative attending the National Foreign Intelligence Board on this occasion, Thomas Rider, restrained DOE experts on enrichment from fully detailing their opposition. Meanwhile, Air Force intelligence also dissented from the judgment that Iraq's program to develop unmanned aerial vehicles was primarily intended to create a capacity to deliver chemical and biological weapons.

Press reports indicate that analysts at the Central Intelligence Agency itself were unhappy with the way some issues were handled, in particular Iraqi nuclear weapons and Baghdad's links with the Al Qaeda terrorist group. As is clear from analysis of the CIA white paper, the Defense Intelligence Agency also lacked the information regarding Iraqi chemical and biological weapons plants needed to sustain the NIE judgment that Baghdad was currently producing and stockpiling these materials.

The NIE concluded with "high confidence" that U.S. intelligence was not detecting portions of the Iraqi weapons programs, that Saddam did have chemical and biological weapons and missiles, that Baghdad was continuing "and in some areas expanding" its weapons programs, and that "Iraq could make nuclear weapons in months to a year once it acquires sufficient weapons-grad [sic] fissile material." The estimate effectively then took back its alarming statement on Iraqi nuclear weapons by declaring U.S. intelligence had "moderate confidence" that Iraq "does not have a nuclear weapon or sufficient material to make one." The NIE projection was for a possible Iraqi nuclear weapon in the 2007–09 time frame. Most critically, the NIE declared it had "low confidence" in claims as to when Saddam would *use* weapons of mass destruction, whether he would make clandestine attacks against the U.S.

homeland, and "whether in desperation Saddam would share chemical or biological weapons with Al Qaeda."

George Tenet chaired the session of the National Foreign Intelligence Board that finalized the Iraq NIE. This review was completed in a single meeting, where such scrubbings often take weeks and numerous sessions of the high-level board to complete. Given the doubts on the subject and its importance, this fact in itself suggests that a directed position may have been involved.

Tenet issued official CIA statements in July and August 2003. Those statements maintain that the process was pristine and CIA's analysts productive and accurate, as Tenet maintained in an earlier statement in the spring of 2003. "We stand behind the judgments of the NIE as well as our analyses on Iraq's programs over the past decade," Tenet declared in his August 11 release. The CIA director maintained the intelligence data on Iraqi biological weapons and missiles had become stronger in recent years and built on a solid historical foundation. New intelligence in 2000 had described the construction of mobile biological weapons plants. On chemical weapons the intelligence community had reached agreement by 1997, Tenet wrote, that Iraq was protecting a "breakout capability" to resume production, and thus it was "not a surprising story" that the 2002 NIE judged that Iraqi production had begun and a stockpile had been accumulated. In the nuclear area Tenet lunged at the inconsistencies in the DOE approach to the national estimate to assert that that agency "*agreed* that reconstitution [of the Iraqi nuclear weapons program] was underway."

Later, the House Permanent Select Committee on Intelligence took a look at how the NIE had been assembled. Chaired by Porter J. Goss, a Florida Republican but a former CIA officer himself, seconded by Jane Harman, a California Democrat who had also sat with Goss on the congressional investigation into the 9/11 attacks, the committee had a good idea how to proceed. They interviewed witnesses and collected enough documentation to fill nineteen thick binders. Their preliminary conclusions were in a letter sent to Tenet on September 25, 2003. In a fashion similar to what is known about the CIA internal inquiry headed by Richard Kerr, they found reliance on past conclusions, fragmentary new evidence, and an assumption that a lack of evidence that something had been destroyed equaled proof that it existed. On the nuclear weapons issue, in particular, "Our examination has identified the relatively fragile nature of this information." On chemical and biological weapons, "The dearth of post-1998 underlying intelligence reflects a weakness in . . . collection." Equally important, "The absence of proof that chemical and biological weapons and their related development programs had been destroyed was considered as proof that they continued to exist." The CIA, which had resisted suggestions in both houses of Congress for wide inquiries into the Iraq intelligence, rejected the House committee's criticism as not having been based "on a detailed inquiry on this study."

Agency officers delivered the completed NIE at the offices of the Senate Select Committee on Intelligence at 10:30 P.M. on the evening of October 1, 2002. The committee would be briefed the next morning by Robert Walpole before anyone had much chance to look at the estimate. An overview was delivered by deputy director for central intelligence John L. McLaughlin. George Tenet did not attend. He would claim afterward that he had had to go to the White House for a long-scheduled meeting.

Meanwhile, the Congress had begun work on a resolution that would permit President Bush to use force against Iraq. Powerful congressmen told the White House they needed public evidence of the threat from Iraq that could be referred to in their deliberations. Until this moment, the administration's stance had been that what Bush said in speeches ought to be sufficient. In addition to the UN General Assembly speech, on September 29 Bush announced a further speech he would give in Cincinnati, and assigned Michael Gerson to write it. People should rely upon what Bush said in those speeches, maintained the White House. The few legislators who wanted more detail were referred to the NIE, which would be available under security safeguards in the vaults of the Senate and House intelligence committees.

That was not enough for a Congress deliberating on war and peace. Senator Bob Graham (D-FL), chairman of the intelligence committee, asked for a public document to inform the debate, which led to the white paper. Thus the white paper's specific purpose was to help the Bush administration secure passage of a war resolution against Iraq. It represented a special effort, a public intelligence estimate of a kind the CIA has produced only a few times in its past, always when an administration wished to persuade Americans of a threat. Notable examples are white papers from the 1980s on an alleged Nicaraguan threat to Central America, and on Soviet laser missile defense capabilities.

Produced under the seal of the Director of Central Intelligence the October 2002 paper "Iraq's Weapons of Mass Destruction Programs," amounted to a twenty-five page condensation of the Iraq NIE. A comparison of the paper's "key judgments" section with the same material from the national estimate shows most of the same elements, often using identical language with numerous glaring exceptions. A detailed examination conducted by analysts Jessica T. Matthews, George Perkovich, and Joseph Cirincione of the Carnegie Endowment for International Peace, identified over a dozen instances in which important qualifiers applied to intelligence judgments in the NIE were dropped from the CIA white paper. This frequently had the effect of converting cautious evaluations into assertions of fact. There are many more problematic differences between the two documents, and within the white paper itself, as the analysis below reveals. Revision, not merely abridgement, occurred between the NIE and the white paper, leading to the suspicion that the Bush administration engaged in the same sort of exercise as Tony Blair's cabinet.

In any case, the sum total of charges leveled hardly justified all-out war: The CIA had caught Saddam making some short-range missiles that went a little farther than the Iraqis claimed. There was reason to believe Saddam was diverting money from foreign income. There was no threat to the homeland of the United States, nor indeed any immediate threat from actual Iraqi weapons of mass destruction. Many of the other charges were demonstrably false. The rest were ambiguous. None was anything the CIA and others had not known about for a long time. All could have been resolved by a process of international inspection to which Iraq had already agreed.

George Bush's war began with the hoodwinking of America, and the claims he made later, and those that others made in Bush's behalf, relied upon the foundation of the CIA white paper. It is crucial to see this paper, and to understand exactly how and where the intelligence books were cooked so that the administration could gain support for the policy it wanted.

The entire CIA white paper is reproduced below. Elements are high-lighted because they require comment, for distortion, exaggeration, because they embody some leap over existing data, or for other reasons, with analysis corresponding to the numbers in the margins of the white paper appearing after the document.

Iraq's Weapons of Mass Destruction Programs

October 2002

Key Judgments

Iraq's Weapons of Mass Destruction Programs

1. Iraq has continued its weapons of mass destruction (WMD) programs in defiance of UN resolutions and restrictions. Baghdad has chemical and biological weapons as well as missiles with ranges in excess of UN restrictions; if left unchecked, it probably will have a nuclear weapon during this decade.

2. Baghdad hides large portions of Iraq's WMD efforts. Revelations after the Gulf war starkly demonstrate the extensive efforts undertaken by Iraq to deny information.

   Since inspections ended in 1998, Iraq has maintained its chemical weapons effort, energized its missile program, and invested more heavily in biological weapons; most analysts assess Iraq is reconstituting its nuclear weapons program.

   • Iraq's growing ability to sell oil illicitly increases Baghdad's capabilities to finance WMD programs; annual earnings in cash and goods have more than quadrupled.

3. • Iraq largely has rebuilt missile and biological weapons facilities damaged during Operation Desert Fox and has expanded its chemical and biological infrastructure under the cover of civilian production.

   • Baghdad has exceeded UN range limits of 150 km with its ballistic missiles and is working with unmanned aerial vehicles (UAVs), which allow for a more lethal means to deliver biological and, less likely, chemical warfare agents.

4. • Although Saddam probably does not yet have nuclear weapons or sufficient material to make any, he remains intent on acquiring them.

   How quickly Iraq will obtain its first nuclear weapon depends on when it acquires sufficient weapons-grade fissile material.

5. • If Baghdad acquires sufficient weapons-grade fissile material from abroad, it could make a nuclear weapon within a year.

   • Without such material from abroad, Iraq probably would not be able to make a weapon until the last half of the decade.

6. — Iraq's aggressive attempts to obtain proscribed high-strength aluminum tubes are of significant concern. All intelligence experts agree that Iraq is seeking nuclear weapons and that these tubes could be used in a centrifuge enrichment program. Most intelligence specialists assess this to be the intended use, but some believe that these tubes are probably intended for conventional weapons programs.

1

7.
— Based on tubes of the size Iraq is trying to acquire, a few tens of thousands of centrifuges would be capable of producing enough highly enriched uranium for a couple of weapons per year.

8. **Baghdad has begun renewed production of chemical warfare agents, probably including mustard, sarin, cyclosarin, and VX.** Its capability was reduced during the UNSCOM inspections and is probably more limited now than it was at the time of the Gulf war, although VX production and agent storage life probably have been improved.

9. • Saddam probably has stocked a few hundred metric tons of CW agents.

   • The Iraqis have experience in manufacturing CW bombs, artillery rockets, and projectiles, and probably possess CW bulk fills for SRBM warheads, including for a limited number of covertly stored, extended-range Scuds.

10. **All key aspects—R&D, production, and weaponization—of Iraq's offensive BW program are active and most elements are larger and more advanced than they were before the Gulf wa r.**

11. • Iraq has some lethal and incapacitating BW agents and is capable of quickly producing and weaponizing a variety of such agents, including anthrax, for delivery by bombs, missiles, aerial sprayers, and covert operatives, including potentially against the US Homeland.

12. • Baghdad has established a large-scale, redundant, and concealed BW agent production capability, which includes mobile facilities; these facilities can evade detection, are highly survivable, and can exceed the production rates Iraq had prior to the Gulf war.

13. **Iraq maintains a small missile force and several development programs, including for a UAV that most analysts believe probably is intended to deliver biological warfare agents.**

14. • Gaps in Iraqi accounting to UNSCOM suggest that Saddam retains a covert force of up to a few dozen Scud-variant SRBMs with ranges of 650 to 900 km.

   • Iraq is deploying its new al-Samoud and Ababil-100 SRBMs, which are capable of flying beyond the UN-authorized 150-km range limit.

   • Baghdad's UAVs—especially if used for delivery of chemical and biological warfare (CBW) agents—could threaten Iraq's neighbors, US forces in the Persian Gulf, and the United States if brought close to, or into, the US Homeland.

   • Iraq is developing medium-range ballistic missile capabilities, largely through foreign assistance in building specialized facilities.

Discussion

Iraq's Weapons of Mass Destruction Programs

In April 1991, the UN Security Council enacted Resolution 687 requiring Iraq to declare, destroy, or render harmless its weapons of mass destruction (WMD) arsenal and production infrastructure under UN or International Atomic Energy Agency (IAEA) supervision. UN Security Council Resolution (UNSCR) 687 also demanded that Iraq forgo the future development or acquisition of WMD.

Baghdad's determination to hold onto a sizeable remnant of its WMD arsenal, agents, equipment, and expertise has led to years of dissembling and obstruction of UN inspections. Elite Iraqi security services orchestrated an extensive concealment and deception campaign to hide incriminating documents and material that precluded resolution of key issues pertaining to its WMD programs.

- Iraqi obstructions prompted the Security Council to pass several subsequent resolutions demanding that Baghdad comply with its obligations to cooperate with the inspection process and to provide United Nations Special Commission (UNSCOM) and IAEA officials immediate and unrestricted access to any site they wished to inspect.

- Although outwardly maintaining the facade of cooperation, Iraqi officials frequently denied or substantially delayed access to facilities, personnel, and documents in an effort to conceal critical information about Iraq's WMD programs.

Successive Iraqi declarations on Baghdad's pre-Gulf war WMD programs gradually became more accurate between 1991 and 1998, but only because of sustained pressure from UN sanctions, Coalition military force, and vigorous and robust inspections facilitated by information from cooperative countries. Nevertheless, **Iraq never has fully accounted for major gaps and inconsistencies in its declarations and has provided no credible proof that it has completely destroyed its weapons stockpiles and production infrastructure**.

- UNSCOM inspection activities and Coalition military strikes destroyed most of its prohibited ballistic missiles and some Gulf war-era chemical and biological munitions, but Iraq still has a small force of extended-range Scud-variant missiles, chemical precursors, biological seed stock, and thousands of munitions suitable for chemical and biological agents.

15. - Iraq has preserved and in some cases enhanced the infrastructure and expertise necessary for WMD production and has used that capability to maintain a stockpile of WMD and to increase its size and sophistication in some areas.

UN Security Council Resolutions and Provisions for Inspections and Monitoring: Theory and Practice

Resolution Requirement	Reality
Res. 687 (3 April 1991) Requires Iraq to declare, destroy, remove, or render harmless under UN or IAEA supervision and not to use, develop, construct, or acquire all chemical and biological weapons, all ballistic missiles with ranges greater than 150 km, and all nuclear weapons-usable material, including related material, equipment, and facilities. The resolution also formed the Special Commission and authorized the IAEA to carry out immediate on-site inspections of WMD-related facilities based on Iraq's declarations and UNSCOM's designation of any additional locations.	Baghdad refused to declare all parts of each WMD program, submitted several declarations as part of its aggressive efforts to deny and deceive inspectors, and ensured that certain elements of the program would remain concealed. The prohibition against developing delivery platforms with ranges greater than 150 km allowed Baghdad to research and develop shorter-range systems with applications for longer-range systems and did not affect Iraqi efforts to convert full-size aircraft into unmanned aerial vehicles as potential WMD delivery systems with ranges far beyond 150 km.
Res. 707 (15 August 1991) Requires Iraq to allow UN and IAEA inspectors immediate and unrestricted access to any site they wish to inspect. Demands Iraq provide full, final, and complete disclosure of all aspects of its WMD programs; cease immediately any attempt to conceal, move, or destroy WMD-related material or equipment; allow UNSCOM and IAEA teams to use fixed-wing and helicopter flights throughout Iraq; and respond fully, completely, and promptly to any Special Commission questions or requests.	Baghdad in 1996 negotiated with UNSCOM Executive Chairman Ekeus modalities that it used to delay inspections, to restrict to four the number of inspectors allowed into any site Baghdad declared as "sensitive," and to prohibit them altogether from sites regarded as sovereign. These modalities gave Iraq leverage over individual inspections. Iraq eventually allowed larger numbers of inspectors into such sites but only after lengthy negotiations at each site.
Res. 715 (11 October 1991) Requires Iraq to submit to UNSCOM and IAEA long-term monitoring of Iraqi WMD programs; approved detailed plans called for in UNSCRs 687 and 707 for long-term monitoring.	Iraq generally accommodated UN monitors at declared sites but occasionally obstructed access and manipulated monitoring cameras. UNSCOM and IAEA monitoring of Iraq's WMD programs does not have a specified end date under current UN resolutions.
Res. 1051 (27 March 1996) Established the Iraqi export/import monitoring system, requiring UN members to provide IAEA and UNSCOM wth information on materials exported to Iraq that may be applicable to WMD production, and requiring Iraq to report imports of all dual-use items.	Iraq is negotiating contracts for procuring—outside of UN controls—dual-use items with WMD applications. The UN lacks the staff needed to conduct thorough inspections of goods at Iraq's borders and to monitor imports inside Iraq.
Res. 1060 (12 June 1996) and Resolutions 1115, 1134, 1137, 1154, 1194, and 1205. Demands that Iraq cooperate with UNSCOM and allow inspection teams immediate, unconditional, and unrestricted access to facilities for inspection and access to Iraqi officials for interviews. UNSCR 1137 condemns Baghdad's refusal to allow entry to Iraq to UNSCOM officials on the grounds of their nationality and its threats to the safety of UN reconnaissance aircraft.	Baghdad consistently sought to impede and limit UNSCOM's mission in Iraq by blocking access to numerous facilities throughout the inspection process, often sanitizing sites before the arrival of inspectors and routinely attempting to deny inspectors access to requested sites and individuals. At times, Baghdad would promise compliance to avoid consequences, only to renege later.
Res. 1154 (2 March 1998) Demands that Iraq comply with UNSCOM and IAEA inspections and endorses the Secretary General's memorandum of understanding with Iraq, providing for "severest consequences" if Iraq fails to comply. **Res. 1194 (9 September 1998)** Condemns Iraq's decision to suspend cooperation with UNSCOM and the IAEA. **Res. 1205 (5 November 1998)** Condemns Iraq's decision to cease cooperation with UNSCOM.	UNSCOM could not exercise its mandate without Iraqi compliance. Baghdad refused to work with UNSCOM and instead negotiated with the Secretary General, whom it believed would be more sympathetic to Iraq's needs.
Res. 1284 (17 December 1999) Established the United Nations Monitoring, Verification, and Inspection Commission (UNMOVIC), replacing UNSCOM; and demanded that Iraq allow UNMOVIC teams immediate, unconditional, and unrestricted access to any and all aspects of Iraq's WMD program.	Iraq repeatedly has rejected the return of UN arms inspectors and claims that it has satisfied all UN resolutions relevant to disarmament. Compared with UNSCOM, 1284 gives the UNMOVIC chairman less authority, gives the Security Council a greater role in defining key disarmament tasks, and requires that inspectors be full-time UN employees.

Since December 1998, Baghdad has refused to allow UN inspectors into Iraq as required by the Security Council resolutions. Technical monitoring systems installed by the UN at known and suspected WMD and missile facilities in Iraq no longer operate. Baghdad prohibits Security Council-mandated monitoring overflights of Iraqi facilities by UN aircraft and helicopters. Similarly, Iraq has curtailed most IAEA inspections since 1998, allowing the IAEA to visit annually only a very small number of sites to safeguard Iraq's stockpile of uranium oxide.

16. **In the absence of inspectors, Baghdad's already considerable ability to work on prohibited programs without risk of discovery has increased, and there is substantial evidence that Iraq is reconstituting prohibited programs. Baghdad's vigorous concealment efforts have meant that specific information on many aspects of Iraq's WMD programs is yet to be uncovered. Revelations after the Gulf war starkly demonstrate the extensive efforts undertaken by Iraq to deny information.**

17. • Limited insight into activities since 1998 clearly show that Baghdad has used the absence of UN inspectors to repair and expand dual-use and dedicated missile-development facilities and to increase its ability to produce WMD.

Nuclear Weapons Program

More than ten years of sanctions and the loss of much of Iraq's physical nuclear infrastructure under IAEA oversight have not diminished Saddam's interest in acquiring or developing nuclear weapons.

18. • Iraq's efforts to procure tens of thousands of proscribed high-strength aluminum tubes are of significant concern. All intelligence experts agree that Iraq is seeking nuclear weapons and that these tubes could be used in a centrifuge enrichment program. Most intelligence specialists assess this to be the intended use, but some believe that these tubes are probably intended for conventional weapons programs.

Iraq had an advanced nuclear weapons development program before the Gulf war that focused on building an implosion-type weapon using highly enriched uranium. Baghdad was attempting a variety of uranium enrichment techniques, the most successful of which were the electromagnetic isotope separation (EMIS) and gas centrifuge programs. After its invasion of Kuwait, Iraq initiated a crash program to divert IAEA-safeguarded, highly enriched uranium from its Soviet and French-supplied reactors, but the onset of hostilities ended this effort. Iraqi declarations and the UNSCOM/IAEA inspection process revealed much of Iraq's nuclear weapons efforts, but Baghdad still has not provided complete information on all aspects of its nuclear weapons program.

• Iraq has withheld important details relevant to its nuclear program, including procurement logs, technical documents, experimental data, accounting of materials, and foreign assistance.

- Baghdad also continues to withhold other data about enrichment techniques, foreign procurement, weapons design, and the role of Iraqi security services in concealing its nuclear facilities and activities.

19.
- In recent years, Baghdad has diverted goods contracted under the Oil-for-Food Program for military purposes and has increased solicitations and dual-use procurements—outside the Oil-for-Food process—some of which almost certainly are going to prohibited WMD and other weapons programs. Baghdad probably uses some of the money it gains through its illicit oil sales to support its WMD efforts.

20. Before its departure from Iraq, the IAEA made significant strides toward dismantling Iraq's nuclear weapons program and unearthing the nature and scope of Iraq's past nuclear activities. In the absence of inspections, however, most analysts assess that Iraq is reconstituting its nuclear program—unraveling the IAEA's hard-earned accomplishments.

Iraq retains its cadre of nuclear scientists and technicians, its program documentation, and sufficient dual-use manufacturing capabilities to support a reconstituted nuclear weapons program. Iraqi media have reported numerous meetings between Saddam and nuclear scientists over the past two years, signaling Baghdad's continued interest in reviving a nuclear program.

Iraq's expanding international trade provides growing access to nuclear-related technology and materials and potential access to foreign nuclear expertise. An increase in dual-use procurement activity in recent years may be supporting a reconstituted nuclear weapons program.

- The acquisition of sufficient fissile material is Iraq's principal hurdle in developing a nuclear weapon.

21.
- **Iraq is unlikely to produce indigenously enough weapons-grade material for a deliverable nuclear weapon until the last half of this decade. Baghdad could produce a nuclear weapon within a year if it were able to procure weapons-grade fissile material abroad.**

22. **Baghdad may have acquired uranium enrichment capabilities that could shorten substantially the amount of time necessary to make a nuclear weapon.**

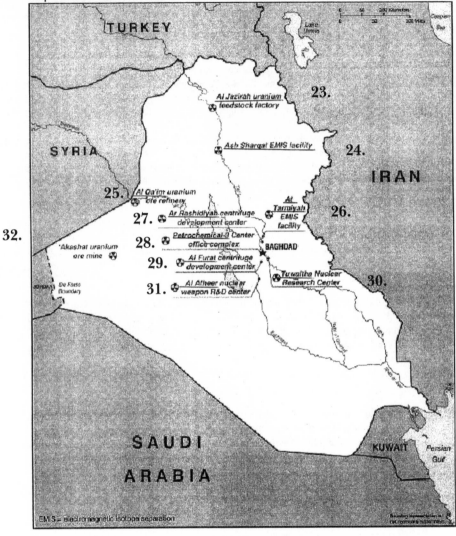

Iraq: Declared Nuclear Facilities

TURKEY

Lake
Urmia

Caspian
Sea

23.

Al Jazirah uranium
feedstock factory

SYRIA

Ash Sharqat EMIS facility

24.

IRAN

25.

Al Qa'im uranium
ore refinery

27. Ar Rashidiyah centrifuge
development center

Al
Tarmiyah
EMIS
facility

26.

32.

28. Petrochemical-3 Center
office complex

BAGHDAD

'Akashat uranium
ore mine

29. Al Furat centrifuge
development center

JORDAN De Facto
Boundary

31. Al Atheer nuclear
weapon R&D center

Tuwaitha Nuclear
Research Center

30.

SAUDI

ARABIA

KUWAIT Persian
Gulf

EMIS = electromagnetic isotope separation

Chemical Warfare Program

Iraq has the ability to produce chemical warfare (CW) agents within its chemical industry, although it probably depends on external sources for some precursors. Baghdad is expanding its infrastructure, under cover of civilian industries, that it could use to advance its CW agent production capability. During the 1980s Saddam had a formidable CW capability that he used against Iranians and against Iraq's Kurdish population. Iraqi forces killed or injured more than 20,000 people in multiple attacks, delivering chemical agents (including mustard agent[1] and the nerve agents sarin and tabun[2]) in aerial bombs, 122mm rockets, and artillery shells against both tactical military targets and segments of Iraq's Kurdish population. Before the 1991 Gulf war, Baghdad had a large stockpile of chemical munitions and a robust indigenous production capacity.

Documented Iraqi Use of Chemical Weapons

Date	Area Used	Type of Agent	Approximate Casualties	Target Population
Aug 1983	Hajj Umran	Mustard	fewer than 100	Iranians/Kurds
Oct-Nov 1983	Panjwin	Mustard	3,000	Iranian/Kurds
Feb-Mar 1984	Majnoon Island	Mustard	2,500	Iranians
Mar 1984	al-Basrah	Tabun	50 to 100	Iranians
Mar 1985	Hawizah Marsh	Mustard/Tabun	3,000	Iranians
Feb 1986	al-Faw	Mustard/Tabun	8,000 to 10,000	Iranians
Dec 1986	Umm ar Rasas	Mustard	thousands	Iranians
Apr 1987	al-Basrah	Mustard/Tabun	5,000	Iranians
Oct 1987	Sumar/Mehran	Mustard/nerve agents	3,000	Iranians
Mar 1988	Halabjah	Mustard/nerve agents	hundreds	Iranians/Kurds

---

[1] Mustard is a blister agent that causes medical casualties by blistering or burning exposed skin, eyes, lungs, and mucus membranes within hours of exposure. It is a persistent agent that can remain a hazard for days.

[2] Sarin, cyclosarin, and tabun are G-series nerve agents that can act within seconds of absorption through the skin or inhalation. These agents overstimulate muscles or glands with messages transmitted from nerves, causing convulsions and loss of consciousness. Tabun is persistent and can remain a hazard for days. Sarin and cyclosarin are not persistent and pose more of an inhalation hazard than a skin hazard.

Chemical-Filled Munitions Declared by Iraq

Iraqi 250-gauge chemical bomb.

Iraqi 500-gauge chemical bombs.

Iraqi DB-2 chemical bomb.

Iraqi R-400 chemical bombs.

Iraqi 155-mm chemical shell.

Iraqi Al Husayn chemical warheads.

122-mm rockets filled with the chemical nerve agent sarin prior to destruction.

Although precise information is lacking, human rights organizations have received plausible accounts from Kurdish villagers of even more Iraqi chemical attacks against civilians in the 1987 to 1988 time frame—with some attacks as late as October 1988—in areas close to the Iranian and Turkish borders.

- UNSCOM supervised the destruction of more than 40,000 chemical munitions, nearly 500,000 liters of chemical agents, 1.8 million liters of chemical precursors, and seven different types of delivery systems, including ballistic missile warheads.

33. More than 10 years after the Gulf war, <u>gaps in Iraqi accounting and current production capabilities strongly suggest that Iraq maintains a stockpile of chemical agents</u>, probably VX,[3] sarin, cyclosarin,[4] and mustard.

- **Iraq probably has concealed precursors, production equipment, documentation, and other items necessary for continuing its CW effort.** Baghdad never supplied adequate evidence to support its claims that it destroyed all of its CW agents and munitions. Thousands of tons of chemical precursors and tens of thousands of unfilled munitions, including Scud-variant missile warheads, remain unaccounted for.

- UNSCOM discovered a document at Iraqi Air Force headquarters in July 1998 showing that Iraq overstated by at least 6,000 the number of chemical bombs it told the UN it had used during the Iran-Iraq War—bombs that remain are unaccounted for.

34. • <u>Iraq has not accounted for 15,000 artillery rockets</u> that in the past were <u>its preferred means for delivering nerve agents</u>, nor has it accounted for about 550 artillery shells filled with mustard agent.

35. • <u>Iraq probably has stocked at least 100 metric tons (MT) and possibly as much as 500 MT of CW agents.</u>

Baghdad continues to rebuild and expand dual-use infrastructure that it could divert quickly to CW production. The best examples are the chlorine and phenol plants at the Fallujah II facility. Both chemicals have legitimate civilian uses but also are raw materials for the synthesis of precursor chemicals used to produce blister and nerve agents. Iraq has three other chlorine plants that have much higher capacity for civilian production; these plants and Iraqi imports are more than sufficient to meet Iraq's civilian

---

36. [3] <u>VX is a V-series nerve agent</u> that is similar to but more advanced than G-series nerve agents in that it causes the same medical effects but is more toxic and much more persistent. Thus, it poses a far greater skin hazard than G-series agents. <u>VX could be used for long-term contamination of territory.</u>
[4] See footnote 5.

needs for water treatment. Of the 15 million kg of chlorine imported under the UN Oil-for-Food Program since 1997, Baghdad used only 10 million kg and has 5 million kg in stock, suggesting that some domestically produced chlorine has been diverted to such proscribed activities as CW agent production.

- Fallujah II was one of Iraq's principal CW precursor production facilities before the Gulf war. In the last two years the Iraqis have upgraded the facility and brought in new chemical reactor vessels and shipping containers with a large amount of production equipment. They have expanded chlorine output far beyond pre-Gulf war production levels—capabilities that can be diverted quickly to CW production. Iraq is seeking to purchase CW agent precursors and applicable production equipment and is trying to hide the activities of the Fallujah plant.

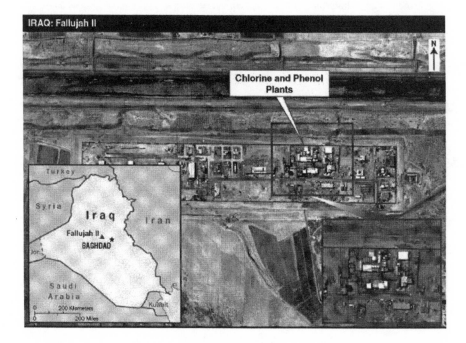

Iraq: CW-Related Production Facilities and Declared Sites of Deployed Alcohol-Filled or Chemical Agent–Filled Munitions During Desert Storm

37.

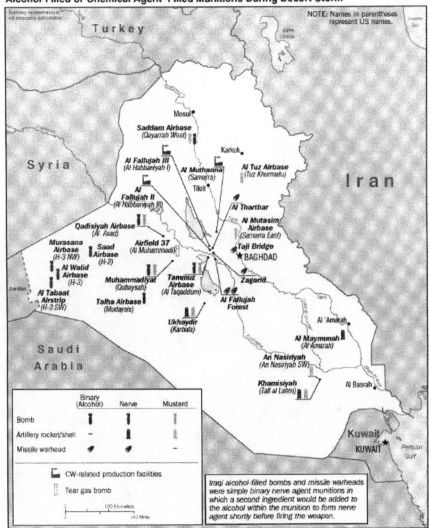

Biological Warfare Program

38. **Iraq has the capability to convert quickly legitimate vaccine and biopesticide plants to biological warfare (BW) production and already may have done so.** This capability is particularly troublesome because Iraq has a record of concealing its BW activities and lying about the existence of its offensive BW program.

After four years of claiming that they had conducted only "small-scale, defensive" research, Iraqi officials finally admitted to inspectors in 1995 to production and weaponization of biological agents. The Iraqis admitted this only after being faced with evidence of their procurement of a large volume of growth media and the defection of

39. Husayn Kamil, former director of Iraq's military industries.

Two R-400A bombs in foreground photographed by UNSCOM inspectors at Murasana Airfield near the Al Walid Airbase in late 1991 bear markings indicating they were to be filled with botulinum toxin. Other bombs appear to have markings consistent with binary chemical agent fill. This evidence contradicted Iraq's declarations that it did not deploy BW munitions to operational airbases and that it destroyed all BW bombs in July 1991—declarations that were subsequently retracted in the face of overwhelming evidence to the contrary.

Iraq: Declared BW-Related Sites

40.

Legend:
- Research/production/filling
- Destroyed by Iraq
- Testing
- Weapon deployment

Al Mansuriyah Railway Tunnel

Al Muthanna

Al Nebai

Khan Bani Saad Airfield

Fallujah III

Tigris Canal

Taji SCP

Fudhaliyah Agricultural and Water Research Center

Airfield 37

Zaghareet

Al Kindi Company for the Production of Veterinary Vaccines and Drugs

BAGHDAD

Dawrah Foot and Mouth Disease Vaccine Production Plant

Al Muhammadiyat

Salman Pak

Amiriyah Serum and Vaccine Institute

Al Hakam facility

Al Aziziyah

Abu Obeydi Airbase

Inset map:
Turkey — Syria — Iraq — Iran
Mosul
Murasana Airfield [a]
Al Walid Airbase
BAGHDAD
Jurf al Sakr Firing Range
Al 'Amarah
An Nasiriyah
Al Chabaish
Saudi Arabia
Kuwait

[a] Not declared by Iraq. Two bombs marked for BW were seen in October 1991 UNSCOM inspection photos.

Iraqi-Acknowledged Open-Air Testing of Biological Weapons		
Location-Date	**Agent**	**Munition**
Al Muhammadiyat – Mar 1988	*Bacillus subtilis*[5]	250-gauge bomb (cap. 65 liters)
Al Muhammadiyat – Mar 1988	*Botulinum toxin*	250-gauge bomb (cap. 65 liters)
Al Muhammadiyat – Nov 1989	*Bacillus subtilis*	122mm rocket (cap. 8 liters)
Al Muhammadiyat – Nov 1989	*Botulinum toxin*	122mm rocket (cap. 8 liters)
Al Muhammadiyat – Nov 1989	Aflatoxin	122mm rocket (cap. 8 liters)
Khan Bani Saad – Aug 1988	*Bacillus subtilis*	aerosol generator – Mi-2 helicopter with modified agricultural spray equipment
Al Muhammadiyat – Dec 1989	*Bacillus subtilis*	R-400 bomb (cap. 85 liters)
Al Muhammadiyat – Nov 1989	*Botulinum toxin*	R-400 bomb (cap. 85 liters)
Al Muhammadiyat – Nov 1989	Aflatoxin	R-400 bomb (cap. 85 liters)
Jurf al-Sakr Firing Range – Sep 1989	Ricin	155mm artillery shell (cap. 3 liters)
Abu Obeydi Airfield – Dec 1990	Water	Modified Mirage F1 drop-tank (cap. 2,200 liters)
Abu Obeydi Airfield – Dec 1990	Water/potassium permanganate	Modified Mirage F1 drop-tank (cap. 2,200 liters)
Abu Obeydi Airfield – Jan 1991	Water/glycerine	Modified Mirage F1 drop-tank (cap. 2,200 liters)
Abu Obeydi Airfield – Jan 1991	*Bacillus subtilis*/Glycerine	Modified Mirage F1 drop-tank (cap. 2,200 liters)

41.

- Iraq admitted producing thousands of liters of the BW agents anthrax,[6] botulinum toxin, (which paralyzes respiratory muscles and can be fatal within 24 to 36 hours), and aflatoxin, (a potent carcinogen that can attack the liver, killing years after ingestion), and preparing BW-filled Scud-variant missile warheads, aerial bombs, and aircraft spray tanks before the Gulf war.

Baghdad did not provide persuasive evidence to support its claims that it unilaterally destroyed its BW agents and munitions. **Experts from UNSCOM assessed that Baghdad's declarations vastly understated the production of biological agents and estimated that Iraq actually produced two-to-four times the amount of agent that it acknowledged producing,** including *Bacillus anthracis*—the causative agent of anthrax—and botulinum toxin.

42. The improvement or expansion of a number of nominally "civilian" facilities that were directly associated with biological weapons indicates that key aspects of Iraq's offensive BW program are active and most elements more advanced and larger than before the 1990-1991 Gulf war.

---

[5] *Bacillus subtilis* is commonly used as a simulant for *B. anthracis*.

[6] An infectious dose of anthrax is about 8,000 spores, or less than one-millionth of a gram in a non immuno-compromised person. Inhalation anthrax historically has been 100 percent fatal within five to seven days, although in recent cases aggressive medical treatment has reduced the fatality rate.

43. • The al-Dawrah Foot-and-Mouth Disease (FMD) Vaccine Facility is one of two known Biocontainment Level-3—facilities in Iraq with an extensive air handling and filtering system. Iraq admitted that before the Gulf war Al-Dawrah had been a BW agent production facility. UNSCOM attempted to render it useless for BW agent production in 1996 but left some production equipment in place because UNSCOM could not prove it was connected to previous BW work. In 2001, Iraq announced it would begin renovating the plant without UN approval, ostensibly to produce a vaccine to combat an FMD outbreak. In fact, Iraq easily can import all the foot-and-mouth vaccine it needs through the UN.

44. • The Amiriyah Serum and Vaccine Institute is an ideal cover location for BW research, testing, production, and storage. UN inspectors discovered documents related to BW research at this facility, some showing that BW cultures, agents, and equipment were stored there during the Gulf war. Of particular concern is the plant's new storage capacity, which greatly exceeds Iraq's needs for legitimate medical storage.

45. • The Fallujah III Castor Oil Production Plant is situated on a large complex with an historical connection to Iraq's CW program. Of immediate BW concern is the

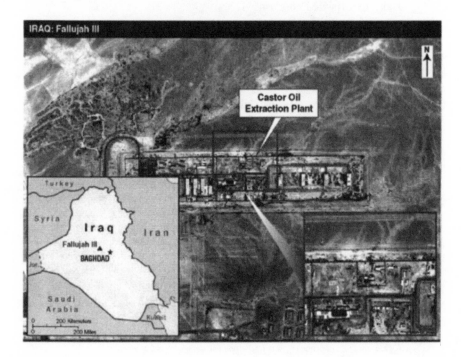

potential production of ricin toxin.[7] Castor bean pulp, left over from castor oil production, can be used to extract ricin toxin. Iraq admitted to UNSCOM that it manufactured ricin and field-tested it in artillery shells before the Gulf war. Iraq operated this plant for legitimate purposes under UNSCOM scrutiny before 1998 when UN inspectors left the country. Since 1999, Iraq has rebuilt major structures destroyed during Operation Desert Fox. Iraqi officials claim they are making castor oil for brake fluid, but verifying such claims without UN inspections is impossible.

In addition to questions about activity at known facilities, **there are compelling reasons to be concerned about BW activity at other sites and in mobile production units and laboratories.** Baghdad has pursued a mobile BW research and production capability to better conceal its program.

46.

- UNSCOM uncovered a document on Iraqi Military Industrial Commission letterhead indicating that Iraq was interested in developing mobile fermentation units, and an Iraqi scientist admitted to UN inspectors that Iraq was trying to move in the direction of mobile BW production.

- Iraq has now established large-scale, redundant, and concealed BW agent production capabilities based on mobile BW facilities.

Ballistic Missile Program

47.

Iraq has developed a ballistic missile capability that exceeds the 150km range limitation established under UNSCR 687. During the 1980s, Iraq purchased 819 Scud B missiles from the USSR. Hundreds of these 300km range missiles were used to attack Iranian cities during the Iran-Iraq War. Beginning in 1987, Iraq converted many of these Soviet Scuds into extended-range variants, some of which were fired at Tehran; some were launched during the Gulf war, and others remained in Iraq's inventory at war's end. Iraq admitted filling at least 75 of its Scud warheads with chemical or biological agents and deployed these weapons for use against Coalition forces and regional opponents, including Israel in 1991.

Most of the approximately 90 Scud-type missiles Saddam fired at Israel, Saudi Arabia, and Bahrain during the Gulf war were al-Husayn variants that the Iraqis modified by lengthening the airframe and increasing fuel capacity, extending the range to 650 km.

Baghdad was developing other longer-range missiles based on Scud technology, including the 900km al-Abbas. Iraq was designing follow-on multi-stage and clustered medium-range ballistic missile (MRBM) concepts with intended ranges up to 3,000 km. Iraq also had a program to develop a two-stage missile, called the Badr-2000, using solid-propellants with an estimated range of 750 to 1,000 km.

---

[7] Ricin can cause multiple organ failure within one or two days after inhalation.

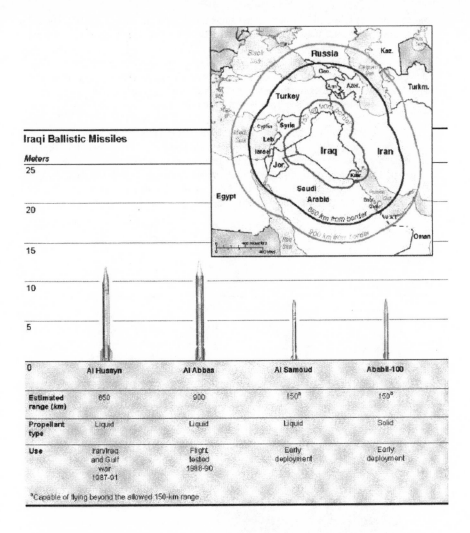

Iraqi Ballistic Missiles

	Al Husayn	Al Abbas	Al Samoud	Ababil-100
Estimated range (km)	650	900	150[a]	150[a]
Propellant type	Liquid	Liquid	Liquid	Solid
Use	Iran/Iraq and Gulf war 1987-91	Flight tested 1988-90	Early deployment	Early deployment

[a]Capable of flying beyond the allowed 150-km range.

- Iraq never fully accounted for its existing missile programs. Discrepancies in Baghdad's declarations suggest that Iraq retains a small force of extended-range Scud-type missiles and an undetermined number of launchers and warheads. Further, Iraq never explained the disposition of advanced missile components, such as guidance and control systems, that it could not produce on its own and that would be critical to developmental programs.

18

48. Iraq continues to work on UN-authorized short-range ballistic missiles (SRBMs)—those with a range no greater than 150 km—that help develop the expertise and infrastructure needed to produce longer-range missile systems. <u>The al-Samoud liquid propellant SRBM and the Ababil-100 solid propellant SRBM, however, are capable of flying beyond the allowed 150km range.</u> Both missiles have been tested aggressively and are in early deployment. Other evidence strongly suggests Iraq is modifying missile testing and production facilities to produce even longer-range missiles.

- The Al-Rafah-North Liquid Propellant Engine Research, Development, Testing, and Evaluation (RDT&E) Facility is Iraq's principal site for the static testing of liquid propellant missile engines. Baghdad has been building a new test stand there that is larger than the test stand associated with al-Samoud engine testing and the defunct Scud engine test stand. The only plausible explanation for this test facility is that Iraq intends to test engines for longer-range missiles prohibited under UNSCR 687.

SA-2 (Al Samoud) Engine Test

Iraq conducted static tests of the SA-2 SAM sustainer engine to support development of the Al Samoud SRBM. This test stand is capable of testing engines for Iraq's UN-authorized liquid-propellant ballistic and anti-ship cruise missiles. The new test stand at Al-Rafah is larger than both this test stand and the defunct Scud engine test stand, indicating Iraqi intentions to test engines for longer-range missiles.

Iraq: Ballistic-Missile-Related Facilities

20

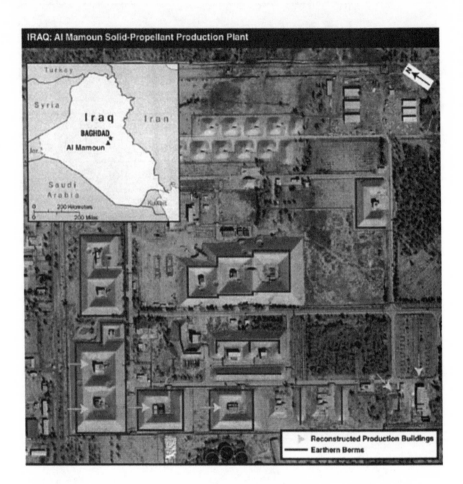

IRAQ: Al Mamoun Solid-Propellant Production Plant

Reconstructed Production Buildings
Earthern Berms

- The Al-Mutasim Solid Rocket Motor and Test Facility, previously associated with Iraq's Badr-2000 solid-propellant missile program, has been rebuilt and expanded in recent years. The al-Mutasim site supports solid-propellant motor assembly, rework, and testing for the UN-authorized Ababil-100, but the size of certain facilities there, particularly those newly constructed between the assembly rework and static test areas, suggests that Baghdad is preparing to develop systems that are prohibited by the UN.

- At the Al-Mamoun Solid Rocket Motor Production Plant and RDT&E Facility, the Iraqis, since the December 1998 departure of inspectors, have rebuilt structures damaged during the Gulf war and dismantled by UNSCOM that originally were built

21

to manufacture solid propellant motors for the Badr-2000 program. They also have built a new building and are reconstructing other buildings originally designed to fill large Badr-2000 motor casings with solid propellant.

- Also at al-Mamoun, the Iraqis have rebuilt two structures used to "mix" solid propellant for the Badr-2000 missile. The new buildings—about as large as the original ones—are ideally suited to house large, UN-prohibited mixers. In fact, the only logical explanation for the size and configuration of these mixing buildings is that Iraq intends to develop longer-range, prohibited missiles.

Iraq has managed to rebuild and expand its missile development infrastructure under sanctions. Iraqi intermediaries have sought production technology, machine tools, and raw materials in violation of the arms embargo.

- The Iraqis have completed a new ammonium perchlorate production plant at Mamoun that supports Iraq's solid propellant missile program. Ammonium perchlorate is a common oxidizer used in solid propellant missile motors. Baghdad would not have been able to complete this facility without help from abroad.

- In August 1995, Iraq was caught trying to acquire sensitive ballistic missile guidance components, including gyroscopes originally used in Russian strategic nuclear SLBMs, demonstrating that Baghdad has been pursuing proscribed, advanced, long-range missile technology for some time. Iraqi officials admitted that, despite international prohibitions, they had received a similar shipment earlier that year.

Unmanned Aerial Vehicle Program and Other Aircraft

49. **Iraq is continuing to develop other platforms which <u>most analysts believe</u> probably are intended for delivering biological warfare agents.** Immediately before the Gulf war, Baghdad attempted to convert a MiG-21 into an unmanned aerial vehicle (UAV) to carry spray tanks capable of dispensing chemical or biological agents. UNSCOM assessed that the program to develop the spray system was successful, but the conversion of the MiG-21 was not. More recently, Baghdad has attempted to convert some of its L-29 jet trainer aircraft into UAVs that can be fitted with chemical and biological warfare (CBW) spray tanks, most likely a continuation of previous efforts with the MiG-21. Although much less sophisticated than ballistic missiles as a delivery platform, an aircraft—manned or unmanned—is the most efficient way to disseminate chemical and biological weapons over a large, distant area.

- Iraq already has produced modified drop-tanks that can disperse biological or chemical agents effectively. Before the Gulf war, the Iraqis successfully experimented with aircraft-mounted spray tanks capable of releasing up to 2,000 liters of an anthrax simulant over a target area. Iraq also has modified commercial crop sprayers successfully and tested them with an anthrax simulant delivered by helicopters.

Iraqi L-29 UAV Test-Bed Aircraft at Samarra East Airbase

- Baghdad has a history of experimenting with a variety of unmanned platforms. Iraq's use of newer, more capable airframes would increase range and payload, while smaller platforms might be harder to detect and therefore more survivable. This capability represents a serious threat to Iraq's neighbors and to international military forces in the region.

- Iraq used tactical fighter aircraft and helicopters to deliver chemical agents, loaded in bombs and rockets, during the Iran-Iraq War. Baghdad probably is considering again using manned aircraft as delivery platforms depending on the operational scenario.

Procurement in Support of WMD Programs

Iraq has been able to import dual-use, WMD-relevant equipment and material through procurements both within and outside the UN sanctions regime. **Baghdad diverts some of the $10 billion worth of goods now entering Iraq every year for humanitarian needs to support the military and WMD programs instead.** Iraq's growing ability to sell oil illicitly increases Baghdad's capabilities to finance its WMD programs. Over the last four years Baghdad's earnings from illicit oil sales have more than quadrupled to about $3 billion this year.

50.

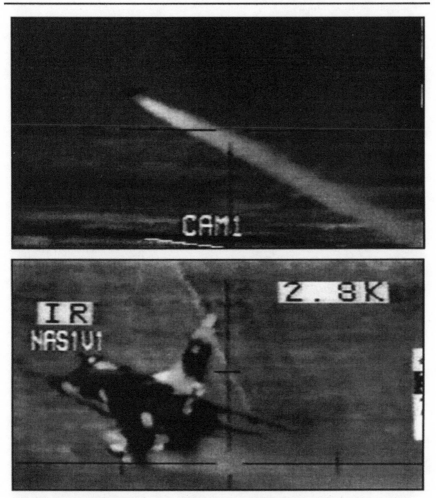

Test of dissemination of BW agents from a modified drop tank carried by a Mirage F1. The drop tank was filled with 1000 liters of slurry Bacillus subtilis, a simulant for B. anthracis, and disseminated over Abu Obeydi Airbase in January 1991. The photo is from a videotape provided by Iraq to UNSCOM.

- UN monitors at Iraq's borders do not inspect the cargo—worth hundreds of millions of dollars—that enters Iraq every year outside of the Oil-for-Food Program; some of these goods clearly support Iraq's military and WMD programs. For example, Baghdad imports fiber-optic communication systems outside of UN auspices to support the Iraqi military.

- Iraq imports goods using planes, trains, trucks, and ships without any type of international inspections—in violation of UN Security Council resolutions.

Even within the UN-authorized Oil-for-Food Program, Iraq does not hide that it wants to purchase military and WMD-related goods. For example, **Baghdad diverted UN-approved trucks for military purposes and construction equipment to rehabilitate WMD-affiliated facilities, even though these items were approved only to help the civilian population.**

- Iraq has been able to repair modern industrial machine tools that previously supported production of WMD or missile components and has imported additional tools that it may use to reconstitute Baghdad's unconventional weapons arsenal.

- On several occasions, Iraq has asked to purchase goods—such as neutron generators and servo valves—that the UN Monitoring, Verification, and Inspection Commission (UNMOVIC) views as linchpins for prohibited Iraqi programs; alternative, non-dual-use items would serve the civilian purpose purportedly intended for this equipment.

UNMOVIC began screening contracts pursuant to UNSCR 1284 in December 1999 and since has identified more than 100 contracts containing dual-use items as defined in UNSCR 1051 that can be diverted into WMD programs. UNMOVIC also has requested that suppliers provide technical information on hundreds of other goods because of concerns about potential misuse of dual-use equipment. In many cases, Iraq has requested technology that clearly exceeds requirements for the stated commercial end-use when it easily could substitute items that could not be used for WMD.

- On some UN contracts, Baghdad claimed that the requested goods are designed to rehabilitate facilities—such as the Al Qa'im phosphate plant and Fallujah—that in the past were used to support both industrial and WMD programs.

CIA White Paper Comments

1. The National Intelligence Estimate (NIE) specifies the years 2007–09 for Iraqi acquisition of a nuclear weapon, a time frame that is far in the future, negating President Bush's contention that Iraq poses an urgent national security threat. (Note that Secretary Rumsfeld's September 19 testimony had already attempted to defuse this objection.) The white paper eliminates the dates, making it possible to fear for tomorrow as well as 2007. In the actual NIE, the text notes right here that there is a dissent by the State Department's Bureau of Intelligence and Research (this would become important during the summer of 2003, when the question arose of National Security Adviser Condoleezza Rice's knowledge of the national estimate). The NIE also states: "We have low confidence in our ability to assess when Saddam would use WMD," an important qualifier that is completely dropped in the CIA white paper.

2. In speeches, public sources, and intelligence reports, much has been made of charges that Iraq practiced deception in its weapons programs to evade UN inspections (and U.S. intelligence). The implication is that deception is illegal and is paired with arms violations. In fact, deception programs are the *norm*, not the exception, in weapons development programs, including America's own, since at least the early 1980s. In the United States, the B-2 bomber, the F-117 fighter, the Trident D-5 missile, warhead development programs, precision guidance programs, not to mention such current programs as research on ballistic missile defenses and "nonlethal" weapons, have all included deception as part of the development program. Deceptive measures have included disguising budget expenditures for programs, creating cover stories to account for revealed information, pretending weapons do not exist, mischaracterizing weapons' characteristics; falsifying test results, deployment dates, and/or numbers of weapons systems; and practical measures (such as building structures, sending phony messages, or creating deceptive documents) intended to give effect to the deceptions. The techniques are identical to those practiced by Iraq.

3. A third-party commentary on this point is furnished by the International Atomic Energy Agency, which noted on July 25, 2002, that there had been construction at Iraqi sites but made a point of acknowledging the impossibility of connecting the building to any particular activity. Here the CIA white paper links the work specifically to missile and biological weapons work, obviously possible only by making the assumption that that is so.

4. In its key judgments the NIE flatly states: "Saddam does not yet have nuclear weapons or sufficient material to make them." The insertion here of the word "probably" in the white paper is designed to heighten public concern.

5. The order of these items is reversed from the body of the white paper itself, placing the scarier nuclear-bomb-within-a-year claim first. That claim is tantamount to saying that if Saddam could acquire a complete nuclear weapon he would have one, which is true of any nation or terrorist group, not merely Iraq. Energetic inspections by the United Nations from November 2002 to March 2003 failed to disclose Iraqi facilities capable of taking newly received high-grade uranium and instantly producing a bomb, or even of enriching uranium to weapons-grade material.

6. The CIA white paper here introduces the subject of the use of aluminum tubes for uranium enrichment by centrifuge (a detailed discussion follows the numbered comments). Note how the white paper disguises dissent to this judgment in the NIE with the "all . . . most" terminology. Knowledge that the Department of Energy, the most expert U.S. agency on centrifuge technology, was among the "some" on the aluminum tubes would have been highly damaging to Bush's case for an urgent Iraqi threat. This information from the NIE was suppressed in the white paper.

7. The NIE observes that 25,000 centrifuges would be capable of producing this amount of fissile material annually by 2007–09. Evidence on Iraqi industrial planning from CIA reports declassified in the mid-1990s shows Baghdad anticipated it would need about five years to achieve a cascade of 1,000 centrifuges. Available portions of the NIE that have been declassified have no information on the rate at which Iraq might be capable of manufacturing and putting into operation large numbers of centrifuges, or how Iraq could have generated the large voltage of electricity necessary to operate them. The white paper also contains no discussion of this crucial point, given that 25,000 represents a huge centrifuge array. The CIA documents from the 90s report that Iraq never operated more than 550 centrifuges in its two plants active before the 1990–91 Gulf War, and had difficulty supplying electricity for that array. (An extended analysis of the Aluminum Tube question follows the numbered comments.)

8. This assertion is not supported by the body of the white paper itself, which claims only that Iraq "has the ability to produce" chemical weapons. Likewise the CIA's description of the threat from Iraq in answers for the record to the Senate Intelligence Committee in April 2002 had read: "Iraq continues to build and expand an infrastructure capable of producing WMD." There was no assertion that actual

production was taking place. (The State Department's Bureau of Intelligence and Research, in February 2002, concurred with this assessment, but also projected that Iraq might be able to resume chemical weapons production within "a few weeks to months.") Postwar U.S. analyses held that Iraq was at least *two years* away from being able to produce sarin nerve gas, and two months from any production capacity for the simpler (but much less lethal) mustard gas.

9. The key judgments in the NIE admit, "we have little specific information on Iraq's [chemical weapons] stockpile." Similarly, a September 2002 operational support study disseminated by the Defense Intelligence Agency observed, "There is no reliable information on whether Iraq is producing and stockpiling chemical weapons," although it estimated that Baghdad "probably" did have chemical agents in munitions and stockpiles of biological agents that could be loaded into munitions. The body of the CIA white paper contains the projection that Iraq has stocked at least 100, and possibly as much as 500, tons of chemical agents. The more ambiguous language here ("a few hundred metric tons") suggests a higher minimum figure. In technical sources it is possible to find estimates that show the amount of chemical agent necessary to saturate one square mile of terrain as high as 100 tons or more. In other words, an Iraqi stockpile of the size claimed represented a very limited capability.

10. Presented in bold type here for greater impact, the sentence is not so rendered in the equivalent section of the NIE. In terms of evidence in this report, the sole evidence presented for production here is the Fallujah III plant, which the report notes was "operated for legitimate purposes under UNSCOM scrutiny before 1998." The report notes the Iraqi government *announced* they would be resuming production at a biological facility to cope with foot-and-mouth disease, but the CIA provides no further information documenting biological weapon production. The evidence for weaponization is presented as a table listing Iraqi weapons tests with various munitions. But the most recent date on the table is January 1991, *before* the Gulf War, which brought UN inspectors to dismantle the then-existing Iraqi weapons infrastructure.

11. None of the Iraqi weaponization tests listed by the CIA ever made use of anthrax, only surrogates. In fact, this report, issued about a year after an episode of near-hysteria in the United States that followed domestic anthrax attacks through the mail, seems to single anthrax out for treatment. The intensely inflamatory phrase "including potentially against the US Homeland" does not appear in the NIE with respect to biological agents at all. In the NIE, this phrase is confined purely to the discussion of Iraqi unmanned aerial vehicles, whose capabilities for chem-

ical or biological weapons delivery were disputed within U.S. intelligence (an extended section on unmanned aerial vehicles follows the numbered comments).

12. An extended discussion of mobile laboratories follows the CIA May 2003 report.

13. The statement in the white paper that "most analysts believe" the Iraqi unmanned aerial vehicles are intended to deliver biological warfare agents covers up the fact that the U.S. Air Force, the service most concerned with the aerial threat, dissented in the NIE on the claimed purpose of the Iraqi vehicles, which lacked the range or payload to be efficient weapons delivery platforms. The Air Force maintained the vehicles were primarily intended for reconnaissance—the same purpose for which the United States uses these craft.

14. The claim of a covert force of Iraqi-improved SCUD medium-range missiles occurs here, in the NIE, in the British white paper, and in many places. This claim is a deduction based entirely on discrepancies between the numbers of missiles Iraq was thought to have acquired, less numbers fired in the Iran-Iraq and Gulf wars, and those accounted for (or destroyed) by UN inspectors. Baghdad itself reported having destroyed a significant number of these missiles in 1992, and whether those claims are accepted is another source for the discrepancy. In its unclassified report to Congress of mid-2002 on international technology acquisition related to weapons of mass destruction, the CIA stated that the United States did not actually know how many missile launchers Iraq might have, or how many warheads there might be to put on top of the rockets (former top Iraqi weapons manager Hussein Kamel, in his 1995 defector debriefing with UN officials, put the number of launchers at two, one of them disassembled). In 1996, UN inspectors, also basing their claims on reporting discrepancies, estimated that between six and sixteen of the SCUD missiles were not accounted for. Few believed Iraqi claims to have destroyed remaining missiles after the Gulf War. That British intelligence puts the number in the "covert force" at twenty and the CIA at several dozen indicates the lack of real intelligence here.

The original SCUD was a Russian-built rocket 38 feet long, 3 feet in diameter, weighing 14,000 pounds. The ones sold to Iraq were a longer-range model that was somewhat larger. Iraq lengthened these missiles to give them more fuel, and made other changes as well. Such weapons were not easy to hide. Neither UN inspectors in 1991–98, in 2002–03, nor American inspectors in 2003 have been able to find any trace of the covert missile force. In this case, the assumption made throughout the Iraq intelligence that accounting discrepancies corresponded to active forces in Saddam's arsenal seems particularly unfounded.

15. The main evidence for Saddam Hussein's "enhanced" infrastructure for producing weapons of mass destruction is the construction that occurred at research and factory sites and the creation of (now disputed) mobile weapons laboratories. Construction alone was inconclusive evidence. As former chief UN weapons inspector Hans Blix expressed in comments in the fall of 2003, American and British intelligence put exclamation points instead of question marks around every indication of activity. An enlarged engine test stand at one of the Iraqi rocket development centers, and new rocket engine production facilities, were definite enhancements. Those are the only ones. There is only circumstantial evidence for any Iraqi weapons stockpile—a few empty chemical artillery shells found by UN weapons inspectors in January 2003, and some overhead pictures and communications intercepts Colin Powell would cite in his Security Council speech of February 2003. Note these latter items of evidence all postdate the October 2002 CIA white paper.

16. That Iraq was engaged in construction was not disputed. The purpose of that work remained the key question. A number of intelligence analyses, both U.S. and British, prior to late 2002 had used the word "reconstitute" in the sense of Iraq maintaining a contingent capability (an ability to resume production in some short period of time), which would have been a deterrent action rather than an offensive one. The usage here is clearly that Baghdad is currently producing weapons, and reflects an assumption as to Iraqi intentions. This imputing of an aggressive intent to Baghdad is a problem throughout this CIA white paper. It is significant that in the NIE, almost all the CIA's predictions in which it had "low confidence" had to do with Saddam's intentions. These least-confidence projections demonstrate that, in fact, the CIA had no idea what Saddam's intentions were.

17. Here the CIA white paper explicitly concedes that it lacks knowledge on the Iraqis ("limited insight into activities since 1998"). Director Tenet insisted on the opposite in August 2003, when in the course of defending the NIE, he went out of his way to comment on sources: "We have had a solid historical foundation and new data that have allowed us to make judgments and attribute high confidence in specific areas. And we had numerous credible sources, including many who provided information after 1998. When inspectors were pushed out in 1998 we did not sit back. Rather we significantly increased our collection efforts throughout the Intelligence Community . . . the fact is we made significant professional progress" (DCI Statement of August 11, 2003). That the white paper's distillation of the NIE admitted to having "limited insight" shows that the CIA's professional progress on Iraq data was really quite narrow. Early reports of the reviews on Iraq intelligence carried out following the war by both the House and

Senate intelligence committees have focused on the very same factor, lack of fresh intelligence after 1998, as a key weakness in the estimates.

18. Here is the substantive text in the paper that underlies the key judgment about the Iraqi procurement of aluminum tubes. A detailed discussion appears below.

19. This text actually has nothing to do with nuclear weapons, but rather summarizes material appearing elsewhere (pp. 23–25). As such, it is an exception to standard drafting practice, in which material in the body of a report is summarized in the "key judgments" section. Items in such reports are rarely repeated at multiple points in the text. The editors of the white paper are attempting to make their charges seem more impressive.

20. The assessment that Iraq is currently reconstituting its nuclear program is based on two flawed sources: Evidence of construction seen in overhead photography was specifically termed ambiguous by the International Atomic Energy Agency, and evidence of Iraq's buying uranium abroad was erroneous, as will be discussed in analysis of President Bush's January 2003 State of the Union speech. The Iraqis separately conducted two tours of the Tuwaitha nuclear facility for reporters in September 2002, before the CIA's national estimate and white paper were completed, producing identical news coverage in which reporters questioned whether any nuclear weapons production could be happening here. Thus, evidence available at the time of the drafting implied the opposite of the U.S. claim of reconstitution. Instead Iraqi press tours were held up in a report from the White House's WHIG unit as well as in a public briefing by the Defense Intelligence Agency in October 2002 as examples of Baghdad's deception techniques. UN inspectors visited all the primary Iraqi nuclear facilities during their November 2002–March 2003 monitoring effort (for example, Tuwaitha at least four times, and Al Tarmiyah, all before December), taking air, water, and soil samples, checking equipment previously tagged by the United Nations, and assessing buildings on the complexes. In January 2003, the International Atomic Energy Agency reported it had conducted 139 new inspections at 109 locations and concluded: "We have found no evidence that Iraq has revived its nuclear weapons program since the elimination of the program in the 1990s" (IAEA Report, January 28, 2003). And in the NIE on which the white paper is based, the State Department's intelligence unit had specifically dissented, using this text: "The activities we have detected do not, however, add up to a compelling case that Iraq is currently pursuing what INR would consider to be an integrated and comprehensive approach to nuclear weapons . . . INR is unwilling to speculate that such an effort began soon after the departure of UN inspectors or to project

a timeline for the completion of activities it does not now see happening" (Iraq NIE Key Judgmdents, October 2002 [declassified July 18, 2003]).

All evidence that has been collected since the Iraq war confirms the lack of any Iraqi nuclear weapons program.

21. Note the structure of this claim. Even in the NIE, the leading judgment is that an Iraqi nuclear capability is remote ("the last half of this decade"), while the menacing immediate Iraqi weapon is contingent upon Saddam acquiring weapons-grade nuclear material abroad. The latter development would be unlikely since highly enriched uranium is tightly controlled, relatively large quantities are necessary for a bomb, and authorities are very sensitive to trafficking in these materials. Completely unaddressed is the question, even assuming Saddam procured the uranium or a complete bomb, of how many nuclear weapons were necessary for Iraq to have a significant capability. A single nuclear bomb is not necessarily a threatening arsenal. It would suffice for just one target. Without survivable command channels, mechanisms for acquiring target intelligence, and delivery systems, a single bomb would be a weapon of desperation, not a flexible military capability.

22. This is another reference to the aluminum tubes imported by Iraq, disguised to sound like a different and additional report.

23. A plant to convert uranium into a gaseous form (uranium hexafluoride) that could then be refined to extract more highly concentrated masses of the element, Jazirah, was heavily bombed in the Gulf War. CIA reports from February and August 1991 differ on the extent of damage, and proliferation expert Joseph Cirincione believes self-inflicted damage from the Iraqi deception program further affected the facility. A July 1991 no-notice inspection by a UN team led by David Kay, then among the early international inspectors, identified the site's function to produce uranium hexafluoride, and it was subsequently under observation.

24. Ash Sharqat is here described as a plant to separate highly enriched uranium by means of electromagnetic separation. In fact, it was originally only a mine. Iraq later began Project 8119 to construct a plant, using Yugoslav plans, identical to a plant constructed at Tarmiya. (Project 8119 was built with different outside dimensions to disguise it from the air—an example of Iraqi deception at work. In another example, Baghdad removed some equipment from the site and laid fresh concrete floors to hide the action.) Ash Sharqat received heavy damage from bombing in 1991 and was subsequently under UN supervision. A CIA report of June 1991 notes that the actual equipment for uranium separation had never been installed before the Gulf War. The British assessment in September 2002 was that the plant had been dismantled by the United Nations, but that starting in 1992 Iraq began

work at the same site on a chemical plant for nitric acid (Project Baiji), useful in creating precursor materials for uranium enrichment, but also for making rocket fuel and explosives (both of which have nothing to do with nuclear weapons). The Defense Intelligence Agency used the fact that Ash Sharkat had controlled access roads and security fences to portray it as an exemplar of Iraqi deception activity in its October 2002 briefing. There is no automatic correlation here, however. Many kinds of facilities have security fences and controlled access. In Iraq those features are characteristic of numerous industrial plants.

25. Al Qa'im, an ore plant from before the 1990–91 war, suffered some damage, then became subject to UN monitors. By 2002 the Defense Intelligence Agency was identifying it as a *chemical*, not nuclear, plant. It underwent an extensive UN inspection on December 10, 2002.

26. Tarmiya is a facility for electromagnetic separation of enriched uranium, built in two stages and opened in February 1990. The CIA estimated that Iraq first succeeded in this kind of enrichment just prior to the Gulf War, a development that likely occurred at Tarmiya. The site had both hot cells and calutrons, the latter in a plant built to Yugoslav plans under Project 411. Initial enrichment was performed here and final enrichment at Tuwaitha. CIA reports in May–June 1991 describe Tarmiya variously as heavily damaged or half-destroyed. Hussein Kamel reported in 1995 that material here had been removed and buried within the past several months. UN inspection teams covered Tarmiya on December 11, 2002, and a reporter who accompanied them described the plant as "destroyed by American bombing during the 1990s" (*New York Times*, December 13, 2002, p. A14).

27. This plant was hit by forty-three U.S. cruise missiles on George Bush's father's last day in office in January 1993. In 1995 Saddam's weapons program manager Hussein Kamel identified Rashidiyah as a research center on centrifuges headed by Dr. Mahdi Obeidi. In May 2003 Obeidi voluntarily went to U.S. occupation forces in Iraq and revealed that the centrifuge plans and prototype equipment were buried in a barrel in his backyard and had been since 1991, on the orders of Qusay Hussein. Rashidiyah could hardly have been an active research center. The CIA confirmed the fact of the materials buried in Obeidi's garden (CIA statement, June 26, 2003). The Bush administration attempted to use this handover as evidence of its claim of an Iraqi weapons program reconstituted as asserted in this CIA white paper. The fact that the centrifuge materials were buried in Obeidi's yard rather speaks against the existence of any active Iraqi weapons program.

28. Naturally among the first sites sealed by UN weapons inspectors in 2002–03.

29. A facility for production of centrifuges, believed built by a German company, Al Furat was under UN supervision from the summer of 1991. This plant figured among the places where satellites spotted new construction after 1998. The CIA assumed Al Furat had a nuclear weapons function in the white paper, but a new wave of UN inspectors, who monitored activity at Al Furat from December 10, 2002, found chemical, not nuclear-related, equipment there.

30. Tuwaitha: Briefly discussed above (#20), Tuwaitha was one of the two most important Iraqi nuclear weapons facilities, location of several research reactors, plutonium extraction, and Group 3Z, some of Iraq's leading nuclear scientists. The facility was bombed by Israel in 1981, and extensively bombed in the 1990–91 Gulf War. The scientists were transferred to Baghdad. Tuwaitha would be closely monitored by the United Nations through 1998, and again in 2002–03. It was described as in dilapidated condition, a status confirmed subsequent to the U.S. invasion, when attention focused on the site owing to extensive reports of looters there.

31. Al Atheer can fairly be described as Iraq's Los Alamos, the country's main nuclear weapons design establishment. Group 4, as the Iraqi unit was known internally, had by the end of 1989 evolved a basic plan for a weapon utilizing an implosion mechanism of yield similar to the Hiroshima bomb, according to documents uncovered by UN inspectors in September 1991. The inspection teams, under David Kay, had found Al Atheer extensively damaged but showed that it had had many of the facilities necessary to a bomb program. UN inspectors destroyed all equipment at the Al Atheer complex in April 1992. In 1995 Hussein Kamel reported that Group 4, under Khalid Sa'id, had first studied a device weighing 12 tons, totally impractical, then one scaled back to 5 tons, also not deliverable by aircraft or missile systems in Saddam's arsenal. In Donald Rumsfeld's September 19 presentation to Congress these studies were transformed into comprehensive "designs" and nothing was said about their impracticality. So little activity was observed at Al Atheer that by 2002 it was not even a high-priority site for weapons inspectors.

32. Overall. The map displaying Iraqi nuclear facilities in the CIA white paper conveys a false sense of precision and an enhanced sense of threat. Facilities named on the map had been destroyed, deactivated, or converted to different uses, and all were subject to a strong regime of UN controls, both through 1998 *and* in 2002–03. This is not the picture of a vigorous nuclear weapons program. Since the Bush administration depended on the alleged nuclear threat as a major leg of its argument for the necessity of attacking Iraq in the near term, the handling of Iraqi nuclear facilities in the CIA white paper must be assessed as highly suspect.

33. The claim of Iraqi possession of a stockpile of biological and chemical weapons is based not on evidence but on assumption. Items not covered by the "gaps in Iraqi accounting" are assumed to reside in the stockpile. "Current production capabilities" are assumed to be used for weapons stockpiling rather than industrial or medical purposes—assumptions identical to those regarding Saddam's possession of a "covert" missile force. The claim to a stockpile is made without any discernible input-output analysis to establish actual or projected Iraqi production. (A different U.S. analysis, the Defense Intelligence Agency's September 2002 report "Iraq: Key Weapons Facilities," explicitly comments: "There is no reliable information on whether Iraq is producing and stockpiling chemical weapons.") The CIA white paper's one caveat—that the evidence only "strongly suggests" Iraqi maintenance of a stockpile—disappears in the Key Judgments section of the paper, the portion authors knew would be the most widely read, to be replaced by "probably," as noted below (#35). In intelligence analysis, "probably" is a term of art, a measure indicating a degree of surety greater than "possibly" but less than "certainly."

34. Here the CIA white paper specifically remarks on, among other things, Iraqi preference for using artillery rockets. This is relevant to the dispute over Baghdad's efforts to acquire aluminum tubes (see analysis on pp. 93–104) because it shows that U.S. intelligence was in fact aware that other possible uses for the tubes reflected an Iraqi weapons preference.

35. The CIA white paper furnishes no basis for its numerical projection of the size of an Iraqi chemical weapons stockpile (100–500 metric tons) in which it nevertheless states relatively high confidence ("probably"). It also offers no characterization of the alleged stockpile. In fact, 100–500 tons, if that amount *was* accurate, would still be a relatively small stockpile. By way of comparison, CIA estimates around the time of the 1990–91 Gulf War were that Iraq maintained a chemical weapons stockpile of 2,000 tons. One plant alone was assessed as capable of adding to that stock at a rate of 720 tons per year. The CIA white paper is also silent as to the shelf life of the Iraqi stockpile, with the public left to suppose that the Iraqi agents were perfectly lethal. In fact the CIA and DIA had doubts about the shelf life of Iraqi chemical agents and disputed this matter throughout the 1990s.

36. For years Baghdad denied that it had produced VX gas. Iraqi weapons program manager Hussein Kamel, who defected in 1995, told UN weapons inspectors that Iraq had made the gas, but destroyed all its stocks and dismantled the equipment for making that agent. The transcript of Kamel's UN interview was avail-

able to the CIA, and its principal contents were passed to the agency in at least two cables in August 1995. Iraq subsequently admitted to having crafted VX but denied having prepared it in suitable form for loading in munitions. UN inspection teams in 1997 found some artillery shells with chemical traces of VX, although there were differences in laboratory results. However, former UN inspector Scott Ritter reports that in 1996 the teams found and destroyed two hundred cases of the glass-lined equipment necessary to produce VX. Ritter is confident Iraq's ability to manufacture VX gas did not survive the loss of that equipment.

37. This map displays an Iraqi chemical capability existing during the 1990–91 Gulf War. While the map is impressive, claims of Iraqi power as of 1991 are not relevant to an evaluation of Iraqi capabilities in 2002. It should be established at whose behest this map was included in the 2002 CIA white paper.

38. This language, clearly intended to heighten readers' concerns, again demonstrates the paucity of hard intelligence that bedevils the CIA white paper and the NIE upon which it is based. Within limits, almost any chemical plant can be configured to manufacture toxic products, the main difference being certain specific equipment or chemical precursors. Two CIA reports issued in 2001 refer to UN inspectors prior to 1998, who had found the Iraqi declarations as to the status of their biological programs incomplete. The inspectors therefore assumed Baghdad had maintained its knowledge base and industrial infrastructure to resume weapons production. As a result, CIA reports express concern that Iraq "may again be producing biological warfare agents." This formula is essentially identical to the one in the CIA white paper. However, had Saddam Hussein reactivated biological agent production lines by early 2001, by late 2002 there surely must have been some hard evidence to attest that development. In short, the assertion is further illustration of how assumptions drove the harsh picture of Iraq presented in the CIA white paper.

39. Here the CIA white paper refers explicitly for the first time to Hussein Kamel, the brother-in-law of Saddam who had managed various aspects of Iraq's weapons programs for many years. Kamel defected in 1995 and provided information to UN inspectors. Kamel was subsequently induced to return to Baghdad, and then murdered by one of Saddam's sons. Kamel is cited repeatedly in Bush's speeches and the other documents included here, but *only* in contexts that call on his authoritative voice to reinforce claims that Iraq possessed powerful weapons of mass destruction. Actually, much of Hussein Kamel's testimony demonstrated the opposite, but the reassuring information Kamel provided is uniformly omitted

from Bush administration presentations, including the CIA white paper. On August 22, 1995, Kamel talked for three hours with senior UN inspectors. Among his revelations were the number of SCUD missile launchers left to Iraq after the Gulf War and unilateral destruction (two); details of various facilities, including nuclear, chemical, and biological; notes on scientists involved in the Iraqi programs; details on uranium enrichment efforts; details on nuclear bomb design (only theoretical studies were performed); confirmation that the number of warheads created for missiles to carry chemical and biological agents was the same (twenty-five) as the U.N. had identified and destroyed; an assertion that Kamel himself had ordered the destruction of stocks of agent, production lines, and missiles; the conversion of a VX plant to manufacture pesticides; and many other details. The Bush administration's treatment of Hussein Kamel's testimony is plainly misleading.

40. Map. As with the previous maps in the CIA white paper, this illustration of the Iraqi biological weapons infrastructure is puffed up considerably, and reflects its status in 1991. The main centers that formed parts of the Iraqi biological weapons complex at that time—Salman Pak, Al Hakam, Al Muthanna, and Samarra—did not figure at all by 2002. UN inspectors destroyed the key equipment at each of these places, sometimes entire facilities, during the 1990s. It is highly suggestive that the body of the CIA paper explicitly discusses only three of the facilities displayed on this map. An indication of the degree of coordination between the CIA and the British intelligence paper is that the British paper covers precisely the same three Iraqi plants.

Immediately after Kamel's defection, and about two weeks prior to the Iraqi official's conversation with U.N. inspectors, senior officers in Baghdad compiled a top secret damage assessment for Saddam's son Qusay Hussein, who had a supervisory role over Iraqi weapons development and deception efforts. Extracted from Saddam's private archives and first reported in the *Washington Post* by correspondent Barton Gellman, the six-page document detailed what Kamel knew and demonstrates that the defector pulled no punches when he spoke to the UN debriefers.

41. This data table looks impressive until one realizes that it lists no Iraqi weapons test since 1991. In particular the list records *no tests at all* for anthrax, the biological weapons specter held up by President Bush at the United Nations, and a primary feature of the charges he leveled in Cincinnati (October 2002), and of those leveled by Colin Powell before the Security Council (February 2003). Anthrax is extremely difficult to work with and literally could not have been weaponized without testing. The listing here of a surrogate (*Bacillus subtilis*) is the kind of thing

done in preparation for a fully worked-up test of the real agent thing. What this table really suggests is that the Gulf War intervened in the Iraqi development program, and that the UN inspectors who moved in afterward effectively cut off Iraqi biological agent weaponization before it could be completed. No American designer would be satisfied with a weapon that had never been fully tested, and for a military establishment to rely on weapons not tested in more than a decade would have been foolhardy. Americans who believed in this aspect of the Iraqi threat were misled.

42. The CIA white paper provides no evidence at all for the allegation that "most elements" of the Iraqi biological weapons program are "more advanced and larger than before the 1990–91 Gulf war." Considering the destruction of whole facilities by the UN inspectors during the 1990s, this seems unlikely. No language in CIA's annual threat estimates for Congress, or its biennial reports on weapons of mass destruction, supports the claim. The British intelligence Iraq paper, in its equivalent passage, says something very different: "Newly purchased equipment and other equipment previously subject to monitoring could be used in a resurgent biological warfare programme."

43. According to reconstructions made from Iraqi declarations to UN inspectors in 1995 and after, Iraq decided to create a facility at Al Dawrah during the summer of 1990. A CIA cable of June 1991 shows the agency was aware of its function by that time. Inspection teams from the United Nations reached differing conclusions, because there was no proof in the early 1990s that biological agents had actually been produced, but monitoring continued. After his defection Hussein Kamel affirmed that Al Dawrah had been active in the Iraqi anthrax program but that all weapons and agents had been destroyed ("Nothing remained," Kamel said).

A UN team under David Kay, visiting Al Dawrah, confirmed evidence of deceptive measures by the Iraqis and also thoroughly checked the negative-air-pressure, high-containment germ laboratory that was a main feature of the facility. In mid-1996 UN teams that included explosives experts and structural engineers deactivated the negative pressure vessel at Al Dawrah, destroyed its large fermenters, tagged the smaller ones, and installed cameras to oversee all tagged equipment. Eleven further teams visited between October 1996 and March 1997.

After the UN inspectors were expelled from Iraq, workers were seen on camera moving equipment outside visual range, which certainly worried the CIA. Its estimate was then based on the assumption that the equipment had been used for biological warfare purposes. When inspectors of the new UN mission visited Al Dawrah on November 28, 2002, they found all the tagged fermenters (one had been moved to another plant but was precisely where the Iraqis said it would be) and other materials. The plant generally was a shambles: after a four-hour inspection the United Nations pronounced it unsuitable for production of either toxins *or* vaccines. Reporters who accompanied the inspectors found Al Dawrah largely in ruins, its main building "little more than a garbage site," with files on the floor gathering dust (*New York Times*, November 29, 2002, p. A20).

44. Amiriyah also had been judged capable of producing biological agents after the Gulf war, but the United Nations could not find evidence that this had been done. Rather it established the facility had been used for research and for storage of agents and seed stocks. The language in the CIA white paper largely copies what is in the British intelligence Iraq paper, except that the British say Amiriyah "has now expanded its storage capacity." The CIA gratuitously adds that this "greatly exceeds Iraq's needs for legitimate medical storage." The CIA's judgment on what level of Iraqi capacity might be legitimate for storage is not explained or substantiated. Amiriyah was inspected by UN teams without incident during the run up to the U.S. invasion.

45. A historical connection is most of what Fallujah had. This was the place where one of the earliest confrontations between a UN inspection team led by David Kay and the Iraqis occurred, in June 1991, a celebrated incident where Iraqis moved prohibited equipment (suspected calutron parts for nuclear enrichment) out the back of the complex while the inspectors were stalled at the front gate. (The Defense Intelligence Agency resurrected this incident when compiling its October 2002 public briefing on Iraqi deception techniques.) In 1993 the United Nations designated certain equipment at Fallujah for elimination, which the Iraqis resisted until after American cruise missile attacks against Iraqi intelligence headquarters in Baghdad, after which the items were quickly moved to the site for destruction. American intelligence agencies were certainly aware of developments at Fallujah since Gerald L. Brubaker, a UN team leader of the mid-1990s, was also liaison between the Pentagon and the UN inspectors. Brubaker participated in the big round of equipment destruction (including the Dawrah vats) that took place at Al Muthanna in 1996. Thus claims are made here by U.S. intelligence about Iraqi capabilities the United States knew had been rendered inoperative.

Note that the wording of the CIA white paper itself admits that Iraq had run Fallujah under UN supervision for legitimate purposes. The CIA statement about verifying claims is a truism. After UN monitors in the new round of inspections mounted a no-notice visit to Fallujah on December 9, 2002, finding intact and unused the two large fermenting vats known to have been left at Fallujah, neither the CIA nor the U.S. government made any effort to correct the record on the charges advanced in this white paper.

46. The question of Iraqi mobile weapons laboratories is analyzed in detail on pp. 283–86.

47. Claims about Iraqi longer-range missiles in this text as well as the chart and map on the following page, like the claims regarding Iraqi nuclear weapons, are advanced without any time frame. The British intelligence paper on Iraq at least puts a date–2007–to the putative threat. Three missiles, two medium- and one long-range, are mentioned in the CIA paper. The Badr-2000 missile here began as a joint development effort between Iraq and Argentina, which called its rocket the Condor. After Argentina canceled its Condor program, the Badr-2000 in Iraq essentially evaporated. Another medium-range program, the Al Abbas, is rated as having been previously flight-tested. The Iraqis are also said to be designing a long-range missile capable of flying 3,000 kilometers. The large engine test stand, later referred to by Colin Powell at the UN Security Council in his notorious February 2003 speech, is suitable for motors in a medium-range missile, which the white paper says Iraq is designing.

The December 2001 NIE on foreign ballistic missile development (whose drafting, like the Iraq NIE's, was supervised by Robert Walpole) noted that Baghdad might be able to test a medium-range missile by "mid-decade," though "this possibility assumed rapid erosion of UN prohibitions and Baghdad's willingness to risk detection of developmental steps, such as static engine-testing, earlier." The NIE judged the flight test of an Iraqi medium-range missile to be likely by 2010, and also concluded that for the first several years following the end of UN sanctions, Iraq would strive to rebuild its short-range missile force to pre-Gulf War levels rather than move to a bigger missile. A test of a long-range rocket "could" happen before 2015, the estimate concluded, but "such a missile almost certainly would fail." Walpole's ballistic missile estimate judged that Iraq was not likely to attempt such a program. This perspective is notably more restrained that the CIA white paper written less than a year later.

In all, the missile evidence is mixed. A threat from Iraqi missiles remained remote, by no means the dark specter held up by the CIA white paper. Iraq had no weapon capability to reach the United States and little even against America's friends in the Near East and south Asia. The UN inspectors confirmed engine test stands and solid-motor casting buildings but no hardware, and none but short-range rockets in the Iraqi arsenal. Following the coalition invasion, technical specialists with the Iraq Survey Group are reported to have found evidence for two solid-fuel and two liquid-fuel missile projects, all with 1,000-km ranges, double the number of medium-range missile programs Iraq was previously thought to have. Two were the same as those the United States featured before the war. The others never progressed beyond the design stage. One literally never progressed beyond pencilled drawings. Indeed, Baghdad was reported to have negotiated with North Korea for medium-range missiles, which would have been unnecessary had its own programs succeeded. On the other hand, there was *no* evidence for the Iraqi long-range missile that could potentially threaten the United States. Former senior Iraqi official Tariq Azziz is reported to have told coalition interrogators that Saddam had believed it was permissible to build the missiles so long as he did not create weapons of mass destruction to put on them.

48. The CIA was correct that these short-range missiles were being deployed. In its December 2001 report to Congress on weapons of mass destruction the agency had already noted the appearance of four Al Samoud transporter-launchers with missiles on them appearing in a December 2000 parade. The CIA was also correct that the Iraqi missiles could fly farther than the 90 miles permitted by UN restrictions. On the other hand—and this is an illustration of how it was simply not possible for Iraq to hide a serious missile development program—when Iraq resumed tests of this missile in May 1999 (the initial flight took place in 1997), U.S. intelligence tracked that and the next seven flight tests and was aware the missile had both propulsion and guidance problems.

   In early 2003 UN inspectors demanded that Saddam Hussein destroy the missiles. Amid much Iraqi groaning, Saddam issued orders for the destruction that February. The fact of the destruction of these missiles did not stop the United States from continuing to assert this substantive breach of UN resolutions. The Bush administration also added a charge—based on no visible evidence—that Saddam was ordering renewed production of the missile elsewhere, even while his wrecking crews were destroying missiles in the glare of journalists' television lights. The short-range missile issue demonstrates that actual Iraqi efforts to disarm made no difference to the U.S. plans to invade Iraq.

49. The phrase "most analysts" here obscures the fact that it was the U.S. Air Force that disagreed with the NIE claims regarding Iraqi unmanned aerial vehicles as chemical and biological weapons carriers. Air Force intelligence believed the craft lacked both the necessary range and desired weight of payload to make them viable as weapon carriers, and thought the Iraqis would use these craft as intelligence-gathering platforms.

50. This is useful information, but it concerns an issue of fundamental policy, not an intelligence question. The easiest remedy for Iraqi diversion of assets into weap-

ons programs was to return to Iraq a strong UN monitoring group that could prevent monetary diversion from resulting in military capabilities. Saddam Hussein agreed to that measure about two weeks prior to the release of this CIA white paper. Ending diversion through invasion of Iraq was a far costlier and more damaging proposition and also resulted in diversion of a different kind, since after the invasion Iraqi income would have to be diverted to rebuilding what was destroyed in the war.

The Aluminum Tubes Question

The single most important factor in the determination of whether Iraq posed a clear and present danger to America in the months and weeks before the U.S. invasion was the question of whether Saddam Hussein possessed nuclear weapons. *That* was something George Bush could get people worked up enough about to support an invasion. By the same token, the political importance of this matter made the intelligence worth fighting about, and that is what happened.

Among the handful of allegations rooted in hard data that the Bush administration relied upon to buttress its charges that Saddam Hussein had nuclear weapons development at the heart of his agenda, near to achievement if not already in hand, was the claim the Iraqis were importing aluminum tubes to use in gas centrifuges. In a centrifuge, the tubes would function as arms of the machine, through which uranium hexafluoride gas would be pumped. Spinning at a very high rate of speed, centrifugal force would push the most potent ("enriched") atoms toward the sides of the tubes, where they could be captured and held in a magnetic field and isolated for further stages of processing until the level of enrichment was sufficient for weapons use. (The term "cascade" that is frequently seen in discussions of this subject denotes both the possibility of multiple production lines and the stages of enrichment, in which parallel sets of centrifuges work with uranium gas at successively higher levels of potency to extract the more highly enriched particles.)

The way the tube allegation surfaced bears every mark of an orchestrated leak by the Bush administration, quite possibly one planned by the

White House Information Group (WHIG). The story went first to Judith Miller, a respected correspondent for the *New York Times*, which published her report on September 8, 2002, stating that Iraq had tried to procure aluminum tubes for its nuclear weapons program. With George W. Bush's UN speech then in draft, containing the same aluminum tube allegation, the administration was preparing the ground for maximum gain from the assertion. During her appearance on a television news program that same day, national security adviser Condoleezza Rice confirmed the story and insisted such aluminum tubes are "only really suited for nuclear weapons programs, centrifuge programs." Appearing on a different television show, Vice President Richard Cheney separately confirmed the press report that Iraq had attempted to buy aluminum tubes for uranium enrichment. Bush gave his speech on September 12, and the following day the WHIG put out one of its Iraq papers that also mentioned the aluminum tubes acquisition.

Iraq did attempt to import the tubes, but for purposes that have been the subject of intense debate. Bush, Cheney, and Rice made out to the public that the tubes were about nuclear weapons. As early as one week after Bush's UN speech, in a report written for his Institute for Science and International Security, David Albright, a physicist who had worked in Iraq as a UN inspector in 1996, and who is probably the most prominent public commentator on Iraqi weapons of mass destruction, disputed the significance of the data. Albright sensibly argued that mere existence of the tubes did not prove that Iraq had a working plant for centrifuge enrichment or give any indication as to a date when such a capability would become available to Baghdad. He also went through details of the tubes' construction, showing that these differed from, and were less advanced than, the specifications of centrifuge designs Iraq had already used in the 1980s. Certain characteristics of the tubes (anodization, thickness of the aluminum, finishing at the ends) would make them even *less* useful in a gas centrifuge. Albright showed convincingly that the tubes were of dubious value as components of centrifuges.

Albright maintained that the anodized coating on the aluminum pipes would make them difficult to weld and thus to use in a centrifuge machine, that the specifications of the pipes were different than those Iraq had used in its centrifuge designs previously, and indeed that Iraq had turned to materials other than aluminum in its efforts to build a centrifuge. As early as April 1992, Albright himself had disclosed that Iraq had secured blueprints for two models of centrifuges designed by the European consortium URENCO, and these used hardened ("maraged") steel or carbon fiber for centrifuge arms, not aluminum. Ten years later there was wide consensus that Baghdad was working from the URENCO designs. Meanwhile, Hussein Kamel told his UN debriefers in August 1995 that the centrifuge project headed by Dr. Obeidi had machines using, in fact, maraged steel and carbon fiber.

In 2000 the CIA learned that Iraq, using an Australian intermediary, was attempting to procure aluminum tubes in China. An agency analyst working on export controls detected this transaction, followed subsequent transactions, and assessed the tubes as being for a nuclear program. The analyst, called "Joe" (the CIA has apparently asked that he be identified no more closely than "Joe T."), had worked as an engineer in the 1980s at the U.S. uranium enrichment facility Oak Ridge. At the Central Intelligence Agency, Joe became an analyst with one of the CIA's fusion information centers, WINPAC, the Weapons Intelligence, Proliferation, and Arms Control center, led by Alan Foley. Joe's intelligence enabled the CIA to intercept one shipment of the tubes, which were photographed and a sample taken, and then to seize another shipment in Jordan in July 2001, when some 3,000 tubes were taken. The last samples seen by one official, as reported in early 2003, bore inscriptions that included the etched word "rocket."

David Albright advanced an alternative explanation for Iraq's interest in the tubes: artillery rockets. The tubes were made of an aluminum-zinc composite, an alloy with a wide range of industrial applications. As reported by Barton Gellman and Walter Pincus (in the *Washington Post* on August 10, 2003), the Italian-designed Medusa artillery rocket has specifications identical to those of the seized tubes. Its body is made from aluminum. In the 1990s Iraq had had an inventory of about 160,000 artillery rockets. When Secretary of State Colin Powell used the example of the tubes himself in February 2003, he made a point of asserting that Iraq had refined its specifications through successive orders of the tubes, claiming this proved their nuclear function. Albright had already commented on this aspect in his initial report for the Institute for Science and International Security in October 2002: the Medusa rockets' specifications had been changed, in precisely the same way, with the modifications related to accidental burn-throughs of the casing at lesser levels of thickness and anodization. By contrast, the pipes in a centrifuge arm have greater thickness and diameter and are not anodized. Iraqi artillery rockets using these tubes were actually offered for sale and exhibited at arms shows in the period before the Iraq war.

The sale angle is a significant one. Postwar investigations would show much of the Iraqi weapons effort had become a "corrupted process," in the words of U.S. Chief Inspector David Kay. He told an audience at the Carnegie Endowment for International Peace that the committees supervising the aluminum tube imports received a percentage of the price. Changing specifications, which required new orders, and increasing tube precision, which increased the price, both increased their take on these deals.

Scientific and engineering investigation by the International Atomic Energy Agency (IAEA) established later that the original tolerances for the tubes were set before 1987, based on "physical measurements from a small number of imported rockets in Iraq's possession," and the tolerances were adjusted later to revitalize the project and improve operational efficiency. The rocket project evidently was kicked from one committee to another in Baghdad and stalled for many years, and the specifications changed when new groups assumed responsibility. In any event, IAEA further found that although Iraq had the manufacturing ability to create high-quality aluminum, it lacked both experience and equipment necessary to craft consistent "flow-formed" pieces to the tolerances necessary for centrifuge parts.

Technical objections made by David Albright and others actually mirrored a dispute within the U.S. intelligence community. Experts at the Z Division of the Lawrence Livermore National Laboratory; at Los Alamos National Laboratory, the U.S. nuclear design specialists; and at Oak Ridge National Laboratory had serious questions about the aluminum pipe theory. Aluminum had not been used in centrifuges since the 1950s. The dimensions of the Iraqi tubes were wrong as well. In late 2001, a former Oak Ridge physicist, Houston G. Wood III, was asked to review the evidence, and concluded that the doubts were well founded.

Some months later, after Bush's UN speech, the intelligence community labored to complete its national intelligence estimate on Iraq's weapons of mass destruction. The draft estimate contained a judgment on the aluminum tubes that followed the opinions of WINPAC analyst "Joe T." Though WIN-PAC's director Alan Foley had a reputation as a straight-shooter, he was not an expert in this field and deferred to the judgment of his line analyst. The State Department's Bureau of Intelligence and Research was prepared to dissent on this issue.

Meanwhile it is the Department of Energy (DOE) that runs Livermore and Los Alamos, the main U.S. nuclear design centers, and Oak Ridge, a vital enrichment facility. The DOE had to make its own assessment about Iraqi aluminum tubes for the estimate—an assessment clearly of central importance to the NIE. The DOE contribution was written mainly by two physicists, William Domke of Livermore and Jeffrey Bedell of Los Alamos. Their analysis dovetailed with the State Department intelligence view—the tubes were not for centrifuges.

At the time, however, the DOE's intelligence chief was really a stand-in from the personnel office, a wholly-unrelated component. While staff wanted to join the Bureau of Intelligence and Research in a dissent, the record shows that this gentleman, Thomas Rider, told senior officials at a DOE preparatory meeting considering the Iraq NIE to drop their opposition to the language in the draft estimate. Rider did take experts from Livermore and Oak Ridge with him to the National Foreign Intelligence Board, but at the session, which took place at the CIA and was chaired by Director Tenet, the DOE man said nothing, and his experts were given no opportunity to comment.

According to George Tenet, analysts at the National Ground Intelligence Center, another of the intelligence community's fusion units supposed to bring together all source information, were also involved in the debate and agreed with the WINPAC assessment rather than that of the DOE experts. The view of the ground warfare analysts was that the aluminum tubes would be a bad choice for rocket motor casings. (Insiders, however, appar-

ently told David Albright as early as the fall of 2002 they doubted the people
at the ground intelligence center had been furnished complete data by the
CIA.) In a March 2003 report, Albright further noted that the aluminum
tubes were apparently *not* made the subject of expert review by an independent panel, as is standard practice in intelligence on disputed technical issues.
During the Cold War, in contrast, the characteristics of Soviet bombers,
missiles, guidance systems, and other items had routinely been examined in
this fashion. A participant in the dispute told Albright that "the administration
could say anything it wanted about the tubes while government scientists
who disagreed were expected to remain quiet."

Director Tenet argues that because analysts from all over agreed that
the tubes *could be* used in a centrifuge (even if extensive modification were
necessary), the debate was simply about intent. That is a painful tautology
since the Bush people were using the tubes *as evidence of intent.* Moreover,
nuclear intent cannot have been true if Iraq lacked the ability to make the
necessary modifications to the tubes. And the main flaw in all this data was
precisely that U.S. intelligence had such poor understanding of Iraq's intentions. To say the debate was over intent is to acknowledge that U.S. intelligence failed to resolve the central issue in contention in its Iraq estimate.

Finally, even if the administration's claims about Iraq's use for aluminum tubes were accurate, they did not add up to the clear and present danger
the Bush White House maintained. In his September 19, 2002, Senate testimony, Secretary Donald Rumsfeld tried to preempt this criticism, arguing
that even if it took the Iraqis five to seven years to craft a bomb, it was
impossible to know whether that interval began in 2002, in 1998, or at some
other date. Rumsfeld's argument glossed over the question of Iraq's ability
to pursue this technology, which had been overestimated in the first place.
In one of his papers, public scientist David Albright calculated that the aluminum tubes might suffice to manufacture about 1,000 centrifuges per year,
and that cascades numbering 3,500 machines could produce about two-thirds
of the fissionable material necessary for a nuclear bomb in a year. Adding
the time to get a production line up and running, that necessary to refine the
remainder of the required highly enriched uranium, and the time required

to build the actual weapon puts the first possible Iraqi nuclear weapon squarely within the five-to-seven-year prediction that Rumsfeld had attempted to denigrate.

That was the worst-case estimate. The Iraqi nuclear program had never attained such a pace. The declassified CIA documents from the early 1990s show that Iraq had never operated more than 550 centrifuges, in a two-stage cascade process. About 500 machines at Rashidiyah performed the initial enrichment, and another 50 at Tuwaitha the final stage. The Iraqis had chronic trouble with electrical supply even at that level of effort. Reports were that the electricity supply problem was solved by construction of new plants just prior to the Gulf War. Then the Gulf War coalition came along and bombed Iraq's electricity infrastructure. The Iraqi electric grid never fully recovered. Indications are that it had reached only about 85 percent of pre-war production when the United States invaded Iraq in 2003. Brownouts and sporadic outages were already endemic in Iraq before the war (and worsened afterward). A major uranium enrichment effort would have added hugely to electric consumption.

David Albright writes of 3,500 centrifuges. The National Intelligence Estimate itself uses the number 25,000. Building up to this production level would have taken much longer than five-to-seven years, could not have been done without relatively early detection, and was certainly not detected in the period after the UN inspectors left Iraq. At that level of activity, the enrichment effort alone would have consumed a significant portion of all electricity generated by Iraq. We also have the evidence of the scientific chief of the centrifuge program at Rashidiyah, Dr. Mahdi Obeidi, who had buried the centrifuge plans and key prototype parts in his backyard—not an action any active manager would take. Clearly the clock had yet to begin ticking on any meaningful Iraqi nuclear weapons program.

The British got at least this part of the Iraq riddle more accurately than the Bush people. In the preparation of their Iraq dossier, lead analyst John Scarlett minimized the importance of the tubes. His report stated "[t]here is no definitive intelligence" that the tubes were intended for centrifuges in a nuclear program.

In the final elaboration of the NIE, the State Department intelligence unit was suspicious of the tube claims. Intelligence and Research chief Carl W. Ford Jr., a former CIA officer (he had once been the NIO for East Asia) who had worked on Capitol Hill and also at the Pentagon, was a Democrat who nevertheless had good relations with figures as diverse as Richard Armitage and Paul Wolfowitz. Ford had been instrumental in shaping the intelligence on the Philippines for the Reagan administration during the crises in that country in the late 1980s. He had later labored under Dick Cheney at the Pentagon, returned to the Hill, then been a Washington lobbyist. Ford called the shots as he saw them. The chief of his military affairs and non-proliferation unit, Greg Thielmann, was of like mind, tight-lipped but analytically rigorous, with decades of experience on weapons intelligence.

State rejected the centrifuge view in the draft NIE, and Ford made his best case in favor of the artillery rocket purpose for the Iraqi aluminum tubes. When he failed to sway the consensus, Intelligence and Research dissented from the estimate, inserting an alternate view (footnote), referred to in the key judgments, but which read at length: "INR is not persuaded that the tubes in question are intended for use as centrifuge rotors. . . . INR considers it far more likely that the tubes are intended for another purpose, most likely the production of artillery rockets. The very large quantities being sought, the way the tubes were tested by the Iraqis, and the atypical lack of attention to operational security in the procurement efforts are among the factors, in addition to the DOE assessments, that lead INR to conclude that the tubes were not intended for use in Iraq's nuclear weapons program." While DOE's scientists felt ignored, their supervisor, Thomas Rider, who had quashed their dissent, was given a performance bonus of $13,000 and went on to another government job. The DOE intelligence directorship was taken over by a former CIA officer, John Russack.

The NIE went to Capitol Hill on October 1, and the CIA white paper followed on the October 4. The Knight-Ridder newspaper chain reported on October 5 that the way the Bush administration flacked the nuclear weapons interpretation of the Iraqi aluminum tubes, while keeping mum on the other view, amounted to its standard procedure on Iraq intelligence, citing several senior officials and intelligence officers as sources. Indeed on October 7, George Bush took the nuclear tubes claim to the public in his Cincinnati speech, which appears later in this narrative. The next day Knight-Ridder noted that intelligence officials "charge that the administration squelches dissenting views, and . . . intelligence analysts are under intense pressure to produce reports supporting the White House argument that Saddam poses such an immediate threat to the United States that pre-emptive military action is necessary."

Bush officials kept up their drumbeat of assertions regarding the aluminum tubes. At a November 15 White House briefing, Condoleezza Rice warned against Saddam Hussein, "a homicidal dictator, armed with a nuclear weapon in the Middle East." In response to Iraqi official statements that the tubes *were* for artillery rockets, presidential spokesman Ari Fleischer declared on December 2, "Iraq did, *in fact* [my italics], seek to buy these tubes for the purpose of producing, not as Iraq now claims conventional forces, but for the purpose of trying to produce nuclear weapons." Fleischer made another similar statement later that month. In actuality both statements went far beyond the facts. Secretary of State Colin Powell, who in congressional testimony on September 19 expressed views at odds with his own INR analysts on Iraq's intent with the tubes, on December 19 told a press conference, "We also know that Iraq has tried to obtain high-strength aluminum tubes, which can be used to enrich uranium in centrifuges."

On January 8, 2003, in his initial briefing for the UN Security Council, Director General Mohammed ElBaradei of the International Atomic Energy Agency (IAEA), reported his preliminary findings regarding nuclear weapons in Iraq. Among other things ElBaradei reported that, although investigation continued, "the IAEA's analysis to date indicates that the specifications of the aluminum tubes sought by Iraq in 2001 and 2002 appear to be consistent with reverse-engineering rockets." A Bush administration official countered, "I think the Iraqis are spinning the IAEA."

The CIA took its best shot at changing the IAEA's mind. CIA's lead analyst on the tubes, WINPAC's "Joe T.", flew to Vienna, where IAEA headquarters is located in a large building complex north of the Danube

River. On January 22, the U.S. embassy hosted a meeting where IAEA officials could listen to the CIA evidence. The CIA brief argued that the aluminum alloy specifications used for the tubes were too fine and too strong for an artillery rocket casing, essentially that it would waste the alloy to use it in this fashion.

The international experts were not moved. On January 27, ElBaradei presented the Security Council with a more extensive report. This time he noted that the IAEA investigation had included inspecting the relevant Iraqi rocket production and storage sites, taking tube samples, interviewing key participants, and reviewing contracts and related documents. His conclusion remained the same: "From our analysis to date it appears that the aluminum tubes would be consistent with the purpose stated by Iraq and, unless modified, would not be suitable for manufacturing centrifuges." An anonymous IAEA official was even more pointed with the *Washington Post* a couple of days before the big report: "It may be technically possible that the tubes could be used to enrich uranium, but you'd have to believe that Iraq deliberately ordered the wrong stock and intended to spend a great deal of time and money reworking each piece."

America's answer came in President George Bush's State of the Union address, given before Congress the next evening. The address, which appears below, blandly repeated the formulaic mantra that Iraq had imported aluminum tubes for its nuclear weapons program. At the United Nations, American ambassador John Negroponte dutifully followed suit, assuring the public on January 29 that the tubes "were designed and were intended for" uranium enrichment, and on January 30 Negroponte reiterated to a Senate panel, "We believe their characteristics are not consistent with a rocket program and are intended for nuclear centrifuges."

Negroponte had appeared before the Senate Foreign Relations Committee with one of his top bosses, Undersecretary of State Richard L. Armitage. The latter appeared to waver somewhat, maybe as a nod toward the State Department's INR, which after all had dissented on this point in the national estimate, saying, "I don't know, perhaps, particularly on the aluminum tubes we miscalculated." The White House reacted immediately.

Spokesman Ari Fleischer, speaking of the claims in Bush's State of the Union address, declared, "The president stands by every word he said."

At the time of these exchanges, the National Security Council staff, the CIA, and the State Department, behind the scenes, were in full battle mode preparing a presentation for Colin Powell to give before the UN Security Council. As will be seen where the Powell speech appears in this narrative, the claim for aluminum tubes went on Powell's list of allegations against Iraq, even though it was known to be contested.

George Tenet also acknowledged that the tube claims were contested when he appeared at the Senate intelligence committee for the CIA's annual global threat briefing on February 11. Tenet attempted to shift the ground by characterizing the Iraqis' style in buying the tubes: "When you look at the clandestine nature of the procurement and how they have tried to deceive what's showing up, and then you look at the other dual-use items they're trying to procure, we think we have stumbled onto one avenue of a nuclear weapons program." What the CIA director did *not* say, and only those senators who had read the footnotes to the Iraq NIE knew, was that the State Department dissent on the aluminum tubes *had explicitly noted* that Iraq had *not* taken its usual care with secrecy in this purchase of tubes, ignoring operational security in the transactions. Actually some of the Iraqi tube orders had been posted on the Internet.

The International Atomic Energy Agency, which received another package of U.S. intelligence data after Powell's Security Council sally, came back with its last word on the aluminum tube controversy on March 7. This time Director General ElBaradei reported: "Based on the available evidence, the IAEA team has concluded that Iraq's efforts to import these aluminum tubes were not likely to have been related to the manufacture of centrifuges and, moreover, that it was highly unlikely that Iraq could have achieved the considerable redesign needed to use them in a revived centrifuge programme."

Reacting to the IAEA report during a television news show, Colin Powell insisted, "We still have an open question with respect to that," and cited new information from a European country, not identified then or after. Leaks from Great Britain, however, revealed that British intelligence, far from supporting the CIA's view, believed the tubes were not for nuclear programs. In fact, the official British intelligence paper on Iraq, which became so controversial because of its alleged "sexed-up" claims about Saddam's programs, had resisted making any equivalent claim about the tubes. On March 10, 2003, just over a week before the United States invaded Iraq, the Institute for Science and International Security was led to pose the question that follows from all this: "A critical question is whether the Bush administration has deliberately misled the public and other governments in playing a 'nuclear card' that it knew would strengthen public support for war."

One additional element, usually covered by the word "other" when U.S. officials made their charges about Iraqi nukes and then insisted the aluminum tubes were not their only evidence, was the question of certain magnets Iraq had imported, which were alleged to be the magnets for the centrifuges. The NIE had this among its data points, and there too the State Department had dissented. The international monitors established that Iraq had bought twelve different kinds of magnets as well as contracting for a magnet factory. The magnets were used in missile guidance systems, industrial machinery, field telephones, and electricity meters, not centrifuges.

Intensely disputed as was the evidence and with the IAEA having reached some definitive conclusions, Vice President Cheney took another shot on March 16, 2003, on the eve of war. "I think Mr. ElBaradei frankly is wrong," Cheney told journalists on the news program *Meet the Press*, asserting, "I believe Saddam Hussein has reconstituted nuclear weapons." Almost exactly six months later, on September 14, on television again for the first time since that appearance, Cheney was asked about his claims from the spring. He had "misspoken," Cheney replied, a nonretraction for a monstrous prevarication.

Unmanned Aerial Vehicles (UAVs)

The CIA white paper makes a great deal out of Iraqi programs to develop unmanned aerial vehicles (UAVs) for the delivery of the alleged stocks of chemical and biological agents Baghdad had accumulated. The report itself discloses that this was nothing new, that indeed Iraqi efforts on UAVs dated to before the Gulf War, and that during the Iran-Iraq war of the 1980s, fighter aircraft had been used to deliver these kinds of weapons. It is important to note that the detailed discussion of the drones toward the end of the CIA white paper provides *no* evidence for the alarming statement in the Key Judgments section of the report that these weapons "could threaten Iraq's neighbors, U.S. forces in the Persian Gulf and the United States, if brought close to, or into, the U.S. Homeland." Within the Key Judgments section itself, the summary line for this item, printed in boldface type, mentions only the most threatening possibility, biological weapons, leaving out the possibility of less exotic chemical agents that is noted below. These are examples of the way the language in the CIA white paper was massaged to emphasize the most alarming potential aspects of the supposed Iraqi military programs.

As noted before, the October white paper is a watered-down version of the still-top-secret NIE, completed only a few days earlier, in which the possibility of Iraqi UAVs used for weapons delivery is indeed featured in the Key Judgments section (the only part of the NIE to have been declassified). However, the threat assessment given the public in the CIA white paper glossed over the fact that U.S. Air Force intelligence and its National Air and Space Intelligence Center had *dissented* from the conclusion about UAVs in the NIE. The Air Force chief, Major General Robert S. Boyd, saw the unmanned vehicles, or drones, as being intended primarily for overhead reconnaissance, arguing based on the small size of the new drone Baghdad had developed. Weapons delivery is an inherent capability of airborne systems, the Air Force conceded, so that could be a secondary mission, language the Air Force agreed to add to its footnote as the estimate was negotiated at the National Foreign Intelligence Board. Boyd thought his dissent had been properly taken into account in the NIE. The CIA white paper, however, implies, but does not state, that dissent existed on this point, noting only that "most" agencies agreed with the assessment the drones were for biological weapons. As with the DOE opinion on centrifuges for Iraqi uranium enrichment, the white paper makes no reference to the fact that the dissenting agency on the

drones was the U.S. intelligence arm with the greatest expertise on the subject. Nor was it noted that the Air Force intelligence view was also prevalent
at the Pentagon's own Ballistic Missile Defense Agency.

The primacy given to biological weapons in the Key Judgments of the
white paper builds on very little information, because the body of the CIA
white paper is notably weak in its discussion of the weaponization of *any* of
these materials. As observed in the page-by-page analysis of the report, no
tests after the Gulf War are listed, nor are there any tests at all of anthrax,
as opposed to simulants. In its claims for a current Iraqi threat, the Bush
administration focused the most on anthrax, clearly fear-mongering in the
wake of the anthrax attacks in the United States after 9/11. George Bush,
Colin Powell, and others would repeatedly give the impression the Iraqis had
been actively improving their weapon, building a stockpile. Yet the Iraqis
would have been foolish to use a changed and modified biological agent
without tests using actual delivery systems and standard equipment. Had
there been such tests the Air Force could not reasonably have tabled the
dissent it did to the national estimate.

Next to the biological claim as a hair-raiser stands the specter of Iraqi
drones attacking the continental United States. This was not merely a claim
made in the CIA white paper. According to Florida Senator Bill Nelson,
speaking to home state journalists in late 2003, a drone attack on the American homeland figured as a prime feature of an intelligence briefing given to
a large group of legislators on Capitol Hill before the vote on the war resolution. Nelson repeated this charge on the floor of the Senate in January
2004: "I was looked at straight in the face and told that UAVs could be
launched from ships off the Atlantic coast to attack eastern seaboard cities of
the United States." Although Senator Nelson declined to specify the exact
date of the briefing or who from the Bush administration participated, CIA
Director George Tenet is known to have met with legislators on October 3,
2002, and to have been at a large congressional briefing with Defense Secretary Rumsfeld a couple of days later. We know from public complaints
made by Senator Tom Daschle in December 2002 that no intelligence briefings occurred between then and mid-December. Thus one of these two meet-

ings had to have been the occasion when the attack on the continental United States was emphasized. Meanwhile Senator Nelson, a former astronaut, is a sophisticate on matters of technology and could hardly have mistaken a claim about a drone threat against the United States for some other point made by CIA briefers.

The assertion that Iraqi unmanned aerial vehicles might attack the American mainland is a hoot. No U.S. authority claims the Iraqi UAVs had ranges longer than about 300 miles, obviously not enough to reach Washington. In fact, at that range no Iraqi drone could even strike Israel. The *only* way in which such an Iraqi craft could hit the American homeland would be to load it up on a ship, cross 7,000 miles of ocean in the face of the U.S. Navy, and launch it a few miles off the American coast, or from some land accommodation in Mexico or Canada. Such a scenario presumes that U.S. intelligence would be unable to accomplish something it is very good at—detecting the movement of suspicious international shipping. It also presumes the U.S. Navy would fail to intercept the shipment over that long distance, that the U.S. Air Force would be unable to destroy the drone in flight, and that the Iraqi handlers would be skilled enough to work with the ultra-dangerous biological weapons without killing themselves at sea. If the Iraqis entrusted the mission to their best scientists, the very movement and concentration of that scientific talent would be another indicator U.S. intelligence could use to discover the plot. If the plan *did* work, it would be strictly a one-shot deal. Iraq would never get away with that again. In short, a UAV attack on the U.S. homeland would have been a stunt, not a serious measure of a threat against which national security managers could plan. As General Boyd said to a reporter when asked about the drone scenario after the war, "We didn't see there was a very large chance they would be used to attack the continental United States. . . . We didn't see them as a big threat to the homeland."

The idea of a potential UAV attack made more sense against troops in the field. Baghdad had a lengthy record in the Iran-Iraq war of using exotic weaponry, particularly chemical weapons (Saddam Hussein used more of them than anyone since World War I). In the Gulf War Iraq apparently at

least toyed with the idea of aerial attack with chemicals. CIA cables from
1991 noted MIG-21 aircraft at an Iraqi base fitted with tanks to carry a
"dirty liquid." A 1992 cable, declassified in the mid-1990s, spoke of Iraq's
planning to execute a biological attack with three MIG-21 spray aircraft, set
to launch following a lead flight bearing conventional explosives, themselves
behind a plane that would scout the target area. According to the cable, the
scout plane was shot down and the mission never carried out. That tale itself
conflicts with other CIA information that Iraq never approved any chemical
attack during the Gulf War.

Another CIA cable from May 1992 notes the discovery of ten drones
that had been concealed at the headquarters building of the Nasir State Establishment for Chemical Industries. By this time Iraq had come under the
intensive scrutiny of UN weapons inspectors, who soon detected Baghdad's
UAV programs as well. The United Nations found that Iraq had experimented with making MIG-21 and Mirage F-1 aircraft into unmanned aerial
vehicles. They decided that Iraqi scientists had failed with the conversion of
the aircraft, but succeeded in modifying drop tanks from the planes as spray
canisters. The United Nations destroyed four such tanks suitable for the
F-1 fighters. Of course, that still left Saddam without a platform. Later UN
inspectors discovered that in 1995 Saddam had issued orders to reinvigorate
UAV research. There was no hard data on what this meant until the
American-British Desert Fox air assault of 1998, which retaliated for the
expulsion of the UN inspectors from Iraq.

On December 17, 1998, a British Tornado attack aircraft dropped its
smart bomb over Talil air base southeast of Baghdad. The projectile sheared
off the roof of a hangar at Talil, revealing to overhead reconnaissance a dozen
Czech-manufactured L-29 trainer aircraft that appeared to have been converted into UAVs. Talil happened to be the same base where the Iraqis had
supposedly planned that biological warfare mission during the Gulf War. The
L-29 trainers became a staple of subsequent intelligence reporting on the Iraqi
unmanned aerial vehicle program.

In 2000 the United States apparently detected flights of the Czech aircraft over Samarra, a standard Iraqi aerial test range. Reporting to Congress

on worldwide acquisition of weapons of mass destruction for the first half of 2001, the CIA noted that the L-29s had been refurbished, and that the planes were believed to have been modified to deliver biological or chemical weapons. The CIA report for the second half of the year actually took a step back from that allegation. Rather than asserting the United States "believed" in this data, the new report merely "suspected" it. On March 19, 2002, Director George Tenet briefed the Senate Armed Services Committee on global threats. With regard to the Iraqi UAV program, he stated that Baghdad "may" have retained a capability for delivering biological or chemical weapons using modified or drone aircraft. Almost seven months later, in his Cincinnati speech, President George Bush referred to the drones as a real threat, "a growing fleet" that could "disperse chemical or biological weapons across broad areas."

In the meantime a fresh contingent of UN weapons inspectors had arrived in Iraq and began a new search. In March 2003, seven to ten days ahead of the U.S. assault on Iraq, the inspectors made a series of discoveries on the unmanned aerial vehicles. At a base near Baghdad and at the Iraqi flight test center of Samarra, inspectors found two different types of Iraqi drones, as well as a chemical tank that had been reconfigured from the fuel cell of an L-29 trainer. The problem was that neither type of unmanned aircraft was capable of carrying the tank. That proved true of all of the sixty drones in the Iraqi fleet. One new prototype drone had first flown just three months earlier. It was nowhere near finishing flight testing, much less load testing, and it had no fittings for the tank. The other UAV, made of balsa wood and aluminum foil, held together with duct tape, sat on a sawhorse. This plane had tiny engines and wooden propellers and could have been a spyplane, as Air Force intelligence believed, but not a weapons carrier. The drones had windows in the underside of the fuselage and fittings for mounting sensors. On the eve of war, the Bush administration did nothing to acknowledge that another of its claims about the Iraqi threat had proven empty. Indeed Colin Powell seemed visibly upset that the monitors had not made more of their discovery. A few days later George Bush went to war.

After the war ended, U.S. intelligence specialists found a set of photos detailing various aspects of the Iraqi UAVs. The pictures confirmed the views held by U.S. Air Force intelligence—the drones were not a threat. In another development, an American site survey team under Lieutenant Colonel Michael Kingsford, sent to the base at Ibn Furnas in June, found five carcasses of drones, mostly burned and blackened things with nine-foot wingspans. A reporter quoted Air Force Captain Libbie Boehm saying, "It could have been a student project, or maybe a model."

In short, if there was an Iraqi program for aerial delivery of bio/chem weapons, it was aimed at the battlefield, utilized conventional aircraft, and did not amount to a clear and present danger to the United States justifying an invasion of Iraq. Yet between the spring and fall of 2002, that is, between Tenet's testimony to Congress on global threats in March and the NIE of September, something happened that resulted in the CIA's taking a much more alarming view of Iraqi UAVs. The data did not change. What changed was President Bush's need to sell his war.

3

Embroidery

Distilled from the National Intelligence Estimate, the twenty-five-page Central Intelligence Agency white paper lacked the nuance and argumentation supplied in the ninety-page estimate. The spin put on the data in the white paper and the sparse description, while aiding in conveying a greater sense of threat, produced a different impression on readers who had also consulted the NIE. The problem would be that the senators and congressmen did read, and the NIE was on file at the intelligence committees of the two houses of Congress. Once President Bush had asked for a resolution authorizing force against Iraq, the intelligence report assumed even greater importance. Senate Intelligence Committee Chairman Bob Graham in particular questioned the one-sided picture in the CIA white paper.

Graham was already irritated by George Tenet's failure to attend the October 2 hearing, when the NIE had first been briefed by the agency. The CIA had not covered issues on which Graham had specifically sought information, such as the impact of a war with Iraq on neighboring states, and it had not furnished a requested NIE on Iraqi conventional capabilities, which would not be finished for weeks yet. Langley had rejected doing any national estimate at all on CIA covert activities in Iraq on the grounds that NIEs measure foreign capabilities, not U.S. operations. (This latter is correct. However, the CIA often did NIEs *in support of* covert plans along the lines of

"Short-Term Prospects for X's Rule in Slobovia." With a secret operation then in preparation in Iraq, compiling such an NIE in this case would be perfectly legitimate. It would not be surprising to learn that such an estimate was done. Whether it was given to the Congress is another matter.) Even the Republican vice-chairman of the committee, Alabama Senator Richard C. Shelby, who thought the intelligence coverage he had seen was adequate, viewed the episode as an index of poor relations between the CIA and Capitol Hill.

Director Tenet tried to mend fences by going to the committee himself on October 3, meeting with Graham and Shelby. The chairman asked for the additional information he wanted. By now Graham was also aware of deficiencies in the NIE on weapons of mass destruction as well. The next day Senator Graham wrote Tenet and asked that the CIA provide more information in unclassified form specifically on its judgments of confidence levels in the national estimate.

The remarks about confidence in the estimate, as the account of its creation showed, included revealing comments that U.S. intelligence had low confidence that Saddam Hussein would use weapons of mass destruction, unless under attack and in extremis. Those same circumstances were deemed to create the situation where Saddam would be most likely to give such weapons to terrorists. There were other points as well, and many of them undercut the case the Bush administration was making on the Iraqi threat.

George Tenet found himself trapped here, even more tightly, between Congress and the White House. President Bush was preparing for a fresh sally, a speech in which his view of the Iraqi threat would be the centerpiece. As the next chapter will detail, the CIA was working at this very moment to dissuade White House speechwriters from using the more lurid of their claims about Saddam. Yet here was the Congress, demanding information that, made public, would show the CIA out of step with the president. Wading through this thicket taxed even Tenet's legendary bureaucratic skills.

Director Tenet's solution took the form of a letter to Senator Graham. Several features of the letter undoubtedly reduced its negative impact (for the CIA) at the White House. First, the agency delayed its response until the instant of the Bush speech, which took place in Cincinnati on October 7. This ensured that its discordant note would play in minor key during the news cycle covering the president's speech. Second, the CIA did not actually release the "confidence levels" discussion from the National Intelligence Estimate. Rather the agency declassified one sentence from the body of the estimate and embroidered upon related material from the Key Judgments. Also released was a short transcribed passage from the secret (closed) hearing of October 2, at which deputy director John McLaughlin and national intelligence officer Robert Walpole had briefed the Senate intelligence committee on the weapons of mass destruction NIE.

Most important, to balance such agency comments as cast doubt on Iraqi weapons usage, Tenet approved including material alleging Iraqi connections with the Al Qaeda terrorist group, another hot-button issue in the prewar concerns of Americans, and a constant theme in Bush administration claims about Iraq.

Having played these two items, the CIA letter boldly refused to disclose anything else, relying upon the supposed need to protect sources and methods. Americans who worry about government secrecy ought to pay attention right here—in this instance the CIA used "sources and methods" to deny information *to the United States Congress,* data specifically relevant to the major decision Congress had been called upon to make. The information in question was from a National Intelligence Estimate, a document that, except in its top-secret, compartmented versions, has been constructed specifically so that sources and methods are not transparent and hence not material to a decision on classification.

Finally, the letter to Senator Graham was not actually signed by Director Tenet, but by John McLaughlin acting for Tenet. That slightly reduced the visibility and credibility of the letter, made it a little less offensive to the Bush White House, and gave Tenet a measure of deniability. If necessary, the CIA director could say he had been busy and the letter had just gotten away from him.

Senator Graham did not think the CIA letter of October 7 responded fully to his needs for intelligence material to support the congressional debate on war and subsequently asked the agency to release more material. Director Tenet refused to do so. The rumor quickly appeared that, after the Bush Cincinnati speech, the White House prohibited the CIA from declassifying any further Iraq material.

Congress released the Graham-Tenet correspondence immediately. Ari Fleischer at the White House told assembled reporters there was no difference between the CIA views expressed therein and the image of Saddam's threat that President Bush articulated in Cincinnati. George Tenet sent a further letter to Graham, not released, to make the same point. Both the original CIA letter and the Cincinnati speech (see the next chapter) are reprinted here.

The entire question of allegations that Saddam had links to Al Qaeda and to the 9/11 attacks is a major issue and is treated as a separate topic below in the analysis of Colin Powell's speech of February 5, 2003.

Central Intelligence Agency

Washington, D.C. 20505

7 October 2002

The Honorable Bob Graham
Chairman
Select Committee on Intelligence
United States Senate
Washington, D.C. 20510

Dear Mr. Chairman:

In response to your letter of 4 October 2002, we have made unclassified material available to further the Senate's forthcoming open debate on a Joint Resolution concerning Iraq.

As always, our declassification efforts seek a balance between your need for unfettered debate and our need to protect sources and methods. We have also been mindful of a shared interest in not providing to Saddam a blueprint of our intelligence capabilities and shortcomings, or with insight into our expectation of how he will and will not act. The salience of such concerns is only heightened by the possibility for hostilities between the U.S. and Iraq.

These are some of the reasons why we did not include our classified judgments on Saddam's decisionmaking regarding the use of weapons of mass destruction (WMD) in our recent unclassified paper on *Iraq's Weapons of Mass Destruction*. Viewing your request with those concerns in mind, however, we can declassify the following from the paragraphs you requested:

1. Baghdad for now appears to be drawing a line short of conducting terrorist attacks with conventional or CBW against the United States.

2. Should Saddam conclude that a US-led attack could no longer be deterred, he probably would become much less constrained in adopting terrorist actions. Such terrorism might involve conventional means, as with Iraq's unsuccessful attempt at a terrorist offensive in 1991, or CBW.

3. Saddam might decide that the extreme step of assisting Islamist terrorists in conducting a WMD attack against the United States would be his last

The Honorable Bob Graham

chance to exact vengeance by taking a large number
of victims with him.

Regarding the 2 October closed hearing, we can
declassify the following dialogue:

Senator Levin: ...If [Saddam] didn't feel threatened, did
not feel threatened, is it likely that he would initiate an
attack using a weapon of mass destruction?

Senior Intelligence Witness: ... My judgment would be
that the probability of him initiating an attack-let me put
a time frame on it-in the foreseeable future, given the
conditions we understand now, the likelihood I think would
be low.

Senator Levin: Now if he did initiate an attack
you've...indicated he would probably attempt clandestine
attacks against us...But what about his use of weapons of
mass destruction? If we initiate an attack and he thought
he was in extremis or otherwise, what's the likelihood in
response to our attack that he would use chemical or
biological weapons?

Senior Intelligence Witness: Pretty high, in my view.

In the above dialogue, the witness's qualifications—"in
the foreseeable future, given the conditions we understand
now"—were intended to underscore that the likelihood of
Saddam using WMD for blackmail, deterrence, or otherwise
grows as his arsenal builds. Moreover, if Saddam used WMD,
it would disprove his repeated denials that he has such
weapons.

Regarding Senator Bayh's question of Iraqi links to al-
Qa'ida. Senators could draw from the following points for
unclassified discussions:

• Our understanding of the relationship between Iraq and
al-Qa'ida is evolving and is based on sources of varying
reliability. Some of the information we have received
comes from detainees, including some of high rank.

• We have solid reporting of senior level contacts between
Iraq and al-Qa'ida going back a decade.

• Credible information indicates that Iraq and al-Qa'ida
have discussed safe haven and reciprocal non-aggression.

4.

5.

The Honorable Bob Graham

- Since Operation Enduring Freedom, we have solid evidence of the presence in Iraq of al-Qa'ida members, including some that have been in Baghdad.

- We have credible reporting that al-Qa'ida leaders sought contacts in Iraq who could help them acquire WMD capabilities. The reporting also stated that Iraq has provided training to al-Qa'ida members in the areas of poisons and gases and making conventional bombs.

- Iraq's increasing support to extremist Palestinians, coupled with growing indications of a relationship with al-Qa'ida, suggest that Baghdad's links to terrorists will increase, even absent US military action.

Sincerely,

George J. Tenet
Director of Central Intelligence

3

Tenet Letter Comments

1. In the Key Judgments of the NIE on Iraqi weapons of mass destruction, declassified in July 2003, this sentence appears immediately following the intelligence community's conclusion that it has "low confidence in our ability to assess when Saddam would use WMD." In George Tenet's letter, the CIA director asserts that Saddam is only temporarily ("for now") exercising forbearance on attacking the United States, a bald declaration of an Iraqi intention, a matter which the NIE explicitly admits the United States does not understand. In the NIE, that language is followed by a series of items indicating that Saddam maintained tight control over his weapons, probably would use chemical or biological agents "when he perceived he irretrievably had lost control of the military and security situation," would more likely use chemicals, and would use them on the battle-field. The NIE conceded a possibility that Saddam might use weapons preemptively, or in the early stages of a war. No language in the estimate credited Saddam with a nuclear weapon. Quotation of the sentence from the NIE that *does* appear in Director Tenet's letter has the effect of making the main subject one of Iraqi offensive action ("terrorist attacks") instead of noting the caution Baghdad had actually shown.

2. The discussion in this paragraph is not very different from the NIE it purports to be summarizing. The letter says that Saddam might initiate a terror offensive with conventional or (alleged) mass destruction weapons if he decided "a U.S.-led attack could no longer be deterred." The estimate says "Iraq would probably attempt clandestine attacks . . . if Baghdad feared an attack that threatened the survival of the regime were imminent or unavoidable, or possibly for revenge." Either way the bottom line stood out that attacking Iraq *increased* the probability of weapons use. Why the CIA felt the NIE language could not simply be given to the Congress is obscure.

3. This sentence is drawn from one of the subordinate items in the NIE's Key Judgments. The quotation is without context, however, and more alarming than the language in the national estimate. The superior clause in the estimate makes clear that its judgment applies to *one particular case*: "Saddam, if sufficiently desperate, might decide that only an organization like al-Qa'ida [Al Qaeda]–with worldwide reach and extensive terrorist infrastructure, and already engaged in a life-and-death struggle against the United States–could perpetrate the type of terrorist attack that he would hope to conduct." Again the NIE foresees the American attack intended by President Bush as not only making weapons use more

likely, but as driving Saddam into the arms of Al Qaeda, both of which Bush policy was ostensibly designed to prevent. This implication was disguised by refusing to permit the public to see the language in the NIE. Congressmen who read the estimate, bound by the strictures of secrecy, could not reveal its contents. No wonder Senator Graham was frustrated.

4. The "senior intelligence witness," in all probability deputy director of central intelligence John McLaughlin, correctly states the view of the NIE that, in effect, the United States will be encouraging the use of weapons of mass destruction by attacking Iraq. This is the portion of the CIA letter most upsetting to the White House. Notice how the letter immediately undercuts the thrust of McLaughlin's testimony by inserting qualifications and adding that Saddam will be more likely to use weapons for blackmail as his arsenal grows (the use of "deterrence" among these functions is puzzling, since Baghdad was already widely understood to be using its weapons potential in this fashion).

5. The material on this page and the next alleging Iraqi links to Al Qaeda forms part of a major subject and will be treated later in the narrative. For the present note that the CIA had not been able to establish any link between Iraq and the September 11 attacks by Al Qaeda, and yet this portion of the letter is presented entirely as if Saddam and Osama bin Laden were cooperating closely. This passage is clearly intended to bolster the White House vision of the Iraqi threat.

4

The Hook

Central Intelligence Agency officials delivered their white paper to Congress on October 4, perfect timing for the Bush administration, as both the Senate and House of Representatives were moving to full-fledged debate on the resolution to give President Bush authority for force in Iraq. Public interest in the debate remained high, with pundits and experts on every side of the issue, but a significant stream of commentary questioned whether Iraq posed any national security threat to the United States. Public opinion remained divided. Those who thought Bush had explained clearly what the problem was with Iraq stood at just 37 percent in early September. Polls taken a couple of weeks later, after Bush's United Nations speech, showed 64 percent of Americans favoring action along the lines of which Bush had spoken, with 57 percent now believing the administration's explanations. The key number, and a real problem given that President Bush already knew there would be little international enthusiasm for his plan to oust Saddam Hussein, was that support among Americans dropped to 33 percent when the question posed was of unilateral American action against Iraq.

To get George Bush to the point where regime change in Baghdad might actually be accomplished, the White House planned to play Congress against the United Nations, using each as a wedge to secure action from the other. The claims about the Iraqi threat were to be the final trump card. Doing nothing could not be an option, to meld statements from Condi Rice, because the alternative could be a mushroom cloud over an American city. But Americans were not yet convinced enough to support unilateral action. President Bush now planned another speech, building upon the CIA white paper, for the October 7, 2002, Cincinnati convention of the Veterans of Foreign Wars.

Now the administration moved quickly to plant in the public mind its own view of the Iraqi threat and its argument that action was needed. The Cincinnati speech would be crucial for several reasons. First, it set up a continuum from Bush's approach to the United Nations and permitted him to link the congressional resolution with UN action, supplying Congress with a seemingly logical reason why they should support the war resolution. Second, it enabled George Bush to use the bully pulpit of the presidency to showcase the supposed Iraqi threat—opinion studies have long shown that presidential assertion is the single most effective form of public persuasion. Third, the speech allowed yet another articulation of a list of particulars about the Iraqi threat, and reiteration again contributes to persuasion. Finally, Bush could use the opportunity to set a series of conditions for Saddam Hussein to meet that would make it almost impossible for Iraq to avert war.

President Bush temporarily muted his demands for regime change in Iraq. On October 1 the president told reporters a military option was not his first choice, "but disarming this man is." Even as American forces began deploying to the Persian Gulf and Kuwait to prepare for the invasion, the White House, Pentagon, and Bush himself were careful to say the president had made no decision on what to do about Iraq. On October 2 spokesman Ari Fleischer artfully referred to covert operations when asked about the potentially high costs of a war: "The cost of one bullet, if the Iraqi people take it upon themselves, is substantially less." In his weekly radio speech on October 5 President Bush added a fresh charge against Baghdad: "We have sources that tell us that Saddam Hussein recently authorized Iraqi field commanders to use chemical weapons—the very weapons the dictator tells us he does not have."

Even as Bush rallied his faithful on the radio that day, in Italy swarms of protesters gathered for demonstrations opposing a war with Iraq. In over a hundred Italian cities and towns from Milan to Rome the demonstrators marched. In Venice some climbed to the roof of the British consulate, and in Rome others were kept away from the U.S. embassy. The next day there were protests against a war across the United States itself. This was an early stirring of a vigorous movement opposed to the war, one that complicated Bush's calculations.

With Congress debating its resolution, Bush employed every argument at his disposal, including a line about enforcement of UN resolutions, to get his message across. Beginning with his UN speech in September, President Bush chose to strengthen his bid for international support by presenting his planned Iraq action as an effort to enforce UN resolutions of the 1990s that created and subsequently extended the mission of the arms inspectors. The argument that Saddam had defied sixteen UN resolutions, failed to cooperate with the United Nations Special Commission (UNSCOM), and defied inspectors by hiding things, and providing incomplete or misleading information, would become a constant refrain. This argument had more resonance in the U.S. Congress than among the international community, but it was really aimed at American public opinion.

The system of economic sanctions the UN used to enforce UNSCOM powers had progressively lost momentum, to the point where Secretary of State Powell had found little enthusiasm for his "smart sanctions" just a year earlier. This occurred in the context of Saddam's having actually expelled the UNSCOM inspectors. Whether UN members felt that UNSCOM had essentially done its job, or had simply lost interest in the entire matter, can be debated. But now, in 2002, the United States had come to the Security Council demanding a fresh inspection resolution that would permit immediate resort to war if Iraq should again obstruct inspectors or fail to comply in any way. At the same time, the United States could not but be aware of the opposition to its course demonstrated in diplomatic exchanges in the first eight months of 2002. A resolution of the type Bush demanded could not be obtained in the United Nations Security Council. The most the administration could hope for would be a mandate on the lines of the compromise suggested by the French and Germans, establishing a new arms monitoring operation, and referring back to the UN for action in case of any violation.

By pitching the Iraq war to the American people as a UN initiative, the Bush administration sought to escape from charges it had taken unilateral action. Negotiations for a UN resolution were useful to the president in Congress. Bush's request for authority to use force would be portrayed as simply creating the mechanism to put teeth into the UN inspection scheme—the hook Bush would use to get his legal authority for war. Some in Congress voted to give Bush that power, taking comfort that the UN would not allow him to exercise it, that the UN would provide checks and balances on American action. President Bush encouraged that impression even as his administration argued at the UN for a Security Council resolution that would permit war at the first sign of Iraqi intransigence, and moved openly to put forces in place for the invasion. The UN angle was thus featured in the speech prepared for President Bush to deliver before the Veterans of Foreign Wars.

(It eventually became abundantly clear that the war had nothing to do with the UN. Asked in February 2003 what would constitute "victory" in Iraq, Condoleezza Rice began by mentioning enforcement of the UN resolution but then stopped, stumped, because there was no real answer to the inevitable follow-up question of how this differed from successful enforcement by means of letting the arms inspectors finish their job. A month later the United States, failing to secure UN approval of a required second resolution—the war approval envisioned in the fall 2002 scheme—went ahead and attacked anyway. Soon enough the United States was saying that there was no place for the UN in its Iraq occupation. Not until Bush's occupation of Iraq had bogged down in a quagmire of poor planning, inadequate forces, contending political movements, and religious and social differences did the United Nations suddenly become relevant to the United States in Iraq, and then it would be as savior for a compromised American operation.)

The UN resolution would be the solution offered by the Bush people in the Cincinnati speech, the hook that made the rest of the sting palatable. That was to be a major component of the address, aimed at convincing

Americans that Bush was not simply out for war. The problem, of course, remained the lack of real menace to America from Saddam Hussein, so the other component of the speech had to be a fresh rendition of the Iraqi threat. The assignment went to chief speechwriter Michael Gerson at the end of September, timing that confirms the speech was laid on when poll results showed public support for U.S. unilateral action to be weak. Gerson's draft drew heavily upon the CIA white paper, but his staff wanted to go farther. The chief speechwriter pulled out the stops, and as this speech went through its drafts, a sexy new bit of data was introduced: an allegation that Iraq had sought to buy uranium ore in Africa. This allegation would cause a ruckus after Bush's 2003 State of the Union address. For now what is significant is that the charge did *not* appear in the final version of the October 7 speech.

Speeches such as the presidential remarks for Cincinnati are typically worked over carefully. The Bush UN address had gone through twenty-five drafts. For the Cincinnati speech there were twenty-eight or twenty-nine. According to Condoleezza Rice's deputy, Stephen J. Hadley, who had charge of clearing national security items in presidential speeches, draft two of the address was the first to include a reference to alleged Iraqi attempts to buy uranium in the African country Niger. The third draft would be the earliest to circulate outside Gerson's speechwriting office, and it contained a charge against Saddam Hussein that combined the Niger uranium and aluminum tubes allegations like this: "And he [Saddam] has not explained his efforts to procure uranium in Africa, or high-strength aluminum tubes suitable for uranium enrichment." That language remained untouched as the Cincinnati speech went through several more drafts. At some point deputy national security adviser Hadley sent a copy to the CIA for comment. That triggered a CIA memorandum on October 5 addressed to both Hadley and Rice. The memo apparently responded to the sixth draft of the speech, because it quoted language from that version, which had specified that Iraq had sought 500 tons of uranium oxide. Speaking on background, a senior White House official later said the CIA objection had been that the charge relied upon a single source, but there was more to it than that. The agency asked that the language be removed because the intelligence community doubted the amount of the purchase. The CIA also noted that it was questionable if such an amount could be bought from Niger in any case. It is still not clear whether the memorandum reminded the White House that the entire matter of the uranium purchase had been disputed in the NIE.

At that moment the planned speech had progressed through more drafts, and another CIA memorandum with additional information sent to Michael Gerson reached the White House with comments on the eighth draft. Gerson had also written a passage regarding Iraq's efforts to develop drone aircraft, which he had called "small planes" in the text, to deliver biological and chemical weapons. The intelligence agencies worried that that language was misleading. At CIA's behest he switched to the awkward military jargon term "unmanned aerial vehicles." As for the Niger uranium, Stephen Hadley reports that the offending language had already been removed from the speech, but at a different point in his description of these events the deputy national security adviser quotes the passage that replaced it, and remained through at least the *fifteenth* draft of Bush's planned speech: "We also note that he [Saddam] has recently sought to procure uranium in Africa and has purchased high-strength aluminum tubes suitable for nuclear weapons production." In short, not much had changed.

It was CIA director George Tenet who stepped into the breach. When John McLaughlin, deputy director of central intelligence, briefed the NIE on Iraqi weapons of mass destruction to the Congress on October 2, and when Tenet himself met with the legislators the next day (according to a July 2003 statement from director Tenet), they had made no mention of the uranium ore question.

In contrast to Tenet's statement, however, the October 5, 2002, CIA memorandum sent to Hadley and Rice on the VFW speech draft reportedly states that the agency had been telling Congress all along that this business of the alleged Iraqi uranium buy from Africa was problematic. It was one of two places where the CIA differed from British intelligence and the British Iraq paper, which gave credence to the Africa uranium story. Journalist Seymour Hersh reports that Tenet and McLaughlin together briefed the Senate intelligence committee on September 24, the day the British paper was released, and that they *did* talk about the uranium. When Tenet saw a draft of the Cincinnati speech that said: "And the [Iraqi] regime has been caught attempting to purchase substantial amounts of uranium oxide from sources in Africa," The CIA director knew President Bush would be on shaky ground in making that claim. He telephoned Hadley at the White House and objected to this language. Impressed with Tenet's determination, Hadley agreed and the uranium language finally disappeared from the prepared text. The allegations about aluminum tubes remained.

The White House put out the word that Bush's Cincinnati VFW speech would be the definitive presentation of the Iraqi threat to America. The Bush Wurlitzer was geared up for the operation. Friendly newspaper columnists were informed that new intelligence had been specially declassified for use in the address. One example cited was the unmanned aerial vehicles charge. (In fact, as seen, this allegation had been in the CIA white paper already made public, as well as in official reports since 2001, and in press reports since 1999.) Nevertheless the speech was not the bombshell the spin doctors had promised. President Bush's speech contained nothing much that was new. What was significant was *how* George Bush made the charges and the fact the president was now enunciating them.

The Cincinnati speech was not carried live on any of the three major U.S. television networks. It did appear on Cable News Network, Fox News Channel and broadcast television, and the MSNBC news channel. Its rated audience of about 17 million beat out the network television programs in that time slot. President Bush was pleased with the result.

document **3.** *George W. Bush's Speech to the Veterans of Foreign Wars, Cincinnati, Ohio, October 7, 2002.*

the **White House**
President George W. Bush

IRAQ **BAGHDAD**   DENIAL AND DECEPTION

For Immediate Release
Office of the Press Secretary
October 7, 2002

President Bush Outlines Iraqi Threat
Remarks by the President on Iraq
Cincinnati Museum Center - Cincinnati Union Terminal
Cincinnati, Ohio

VIDEO Multimedia
President's Remarks
🖻 view
🔊 listen

8:02 P.M. EDT

THE PRESIDENT: Thank you all. Thank you for that very gracious and warm Cincinnati welcome. I'm honored to be here tonight; I appreciate you all coming.

Tonight I want to take a few minutes to discuss a grave threat to peace, and America's determination to lead the world in confronting that threat.

1. The threat comes from Iraq. It arises directly from the Iraqi regime's own actions -- its history of aggression, and its drive toward an arsenal of terror. Eleven years ago, as a condition for ending the Persian Gulf War, the Iraqi regime was required to destroy its weapons of mass destruction, to cease all development of such weapons, and to stop all support for terrorist groups. The Iraqi regime has violated all of those obligations. It possesses and produces chemical and biological weapons. It is seeking nuclear weapons. It has given shelter and support to terrorism, and practices terror against its own people. The entire world has witnessed Iraq's eleven-year history of defiance, deception and bad faith.

We also must never forget the most vivid events of recent history. On September the 11th, 2001, America felt its vulnerability -- even to threats that gather on the other side of the earth. We resolved then, and we are resolved today, to confront every threat, from any source, that could bring sudden terror and suffering to America.

2. Members of the Congress of both political parties, and members of the United Nations Security Council, agree that Saddam Hussein is a threat to peace and must disarm. We agree that the Iraqi dictator must not be permitted to threaten America and the world with horrible poisons and diseases and gases and atomic weapons. Since we all agree on this goal, the issues is : how can we best achieve it?

Many Americans have raised legitimate questions: about the nature of the threat; about the urgency of action -- why be concerned now; about the link between Iraq developing weapons of terror, and the wider war on terror. These are all issues we've discussed broadly and fully within my administration. And tonight, I want to share those discussions with you.

3. First, some ask why Iraq is different from other countries or regimes that also have terrible weapons. While there are many dangers in the world, the threat from Iraq stands alone -- because it gathers the most serious dangers of our age in one place. Iraq's weapons of mass destruction are controlled by a murderous tyrant who has already used chemical weapons to kill thousands of people. This same tyrant has tried to dominate the Middle East, has invaded and brutally occupied a small neighbor, has struck other nations without warning, and holds an unrelenting hostility toward the United States.

4. By its past and present actions, by its technological capabilities, by the merciless nature of its regime, Iraq is unique. As a former chief weapons inspector of the U.N. has said, "The fundamental problem with Iraq remains the nature of the regime, itself. Saddam Hussein is a homicidal dictator who is addicted to weapons of mass destruction."

5. Some ask how urgent this danger is to America and the world. The danger is already significant, and it only grows worse with time. If we know Saddam Hussein has dangerous weapons today -- and we do -- does it make any sense for the world to wait to confront him as he grows even stronger and develops even more dangerous weapons?

6. In 1995, after several years of deceit by the Iraqi regime, the head of Iraq's military industries defected. It was then that the regime was forced to admit that it had produced more than 30,000 liters of anthrax and other deadly biological agents. The inspectors, however, concluded that Iraq had likely produced two to four times that amount. This is a massive stockpile of biological weapons that has never been accounted for, and capable of killing millions.

7. We know that the regime has produced thousands of tons of chemical agents, including mustard gas, sarin nerve gas, VX nerve gas. Saddam Hussein also has experience in using chemical weapons. He has ordered chemical attacks on Iran, and on more than forty villages in his own country. These actions killed or injured at least 20,000 people, more than six times the number of people who died in the attacks of September the 11th.

And surveillance photos reveal that the regime is rebuilding facilities that it had used to produce chemical and biological weapons. Every chemical and biological weapon that Iraq has or makes is a direct violation of the truce that ended the Persian Gulf War in 1991. Yet, Saddam Hussein has chosen to build and keep these weapons despite international sanctions, U.N. demands, and isolation from the civilized world.

8.
9. Iraq possesses ballistic missiles with a likely range of hundreds of miles -- far enough to strike Saudi Arabia, Israel, Turkey, and other nations -- in a region where more than 135,000 American civilians and service members live and work. We've also discovered through intelligence that Iraq has a growing fleet of manned and unmanned aerial vehicles that could be used to disperse chemical or biological weapons across broad areas. We're concerned that Iraq is exploring ways of using these UAVS for missions targeting the United States. And, of course, sophisticated delivery systems aren't required for a chemical or biological attack; all that might be required are a small container and one terrorist or Iraqi intelligence operative to deliver it.

And that is the source of our urgent concern about Saddam Hussein's links to international terrorist groups. Over the years, Iraq has provided safe haven to terrorists such as Abu Nidal, whose terror organization carried out more than 90 terrorist attacks in 20 countries that killed or injured nearly 900 people, including 12 Americans. Iraq has also provided safe haven to Abu Abbas, who was responsible for seizing the Achille Lauro and killing an American passenger. And we know that Iraq is continuing to finance terror and gives assistance to groups that use terrorism to undermine Middle East peace.

10. We know that Iraq and the al Qaeda terrorist network share a common enemy -- the United States of America. We know that Iraq and al Qaeda have had high-level contacts that go back a decade. Some al Qaeda leaders who fled Afghanistan went to Iraq. These include one very senior al Qaeda leader who received medical treatment in Baghdad this year, and who has been associated with planning for chemical and biological attacks. We've learned that Iraq has trained al Qaeda members in bomb-making and poisons and deadly gases. And we know that after September the 11th, Saddam Hussein's regime gleefully celebrated the terrorist attacks on America.

11. Iraq could decide on any given day to provide a biological or chemical weapon to a terrorist group or individual terrorists. Alliance with terrorists could allow the Iraqi regime to attack America without leaving any fingerprints.

12. Some have argued that confronting the threat from Iraq could detract from the war against terror. To the

contrary; confronting the threat posed by Iraq is crucial to winning the war on terror. When I spoke to Congress more than a year ago, I said that those who harbor terrorists are as guilty as the terrorists themselves. Saddam Hussein is harboring terrorists and the instruments of terror, the instruments of mass death and destruction. And he cannot be trusted. The risk is simply too great that he will use them, or provide them to a terror network.

Terror cells and outlaw regimes building weapons of mass destruction are different faces of the same evil. Our security requires that we confront both. And the United States military is capable of confronting both.

13. Many people have asked how close Saddam Hussein is to developing a nuclear weapon. Well, we don't know exactly, and that's the problem. Before the Gulf War, the best intelligence indicated that Iraq was eight to ten years away from developing a nuclear weapon. After the war, international inspectors learned that the regime has been much closer -- the regime in Iraq would likely have possessed a nuclear weapon no later than 1993. The inspectors discovered that Iraq had an advanced nuclear weapons development program, had a design for a workable nuclear weapon, and was pursuing several different methods of enriching uranium for a bomb.

Before being barred from Iraq in 1998, the International Atomic Energy Agency dismantled extensive nuclear weapons-related facilities, including three uranium enrichment sites. That same year, information from a high-ranking Iraqi nuclear engineer who had defected revealed that despite his public promises, Saddam Hussein had ordered his nuclear program to continue.

The evidence indicates that Iraq is reconstituting its nuclear weapons program. Saddam Hussein has held numerous meetings with Iraqi nuclear scientists, a group he calls his "nuclear mujahideen" -- his nuclear holy
14. warriors. Satellite photographs reveal that Iraq is rebuilding facilities at sites that have been part of its nuclear program in the past. Iraq has attempted to purchase high-strength aluminum tubes and other equipment needed for gas centrifuges, which are used to enrich uranium for nuclear weapons.

If the Iraqi regime is able to produce, buy, or steal an amount of highly enriched uranium a little larger than a single softball, it could have a nuclear weapon in less than a year. And if we allow that to happen, a terrible line would be crossed. Saddam Hussein would be in a position to blackmail anyone who opposes his aggression. He would be in a position to dominate the Middle East. He would be in a position to threaten America. And Saddam Hussein would be in a position to pass nuclear technology to terrorists.

15. Some citizens wonder, after 11 years of living with this problem, why do we need to confront it now? And there's a reason. We've experienced the horror of September the 11th. We have seen that those who hate America are willing to crash airplanes into buildings full of innocent people. Our enemies would be no less willing, in fact, they would be eager, to use biological or chemical, or a nuclear weapon.

16. Knowing these realities, America must not ignore the threat gathering against us. Facing clear evidence of peril, we cannot wait for the final proof -- the smoking gun -- that could come in the form of a mushroom cloud. As President Kennedy said in October of 1962, "Neither the United States of America, nor the world community of nations can tolerate deliberate deception and offensive threats on the part of any nation, large or small. We no longer live in a world," he said, "where only the actual firing of weapons represents a sufficient challenge to a nations security to constitute maximum peril."

Understanding the threats of our time, knowing the designs and deceptions of the Iraqi regime, we have every reason to assume the worst, and we have an urgent duty to prevent the worst from occurring.

Some believe we can address this danger by simply resuming the old approach to inspections, and applying diplomatic and economic pressure. Yet this is precisely what the world has tried to do since 1991. The U.N. inspections program was met with systematic deception. The Iraqi regime bugged hotel rooms and offices of inspectors to find where they were going next; they forged documents, destroyed evidence, and developed mobile weapons facilities to keep a step ahead of inspectors. Eight so-called presidential palaces were declared off-limits to unfettered inspections. These sites actually encompass twelve square miles, with hundreds of structures, both above and below the ground, where sensitive materials could be hidden.

The world has also tried economic sanctions -- and watched Iraq use billions of dollars in illegal oil revenues to fund more weapons purchases, rather than providing for the needs of the Iraqi people.

The world has tried limited military strikes to destroy Iraq's weapons of mass destruction capabilities -- only to see them openly rebuilt, while the regime again denies they even exist.

The world has tried no-fly zones to keep Saddam from terrorizing his own people -- and in the last year alone, the Iraqi military has fired upon American and British pilots more than 750 times.

After eleven years during which we have tried containment, sanctions, inspections, even selected military action, the end result is that Saddam Hussein still has chemical and biological weapons and is increasing his capabilities to make more. And he is moving ever closer to developing a nuclear weapon.

Clearly, to actually work, any new inspections, sanctions or enforcement mechanisms will have to be very different. America wants the U.N. to be an effective organization that helps keep the peace. And that is why we are urging the Security Council to adopt a new resolution setting out tough, immediate requirements. Among those requirements: the Iraqi regime must reveal and destroy, under U.N. supervision, all existing weapons of mass destruction. To ensure that we learn the truth, the regime must allow witnesses to its illegal activities to be interviewed outside the country -- and these witnesses must be free to bring their families with them so they all beyond the reach of Saddam Hussein's terror and murder. And inspectors must have access to any site, at any time, without pre-clearance, without delay, without exceptions.

17. The time for denying, deceiving, and delaying has come to an end. Saddam Hussein must disarm himself -- or, for the sake of peace, we will lead a coalition to disarm him.

Many nations are joining us in insisting that Saddam Hussein's regime be held accountable. They are committed to defending the international security that protects the lives of both our citizens and theirs. And that's why America is challenging all nations to take the resolutions of the U.N. Security Council seriously.

18. And these resolutions are clear. In addition to declaring and destroying all of its weapons of mass destruction, Iraq must end its support for terrorism. It must cease the persecution of its civilian population. It must stop all illicit trade outside the Oil For Food program. It must release or account for all Gulf War personnel, including an American pilot, whose fate is still unknown.

19. By taking these steps, and by only taking these steps, the Iraqi regime has an opportunity to avoid conflict. Taking these steps would also change the nature of the Iraqi regime itself. America hopes the regime will make that choice. Unfortunately, at least so far, we have little reason to expect it. And that's why two administrations -- mine and President Clinton's -- have stated that regime change in Iraq is the only certain means of removing a great danger to our nation.

20. I hope this will not require military action, but it may. And military conflict could be difficult. An Iraqi regime faced with its own demise may attempt cruel and desperate measures. If Saddam Hussein orders such measures, his generals would be well advised to refuse those orders. If they do not refuse, they must understand that all war criminals will be pursued and punished. If we have to act, we will take every precaution that is possible. We will plan carefully; we will act with the full power of the United States military; we will act with allies at our side, and we will prevail. (Applause.)

There is no easy or risk-free course of action. Some have argued we should wait -- and that's an option. In my view, it's the riskiest of all options, because the longer we wait, the stronger and bolder Saddam Hussein will become. We could wait and hope that Saddam does not give weapons to terrorists, or develop a nuclear weapon to blackmail the world. But I'm convinced that is a hope against all evidence. As Americans, we want peace -- we work and sacrifice for peace. But there can be no peace if our security depends on the will and whims of a ruthless and aggressive dictator. I'm not willing to stake one American life on trusting Saddam Hussein.

Failure to act would embolden other tyrants, allow terrorists access to new weapons and new resources, and make blackmail a permanent feature of world events. The United Nations would betray the purpose of its founding, and prove irrelevant to the problems of our time. And through its inaction, the United States would resign itself to a future of fear.

That is not the America I know. That is not the America I serve. We refuse to live in fear. (Applause.) This nation, in world war and in Cold War, has never permitted the brutal and lawless to set history's course. Now, as before, we will secure our nation, protect our freedom, and help others to find freedom of their own.

21. Some worry that a change of leadership in Iraq could create instability and make the situation worse. The situation could hardly get worse, for world security and for the people of Iraq. The lives of Iraqi citizens would improve dramatically if Saddam Hussein were no longer in power, just as the lives of Afghanistan's citizens improved after the Taliban. The dictator of Iraq is a student of Stalin, using murder as a tool of terror and control, within his own cabinet, within his own army, and even within his own family.

On Saddam Hussein's orders, opponents have been decapitated, wives and mothers of political opponents have been systematically raped as a method of intimidation, and political prisoners have been forced to watch their own children being tortured.

America believes that all people are entitled to hope and human rights, to the non-negotiable demands of human dignity. People everywhere prefer freedom to slavery; prosperity to squalor; self-government to the rule of terror and torture. America is a friend to the people of Iraq. Our demands are directed only at the regime that enslaves them and threatens us. When these demands are met, the first and greatest benefit will come to Iraqi men, women and children. The oppression of Kurds, Assyrians, Turkomans, Shi'a, Sunnis and others will be lifted. The long captivity of Iraq will end, and an era of new hope will begin.

Iraq is a land rich in culture, resources, and talent. Freed from the weight of oppression, Iraq's people will be able to share in the progress and prosperity of our time. If military action is necessary, the United States and our allies will help the Iraqi people rebuild their economy, and create the institutions of liberty in a unified Iraq at peace with its neighbors.

22. Later this week, the United States Congress will vote on this matter. I have asked Congress to authorize the use of America's military, if it proves necessary, to enforce U.N. Security Council demands. Approving this resolution does not mean that military action is imminent or unavoidable. The resolution will tell the United Nations, and all nations, that America speaks with one voice and is determined to make the demands of the civilized world mean something. Congress will also be sending a message to the dictator in Iraq: that his only chance -- his only choice is full compliance, and the time remaining for that choice is limited.

Members of Congress are nearing an historic vote. I'm confident they will fully consider the facts, and their duties.

The attacks of September the 11th showed our country that vast oceans no longer protect us from danger. Before that tragic date, we had only hints of al Qaeda's plans and designs. Today in Iraq, we see a threat whose outlines are far more clearly defined, and whose consequences could be far more deadly. Saddam Hussein's actions have put us on notice, and there is no refuge from our responsibilities.

We did not ask for this present challenge, but we accept it. Like other generations of Americans, we will meet the responsibility of defending human liberty against violence and aggression. By our resolve, we will give strength to others. By our courage, we will give hope to others. And by our actions, we will secure the peace, and lead the world to a better day.

the responsibility of defending human liberty against violence and aggression. By our resolve, we will give strength to others. By our courage, we will give hope to others. And by our actions, we will secure the peace, and lead the world to a better day.

May God bless America. (Applause.)

END 8:31 P.M. EDT

Bush Cincinnati Speech Comments

1. The phrase "arsenal of terror" referred to Baghdad's weapons inventory but could be interpreted as Saddam's giving support to terrorists like Al Qaeda, which President Bush suggests directly later in the speech. This was clever phrasing.

2. There is no evidence that Saddam Hussein *ever* threatened America or the world with poisons, diseases, gases, or nuclear weapons. Analysis of the CIA white paper (pp. 77-93) showed conclusively the weaknesses in U.S. intelligence claims regarding an Iraqi nuclear weapons program and highlighted the thin information available on allegations that Baghdad possessed chemical or biological weapons. President Bush twice ("we agree," "we all agree") attempts to invoke universal approval of his claims and goals, as if there is no doubt about the nature of the Iraqi threat.

3. This part of Bush's speech attempts a defense against those who believe there were greater or more immediate problems for the United States than Iraq, in particular North Korea, which the CIA had assessed since 1995 as having one or two actual nuclear weapons, which was working on a missile with range sufficient to reach the United States, and which was actually *saying in public* at this time that it had weapons. North Korea had a real claim to U.S. attention. Iraq continued to have *no* assessed nuclear weapon and the NIE projected that it could not until 2007-09. Iran was also assessed by the CIA as having a more active nuclear program than Iraq and had longer-range missiles imported from China. A reasonable assessment of threats to American security could put Al Qaeda, North Korea, and Iran *all* ahead of Iraq. Bush's specific defense—that Saddam is a "murderous tyrant"—distinguishes a leader not materially different from North Korea's Kim Jong Il or from many dictators with whom the United States, in fact, maintained friendly relations.

4. As just noted, Iraq was by no means unique.

5. Here President Bush guarantees the accuracy of the intelligence on Iraq, which in fact amounted to conjecture. The stream of direct, on-the-ground evidence had ended in 1998 with the departure of UN weapons inspectors. Sources of information since then included satellite photographs, which could not show what went on inside buildings; defectors, who had agendas of their own; communications intelligence in limited quantities; and Iraqi official statements, plus other open source material. All of that remained subject to interpretation. Thus, on the

most basic level, the Bush administration oversold the certainty of its intelligence knowledge from the outset of the Iraq affair.

6. This is a reference to Hussein Kamel. Note here and elsewhere the frequency with which the Bush administration brings up Kamel when it seems advantageous but never when his revelations detract from their case. With respect to these two paragraphs, for example, Kamel had told UN inspectors that Saddam ordered the destruction of all the chemical and biological weapons stocks. As for President Bush's actual statement, here he alleges that the UN had reached an affirmative conclusion that Iraq had manufactured a quantity of biological agents significantly greater than the listed amount. In fact, international inspectors had reported that unaccounted precursor materials offered the *potential* for production of larger quantities of agents.

7. Bush refers to Saddam's campaign against the Kurds, in which the most important chemical attacks occurred at Halabja and other villages. In contrast to the number 20,000 cited here, estimates of casualties generally range from 5,000 to 8,000. The higher number may be associated with the entire civil war between Baghdad and the Kurds. It should also be noted that even in regard to Halabja there is not full agreement among intelligence analysts. Some CIA reports indicate that refugees who fled across the border into Turkey, saying they had been gassed, did not have symptoms of gas-induced sickness. The CIA and DIA had differences as well over gases employed (whether toxic or not), and even whether the attacks had been made by Iraq or Iran, with which Saddam was at war at the time. Estimates of Iranian chemical casualties in that war—upwards of 50,000— far exceed those killed at Halabja. This is not to excuse Saddam's horrific actions at Halabja and elsewhere, but to illustrate how Bush misemployed statistics.

8. Missiles that fly hundreds of miles can mean only the alleged "covert force" of modified SCUD-type missiles. As noted previously, the only evidence for these rockets was discrepancies in tallies of missiles bought, expended, and destroyed by UN monitors and the Iraqis themselves. This is a good example of conjecture in intelligence.

9. The "growing fleet" of aerial vehicles is examined in detail above, in the analysis that follows the CIA white paper.

10. Iraqi relations with Al Qaeda are a major subject and will be covered in a section that follows Secretary of State Colin Powell's UN Security Council presentation, below.

11. This is Bush's scariest claim. The charge presupposes the existence of Iraqi biological or chemical agents in usable form that would be practical for terrorists to handle and deploy. That is a level beyond standard military weaponry. No evidence of such weapons has been found from that day to this.

12. The Iraq operation could and did detract from the terror war.

13. The notion that America should launch a war because "we don't know exactly, and that's the problem" is of *great* concern. The entire question of "preemption" in security theory is bound up in the expectation that force may be used if an adversary has launched its attack or it is certain that the adversary is at the point of attacking, and force may deflect an attack or reduce its impact. Here George Bush speaks of American action in a case of *uncertainty* and indeed justifies action *because* of that uncertainty. To call what happened in Iraq "preemptive self-defense," as the Bush administration has done, is disingenuous at best. If no Iraqi weapons of mass destruction are ultimately found, it will be seen as deceitful.

14. This discussion of the Iraqi nuclear program gives the impression that it is powerful and ongoing. Our analysis of the CIA white paper showed this was far from accurate. Before the Gulf War, the Iraqi program had been estimated to employ 7,000 scientific and engineering personnel and 20,000 workers. Nothing like that had since been claimed, even by the Bush administration. As for Saddam's "nuclear mujahideen," the CIA had evidence of *one* Saddam meeting with his scientists, probably because articles in the Iraqi press mentioned such an encounter. The president resorts to characterizing the questionable charge that Iraq was buying aluminum tubes (analyzed on pp. 93–104) as concrete evidence of its nuclear progress. The specter of an Iraqi nuclear weapon in less than a year is a specific reference to the NIE's worst case, in which Iraq manages to obtain ready-to-use enriched uranium from abroad and has already prepared a bomb assembly. The majority consensus within U.S. intelligence is that *even* with a reconstituted nuclear program, an Iraqi nuclear capability remained unlikely before the 2007–2009 time period. That judgment supported a UN-backed course of inspections and disarmament, in contrast to the urgent action President Bush is demanding here.

15. Here President Bush insinuates. The fact of the September 11 attacks on the United States, whatever weapons enemies might be using against the United States, has nothing to do with American policy vis-à-vis the sovereign state of Iraq.

16. Bush uses the image of the smoking gun "that could come in the form of a mushroom cloud," first articulated by Condoleezza Rice a month earlier, and he

also evokes the heroics of John Kennedy in the Cuban Missile Crisis, to complete his insinuation: the Iraqi threat is as critical for the United States as the most intense crisis of the Cold War.

17. President Bush makes explicit his threat of war on Iraq.

18. Note that *none* of the UN resolutions President Bush claimed to be solely interested in enforcing demanded anything other than disarmament. Here Bush inserts additional conditions that reveal his demands as an ultimatum: Baghdad is required to fulfill both foreign policy (regulation of its contact with terrorist organizations, curtailment of illicit trade, Gulf War accounting) and internal ("cease the persecution of its civilian population") conditions to satisfy U.S. demands. It was highly unlikely Saddam Hussein would agree to any such conditions, as Bush well knew. In essence, President Bush designed a set of demands likely to ensure a war. As desirable as it was to get the Saddam regime to end its domestic repression and manipulation of the sanctions system, to proceed in this fashion was a clear interference in the internal affairs of a sovereign nation, prohibited by both the UN Charter and U.S. law.

19. President Bush here reveals that regime change continues to be his objective. Invoking continuity with the Clinton administration, which pursued a covert operation to overthrow Saddam that was as objectionable as Bush's policy here, does not excuse his own behavior. Bush's rhetoric suggested that Saddam Hussein's government could do all that he demanded and still preserve itself, but that language exists here primarily to avoid the charge that Bush planned coercively to unseat a sovereign ruler.

20. President Bush's threat to hold Iraqi commanders for prosecution at war crimes trials is additional evidence that the aim of this speech was to rally support for war, not to implant a fresh UN weapons-monitoring authority.

21. President Bush recognized, *before* the Iraq war, the possibility that regime change would create unstable leadership in Iraq and make the situation worse. When precisely that occurred after the April 2003 fall of Baghdad, Bush first denied the reality, then did nothing to take responsibility for the mess or to make accountable those senior officials of his own administration whose myopic planning and grandiose visions of a transformed Middle East led to the Iraq disaster, then changed willy-nilly his plans for occupation and a transfer of political power to Iraqis not once but several times.

22. President George Bush here plays the part of confidence man. He deftly inserts the hook, telling Americans that the reason he wants a congressional resolution

authorizing force against Iraq is simply to enforce, if necessary, a UN resolution. The resolution would be used as the legal authority for an invasion the UN *had not* approved. Moreover, the sole reason the UN Security Council did not actually *reject* the U.S.-led invasion was that it never had the opportunity: Great Britain, acting under American instructions, took off the table a draft resolution for war once it became clear that it could not secure a Security Council approval.

Bush's statement that military action was not imminent was accurate because the U.S. buildup in the Persian Gulf and Kuwait at this point had just begun. The assertion that war with Iraq would not be "unavoidable" is a judgment call. The entire logic of this speech seems to signify that any combination of concessions one might expect from Saddam Hussein would not be sufficient to prevent a U.S. invasion.

5

The Shutout

Much can be said of the congressional debate on war powers that President Bush sought to influence with his Cincinnati speech, and many ordinary Americans found ways to express their views. There were marches and demonstrations, huge advertisements in major newspapers, pundits endlessly expressing opinions on radio, on television, and on the pages of the print media. Yet in the wake of President Bush's Cincinnati speech, large majorities in both houses of Congress voted for the war resolution. The House of Representatives passed the bill on October 10, the Senate a nearly identical text the next day.

The result became the Authorization for Use of Military Force against Iraq Resolution (Public Law 107-243). It enabled the president to use American armed forces as he deemed necessary and appropriate both to enforce "all relevant United Nations Security Council resolutions," and to defend the national security of the United States "against the continuing threat posed by Iraq." No part of the law permitted war for the purpose of regime change, to enforce internal changes on Iraqi government behavior, or to obtain any of the other conditions George Bush had posed in his Cincinnati speech. On the contrary, the authority to use force was explicitly linked to the sole question of the alleged Iraqi weapons.

If Iraq had no weapons of mass destruction, under the relevant UN mandate, Baghdad would then be considered disarmed, the resolutions fulfilled, and the authorization for war voted by the U.S. Congress would expire with them. Similarly, if Iraq had no weapons, it posed no threat to American national security, and the grant of war power to Bush evaporated the same way.

Thus the question of whether or not Iraq possessed weapons of mass destruction, far from some academic exercise, lay at the heart of the administration's entire enterprise. To make war on Saddam Hussein *required* asserting an Iraqi threat and, conversely, necessitated avoiding a determination by any authoritative body—such as the UN weapons inspectors—that Baghdad had been effectively disarmed.

George Bush's confidence game involved making sure the allegations against Iraq stuck. That meant constantly reinforcing his administration's claims about Iraqi weapons, shutting out the UN arms inspectors, and maintaining that Iraq was not complying with UN resolutions. Emblematic of the Bush administration's stance is the one-page "fact sheet" authored by the State Department and the CIA and issued in December 2002 (reproduced below). The fact sheet strained to find sins of omission in the huge declaration regarding its military capacity that Baghdad submitted to the UN. It would also mean, as we shall see, ensuring that UN arms inspectors *did not* complete their job of disarming Baghdad. This shutout of the inspectors would be a necessary condition for the war on Iraq to take place.

As the Clock Ticks

Bush administration claims regarding Iraqi weapons may have been critical to the push for war, but they were never uncontested. What made the Central Intelligence Agency reporting especially important to the political debate was the sense that the CIA could serve as arbiter between the factions—with its expertise and secret knowledge, the agency could be the authoritative source lending weight to Bush's claims. Administration opponents, well aware of the traction President Bush had gotten from the CIA white paper, were quick to seize upon the letter Director George Tenet had sent to Congress on October 7 as showing a less stark picture than Bush portrayed. Bush allies rallied to defend the claims about Iraqi weaponry. The president's Cincinnati speech ultimately did not settle these issues.

As disputes over the intelligence bubbled, political controversy continued to roil over the Iraq option. The Norwegian Nobel Committee took a hand with a highly unusual public statement in connection with their award of a Peace Prize to former President Jimmy Carter, declaring the prize "can and must be seen as criticism of the line the current U.S. administration has taken on Iraq." Simultaneously a coalition of more than sixty religious groups in both the United States and Great Britain issued a declaration denouncing the concept of preemptive war on religious, moral, and practical grounds. On October 12 there were widespread protest marches in France, and on the 26th similar demonstrations took place throughout the United States. In the largest antiwar march on Washington since the Vietnam era, between one and two hundred thousand protestors descended upon the nation's capital.

Military preparations continued in tandem with the Bush administration's effort to create the political conditions necessary for an intervention. In mid-September General Tommy Franks of the Central Command (CENT-COM) presented President Bush the latest version of his operations plan. Shortly thereafter Franks left on a visit to the Middle East, where the United States was preparing air bases in Qatar and Oman to compensate for Saudi Arabia's refusal to permit the major bases on its soil to be used in a war. Diplomacy with the Saudis eventually wore down that opposition enough to enable the United States to use those airfields for combat support, if not combat purposes—air refueling, intelligence missions, and defensive air patrols would continue to fly out of Saudi bases, as would the daily flights enforcing the no-fly zones. The latter missions frequently involved bombing and would in fact be used to disrupt Iraq's air defenses and command networks in the months before war actually began.

General Franks reached Kuwait on September 19. There he held a conference among senior commanders. A forward headquarters for CENT-

COM, now planned for deployment to Qatar, was scheduled to be in place by November, and General Franks arranged for military exercises to rehearse the war plan. Advance parties of construction, transportation, and logistics units that would be required to prepare for the deployment of major ground and air forces were slated for movement to the Persian Gulf. By mid-October Franks had returned to the Middle East, this time to Jordan. The United States never would convince Jordan to take any big role in its "coalition of the willing," but the Jordanians did offer limited cooperation, including holding exercises in which U.S. special operations forces sharpened the skills they would use in the Iraq war. The Jordanians accepted deployment of U.S. antimissile batteries that were intended to help blunt any Iraqi missile attack on Israel. President Bush held direct talks with the Israelis themselves on October 16, with the object of getting Prime Minister Ariel Sharon's government to stay out of the war, even if Iraqis launched rocket attacks on Israel. Sharon accepted more American antimissile batteries and agreed on nonintervention in principle, but reserved his options if the Iraqis did attack.

Diplomatic moves at this time indicate that the United States had arrived at the stage of finalizing its war plan for Iraq. At a news conference on November 7 Bush confidently declared "The outcome of the current crisis is already determined: the full disarmament of Iraq will occur." The president also asserted that the United States and its allies would "move swiftly with force to do the job." Ten days later, just before leaving on a trip to Eastern Europe, where Bush would enjoy the most enthusiasm for his policy, the president threatened that if Saddam did not disarm Iraq, "We will lead a coalition of the willing and disarm him." Hinting at his ulterior aims, in a talk in Rumania on November 22, President Bush added: "Aggressive dictators cannot be appeased or ignored, they must always be opposed."

The military forces began to move. At the end of November and the beginning of December the CIA held a crucial conference with CENTCOM's intelligence staffs and key commanders to review all their information about Iraq. George Tenet and John McLaughlin personally hosted the military officers. The group identified what they still needed to know about Saddam's forces. The CIA detailed the collection resources that could be assigned to each intelligence question, and the "spooks" and generals together decided where they would accept the existing uncertainties and how they would distribute the resources to settle the key questions.

The intelligence would be plugged into the military exercise Internal Look, beginning on December 9. The exercise simulated the invasion of Iraq. The more CENTCOM intel people saw, the less confidence they had in Washington's holdings. When it came to the matter of nailing down exactly which Iraqi sites held weapons of mass destruction, what weapons were stored at the sites, and so on, one CENTCOM planner characterized the intelligence to *Newsweek*: "It was crap." The places were for the most part the same ones the military had been dealing with throughout the 1990s, many of them bombed repeatedly by now, shown in bright light by spy satellite photos. The officer continued: "What was inside the structures was another matter." The military needed to know in order to minimize the collateral damage and to plan the right weapons to use in particular strikes. "We asked, 'Well, what agents are in these buildings? Because we need to know.' And the answer was, 'We don't know.'" Obviously, key intelligence questions remained to be solved.

Deputy Secretary of Defense Paul Wolfowitz had gone to Turkey the previous summer. He returned there at the beginning of December, insisting in public that Turkish support was guaranteed even while there were plenty of Turkish officials saying the opposite. The United States needed transit rights through Turkey, and the use of Turkish ports, airfields, and military bases, to sustain a northern front in the attack on Iraq. Wolfowitz went from Ankara to Brussels, where he asked North Atlantic Treaty Organization countries to commit troops to the Iraq invasion and also to help shield Turkey from any Iraqi retaliation. Wolfowitz failed in both endeavors. Turkey would not aid the invasion. Last minute offers of U.S. money did not sway a Turkish public overwhelmingly opposed to war. American diplomats also largely failed in their appeals to more than fifty nations to contribute forces to the coalition of the willing. Except for Great Britain, an ally from the start, there were few adherents. Australia contributed a couple of thousand military personnel and a couple of warships, and New Zealand made a token addition

to that. Poland sent a handful of commandos. As noted above, the Czech
Republic, which had had a chemical protection unit in Kuwait since the Gulf
War, permitted that unit to stay on for the new war, but only in Kuwait and
only for defensive purposes. Even so, it had to replace a number of soldiers
who wanted no part of the new adventure. To impress the public with its
international support, the Bush administration took to citing as military contributions the liaison officers various nations assigned to CENTCOM to coordinate multilateral matters, enabling Washington to claim their nations as
participants. That was the coalition of the willing.

As the days passed, public criticism in the United States of the Bush
administration's course on Iraq broadened to engage its actions on several
levels. Occasional leaks on the military planning against Iraq, then the openly
announced beginnings of the U.S. deployment to the Persian Gulf, brought
an outpouring of comment on the perceived nature of the operational concept. Whether coalition forces would be prepared for city fighting, the effect
of the alleged chemical weapons on the conflict, the cost of a war—all became
points in the debate. War commentary became widespread enough that U.S.
military planners took advantage of it to float certain stories in early November as part of a psychological warfare gambit, deliberately detailing an invasion larger in scope than what was intended to instill fear in Saddam's
commanders. The thinness of international support for President Bush also
did not go unnoticed. Administration supporters followed the Bush claims
on intelligence and insisted the Iraqi threat had become too serious to deal
with except by force, while paradoxically arguing that an invasion would be
a "cakewalk." They also maintained that UN inspectors could not be relied
upon to disarm Iraq since they, supposedly, would be bamboozled by Baghdad's deceptive measures.

Beyond the public debate, waves of protest gathered. Indeed the months
leading up to the Iraq war witnessed the largest sustained global opposition
to a foreign policy yet recorded. On November 9 demonstrations took place
throughout Italy, with half a million people marching in Florence alone. On
the 10th in the United States, there were protests at more than a hundred
places in thirty-seven states, building toward International Human Rights

Day. A month later, on the day itself, coordinated protests in America included one hundred and fifty events. Cities and towns throughout the United
States began passing official resolutions opposing a war. When the City
Council in Chicago passed such a resolution on January 16, 2003, it became
the largest city yet and the twenty-third overall to take this position (ultimately over a hundred cities would go on record, as well as some state
legislatures; no jurisdiction passed any resolution in favor of war with Iraq).

As he had used the United Nations initiative to achieve approval of war
power by Congress, so too did President Bush use the UN card to trump
public protests. From Washington's standpoint, the problem with UN inspections remained one of achieving a formula that would enable the United
States to act at will. Iraq's acceptance of a new UN arms monitoring authority
on September 17, 2002, made that task more difficult, as did the paucity of
international support for the U.S. position. American negotiators led by ambassador John D. Negroponte sought approval of a scheme permitting war
after any determination that Iraq was in defiance of Security Council resolutions, without further reference to any body, including the Security Council. For approval of such a formula, the United States needed not only a
majority vote of the fifteen member states on the Security Council, but the
affirmative vote of all the five permanent members (United States, United
Kingdom, France, Russia, People's Republic of China), who thus exercise a
veto power. As it developed, a formula agreed between the United States
and Britain stood to be vetoed three ways and might not gain even a simple
majority.

This impasse continued through mid-October, when Washington
backed off somewhat, offering to drop the provision in the resolution providing for resort to war without further reference to the UN. After informal
discussions, on October 17 the Americans agreed to a two-stage approach,
under which there would have to be a second Security Council resolution.
Four days later ambassador Negroponte tabled a draft resolution to this effect. The United States also abandoned its insistence that American intelligence experts be included in the new UN disarmament mission. Russia and
France continued to worry that the mechanism effectively had war as its

default value, rather than referring a violation to the UN for a decision on whether to trigger a war. Several nations worried that the UN monitors would not be allowed enough time to decide whether Iraq had disarmed.

By late October, after some editing of the new draft, perceptions were that most members had lined up in favor of the latest version. Syria continued to object that the Security Council resolution remained too negative; that is, it was all about Iraqi compliance and made no mention of lifting the economic sanctions that originally were supposed to disappear once Baghdad had completed its disarmament. Those objections were met. By unanimous vote on November 8 the Security Council passed Resolution 1441 ordering the United Nations Monitoring Inspection and Verification Commission (UNMOVIC), to return to Iraq and handle disarmament in areas other than nuclear weapons, which would fall under the International Atomic Energy Agency (IAEA).

Meanwhile in Baghdad Saddam Hussein was responding positively to diplomatic pressure from the United Nations. While Saddam had agreed in September that the UN inspectors could return, in the days afterward he attempted to limit their activities in ways that had stymied UN inspection missions in the 1990s. But UNMOVIC, successor to the earlier organization, had long planned its return to Iraq and now took care to create favorable conditions for its inspections. In sharp negotiations, director general Hans Blix hammered out guidelines with the Iraqi government. The Iraqis agreed to no-notice inspections. Attempting to influence international public opinion, they took reporters on tours of some of the sites alleged to be Iraqi weapons production and storage sites. In October the Iraqis abandoned an effort to exclude from inspection Saddam's presidential palaces, which had been a source of the breakdown in 1997–98. Even though the Iraqi parliament rejected intrusive inspections in its debate in early November, Saddam Hussein ruled that the UN monitors had to be admitted. Arrangements for housing, for reopening the old UN offices, for security, were made. An Iraqi foreign ministry letter on November 14 finalized the arrangements. Iraq was to provide a comprehensive declaration of its arms as well as its production infrastructure on December 8.

Blix had already assembled a cadre of 220 experts and wanted to put groups of 80 at a time into Iraq. By December Blix had hopes for 100 inspectors in-country, and not long afterward for a total staff of 350. By late January, Blix had the inspectors, an air staff of 60, and an overall complement of 260 persons. The mission would grow and acquire bases in Iraqi cities other than Baghdad. An advance team reached Baghdad on November 18, with the first expert group following on November 25. Actual inspections began two days later. The inspectors had a huge archive of material from the UN mission of the 1990s, including inventories of marked and tagged equipment, records of previous inspections, and millions of pages of Iraqi government declarations or seized documents. Helicopters gave the inspectors an immediate aerial capability, and the first aerial inspection flight took place on January 5, 2003. The UNMOVIC inspectors also enjoyed the ability to call on the United States for high-altitude overhead photography carried out by U-2 aircraft (the UN inspection mission that had ended in 1998 benefited from U-2 coverage also—the planes painted in UN white and blue colors—at a rate of a flight every other day; UNMOVIC undoubtedly had an even higher flight tempo).

Alongside Hans Blix and his UNMOVIC inspectors stood director general Mohammed ElBaradei of the International Atomic Energy Agency (IAEA), who participated equally in the Iraq mission. Some synergistic benefit accrued from having the two missions, which could share information and clues. A number of the Iraqi sites on the inspection lists were former nuclear facilities reoriented to chemical plants. Since experience from the 1990s indicated the Iraqis had at times hidden nuclear equipment in chemical plants, monitors enjoyed a certain overlap in terms of their inspections. The list of prospective sites to check numbered approximately 550.

The UN inspectors moved quickly to establish their activity. The very first inspections were no-notice surveys. Some of the top facilities, such as the missile plant at Al Rafah, were checked immediately. Inspections rapidly were extended outside the environs of Baghdad. Presidential palaces were checked beginning on December 3. In contrast to the 1990s, the Iraqis acquiesced in the inspections and did not attempt to be obstructive. Even Saddam's palaces opened their gates without significant delays when the UN jeeps drew up in front of them. Iraq also complied with the December 8 deadline to furnish a comprehensive declaration on its weapons and programs (see below for a detailed discussion). The only instance of denied access recorded occurred on December 12 when a vault at one site could not be opened, but it was established that local Iraqi representatives lacked keys to the locks, and the Iraqis stood by as inspectors sealed the vault. Monitors returned the next day, broke the seals, and inspected the contents.

Issues did arise in the course of the inspections, and both Blix and ElBaradei would report to the Security Council times when they were at odds with Iraqi authorities, but in each case Baghdad gave way. In December there arose a question of lists of Iraqi scientists associated with all the weapons of mass destruction programs (one complaint would be that the lists were woefully incomplete), then whether scientists could be interviewed privately, then if they could be interviewed abroad. Lasting through February 2003 the question of the scientists would be the most contentious of all. Next to it was probably the issue of aerial flights, including both the helicopters and U-2s. Baghdad refused to guarantee that a UN aircraft might not be targeted accidentally by Iraqi air defenses. On March 11 Baghdad actually scrambled a couple of interceptor jets against one of the high-altitude UN flights. But after complaints from Hans Blix, the Iraqis promised to do better, and for the most part they did. The Iraqis also liked to send escort choppers with the UN ships on aerial inspection. When monitors wanted to go into the no-fly zones enforced by the Americans and British, that posed the immediate danger that Anglo-American aircraft might attack the Iraqi helicopters and involve the UN in the fray. The Iraqis stopped their escorts into the zones.

Perhaps the most significant test of Iraqi compliance entailed Baghdad's tactical missiles. Monitors checked them out and counted them, but the capabilities of the system were in dispute. The Security Council resolutions restricted Baghdad to missiles of no more than 90 miles in range. The CIA had been reporting for several years that the missiles could exceed that range, and the UN inspectors agreed. A technical panel formed to evaluate the Al Samoud missiles and indeed concluded the missiles exceeded the permissible range. The inspectors ordered that the missiles be destroyed. Saddam Hussein issued a ban on all weapons of mass destruction on February 15, and affirmed the offending missiles would be destroyed beginning on March 1. The Iraqis were still breaking up these missiles when the war began.

The inspectors did discover some prohibited weapons. Specifically, in January, at two munitions storage sites, some gas warheads were found. These were for 122-mm artillery rockets that Baghdad had not declared in its comprehensive listing the preceding month. In one case there were a dozen warheads, in the other four more. The UN promptly destroyed the warheads. When UNMOVIC encountered unmanned aerial vehicles, the notorious drone aircraft, those were destroyed as well. In short, the actual progress of inspections permits a reasonable conclusion that, given sufficient time, Iraq would have been fully deprived of any weapons of mass destruction it possessed as well as any capacity to manufacture them.

The most distressing element in the picture was the behavior of the United States. For months the Americans kept demanding more, keeping the goalposts so high the Iraqis could hardly hope to reach them—for example, the Bush people's demands for interviews with Iraqi scientists, then that these take place outside Iraq, and then the U.S. attempt to write this requirement right into the Security Council resolution setting up the new UN inspections. This matter of interviews could not be solved to the satisfaction of all. The Bush administration essentially said it would not believe any report on Iraqi weapons not based on out-of-the-country interviews. Such interviews required Iraqi citizens to leave their homes and uproot their families (one could not be sure of Saddam's reaction) and involved a betrayal of Iraqi nationalism. Exposure to CIA recruitment efforts while outside Iraq for these interviews increased Saddam's fears of disloyalty, further diminishing the scientists' life expectancy in Baghdad. It is not surprising that no Iraqi scientists chose to come forward in this manner.

The Bush approach was also to construe *any* violation of Resolution 1441 as a "material breach" justifying full-scale war. Washington failed to get the single-step-to-war arrangement it originally sought, but the compromise was to insert very threatening "material breach" language that attempted to build an implicit basis for war. Thus the handful of 122-mm artillery rockets the monitors found constituted a "material breach." Then the Americans tried to extend the resolution's scope beyond the disarmament system, claiming that the U.S. and British flights in the no-fly zones were somehow part of the information apparatus of the UN inspection mission, and firing on them was also a "material breach" of the Security Council resolution. Since air missions in the no-fly zones were being used to mount a low-intensity offensive air campaign, this amounted to demanding Iraq's acquiescence in its own destruction. In actuality the CENTCOM flights had nothing to do with the UN inspectors and were not providing any support to them. The no-fly zones had been established unilaterally by the United States and Great Britain after the Gulf War as a response to civil war in Iraq. They were not even recognized by the UN.

Symptomatic of the Bush administration approach would be its handling of the voluminous declaration of weapons and programs that Iraq submitted to the UN on December 8 to comply with the Security Council resolution. All fifteen members of the Council were equally entitled to view the 12,000-page document. Instead the United States took the copy that was sent to New York. For a brief moment it seemed the Americans might return to the UN only selected portions of Baghdad's declaration. This idea evaporated because Security Council members were not only clearly legally entitled to the material, they could get fresh copies from UNMOVIC in Baghdad.

The Iraqi document, as described by UN officials and American diplomats, was certainly incomplete despite its length. The comprehensive disclosure apparently consisted of a compilation of earlier reports previously given to the UN plus a certain amount of new material. It was contradictory in places, omitted some items weapons monitors already had, and had clearly been thrown together to meet the submission deadline. That did not necessarily mean it had no value. New material could be compared with what was already on file, and the UN inspectors had their own records for comparison as well. The sum provided a baseline for UNMOVIC inspections. Senior Bush aides, however, eager to discredit the declaration, were soon labeling it as disinformation. The morning of December 18, a national security meeting of the Principals Group at the White House debated whether to charge the Iraqi declaration itself was a material breach of the UN resolution. The case could not be made clearly because the Baghdad papers contained omissions but not obvious prevarications. This charge would be made anyway.

The State Department sent its top nonproliferation official, John S. Wolf, to New York to meet with Hans Blix at the UN. Wolf detailed the American view of what was still lacking in the Iraqi disclosures. Wolf's presentation has been described as an outline accompanied by examples, not an analysis backed by CIA intelligence data. If so, it is very likely that the presentation followed the substance of the U.S. document "Illustrative Examples" that is reprinted below.

Acting for the inspectors, Blix issued a statement from New York on December 19. He noted places where material previously provided to UN inspectors did not appear in the comprehensive declaration, but also some where Baghdad had furnished additional explanations, including "non-weapons-related activity," presumably material on how the functions of various plants had nothing to do with weapons of mass destruction. He noted one area, Iraq's account of its destruction of anthrax it had possessed, as being inaccurate based on information in UNMOVIC's possession. On the other hand, Iraq *did* provide material in its declaration pertinent to the aluminum tube issue, in describing its artillery rocket programs. Blix covered chemical and biological weapons and missiles, overall not finding much new information. But he also noted that "Iraq continues to state in the declaration, as it has consistently done . . . that there were no weapons of mass destruction in Iraq when inspectors left at the end of 1998, and that none have been designed, procured, produced, or stored in the period since then."

For Colin Powell, Iraq's denial became the centerpiece for his denunciation of the Baghdad papers, made at a press conference the same day. Secretary of State Powell saw the denial as the most brazen act of all. The declaration, "consistent with the Iraqi regime's past practices," amounted to deception, Powell asserted. It was a game. "These are material omissions that, in our view, constitute another material breach," the secretary thundered.

To buttress Powell's statements, the State Department issued a one-page statement titled "Illustrative Examples of Omissions from the Iraqi Declaration to the United Nations Security Council." Issued as a fact sheet by the Office of the Spokesman of the department, the aggressive tone exceeded even Colin Powell's rhetoric. It demanded answers to why Iraq's declaration did not fit Bush administration perceptions in eight areas relating to various weapons categories. While the statement appeared on State Department letterhead, three months later, in answer to questions from Representative Henry A. Waxman (D-CA), the department admitted the fact sheet was produced jointly by the State Department and the Central Intelligence Agency.

During his press conference, secretary Powell had insisted that the "pattern" of omissions in the Baghdad papers "is not the result of accidents or editing oversights or technical mistakes." Exactly the same can be said about the State/CIA fact sheet of December 19, 2002. The document did not analyze the contents of the Iraqi declaration. Rather, it hit the *same points featured in all the previous U.S. litanies* of charges about the supposed Iraqi threat. This was no accident. The Bush administration focused on making its case, not on constructive criticism that might induce Baghdad to perfect its disclosures.

The "Illustrative Examples" document is reprinted below. Among other points of interest, the paper represents the first public surfacing of the charge that Iraq had sought uranium ore in the African nation of Niger. The charge had appeared in the classified NIE, was disputed even then, and was considered so weak that CIA Director George Tenet had labored to ensure President Bush did not use it in his speech in Cincinnati. The fact that the Niger charge appears publicly at this moment in December 2002, reflects a deliberate decision at the highest level of the Bush administration. It is notable that the National Security Council Principals Group, which had considered the U.S. response to the Iraqi declaration, included Vice President Cheney, perhaps the most senior proponent of the Niger uranium allegation.

The other items in the fact sheet are a mixture of assertions that are sometimes accurate, at times speculative, and in some cases simply statements of intelligence projections. Every allegation (except for the Niger uranium) was an old one, long discussed in U.S. intelligence circles; none constituted a fresh point raised for the first time as a result of the Iraqi declaration. All are subject to the assumption that wherever discrepancies exist, Iraq is assumed to have the weapons or chemicals in dispute. In the Bush administration's collective imagination, Baghdad had perfect records and its failure to supply them could only mean that Iraq had hidden real capabilities.

U.S. DEPARTMENT *of* STATE

Fact Sheet
Office of the Spokesman
Washington, DC
December 19, 2002

Illustrative Examples of Omissions From the Iraqi Declaration to the United Nations Security Council

Anthrax and Other Undeclared Biological Agents

1.
- The UN Special Commission concluded that Iraq did not verifiably account for, at a minimum, 2160kg of growth media.
- This is enough to produce 26,000 liters of anthrax — 3 times the amount Iraq declared; 1200 liters of botulinum toxin; and, 5500 liters of clostridium perfrigens — 16 times the amount Iraq declared.
- *Why does the Iraqi declaration ignore these dangerous agents in its tally?*

Ballistic Missiles

2.
- Iraq has disclosed manufacturing new energetic fuels suited only to a class of missile to which it does not admit.
- Iraq claims that flight-testing of a larger diameter missile falls within the 150km limit. This claim is not credible.
- *Why is the Iraqi regime manufacturing fuels for missiles it says it does not have?*

Nuclear Weapons

3.
- The Declaration ignores efforts to procure uranium from Niger.
- *Why is the Iraqi regime hiding their uranium procurement?*

VX

4.
- In 1999, UN Special Commission and international experts concluded that Iraq needed to provide additional, credible information about VX production.
- The declaration provides no information to address these concerns.
- *What is the Iraqi regime trying to hide by not providing this information?*

Chemical and Biological Weapons Munitions

5.
- In January 1999, the UN Special Commission reported that Iraq failed to provide credible evidence that 550 mustard gas-filled artillery shells and 400 biological weapon-capable aerial bombs had been lost or destroyed.
- The Iraqi regime has never adequately accounted for hundreds, possibly thousands, of tons of chemical precursors.
- *Again, what is the Iraqi regime trying to hide by not providing this information?*

Empty Chemical Munitions

6.
- There is no adequate accounting for nearly 30,000 empty munitions that could be filled with chemical agents.
- *Where are these munitions?*

Unmanned Aerial Vehicles (UAV) Programs

7.
- Iraq denies any connection between UAV programs and chemical or biological agent dispersal. Yet, Iraq admitted in 1995 that a MIG-21 remote-piloted vehicle tested in 1991 was to carry a biological weapon spray system.
- Iraq already knows how to put these biological agents into bombs and how to disperse biological agent using aircraft or unmanned aerial vehicles.
- *Why do they deny what they have already admitted? Why has the Iraqi regime acquired the range and auto-flight capabilities to spray biological weapons?*

Mobile Biological Weapon Agent Facilities

8.
- The Iraqi declaration provides no information about its mobile biological weapon agent facilities. Instead it insists that these are "refrigeration vehicles and food testing laboratories."
- *What is the Iraqi regime trying to hide about their mobile biological weapon facilities?*

Summary

None of these holes and gaps in Iraq's declaration are mere accidents, editing oversights or technical mistakes: they are material omissions.

State Department/CIA Fact Sheet Comments

1. Strictly speaking, the numbers used in this fact sheet did *not* come from the UN Special Commission but rather are based on the calculations in the British Iraq white paper, which credited Iraq with growth medium sufficient to produce 25,500 liters. Iraq had previously admitted to the UN production of 8,500 liters of anthrax, which it claimed had been destroyed. In his Cincinnati speech, George Bush put the amount at 30,000 liters, higher than what is here, then asserted that *inspectors* (presumably the UN) had concluded "Iraq had likely produced two to four times that amount," for the astonishing total of 60,000–120,000 liters of anthrax. But the UN reports cite only the 8,500 number. In this case the fact sheet actually supplies a correction for Bush's wild exaggeration of October, but it attributes the data to an international source (the UN) rather than a partner in the plan to rid Iraq of Saddam Hussein. The botulinum and clostridium estimates are new here.

2. The missile fuel statement is likely a reference to roughly 400 tons of fuel for SCUD missiles. Existence of the fuel was known to the UN before 1998. This is a subtle reference to the alleged "covert" missile force.

   The larger-diameter missile in question was the Al Samoud, which Iraq discussed in its comprehensive declaration. In fact *it was the Iraqi report itself,* which furnished the fresh data on missile diameter (760 mm vs. 500 mm), the number of tests that had exceeded the UN range standard (13) and by how much (24 miles, to a total range of 114 miles), that confirmed these rockets exceeded permissible ranges. This was a "material breach," but this short-range rocket would not threaten New York or Washington.

3. The Niger uranium claim was a fabrication of which the U.S. government was aware *before* the drafting of this State Department/CIA statement. It is not surprising that the Iraqi government declaration said nothing about a fabricated allegation about which it was ignorant. For the United States to publicly charge Baghdad with a "material breach" based on this shows the true purpose of the "Illustrative Examples" document.

4. This allegation regarding the highly toxic gas VX is remarkable for its inconsequentiality. In the October 2002 NIE, the U.S. services judged that Iraq actually had VX in current production. Yet September 2003 testimony by senior British intelligence official John Scarlett (in the Hutton inquiry into the death of a British weapons scientist and the preparation of the British Iraq dossier) revealed that *British* intelligence had written into a report on Iraq prepared in March, 2002 a

strong statement that Iraq was producing VX gas, but downgraded the claim to "might" because this represented the most the intelligence data would sustain. Scarlett was the author of the British Iraq dossier, and that September 2002 document went no farther than asserting that Iraq had a capability to produce VX. It is also relevant that former UN weapons monitor Scott Ritter said in an interview with *The Guardian* (September 19, 2002) that when inspectors found and destroyed 200 crates filled with glass-lined VX production equipment in 1996, Iraq's ability to manufacture that substance disappeared.

5. Iraq's explanation for the shells provided in 1998 and earlier was that they had been lost in the wake of the Gulf War, and of the bombs, that they were destroyed secretly. There had often been exchanges with Baghdad about the fate of precursor chemicals. One could (and might) choose not to believe Iraq's explanations, or wish the Iraqis kept better records (or had not destroyed them), but this State/CIA fact sheet is essentially accusing Iraq of not providing any such explanations.

6. The number 31,658 munitions, already available in 1998 data, again had already been the subject of exchanges. Iraqi explanations were that some had been destroyed in coalition bombing in the Gulf War, some had been lost, and the rest thrown away.

7. Unmanned aerial vehicles have already been examined in detail. The U.S. Air Force did not believe in the threat the fact sheet is portraying here.

8. On the mobile labs see the detailed analysis in Chapter 7.

The Tale

Most cynical of all the aspects of President Bush's policy in the months leading up to the Iraq war would be his approach to finding out what weapons of mass destruction actually existed in that Persian Gulf state. Here also the direct control by Bush White House people would be at its most visible. Condoleezza Rice and the National Security Council staff took on an operational role. Some activities, like the Bush propaganda Wurlitzer coordinated by the White House Information Group (WHIG), the intense scrutiny of many aspects of the intelligence effort by Vice President Richard B. Cheney, and the unusually public profile of National Security Adviser Rice, have already been mentioned. Now they assumed even greater importance. As the United States moved toward war—directives for the deployment of major combat forces to the Gulf would be issued by secretary Rumsfeld just a week after the State/CIA fact sheet was issued—the Bush administration's struggle to shape domestic and international opinion required an all-out effort.

The National Security Council (NSC) staff and national security adviser Condoleezza Rice would be central to this phase of the operation. Rice not only acted as an advocate for policy before the public to a greater degree than any predecessor, she became the first adviser to deal openly with a subordinate UN body, in this case Hans Blix's UNMOVIC, in an attempt to influence its activities. Rice's staff continued to regulate the message flowing to the American people, as did the WHIG operation that combined Bush's political and NSC staffs. All of this aimed toward a crucial period of two days toward the end of January 2003, when Bush would present his State of the Union speech, and, almost simultaneously, Hans Blix would report to the UN Security Council on what his inspectors had discovered about weapons of mass destruction in Iraq.

Osama bin Laden was known for his multiple simultaneous terrorist attacks. George Bush liked to mount multiple simultaneous strikes on public opinion. In Washington on December 2, 2002, national security adviser Condoleezza Rice participated in one more of these exercises, when she gave a speech about Iraq, coordinated with Vice President Cheney speaking in Denver and deputy secretary of defense Paul Wolfowitz in London. All used the theme of expressing doubt Iraq would cooperate with the weapons inspectors. At the White House, spokesman Ari Fleischer added to the fire, implying that any denial by Saddam that he possessed weapons of mass destruction would be a new deception. The WHIG put out another of its anti-Iraq studies, complementing the early December speechifying. This one was titled "Apparatus of Lies: Saddam's Disinformation and Propaganda, 1990–2003."

Before her public appearance Rice held a quiet meeting with UN chief inspector Hans Blix, insisting the UN stiffen its demands on Baghdad for

Iraqi scientists to be sent outside the country for interviews. The quiet meeting proved even more important than Rice's public remarks, and would be followed by repeated Rice trips to see Blix in New York. This was unprecedented. Never had a national security adviser to the President of the United States carried out a specific mission to an independent agency of the UN with specific operational goals.

Director general Blix wrestled with a problem of his own. The drumbeat of Bush administration public commentary had been uniformly negative. Washington wanted, or at least said it wanted, more inspections, faster inspections, more comprehensive inspections, at a time when the UNMOVIC group in Iraq had only recently arrived, was still getting up to speed, and had just over a week of visits under its belt. The Americans were making all kinds of confident assertions of what Iraq's weapons of mass destruction were. Hans Blix wanted to find them. Blix had received U.S. intelligence briefings before, but all at a general level. He wanted the real skinny—hard data on targets his inspectors could go out and find. Indications are that Hans Blix hesitated for some time before asking the United States for that information. It is likely that Blix raised the matter informally with Rice in Washington on December 2. In any case, UNMOVIC made an official request four days later. Disturbingly, Blix felt the need to make these specific requests even though section 10 of Security Council Resolution 1441, the very UN inspection authority that Washington relied on and needed for war, called upon member states to provide the international inspectors with all available intelligence help.

The request opened Blix up to new pressures. Bush administration officials wanted inside reports back from UNMOVIC in exchange for their intelligence, since that could be important in a war. The Americans were also angry. Testifying for an official Australian investigation of the pre-Iraq war intelligence, Blix's predecessor, the Australian Richard Butler, had a fine appreciation of the UNMOVIC director's plight. "That was a tough call for him to make politically," Butler told the parliamentary inquiry. "The Americans were extremely angry with him for doing that—in public. I am not making that up—they got very angry with him." By publicly asking for the

U.S. intelligence, in fact, Blix had lifted the veil ever so slightly on the true Bush administration attitude toward the inspections. There was ridicule of Blix among the Bush people, both on a personal level and as someone who could not get the job done without American help. Hans Blix himself commented on the matter shortly before his retirement in the summer of 2003. "I have my detractors in Washington," Blix said to a British journalist. "There are bastards who spread things around, of course, who planted nasty things in the media."

For better or worse, Blix did what he had to, then awaited the results. And waited. Then he waited some more. Two weeks after the UNMOVIC request, at the December 19 press conference where Secretary Powell accused Baghdad of a fresh "material breach" with its disclosure data, Powell also said the United States was now prepared to share intelligence with the UN. But the flow of information did not actually start until early January, and even then Powell admitted that U.S. intelligence would withhold some of its more sensitive data. Once the flow began, Hans Blix told reporters, "It is a little opaque." In a context where U.S. intelligence had current knowledge and awareness, not some obscure subject where data needed to be dug out of old files, and where the United States was insisting on a very tight time limit for the UN inspectors to report, arrangements for a limited intelligence flow had taken more than a month.

Visiting the home of one named scientist, the UN inspectors found several thousand pages of documents bearing primarily on Iraqi efforts to enrich uranium by laser separation, a method Baghdad had discontinued more than a decade earlier when Iraq succeeded with electromagnetic methods. This would be ballyhooed as a fruit of intelligence sharing, though later reports attributed the tip to the British, not the United States.

Thus the Bush administration, which had been insisting that the Iraqi threat was urgent enough to justify high-priority, intrusive inspections by a disarmament commission, dallied for weeks in assisting that monitoring group. Moreover, as would become evident when Colin Powell addressed the Security Council a couple of months later, the United States specifically trained the cameras and ears of its spy satellites on Iraq the very moment the UNMOVIC inspections began. On December 21, President Bush, Condi Rice, and George Tenet sat down in the Oval Office to listen to tapes of Iraqi radio communications recorded by the satellites during some of these inspections. Yet none of this data was made available to UNMOVIC.

In contrast with the slow response to UNMOVIC's appeals for help, Washington moved rapidly ahead with war preparations during this same period. General Franks tested his plan with an exercise held at command posts in the Gulf and at home. Secretary Rumsfeld signed deployment orders for large combat forces just before Christmas, and additional personnel of the Reserves and National Guard were mobilized just after that holiday. The newspapers contained hints that Bush would make his final decision on a war in late January.

Only days after the Bush administration began handing over some of its data on Iraq, Condi Rice went to New York and met with Blix again. Now she wanted the *quo* for the *quid*. The UNMOVIC director had made his first substantive report to the Security Council on January 9, a workman-like briefing, partly about the monitors setting up shop, partly analysis of the Iraqi disclosure, and just a little bit on early inspections. The White House countered that afternoon when spokesmen Ari Fleischer declared, "We know for a fact there are weapons there." A more ambitious interim report from Blix was due on January 27, and Rice wished to ensure the new report would be tougher on Baghdad, helping shape the political situation that would obtain when President Bush made his choice.

The second Rice–Blix encounter took place on January 14. By then another Bush information blitz was in train, timed to build up to the president's State of the Union address on January 28. Condoleezza Rice's part, the article "Why We Know Iraq Is Lying," appeared as an op-ed piece in the *New York Times* on January 23. The WHIG unit at the White House simultaneously put out another of its papers called "What Does Disarmament Look Like?" Using much identical language, both pieces argued that Iraqi behavior was far different from that of other nations that had truly rid themselves of weapons of mass destruction, such as South Africa, Kazakhstan, and the Ukraine (the choice of the Ukraine as a model is interesting, given that the Bush administration was furious at the Ukrainians for selling air defense radar equipment and other military items to Iraq). As Rice put it in the conclusion to her column, "Iraq is still treating inspections as a game. It should know that time is running out."

Paul Wolfowitz followed up with a speech to the Council on Foreign Relations in New York. The title? What else—"Iraq—What Does Disarmament Look Like?" Answering questions following his delivery, Wolfowitz insisted that what the United States said about Iraq had mostly been based upon hard intelligence from multiple sources.

Meanwhile a couple of discoveries by UNMOVIC inspectors in Iraq seemed to lend substance to Bush administration charges, and appeared just in time to put weight into the White House products just cited. In two separate incidents, monitors found chemical warheads for 122-mm artillery rockets in different Iraqi munitions depots, a dozen in one lot and four more in the other. Oddly enough, when these prohibited chemical warheads were uncovered, the Bush administration *did not* make *any* immediate claim to a material breach of Resolution 1441. Other than using the warheads as examples in Rice's column, Bush's State of the Union address, and Colin Powell's UN speech, the 122-mm rockets were ignored, their value as verified violations cast aside. Could that have been because it was these self-same rockets for which the Iraqis had bought aluminum tubes and that Bush was claiming—and would say again in a few days' time—were for nuclear weapons programs? Focusing attention on the rockets could have led to the unraveling of the Bush administration's allegations regarding Iraq's alleged nuclear program.

In any case, the story of Condoleezza Rice and Hans Blix had yet to play out fully. Blix and Mohammed ElBaradei of the International Atomic Energy Agency reported to the Security Council as anticipated on January 27. Their reports were not everything the Bush people could want. The upshot would be a third meeting between Rice and Blix on February 11, which, according to UN sources, did not go well. No doubt the tempest related to Blix's refusal to report an Iraqi threat of dimensions that matched the picture purveyed in Washington. Blix reported to the UN again three days later, and again at the beginning of March, neither time making the Iraqis out as much of a threat, more concerned with assuring the smooth functioning of the inspections than exaggerating the scale of the problem.

On March 6, CIA director Tenet sent a letter up to Capitol Hill certifying that data had been turned over to the UN. He implied the material covered all the high-value and moderate-value sites as well as a large majority of even the lowest-priority locations. In slightly over three months, the data handed over remained relatively limited. Press reports put roughly 1,000 Iraqi place names, overall, on the site lists UNMOVIC used for its planning. According to figures declassified at the behest of Senator Carl Levin (D-MI) of the Senate Intelligence Committee, however, U.S. intelligence named only 550 sites to Hans Blix, including 150 as most highly suspect. A smaller (but still secret number) were high- and medium-priority sites (as with America's new color-coded system of terror warnings, there are apparently no "low" priorities). The CIA provided additional information on a smaller (but classified) number of medium- and high-priority sites, and full briefing packages on another smaller (and classified) number of locations. In other words, some few sites were detailed in files turned over to the UN, but by far the largest number of inspection targets were covered only by their names appearing on U.S. lists. In addition, the last set of CIA materials arrived on March 11, so close to the U.S. attack that, as a practical matter, not much inspecting could be accomplished. In an interview with the BBC some months later Hans Blix recounted that his inspectors visited a great many of the sites that had been suggested by U.S. (and British) intelligence and at only three places did UNMOVIC find anything—*and* the finds were unrelated to weapons of mass destruction.

In short, the promised U.S. intelligence cooperation proved too little, too late. One can conclude that the cooperation effort failed due to incompetence, in which case heads ought to have rolled—but none did. Or it is possible that the administration's whole collaboration with the UN inspectors had become hopelessly bollixed up by interagency jealousies. But the most likely explanation is that intelligence liaison remained slow and limited because that was the way George Bush wanted it.

While the Bush administration–UNMOVIC relationship unraveled, Washington continued the campaign that had begun with the Rice-Wolfowitz media blitz contrasting Iraq with truly disarmed nations, and would continue with President Bush's State of the Union address and Colin Powell's presentation to the Security Council on February 5. These last two were prepared in parallel, as the administration's need to build new support had become glaring. A massive march on Washington by protesters had put 300,000 demonstrators on the streets of Washington in subfreezing weather. A *Washington Post*/ABC poll out on January 21 showed that Americans were essentially deadlocked on the basis for war (48 percent believing there was sufficient evidence, 47 percent that there was not) and, even more disturbing to Bush, that an overwhelming majority (69 percent) believed the UN inspectors should have the time they needed, ranging from several months to however much was needed, as against just 26 percent who felt the inspections ought to be restricted to a few weeks' time. Worst of all, approval ratings for President Bush had fallen to the lowest levels since before the September 11 attacks. A different poll, from the Pew Trust, found a majority (53 percent) thought the Bush administration had not made a sufficient case to justify war.

Also advancing rapidly were war preparations. At the National Security Agency, director General Michael Haydon met with CENTCOM intelligence chiefs to finalize details of communications interception in support of the forces. In Washington on January 20, the day after the massive march, President Bush ordered the creation of an organization to plan for postwar Iraq. Bush gave the job to the Pentagon, which had no experience in this area, even though the State Department also made a bid and had had a Future of Iraq Project staffed by Iraqi exiles in place for nearly a year. Postwar planning took place under leadership of an NSC subcommittee chaired by deputy national security adviser Stephen J. Hadley, the same official who became caught up in the firestorm that engulfed the State of the Union address.

President George Bush's State of the Union address would become hugely controversial afterward. This was because of the so-called "Sixteen Words," the statement the speech contained alleging that Saddam Hussein had fueled his nuclear weapons program with uranium from Niger. Because the administration's defense against this controversy centers on the contention that the inclusion of the statement was an innocent error of coordination between Stephen Hadley of the NSC staff and Director Tenet of the CIA, and their subordinates, it is important to reconstruct the genesis of the speech as closely as possible at this writing.

The White House subsequently worked hard to isolate the incident as a technical error with no relation to the president. This is questionable for several reasons. Bush worked extensively on the speech; the White House's own Web site, in the halcyon days immediately afterward, featured a photo montage of President Bush with pencil poised over the text. As early as mid-December, Bush held an initial meeting with chief speechwriter Michael Gerson, communications director Dan Bartlett, and their aides to sketch out broad outlines. Iraq remained on the front burner throughout this period. It was precisely at this time that the United States needed to counter the Iraqi comprehensive disclosure—and it was in the December 19 State/CIA fact sheet that the Niger uranium allegation first surfaced.

President Bush approved a short outline written up from the original discussion upon his return from Christmas vacation in Crawford. He marked up a draft on January 17, and held a rehearsal using a teleprompter a week later, with a second on January 25. Because of his Cincinnati address to the VFW, which originally had the uranium charge in it, which Bush had seen in multiple drafts, and from which the uranium charge was ultimately removed, there is a reasonable expectation the president would have remembered this controversial item. In Bush's actual delivery of the speech, he did not simply recite the line from the text. Instead of his usual flat enunciation, he came up with one of the more dramatic renditions in the address, rising to a crescendo: "The British government has learned that Saddam Hussein recently sought significant quantities of uranium . . . from *Africa!*" The president had clearly labored to craft this delivery. He *knew* the point to be a key one, and that also speaks to his knowledge of the subject.

The question of how the "Sixteen Words" got into the speech breaks down into two parts: where the idea came from, and how the uranium charge came to assume the form it took in the text. (The specifics of the intelligence issue over the uranium charge will be treated in a major section following the speech itself.)

It is speculative but entirely possible that President Bush wanted the Niger uranium charge in his State of the Union address from the beginning. In India, there have been published reports that attribute the idea to Paul Wolfowitz. It is true that at the Council on Foreign Relations on January 23 Wolfowitz mentioned the uranium issue, but the context amounted to a reference to the charge as it appeared in the State/CIA fact sheet. Secretary Powell used the uranium charge in his speech to global financial magnates at Davos, Switzerland, on January 26. But that was late in the speech-writing process for this passage to arrive on the scene. Six months later, attempting to defend Bush in the "Sixteen Words" controversy, a (proverbial) "senior White House official" who had the speechwriting staff under his purview, quite probably Chief of Staff Andrew H. Card. Jr., described the process as an open one. In "Card's" (we shall give the official that name) version the writers pile up a stack of source material, go through it, then come up with a draft on which opinions are then gathered until the draft is satisfactory to the various people concerned. Of course the big pile included the Iraq National Intelligence Estimate. "Card" specifically said on July 18, 2003, following a question from a reporter, that it was his understanding that "no senior White House officials gave the speechwriters even any list, any idea of what they wanted to be included from the NIE." But the Niger uranium claim was a main point in the state/CIA fact sheet criticizing the Iraqi weapons declaration, and that fact sheet had to be near the top of the pile of the writers' source materials.

Chief speechwriter Michael Gerson, an evangelical like the president and Card (a Methodist), had a fine instinct for the jugular. Gerson was the one who, reaching back to Reagan days, had pulled up the word "evil" to christen the "Axis of Evil" that had had tremendous impact in the president's State of the Union a year earlier. Gerson had also drafted Bush's October speech in Cincinnati, when the Niger uranium allegation had been in many drafts of the text but was taken out at the behest of the CIA. The agency had addressed a memo directly to Gerson on the subject. That too should have formed part of his pile of source material. Gerson may have thought the appearance of the charge in the State/CIA fact sheet made it legitimate, although by its own account the White House insists on absolute accuracy for a presidential speech. Or he may have lamented its removal in October and in January been determined to get the uranium charge in. More likely Gerson had been instructed to put in the Niger uranium. In any case, the "Sixteen Words" went into the State of the Union draft.

Given the political problem that the Niger allegations became, one has to ask how the speechwriters could have missed seeing the issue was in dispute, *unless* they had orders to put the item in. The national estimate had the issue in dispute and at least two CIA memoranda from October 2002 raised questions about the charge. Separately, there were CIA reports and State Department cables from the field that discredited the original reports. Months afterward, Gerson would claim he had found one of the CIA memos in his files, but that he had no memories from the time. This is remarkable because of the byplay from the Cincinnati speech. At the time of the Cincinnati speech, Gerson had been interviewed for a profile in the *Washington Post* and had talked about *another* objection the CIA had had (on unmanned aerial vehicles) regarding his text. The speechwriter had actually bragged about the vetting procedure. It is unlikely he would have forgotten the set of issues that had bothered the CIA when he returned to writing about the same subject.

Backstopping the process, Stephen Hadley of the NSC staff should have blown the whistle. A man who prided himself on deliberateness, the fifty-four-year-old Hadley used the lexicon of a management consultant, though by training he was a lawyer. He had picked up the vocabulary as a member of Brent Scowcroft's consulting firm. He had also been a partner with the well-known Washington law firm Shea and Gardner. Hadley could have blown the whistle and made it stick. Stephen Hadley also happened to be a Dick Cheney man. He had been a team member for the group that supervised the Pentagon's transition to the first Bush administration, from which Cheney, at that time the secretary of defense, had selected Hadley to head up his international security policy shop. Appointed deputy national security adviser in the second, Hadley endured inevitable jokes about being Dick Cheney's man on the NSC staff.

Somewhere along the way Hadley's smooth edges had worn away. A moderate on arms control while on President Gerald Ford's NSC staff, Hadley in the Cheney Pentagon became much more the hardliner. He acquired neo-con friends like Kenneth Adelman and Richard Perle, whom he succeeded at the Department of Defense. In the second Bush administration, of course, Dick Cheney had no need of a man on the NSC staff. It would be more accurate to say Cheney had his own NSC staff which influenced the traditional one, on which Stephen Hadley functioned as a like-minded operator.

At the NSC Hadley saw himself as the manager who kept the trains running while Condi Rice ran the front office, but the traffic cop role is belied by the "Sixteen Words" episode. September 11 made Hadley a card carrying member of the new interventionist movement in the White House, and he became involved intensely in the maneuvers leading up to the Afghan war. Only a month later, a letter to the UN over the signature of U.S. ambassador John D. Negroponte contained inflammatory language about self-defense requiring action with respect to other states and organizations. The letter caused embarrassment to Negroponte, who had seen the final draft before it left State and knew that language had not been in there. The words were an early formulation of Bush's doctrine of preemption and had been inserted by Hadley at the NSC. In September 2002 Hadley had participated in both the prebriefs and the summit meeting between President Bush and Prime Minister Tony Blair at Camp David. Immediately afterward, as noted earlier, Bush had gone before the press and misrepresented reports of the International Atomic Energy Agency (IAEA) to suggest the IAEA was currently reporting an active nuclear program by Baghdad and that that was sufficient reason to attack Iraq.

Then there was the Cincinnati VFW speech a month later. In that case, the Niger uranium allegations had been the specific subject of objections from the CIA. Steve Hadley, like Mike Gerson, had been the recipient of memoranda on that very issue, and Hadley had had it out on the telephone with

George Tenet. There was also the NIE, in which the uranium claims had been an issue, and which certainly went to Hadley at the White House. Once the "Sixteen Words" had triggered a storm of political criticism, Hadley would be sandbagged into an on-the-record press conference. His explanation would be that he had forgotten the events of October. Granted that several months had passed, this explanation is still not credible. The Bush administration charges against Iraq constantly hammered at the same points, so the addition of a new one had to be noticed. More important, the issue of responding to the UN inspections and the Baghdad declaration, quite important at the White House, had happened just a few weeks before, and had marked the occasion for unveiling the uranium ploy. What the State of the Union represented was the opportunity to move the charge to a much higher level by giving it the immense visibility of a major presidential address.

Condoleeza Rice could also have saved President Bush from the "Sixteen Words," if that had been something important to do. "Andrew Card's" later explanation that neither Rice nor the president had read the NIE and therefore neither of them knew the Niger uranium story was, as the State Department intelligence bureau's dissent put it, "dubious." Rice herself later tried to shift blame to the CIA, saying that if George Tenet had asked for the language to be out of the speech it would have been, holding Cincinnati up as the example. The national security adviser also pleaded ignorance, maintaining that someone at lower levels might have known the uranium thing was questionable, but she did not. It is not altogether implausible that Rice did not read NIEs, especially ones the White House had not wanted (and it is pretty certain that Bush did not read them), but it was Rice's *job* to be on top of the intelligence, and it would be unlikely she had not read at least the Key Judgments section, where the dissent was alluded to. Rice had also been an addressee for at least one of the CIA memos on getting the uranium story out of the Cincinnati VFW speech. *And* the response to the Baghdad declaration had involved at least one meeting of the Principals Group of the NSC, which Rice chaired, and probably a meeting of the full National Security Council, of which she was an active member. Part of the response had been to surface the uranium story. Rice's claim to ignorance is not tenable.

The logical conclusion from all this is that the State of the Union address contained the allegation that Saddam sought uranium ore in Africa because President George Bush wanted it to be there.

That conclusion is only reinforced by the story of what happened in the final twenty-four hours before the speech. The morning of January 27 the UN chief inspectors reported to the Security Council. Hans Blix, Condi Rice's efforts notwithstanding, reported no Iraqi weapons of mass destruction found despite 300 visits to 230 different sites. In all, what had been uncovered were the (fewer than twenty) artillery rocket warheads, a small quantity of a precursor chemical for mustard gas, the Al Samoud missiles, which at that time Iraq had yet to agree to destroy, some repaired chemical equipment at Al Fallujah, and the seizure of documents on laser separation of uranium isotopes at the home of an Iraqi scientist. These items posed some concern but no material breach sufficient to justify war. Of overriding import were the comments of Mohammed ElBaradei of the IAEA. His monitors had inspected 106 sites and made 139 visits, and ElBaradei reported IAEA had "made good progress in our knowledge of Iraq's nuclear capabilities." The body of the IAEA report discredited the Bush administration's claims regarding Iraq's importing aluminum tubes, finding no connection between those and any nuclear enrichment effort. The bottom line held no promise for the Bush people: "We have to date found no evidence that Iraq has revived its nuclear weapons program since the elimination of the program in the 1990s."

With just over twenty-four hours to go before Bush's State of the Union address, the world had been told by the UN inspectors that there was *no* Iraqi nuclear program and precious little in terms of *anything* that could be construed as weapons of mass destruction. The horror among White House and NSC staff must have been palpable. That led to frantic activity. According to senior administration official "Andrew Card," the White House communications staff now decided to change the State of the Union draft so as to attribute each of its statements about Saddam's Iraq to a specific source. Three lines of the speech were changed, resulting in the "Sixteen Words" storm.

As befits a presidency on the defensive for its contriving of an Iraq crisis, even at this writing the story of the speech remains murky. Despite their explanations, neither "Andrew Card," Stephen Hadley, nor George Tenet has precisely described the process of agency clearance on the State of the Union. Though the CIA commented on the Cincinnati VFW speech beginning with its sixth draft (of 28 or 29), and also had very early input on some of the (at least) 25 drafts of the Bush UN speech, for this address Director Tenet has revealed (in a July 2003 statement), "Portions of the State of the Union speech draft came to the CIA for comment shortly before the speech was given." Senior source "Card" identifies this as happening on January 27, the day before the speech. Hadley glosses over the point, suggesting that the CIA fact-checked as many as thirty items about weapons of mass destruction, but gives no timing. We are left with the suspicion that the CIA might never have seen the State of the Union draft *until* Gerson began making last-minute changes and the NSC staff had to run them by the agency. If this was true, the most likely reason would have been exactly *because* the CIA had pushed the White House to take the uranium story out of the Cincinnati speech in October.

More likely it was the "Sixteen Words" the agency never saw. Bush administration officials, attempting to explain what happened, agree that an NSC staffer called the CIA and asked for clearance for the sentence in the speech. The staffer, Robert G. Joseph, was senior specialist on counterproliferation at the NSC. He spoke to the director of Tenet's Weapons Intelligence, Nonproliferation, and Arms Control Center (WINPAC), Alan Foley. Joseph faxed over the language. They had a conversation. Agreement ends there.

According to reports of Foley's testimony six months later before the Senate intelligence committee, when the WINPAC director saw the State of the Union language, he told Joseph that U.S. intelligence could not be certain of the veracity of the Niger uranium story, and he certainly did not want a specific amount of ore mentioned in the speech since that might jeopardize the source of the data. Joseph agreed to delete those things, but then suggested that instead the speech could say "Africa" and refer to the British government, which had included the uranium in its published Iraq intelligence paper. Foley objected that, though this was accurate, the CIA had actually told the British of their own doubts and asked John Scarlett to remove the offending item from the British dossier. Scarlett had refused to do so, arguing that SIS, in contrast to CIA, was confident in their data on the issue. Bob Joseph finally asked whether it was correct to say that British intelligence had reported that information. Foley had to reply yes. Joseph took that as a CIA approval, and the White House ran with the ball. The State of the Union as President Bush delivered it was redrafted to attribute the item to the British.

According to senior White House aide "Andrew Card," that had not been the conversation at all. Robert Joseph had no recollection that CIA had raised any objection to the British paper being cited. Stephen Hadley, Joseph's direct superior with respect to the speech, also maintains that Joseph does not remember—"he's not saying it didn't happen, he's saying he does not recall"—but sets the entire conversation within a larger context, one in which Joseph and Foley were going through the speech draft and reviewing each of the president's planned allegations in turn.

What to make of all this is among the important questions in the hoodwinking of America. There had been plenty of selective amnesia in the Watergate scandal and the Iran-Contra affair. It is disturbing to see it again in Bush's confidence game leading up to the Iraq war.

The CIA and its WINPAC center did their best to keep President Bush from uttering the statement that pulled the pin on a political hand grenade. The WINPAC analysts must have shuddered a few months later when their top boss, director Tenet, nevertheless shouldered the blame for the appearance of the uranium story in the State of the Union. Tenet's July 11, 2003, statement shows the length to which he would go to keep President Bush's confidence, and it must have cost him esteem at CIA and broken morale among agency analysts. Tenet's words are worth recording for posterity: "Legitimate questions have arisen about how remarks on alleged Iraqi attempts to obtain uranium in Africa made it into the President's State of the Union speech. Let me be clear about several things. First, CIA approved the President's State of the Union address before it was delivered. Second, I am responsible for the approval process in my agency. And third, the President has every reason to believe the text presented to him was sound. These sixteen words should never have been included in the text written for the President."

In contrast with the CIA, which tried to save Bush from his false move and then helpfully took the responsibility, the White House offered a host of obfuscatory explanations and defenses. The senior official whose responsibilities included the speechwriting staff made the gaffe out to be a minor editorial mistake made while changing the attribution of items in the speech. Speechwriter Gerson, who had had trouble with the uranium story only three months before, professed not to remember an issue that had led to memos from the CIA, then not to recall the memos themselves until he accidentally came across them—the evening *after* the senior official's news conference explaining the mess. Then there is Condoleezza Rice, who evaded the issue, tried to put it all on the CIA, injected confusion by mixing up the Cincinnati and State of the Union speeches, and finally had her deputy make her apologies as an aside while himself eating crow. After that we have the deputy, Stephen Hadley, whose own amnesia involved his conversation with George Tenet and the CIA memoranda he had received when the agency succeeded in getting the same uranium story taken out of the Cincinnati VFW speech. When all else failed, the White House resorted to claiming that because the British *had* put something about uranium in *their* Iraq paper, it was all right to put a fraudulent allegation in an American State of the Union address.

In May 2003 the President's Foreign Intelligence Advisory Board (PFIAB), led by General Brent Scowcroft, undertook an investigation of the appearance of the "Sixteen Words" in the State of the Union address. Their conclusion, described by *Washington Post* reporter Walter Pincus shortly before Christmas, was that although no deliberate effort had been made to fabricate the story, the White House had been so eager "to grab onto something affirmative" about Iraqi nuclear weapons that it had disregarded CIA warnings regarding the information. The desire to avoid any public admission of this drive, which followed directly from Bush's strategy to shape the politics of war, contributed mightily to the outbreaks of amnesia once it became time to explain what had happened with the State of the Union.

Prominent among the amnesia victims would be Ambassador Robert G. Joseph, the final link in the White House chain. We may gain a sense of the mindset at the White House by taking a look at Joseph. A rancher, from the Dakota Badlands rather than Texas, Joseph's ambitions led him to the University of Chicago and to Columbia, places at which he made connections key to arriving at 1600 Pennsylvania Avenue. At Chicago, Joseph had taken classes with Albert Wohlstetter, patron saint of Richard Perle, who first hired Joseph into the Office of the Secretary of Defense. At the Pentagon, he met and worked for Steve Hadley, who succeeded Perle and later pulled Joseph into the Bush (I) administration. At Columbia, Joseph had known Zalmay Khalilzad, America's Afghan. Khalilzad and Perle both pitched in as foreign policy advisers in George W. Bush's presidential campaign, part of the brain trust headed by Condoleezza Rice. Joseph did chores and had people perfectly placed to pitch him on high. He joined the Rice staff the day of the inauguration.

Joseph's progress also shows signs of the malleability that at times afflicts defense intellectuals. Arabic was his language at school because security studies had become overpopulated in those Cold War years by Russian specialists. But of course it *was* the Cold War then, and Soviet affairs remained the main show, and there Joseph spent the bulk of his career. In the Pentagon Joseph worked on arms control policy and nuclear force issues. Asked to head the American delegation to the U.S.-Russian Consultative Commission on Nuclear Testing, he became an ambassador. Later, Joseph served as chief U.S. delegate to the Standing Consultative Commission that monitored implementation of the Anti-Ballistic Missile Treaty. During the Clinton years, especially the second term, the notion of "counterproliferation" became a catchword in defense circles, and Joseph went to head a center for counterproliferation studies at the National Defense University, formed at a time that war college was trying to reach beyond its academic role.

Bob Joseph had been a moderate early on, though inclined to the dark sides of issues. A typical example occurred in graduate school. In the late 1970s, a private corporation called OTRAG formed to develop rockets, much like the various companies today that market satellite launch services. This corporation worked on a rocket design and tested it in Zaire. Joseph saw in OTRAG a stalking horse for Libyan dictator Muammar Qadhafi, worried about Libyan nuclear capability, and argued the burden of proof should be on those who saw no threat, not the other way around. Otherwise OTRAG had to be seen as a Libyan missile program. Of course OTRAG eventually collapsed of its own lack of weight. But the logic of the argument would be identical to what the Bush people used with Saddam Hussein: Baghdad had the weapons of mass destruction and the United States should cease and desist only if others could prove the negative.

In the real world, proving the negative would be impossible, or at least not possible to the satisfaction of George W. Bush. The president had no intention of becoming convinced, because his claims about Iraqi weapons were instrumental to his real schemes for Baghdad. Bush needed those claims to induce the American people to accept a war.

Ambassador Joseph would be on board for the Iraq adventure. In remarks for the Institute for Foreign Policy Analysis in October of 2002 he explained that preemptive attack (called "defense" in the Bush White House) is a good and necessary thing, a natural consequence of international law, in which states have always had the right to take action when faced with imminent danger. Three months later, with the State of the Union address, Joseph's mission in gaining CIA approval of the threat claims in the speech text would be to provide language demonstrating that the danger was, in fact, imminent.

The portions of President Bush's State of the Union address that concern Iraq are reprinted below. The question of the Niger uranium purchase, and the intelligence issue that revolved around it, is the subject of a major analysis section that appears where the narrative resumes following the speech text.

document 5. *State of the Union.*

the *White House*
President George W. Bush

For Immediate Release
Office of the Press Secretary
January 28, 2003

President Delivers "State of the Union"
The U.S. Capitol

9:01 P.M. EST

THE PRESIDENT: Mr. Speaker, Vice President Cheney, members of Congress, distinguished citizens and fellow citizens: Every year, by law and by custom, we meet here to consider the state of the union. This year, we gather in this chamber deeply aware of decisive days that lie ahead.

You and I serve our country in a time of great consequence. During this session of Congress, we have the duty to reform domestic programs vital to our country; we have the opportunity to save millions of lives abroad from a terrible disease. We will work for a prosperity that is broadly shared, and we will answer every danger and every enemy that threatens the American people. (Applause.)

In all these days of promise and days of reckoning, we can be confident. In a whirlwind of change and hope and peril, our faith is sure, our resolve is firm, and our union is strong. (Applause.)

This country has many challenges. We will not deny, we will not ignore, we will not pass along our problems to other Congresses, to other presidents, and other generations. (Applause.) We will confront them with focus and clarity and courage.

During the last two years, we have seen what can be accomplished when we work together. To lift the standards of our public schools, we achieved historic education reform -- which must now be carried out in every school and in every classroom, so that every child in America can read and learn and succeed in life. (Applause.) To protect our country, we reorganized our government and created the Department of Homeland Security, which is mobilizing against the threats of a new era. To bring our economy out of recession, we delivered the largest tax relief in a generation. (Applause.) To insist on integrity in American business we passed tough reforms, and we are holding corporate criminals to account. (Applause.)

Some might call this a good record; I call it a good start. Tonight I ask the House and Senate to join me in the next bold steps to serve our fellow citizens.

Our first goal is clear: We must have an economy that grows fast enough to employ every man and woman who seeks a job. (Applause.) After recession, terrorist attacks, corporate scandals and stock market declines, our economy is recovering -- yet it's not growing fast enough, or strongly enough. With unemployment rising, our nation needs more small businesses to open, more companies to invest and expand, more employers to put up the sign that says, "Help Wanted." (Applause.)

Jobs are created when the economy grows; the economy grows when Americans have more money to spend and invest; and the best and fairest way to make sure Americans have that money is not to tax it away in the first place. (Applause.)

I am proposing that all the income tax reductions set for 2004 and 2006 be made permanent and effective this year. (Applause.) And under my plan, as soon as I sign the bill, this extra money will start showing up in workers' paychecks. Instead of gradually reducing the marriage penalty, we should do it now. (Applause.) Instead of slowly raising the child credit to $1,000, we should send the checks to American families now. (Applause.)

The tax relief is for everyone who pays income taxes -- and it will help our economy immediately: 92 million Americans will keep, this year, an average of almost $1,000 more of their own money. A family of four with an income of $40,000 would see their federal income taxes fall from $1,178 to $45 per year. (Applause.) Our plan will improve the bottom line for more than 23 million small businesses.

You, the Congress, have already passed all these reductions, and promised them for future years. If this tax relief is good for Americans three, or five, or seven years from now, it is even better for Americans today. (Applause.)

We should also strengthen the economy by treating investors equally in our tax laws. It's fair to tax a company's profits. It is not fair to again tax the shareholder on the same profits. (Applause.) To boost investor confidence, and to help the nearly 10 million senior who receive dividend income, I ask you to end the unfair double taxation of dividends. (Applause.)

Lower taxes and greater investment will help this economy expand. More jobs mean more taxpayers, and higher revenues to our government. The best way to address the deficit and move toward a balanced budget is to encourage economic growth, and to show some spending discipline in Washington, D.C. (Applause.)

We must work together to fund only our most important priorities. I will send you a budget that increases discretionary spending by 4 percent next year -- about as much as the average family's income is expected to grow. And that is a good benchmark for us. Federal spending should not rise any faster than the paychecks of American families. (Applause.)

A growing economy and a focus on essential priorities will also be crucial to the future of Social Security. As we continue to work together to keep Social Security sound and reliable, we must offer younger workers a chance to invest in retirement accounts that they will control and they will own. (Applause.)

Our second goal is high quality, affordable health care for all Americans. (Applause.) The American system of medicine is a model of skill and innovation, with a pace of discovery that is adding good years to our lives. Yet for many people, medical care costs too much -- and many have no coverage at all. These problems will not be solved with a nationalized health care system that dictates coverage and rations care. (Applause.)

Instead, we must work toward a system in which all Americans have a good insurance policy, choose their own doctors, and seniors and low-income Americans receive the help they need. (Applause.) Instead of bureaucrats and trial lawyers and HMOs, we must put doctors and nurses and patients back in charge of American medicine. (Applause.)

Health care reform must begin with Medicare; Medicare is the binding commitment of a caring society. (Applause.) We must renew that commitment by giving seniors access to preventive medicine and new drugs that are transforming health care in America.

Seniors happy with the current Medicare system should be able to keep their coverage just the way it is. (Applause.) And just like you -- the members of Congress, and your staffs, and other federal employees -- all seniors should have the choice of a health care plan that provides prescription drugs. (Applause.)

My budget will commit an additional $400 billion over the next decade to reform and strengthen Medicare. Leaders of both political parties have talked for years about strengthening Medicare. I urge the members of this new Congress to act this year. (Applause.)

To improve our health care system, we must address one of the prime causes of higher cost, the constant threat that physicians and hospitals will be unfairly sued. (Applause.) Because of excessive litigation, everybody pays more for health care, and many parts of America are losing fine doctors. No one has ever been healed by a frivolous lawsuit. I urge the Congress to pass medical liability reform. (Applause.)

Our third goal is to promote energy independence for our country, while dramatically improving the environment. (Applause.) I have sent you a comprehensive energy plan to promote energy efficiency and conservation, to develop cleaner technology, and to produce more energy at home. (Applause.) I have sent you Clear Skies legislation that mandates a 70-percent cut in air pollution from power plants over the next 15 years. (Applause.) I have sent you a Healthy Forests Initiative, to help prevent the catastrophic fires that devastate communities, kill wildlife, and burn away millions of acres of treasured forest. (Applause.)

I urge you to pass these measures, for the good of both our environment and our economy. (Applause.) Even more, I ask you to take a crucial step and protect our environment in ways that generations before us could not have imagined.

In this century, the greatest environmental progress will come about not through endless lawsuits or command-and-control regulations, but through technology and innovation. Tonight I'm proposing $1.2 billion in research funding so that America can lead the world in developing clean, hydrogen-powered automobiles. (Applause.)

A single chemical reaction between hydrogen and oxygen generates energy, which can be used to power a car -- producing only water, not exhaust fumes. With a new national commitment, our scientists and engineers will overcome obstacles to taking these cars from laboratory to showroom, so that the first car driven by a child born today could be powered by hydrogen, and pollution-free. (Applause.)

Join me in this important innovation to make our air significantly cleaner, and our country much less dependent on foreign sources of energy. (Applause.)

Our fourth goal is to apply the compassion of America to the deepest problems of America. For so many in our country -- the homeless and the fatherless, the addicted -- the need is great. Yet there's power, wonder-working power, in the goodness and idealism and faith of the American people.

Americans are doing the work of compassion every day -- visiting prisoners, providing shelter for battered women, bringing companionship to lonely seniors. These good works deserve our praise; they deserve our personal support; and when appropriate, they deserve the assistance of the federal government. (Applause.)

I urge you to pass both my faith-based initiative and the Citizen Service Act, to encourage acts of compassion that can transform America, one heart and one soul at a time. (Applause.)

Last year, I called on my fellow citizens to participate in the USA Freedom Corps, which is enlisting tens of thousands of new volunteers across America. Tonight I ask Congress and the American people to focus the spirit of service and the resources of government on the needs of some of our most vulnerable citizens -- boys and girls trying to grow up without guidance and attention, and children who have to go through a prison gate to be hugged by their mom or dad.

I propose a $450-million initiative to bring mentors to more than a million disadvantaged junior high students and children of prisoners. Government will support the training and recruiting of mentors; yet it is the men and women of America who will fill the need. One mentor, one person can change a life forever. And I urge you to be that one person. (Applause.)

Another cause of hopelessness is addiction to drugs. Addiction crowds out friendship, ambition, moral conviction, and reduces all the richness of life to a single destructive desire. As a government, we are fighting illegal drugs by cutting off supplies and reducing demand through anti-drug education programs. Yet for those already addicted, the fight against drugs is a fight for their own lives. Too many Americans in search of treatment cannot get it. So tonight I propose a new $600-million program to help an additional 300,000 Americans receive treatment over the next three years. (Applause.)

Our nation is blessed with recovery programs that do amazing work. One of them is found at the Healing Place Church in Baton Rouge, Louisiana. A man in the program said, "God does miracles in people's lives, and you never think it could be you." Tonight, let us bring to all Americans who struggle with drug addiction this message of hope: The miracle of recovery is possible, and it could be you. (Applause.)

By caring for children who need mentors, and for addicted men and women who need treatment, we are building a more welcoming society -- a culture that values every life. And in this work we must not overlook the weakest among us. I ask you to protect infants at the very hour of their birth and end the practice of partial-birth abortion. (Applause.) And because no human life should be started or ended as the object of an experiment, I ask you to set a high standard for humanity, and pass a law against all human cloning. (Applause.)

The qualities of courage and compassion that we strive for in America also determine our conduct abroad. The American flag stands for more than our power and our interests. Our founders dedicated this country to the cause of human dignity, the rights of every person, and the possibilities of every life. This conviction leads us into the world to help the afflicted, and defend the peace, and confound the designs of evil men.

In Afghanistan, we helped liberate an oppressed people. And we will continue helping them secure their country, rebuild their society, and educate all their children -- boys and girls. (Applause.) In the Middle East, we will continue to seek peace between a secure Israel and a democratic Palestine. (Applause.) Across the Earth, America is feeding the hungry -- more than 60 percent of international food aid comes as a gift from the people of the United States. As our nation moves troops and builds alliances to make our world safer, we must also remember our calling as a blessed country is to make this world better.

Today, on the continent of Africa, nearly 30 million people have the AIDS virus -- including 3 million children under the age 15. There are whole countries in Africa where more than one-third of the adult population carries the infection. More than 4 million require immediate drug treatment. Yet across that continent, only 50,000 AIDS victims -- only 50,000 -- are receiving the medicine they need.

Because the AIDS diagnosis is considered a death sentence, many do not seek treatment. Almost all who do are turned away. A doctor in rural South Africa describes his frustration. He says, "We have no medicines. Many hospitals tell people, you've got AIDS, we can't help you. Go home and die." In an age of miraculous medicines, no person should have to hear those words. (Applause.)

AIDS can be prevented. Anti-retroviral drugs can extend life for many years. And the cost of those drugs has dropped from $12,000 a year to under $300 a year -- which places a tremendous possibility within our grasp. Ladies and gentlemen, seldom has history offered a greater opportunity to do so much for so many.

We have confronted, and will continue to confront, HIV/AIDS in our own country. And to meet a severe and urgent crisis abroad, tonight I propose the Emergency Plan for AIDS Relief -- a work of mercy beyond all current international efforts to help the people of Africa. This comprehensive plan will prevent 7 million new

AIDS infections, treat at least 2 million people with life-extending drugs, and provide humane care for millions of people suffering from AIDS, and for children orphaned by AIDS. (Applause.)

I ask the Congress to commit $15 billion over the next five years, including nearly $10 billion in new money, to turn the tide against AIDS in the most afflicted nations of Africa and the Caribbean. (Applause.)

This nation can lead the world in sparing innocent people from a plague of nature. And this nation is leading the world in confronting and defeating the man-made evil of international terrorism. (Applause.)

There are days when our fellow citizens do not hear news about the war on terror. There's never a day when I do not learn of another threat, or receive reports of operations in progress, or give an order in this global war against a scattered network of killers. The war goes on, and we are winning. (Applause.)

To date, we've arrested or otherwise dealt with many key commanders of al Qaeda. They include a man who directed logistics and funding for the September the 11th attacks; the chief of al Qaeda operations in the Persian Gulf, who planned the bombings of our embassies in East Africa and the USS Cole; an al Qaeda operations chief from Southeast Asia; a former director of al Qaeda's training camps in Afghanistan; a key al Qaeda operative in Europe; a major al Qaeda leader in Yemen. All told, more than 3,000 suspected terrorists have been arrested in many countries. Many others have met a different fate. Let's put it this way -- they are no longer a problem to the United States and our friends and allies. (Applause.)

We are working closely with other nations to prevent further attacks. America and coalition countries have uncovered and stopped terrorist conspiracies targeting the American embassy in Yemen, the American embassy in Singapore, a Saudi military base, ships in the Straits of Hormuz and the Straits the Gibraltar. We've broken al Qaeda cells in Hamburg, Milan, Madrid, London, Paris, as well as, Buffalo, New York.

We have the terrorists on the run. We're keeping them on the run. One by one, the terrorists are learning the meaning of American justice. (Applause.)

As we fight this war, we will remember where it began -- here, in our own country. This government is taking unprecedented measures to protect our people and defend our homeland. We've intensified security at the borders and ports of entry, posted more than 50,000 newly-trained federal screeners in airports, begun inoculating troops and first responders against smallpox, and are deploying the nation's first early warning network of sensors to detect biological attack. And this year, for the first time, we are beginning to field a defense to protect this nation against ballistic missiles. (Applause.)

I thank the Congress for supporting these measures. I ask you tonight to add to our future security with a major research and production effort to guard our people against bioterrorism, called Project Bioshield. The budget I send you will propose almost $6 billion to quickly make available effective vaccines and treatments against agents like anthrax, botulinum toxin, Ebola, and plague. We must assume that our enemies would use these diseases as weapons, and we must act before the dangers are upon us. (Applause.)

Since September the 11th, our intelligence and law enforcement agencies have worked more closely than ever to track and disrupt the terrorists. The FBI is improving its ability to analyze intelligence, and is transforming itself to meet new threats. Tonight, I am instructing the leaders of the FBI, the CIA, the Homeland Security, and the Department of Defense to develop a Terrorist Threat Integration Center, to merge and analyze all threat information in a single location. Our government must have the very best information possible, and we will use it to make sure the right people are in the right places to protect all our citizens. (Applause.)

Our war against terror is a contest of will in which perseverance is power. In the ruins of two towers, at the western wall of the Pentagon, on a field in Pennsylvania, this nation made a pledge, and we renew that pledge tonight: Whatever the duration of this struggle, and whatever the difficulties, we will not permit the triumph of violence in the affairs of men -- free people will set the course of history. (Applause.)

1. Today, the gravest danger in the war on terror, the gravest danger facing America and the world, is outlaw regimes that seek and possess nuclear, chemical, and biological weapons. These regimes could use such weapons for blackmail, terror, and mass murder. They could also give or sell those weapons to terrorist allies, who would use them without the least hesitation.

This threat is new; America's duty is familiar. Throughout the 20th century, small groups of men seized control of great nations, built armies and arsenals, and set out to dominate the weak and intimidate the strong. In each case, their ambitions of cruelty and murder had no limit. In each case, the ambitions of Hitlerism, militarism, and communism were defeated by the will of free peoples, by the strength of great alliances, and by the might of the United States of America. (Applause.)

2. Now, in this century, the ideology of power and domination has appeared again, and seeks to gain the ultimate weapons of terror. Once again, this nation and all our friends are all that stand between a world at peace, and a world of chaos and constant alarm. Once again, we are called to defend the safety of our people, and the hopes of all mankind. And we accept this responsibility. (Applause.)

3. America is making a broad and determined effort to confront these dangers. We have called on the United Nations to fulfill its charter and stand by its demand that Iraq disarm. We're strongly supporting the International Atomic Energy Agency in its mission to track and control nuclear materials around the world. We're working with other governments to secure nuclear materials in the former Soviet Union, and to strengthen global treaties banning the production and shipment of missile technologies and weapons of mass destruction.

In all these efforts, however, America's purpose is more than to follow a process -- it is to achieve a result: the end of terrible threats to the civilized world. All free nations have a stake in preventing sudden and catastrophic attacks. And we're asking them to join us, and many are doing so. Yet the course of this nation does not depend on the decisions of others. (Applause.) Whatever action is required, whenever action is necessary, I will defend the freedom and security of the American people. (Applause.)

Different threats require different strategies. In Iran, we continue to see a government that represses its people, pursues weapons of mass destruction, and supports terror. We also see Iranian citizens risking intimidation and death as they speak out for liberty and human rights and democracy. Iranians, like all people, have a right to choose their own government and determine their own destiny -- and the United States supports their aspirations to live in freedom. (Applause.)

On the Korean Peninsula, an oppressive regime rules a people living in fear and starvation. Throughout the 1990s, the United States relied on a negotiated framework to keep North Korea from gaining nuclear weapons. We now know that that regime was deceiving the world, and developing those weapons all along. And today the North Korean regime is using its nuclear program to incite fear and seek concessions. America and the world will not be blackmailed. (Applause.)

4. America is working with the countries of the region -- South Korea, Japan, China, and Russia -- to find a peaceful solution, and to show the North Korean government that nuclear weapons will bring only isolation, economic stagnation, and continued hardship. (Applause.) The North Korean regime will find respect in the world and revival for its people only when it turns away from its nuclear ambitions. (Applause.)

Our nation and the world must learn the lessons of the Korean Peninsula and not allow an even greater threat to rise up in Iraq. A brutal dictator, with a history of reckless aggression, with ties to terrorism, with great potential wealth, will not be permitted to dominate a vital region and threaten the United States. (Applause.)

5. Twelve years ago, Saddam Hussein faced the prospect of being the last casualty in a war he had started and lost. To spare himself, he agreed to disarm of all weapons of mass destruction. For the next 12 years, he systematically violated that agreement. He pursued chemical, biological, and nuclear weapons, even while inspectors were in his country. Nothing to date has restrained him from his pursuit of these weapons -- not economic sanctions, not isolation from the civilized world, not even cruise missile strikes on his military facilities.

Almost three months ago, the United Nations Security Council gave Saddam Hussein his final chance to disarm. He has shown instead utter contempt for the United Nations, and for the opinion of the world. The 108 U.N. inspectors were sent to conduct -- were not sent to conduct a scavenger hunt for hidden materials across a country the size of California. The job of the inspectors is to verify that Iraq's regime is disarming. It is up to Iraq to show exactly where it is hiding its banned weapons, lay those weapons out for the world to see, and destroy them as directed. Nothing like this has happened.

6. The United Nations concluded in 1999 that Saddam Hussein had biological weapons sufficient to produce over 25,000 liters of anthrax -- enough doses to kill several million people. He hasn't accounted for that material. He's given no evidence that he has destroyed it.

7. The United Nations concluded that Saddam Hussein had materials sufficient to produce more than 38,000 liters of botulinum toxin -- enough to subject millions of people to death by respiratory failure. He hadn't accounted for that material. He's given no evidence that he has destroyed it.

8. Our intelligence officials estimate that Saddam Hussein had the materials to produce as much as 500 tons of sarin, mustard and VX nerve agent. In such quantities, these chemical agents could also kill untold thousands. He's not accounted for these materials. He has given no evidence that he has destroyed them.

U.S. intelligence indicates that Saddam Hussein had upwards of 30,000 munitions capable of delivering chemical agents. Inspectors recently turned up 16 of them -- despite Iraq's recent declaration denying their existence. Saddam Hussein has not accounted for the remaining 29,984 of these prohibited munitions. He's given no evidence that he has destroyed them.

From three Iraqi defectors we know that Iraq, in the late 1990s, had several mobile biological weapons labs. These are designed to produce germ warfare agents, and can be moved from place to a place to evade inspectors. Saddam Hussein has not disclosed these facilities. He's given no evidence that he has destroyed them.

9. The International Atomic Energy Agency confirmed in the 1990s that Saddam Hussein had an advanced nuclear weapons development program, had a design for a nuclear weapon and was working on five different methods of enriching uranium for a bomb. The British government has learned that Saddam Hussein recently sought significant quantities of uranium from Africa. Our intelligence sources tell us that he has attempted to purchase high-strength aluminum tubes suitable for nuclear weapons production. Saddam Hussein has not credibly explained these activities. He clearly has much to hide.

The dictator of Iraq is not disarming. To the contrary; he is deceiving. From intelligence sources we know, for instance, that thousands of Iraqi security personnel are at work hiding documents and materials from the U.N. inspectors, sanitizing inspection sites and monitoring the inspectors themselves. Iraqi officials accompany the inspectors in order to intimidate witnesses.

10. Iraq is blocking U-2 surveillance flights requested by the United Nations. Iraqi intelligence officers are posing as the scientists inspectors are supposed to interview. Real scientists have been coached by Iraqi officials on what to say. Intelligence sources indicate that Saddam Hussein has ordered that scientists who cooperate with U.N. inspectors in disarming Iraq will be killed, along with their families.

11. Year after year, Saddam Hussein has gone to elaborate lengths, spent enormous sums, taken great risks to build and keep weapons of mass destruction. But why? The only possible explanation, the only possible use he could have for those weapons, is to dominate, intimidate, or attack.

12. With nuclear arms or a full arsenal of chemical and biological weapons, Saddam Hussein could resume his ambitions of conquest in the Middle East and create deadly havoc in that region. And this Congress and the America people must recognize another threat. <u>Evidence from intelligence sources, secret communications, and statements by people now in custody reveal that Saddam Hussein aids and protects terrorists, including members of al Qaeda.</u> Secretly, and without fingerprints, he could provide one of his hidden weapons to terrorists, or help them develop their own.

Before September the 11th, many in the world believed that Saddam Hussein could be contained. But chemical agents, lethal viruses and shadowy terrorist networks are not easily contained. Imagine those 19 hijackers with other weapons and other plans -- this time armed by Saddam Hussein. It would take one vial, one canister, one crate slipped into this country to bring a day of horror like none we have ever known. We will do everything in our power to make sure that that day never comes. (Applause.)

Some have said we must not act until the threat is imminent. Since when have terrorists and tyrants announced their intentions, politely putting us on notice before they strike? If this threat is permitted to fully and suddenly emerge, all actions, all words, and all recriminations would come too late. Trusting in the sanity and restraint of Saddam Hussein is not a strategy, and it is not an option. (Applause.)

The dictator who is assembling the world's most dangerous weapons has already used them on whole villages -- leaving thousands of his own citizens dead, blind, or disfigured. Iraqi refugees tell us how forced confessions are obtained -- by torturing children while their parents are made to watch. International human rights groups have catalogued other methods used in the torture chambers of Iraq: electric shock, burning with hot irons, dripping acid on the skin, mutilation with electric drills, cutting out tongues, and rape. If this is not evil, then evil has no meaning. (Applause.)

And tonight I have a message for the brave and oppressed people of Iraq: Your enemy is not surrounding your country -- your enemy is ruling your country. (Applause.) And the day he and his regime are removed from power will be the day of your liberation. (Applause.)

The world has waited 12 years for Iraq to disarm. America will not accept a serious and mounting threat to our country, and our friends and our allies. The United States will ask the U.N. Security Council to convene on February the 5th to consider the facts of Iraq's ongoing defiance of the world. Secretary of State Powell will present information and intelligence about Iraqi's legal -- Iraq's illegal weapons programs, its attempt to hide those weapons from inspectors, and its links to terrorist groups.

We will consult. But let there be no misunderstanding: If Saddam Hussein does not fully disarm, for the safety of our people and for the peace of the world, we will lead a coalition to disarm him. (Applause.)

Tonight I have a message for the men and women who will keep the peace, members of the American Armed Forces: Many of you are assembling in or near the Middle East, and some crucial hours may lay ahead. In those hours, the success of our cause will depend on you. Your training has prepared you. Your honor will guide you. You believe in America, and America believes in you. (Applause.)

Sending Americans into battle is the most profound decision a President can make. The technologies of war have changed; the risks and suffering of war have not. For the brave Americans who bear the risk, no victory is free from sorrow. This nation fights reluctantly, because we know the cost and we dread the days of mourning that always come.

We seek peace. We strive for peace. And sometimes peace must be defended. A future lived at the mercy of terrible threats is no peace at all. If war is forced upon us, we will fight in a just cause and by just means -- sparing, in every way we can, the innocent. And if war is forced upon us, we will fight with the full force and might of the United States military -- and we will prevail. (Applause.)

And as we and our coalition partners are doing in Afghanistan, we will bring to the Iraqi people food and medicines and supplies -- and freedom. (Applause.)

Many challenges, abroad and at home, have arrived in a single season. In two years, America has gone from a sense of invulnerability to an awareness of peril; from bitter division in small matters to calm unity in great causes. And we go forward with confidence, because this call of history has come to the right country.

Americans are a resolute people who have risen to every test of our time. Adversity has revealed the character of our country, to the world and to ourselves. America is a strong nation, and honorable in the use of our strength. We exercise power without conquest, and we sacrifice for the liberty of strangers.

Americans are a free people, who know that freedom is the right of every person and the future of every nation. The liberty we prize is not America's gift to the world, it is God's gift to humanity. (Applause.)

We Americans have faith in ourselves, but not in ourselves alone. We do not know -- we do not claim to know all the ways of Providence, yet we can trust in them, placing our confidence in the loving God behind all of life, and all of history.

May He guide us now. And may God continue to bless the United States of America. (Applause.)

END 10:08 P.M. EST

State of the Union Comments

1. President Bush here implies that there is no distinction between states and terrorist groups. It is a subtle way to link Saddam Hussein's Iraq with Osama bin Laden's Al Qaeda without presenting evidence, and also a scare tactic. The phrase "outlaw regimes" (rendered on other occasions as "outlaw states") also begs for examination. Regardless of how oppressive governments have been in *any* of the nations that Bush grouped as an "Axis of Evil" in 2002 (Iraq, Iran, North Korea), no legal proceeding in any international body or nation has declared these states "outlaws." In international law, every state has equal legitimacy and standing. George Bush has unilaterally declared these nations "outlaws."

2. President Bush here suggests an ultimate conflict, like the struggles he has invoked in the previous text with Hitler or in the Cold War. No such conflict actually existed with Iraq. Saddam Hussein's Ba'athist movement in Iraq had no particular "ideology of power and domination," no march to take over the world. Even Bin Laden's Al Qaeda has a religious agenda which, though it operates in many respects like an ideology, is about instituting a religious revolution, not domination and power. At a minimum this is overblown rhetoric. Its aim is to group Saddam's Iraq together with Bin Laden's Al Qaeda and insinuate that Iraq forms part of a global threat.

3. President Bush's claim of strong support for the international weapons monitors does not match actual U.S. behavior vis-à-vis the IAEA and UNMOVIC, as the narrative above has shown in some detail.

4. Note the inversion of the magnitude of the supposed threats. The CIA has believed North Korea to have one or two nuclear weapons since the mid-1990s. North Korea has also flight-tested a missile to an actual range greater than 1,000 miles, and was estimated to be designing a missile capable of reaching the western part of the United States. During the prelude to the Iraq war, North Korea publicly admitted to having nuclear weapons, stated it would restart fissile materials production and abrogate its moratorium on missile flight tests, and made verbal threats against the United States. Granted that these developments have been assessed as bids to get Washington's attention, North Korea had far more significant capabilities, the criteria on which the Bush administration based its policies. Yet here Iraq can be "an even greater threat."

5. UN Security Council resolution 687, originally establishing the Iraq disarmament commission, the requirements Saddam was to fulfill, and the economic sanctions,

had been passed on April 3, 1991. As of the State of the Union, only eleven years had passed, a number President Bush had cited correctly in his UN General Assembly and Cincinnati speeches in September–October 2002. The Bush administration's drive to maximize its charges against Iraq applied even to simple matters.

6. Anthrax is a biological agent (weapon); "weapons" do not produce anthrax. If the error was inadvertent, it indicates a careless approach to this serious question; if deliberate, it is further evidence of how Bush was appealing to fear. In his Cincinnati speech, Bush had said the UN had concluded Iraq had sufficient precursors to produce 60,000–120,000 liters of anthrax, a wild exaggeration that someone clearly caught. It is reported here as 25,000 liters.

7. The correction in the anthrax number is matched here by a fresh misrepresentation, this time of the administration's own numbers. Six weeks earlier, on December 19, 2002, the State/CIA fact sheet item on botulinum toxin claimed Iraq had enough materials to produce 1,200 liters of the toxin. The 1,200 figure would be repeated without change in the WHIG paper "What Does Disarmament Look Like," which the White House released just days before the State of the Union speech. The increase here is more than *3,000 percent*. In the desire to pin black hats on the Iraqis, either the president misspoke, his speechwriters exaggerated wildly, or the administration purposefully went beyond any of its intelligence data.

8. The U.S. National Intelligence Estimate projected the Iraqi chemical stockpile with some confidence ("probably") at 100 tons and with much less confidence ("possibly") at up to 500 tons. The language in the State of the Union address obscures the lower figure and suggests greater confidence overall, with the scarier higher figure the only number mentioned. (This topic is discussed in some detail in coverage of the CIA white paper above. For a discussion of the 30,000 munitions in the next paragraph see the section on the State Department/CIA fact sheet.)

9. This passage became infamous as the "Sixteen Words." A major analysis of this issue follows this speech. Bush then proceeds to add the aluminum tubes claim for his grand slam. On the general issue of uranium enrichment, methods include gaseous diffusion, electrolytic separation, centrifuge, electromagnetic (using calutrons), and laser separation. Iraq in 2002 was not utilizing five methods of enrichment, nor had it been doing so even in the 1990s as Bush avers. The operative word in Bush's sentence in the State of the Union has to be "was." Iraq had abandoned laser methods before the Gulf War of 1990–91, had never

done serious work on gaseous diffusion or electrolytic methods, had buried its centrifuge plans, and imports of aluminum tubes and magnets (for purposes that remain in dispute) were the sole evidence of work on electromagnetic separation.

10. Iraq was negotiating with the UN inspectors on rules to govern U-2 flights, and the matter remained in contention for over a month after this speech. There was some substance to the U.S. objections here, but immediately thereafter President Bush makes fresh extravagant claims about Saddam ordering the murder of scientists who allow themselves to be interviewed by the UN inspectors.

11. Domination was not the only possible purpose for Iraqi weapons of mass destruction. Prestige is often cited as a possible reason for acquiring nuclear weapons, as is deterrence. As CIA director Tenet put it to the Senate Armed Services Committee in his annual testimony on global threats, just six months before the September 11 attacks, Saddam could be seeking "a renewed WMD capability both for credibility and because every other strong regime in the area either has it or is pursuing it." Incidentally, at that time, hardly a year before Iraq would be claimed as the paramount threat to the United States, the CIA assessed the Iraqi economic infrastructure as "in long-term decline." A few months after the U.S. invasion, a former UN chief inspector speculated that Saddam might have wanted to pretend to weapons of mass destruction, that is, leverage the fears that ambiguity about his weapons created abroad, as a way to deter enemies. If so, that was a serious miscalculation.

12. Allegations regarding Saddam's relationships with terrorists, particularly Al Qaeda, are an important subject and are addressed following our presentation of the UN Security Council speech by secretary of state Colin Powell below.

The Uranium from Niger

Coming back to work after the New Year, Niger diplomats in Rome discovered on January 2, 2001, that a break-in had taken place at their embassy. A watch and two bottles of perfume were missing and the office had been scoured pretty thoroughly. The real target of the burglary may have been official stationary and letterheads. In any case, some rogue concocted a set of five documents and sold them to the Italian military intelligence service. A couple of years earlier Wissam al-Zahawie, Iraq's ambassador to Italy, had visited four West African nations including Niger. The documents purported to be official correspondence from the Niger government of that time concerning a sale of 500 tons of uranium ore to Iraq. One version of the story has it that the Italian intelligence service, known as SISMI, purchased the documents from a Niger diplomat eager to make a buck and aware of Al-Zahawie's trip. In any case, SISMI passed along the substance of the report to British and U.S. intelligence. An official statement from CIA director Tenet in July 2003 confirms that the CIA received "fragmentary intelligence" about an Iraqi uranium deal in Africa in late 2001 and early 2002.

The CIA was still wrestling with what to do with this information in February 2002, when Vice President Richard Cheney's office asked for its evaluation of the report. The agency decided to make a more thorough investigation, sending someone to Niger to check the reports out on the ground. According to columnist Robert D. Novak, agency officer Valerie Plame suggested her husband, Joseph C. Wilson, for the mission. Wilson, a retired diplomat, had been U.S. chargé in Baghdad just before the Gulf War and was instrumental in securing the release of American hostages then held by Saddam. He had worked at the White House on African affairs with the Clinton NSC staff, then as ambassador to Gabon, from where he retired in 1998. Most important, Wilson had served in Niger early in his State Department career. All these things made him a good choice for the inquiry mission. Officials at CIA, questioned by Novak about the idea that Plame had suggested to her husband, responded that Wilson had been selected by agency counterproliferation officials. Most likely that would have been Alan Foley of WINPAC. Uncomfortable with meddling from Vice President Cheney, Foley had gone to a former official who had a good reputation with the president's father and whose report might be expected to pass unchallenged. Plame was simply asked to contact her husband. Either way, Wilson took on the assignment.

Ambassador Wilson confirms that Plame merely contacted him on behalf of the CIA. At first asked merely to share his expertise on Niger, which was considerable, Wilson went to CIA headquarters and met with a group of about a dozen people, some from CIA, some from the State Department.

He recounts that he recognized no one, though a couple of participants introduced themselves as having attended other briefings he had presented. Afterward Wilson was asked to take on the mission. He made the trip after consulting with the State Department, and met with U.S. ambassador to Niger Barbro Owens-Kirkpatrick the morning after his arrival in late February 2003. For the next eight days Wilson met with Niger government officials, former officials, embassy officers, and persons in the uranium industry. Owens-Kirkpatrick knew about the rumored uranium deal and believed she had already debunked it in her cables to Washington. Wilson met with his contacts, among whom one former official said he was not aware of any deal signed by Niger and Iraq during his tenure. The same official stated he had been approached in June 1999 by a businessman who asked him to meet with an Iraqi delegation with a view to increasing trade between the countries, which he interpreted as an approach regarding uranium. Overall, however, Wilson found no substance to the reports, and returned to Washington early in March.

In the summer of 2003, after the "Sixteen Words" from the State of the Union address became controversial, Bush administration officials anonymously claimed the CIA had never shared its doubts about the uranium story. That brought an instant counter from the agency, a leak that in fact a two-page report had been circulated in Washington on March 9. In the war of leaks that then embroiled the capital it came out that the CIA report may not have seemed authoritative because it did not mention ambassador Wilson by name or detail his investigative efforts. But the report did circulate, and there were also the cables from ambassador Owens-Kirkpatrick. Wilson himself did not write a detailed report, but he recounted his mission in detail both to a CIA reports officer and at the State Department. He believes there must have been at least three documents in addition to the CIA report: a set of observations from Owens-Kirkpatrick based on their conversations before and after his investigation, a record of his State Department debriefing, and the reply made to Vice President Cheney based on his mission at the behest of the CIA (the latter, Wilson acknowledges, could have been an oral briefing). There may also have been a report from Marine General Carlton Fulford, who had passed through Niger when ambassador Owens-Kirkpatrick had originally been looking into this matter, and who had reportedly agreed with her conclusion there was no substance to the claims.

In any case, the rumored Iraqi deal was unlikely on its face. Uranium—high-grade ore, to be sure—had been discovered in Niger in the 1960s a couple of hundred miles north of the town of Agades. A mining company, Somair, formed as a joint venture between the Niger government and French interests, including as a shareholder the French Atomic Energy Commission. Site preparations for a strip mine began in 1968, and the first ore extraction came two years later. A new consortium, Cominak, including Spanish, German, and Japanese interests, started a second mine later. With public unease regarding nuclear power, the market for uranium came near collapse during the 1980s, with the net result that the owners of these mines monopolized their output. Moreover, all the governments involved cooperate with the International Atomic Energy Agency, which is very good at tracking inventories of fissile materials worldwide. These consortia operated without direct participation by the Nigerien government. Their partners set production objectives at annual meetings, then reviewed progress every two months or so. The government of Niger merely collected taxes on the output. Ambassador Wilson succinctly states in an opinion piece in the *New York Times* the difficulties that would have faced Iraq if it had wanted some of the ore: "Because the two mines are closely regulated, quasi-governmental entities, selling uranium would require the approval of the minister of mines, the prime minister, and probably the president. In short, there's simply too much oversight over too small an industry for a sale to have transpired." Any such transaction would also have had to be published in the official journal of the Niger government. In addition the Niger ore output was already under contract for years into the future, primarily to France and Japan. Wilson spoke to officials whose signatures would have been required for such a transaction, and all denied any such thing had occurred. Officials also explained to him how it would be practically impossible to divert uranium ore illicitly.

The story next unfolds in London where, in June, the British heard something about uranium from Niger. The British signals intelligence service,

Government Communications Headquarters (GCHQ), had some intercepts from the Iraqi ambassador's 1999 visit that lent credence to the report. From early September the highest British intelligence analytical authority, the Joint Intelligence Committee (JIC), under John Scarlett, in collaboration with prime minister Tony Blair's staff at 10 Downing Street, were assembling their Iraq dossier. Scarlett and JIC were in touch with the CIA about the prospective British dossier, and analysts at WINPAC noted a reference to the uranium transaction. The CIA recommended to the British that this material be deleted from the dossier. The British replied they were confident in their intelligence and kept the item in their paper. Scarlett also resisted pressure coming in the other direction. About a week before the British moved to publication, Alastair Campbell, communications director for 10 Downing Street, in his role shepherding the dossier in the direction Tony Blair wanted, tried to get Scarlett to revise the draft to say Iraq had actually procured the uranium ore. Scarlett insisted the evidence could not sustain such a claim. The British paper published on September 24 contained two references to the ore, in the body of the paper and in the executive summary. The latter reads, among the bullets of what Iraq had supposedly done, "sought significant quantities of uranium from Africa, despite having no active civil nuclear power program that could require it." (Note the wording of the first part of this item, which is identical to what President Bush said in his State of the Union address. The British *did not* say, however, that Iraq had done that "recently," as Bush did. Actually Iraq had bought some uranium ore from Niger in the 1980s.)

Unlike the United States, where public investigation of the CIA white paper or the other intelligence items involved in the hoodwinking has been resisted, in Great Britain there has been an official parliamentary inquiry into the Iraq dossier. The Intelligence and Security Committee of Parliament finds that "the claim that Iraq had expressed an intention to obtain uranium in Africa was not included in JIC assessments prior to September 2002." The explanation provided by the Secret Intelligence Service (SIS) was that the information came to it in June and the JIC made no analyses between then and the September dossier, when there was also a second piece of intelligence. Sir Richard Dearlove, the director of SIS, attributed his information to two sources, one of them documentary. The report notes: "The sources were uncertain whether contracts had been signed or if uranium had actually been shipped to Iraq." The SIS continues to believe its information and the parliamentary committee found its basis reasonable.

The timing and nature of the intelligence to the British is the key to understanding these conclusions. Information from June corresponds to the time when the Italian intelligence service could have been circulating the substance of the Niger material without the documentation. France, the former colonial power in Niger, also had major sources in that country and could alternatively have been the source for the June report. The September time frame was when documents were becoming available, which SIS may have acquired either from the Italian service or from a journalist (about which more in a moment). It is noteworthy that once the purported uranium deal documents had been discredited by the International Atomic Energy Agency, the source that had given the documents to SIS and had been asked to check their authenticity had not, by the fall of 2003, been able to do so. These indications suggest that SIS holds to its position owing to its confidence in liaison relationships with sister services, not because of the veracity of the reports themselves.

Meanwhile in America, the intelligence community was moving to complete its National Intelligence Estimate (NIE) on Iraq's weapons of mass destruction, as we have seen earlier. The NIE contained several paragraphs in its discussion of the Iraqi uranium ore stockpile, and reference to the Niger story appeared in that passage. In his statement, director Tenet quotes those references: "A foreign government service reported that as of early 2001, Niger planned to send several tons of pure 'uranium' (probably yellowcake) to Iraq. As of early 2001, Niger and Iraq reportedly were still working out the arrangements for this deal, which could be for up to 500 tons of yellowcake." The State Department's Bureau of Intelligence and Research dissented from this text, terming the report "highly dubious." Even the consensus view of the NIE admitted, "We do not know the status of this arrangement."

Much as the British had used the Niger story, so too did the Bush administration. Secretary of State Colin Powell has been identified as mentioning it in a closed hearing on Capitol Hill on September 26. It is disturbing that Powell was favorably citing a report that his own intel people found dubious. Although Tenet has denied this, multiple sources maintain that Tenet and his deputy, John McLaughlin, referred to Niger uranium in two congressional briefings shortly before the Powell appearance. That was on September 24. National Intelligence Officer Robert Walpole, lead drafter of the NIE, attended that briefing and answered questions, one of which concerned the CIA's view of the Niger uranium allegation in the British dossier. There are conflicting accounts of what Walpole said. Two sources maintain that Walpole expressed no doubts about the information in the British report. Another source, at CIA, apparently told reporters of questions regarding the accuracy of the British claim. And then there would be the presidential speech to the Veterans of Foreign Wars at Cincinnati scheduled for October 7. That Tenet and CIA worked to keep the Niger story out of that speech (see Chapter 4) is an indication that the uranium report was deemed unable to withstand public scrutiny.

Director Tenet insisted in his July 2003 statement that the Niger story was just not that important. It did not figure among the six reasons the NIE gave for its key judgment that Iraq had reconstituted its nuclear weapons program, and the Niger uranium got no mention in the CIA white paper "because it was not fundamental to the judgment that Iraq was reconstituting its nuclear weapons program." But at the White House, Niger represented a scare story that could make its case for war more concrete. That was why it appeared in drafts of the Cincinnati speech, and arguably why it reappeared in the State of the Union afterward.

Tenet also admits, "We had questions about some of the reporting," a clear allusion to the Wilson mission, the attempt to get the British not to use the material, and the disputed national estimate. Those doubts would only increase. It turns out an Italian journalist had the same information that Italian intelligence had acquired. Elisabetta Burba of the newsweekly *Panorama* got documents referring to a sale of uranium ore by Niger to Iraq. Burba was initially unable to confirm the papers. Whether concocted by a Niger diplomat on the make or, according to another version, by former CIA officers who wanted the Bush people to fool themselves with the fabrication and then be embarrassed by the hoax, the documents gave the Niger story new legs. Though tempted by the potential for a worldwide scoop, Burba herself understood that publishing a hoax could end her career. Her editor wanted authentication, so Burba gave copies of the documents to the U.S. embassy in Rome on October 11. Then she traveled to Niger to investigate, in much the same way as had Joseph Wilson. Meanwhile, the U.S. ambassador handed copies of the documents to the CIA chief of station, who for some reason never forwarded the Niger documents to headquarters. Nevertheless, it is reported that on October 16 in Washington, the State Department's Bureau of Intelligence and Research circulated copies of the documents to agencies including the CIA, with the comment that they seemed to be of "dubious authenticity." The later White House claim that the CIA did not have these documents when the State of the Union was being drafted is thus demonstrably false.

The question then becomes: How could the State Department and the CIA agree to such an item in the fact sheet they released on December 19 to discredit Baghdad's comprehensive disclosure? We now know that State's intelligence branch thought the Niger story hokey enough both to dissent on an NIE and to include a disclaimer with the documents it circulated, and that the department had received rejections of the story both from its ambassador to Niger and from Joseph Wilson. The CIA's center, WINPAC, had that same data, and George Tenet tells us, had questions about the reporting on Niger. My speculation would be that the answer involves the White House.

Both Niger and Iraq denied having any dealings on uranium as soon as the fact sheet appeared.

All of which brings us back to the January 2003 State of the Union address and the "Sixteen Words." When he heard Bush's words, recently retired State Department intelligence analyst Greg Thielmann was astonished. He recounts his reaction to reporters for *Newsweek*: "Not that stupid piece of garbage. My thought was, how did that get into the speech?" The preparation and delivery of that speech have already been described. What is important here is that the occasion represented the second instance of the Bush administration's using the Niger story, and that had international repercussions. In Vienna at the International Atomic Energy Agency (IAEA), Mohamed El-Baradei had requested copies of the Niger documents as soon as the United States issued its December fact sheet. ElBaradei received nothing between then and the State of the Union address, a period of more than a month, except assurances from the U.S. embassy that his request had been forwarded to Washington. ElBaradei promptly renewed his request after the State of the Union. On February 4, the head of IAEA's Iraq Nuclear Verification Office, Jacques Baute, was about to leave for New York to join ElBaradei and hear Colin Powell's presentation to the Security Council when his office finally received an oral briefing from the Americans on the Niger documents. Just a briefing, no documents. Baute made an official complaint through UN-MOVIC, again asking for the documents. The IAEA actually received the papers while Baute was in America. The United States provided no specific comments with them.

With another interim report on the Iraq inspections due in mid-February, it was not until later in the month that Baute was able to focus on the authenticity of the Niger documents. The material included an alleged agreement for the delivery of two lots of 500 tons of ore each, over a two-year span. Checking records and making commercial inquiries, Baute established within ten days that the alleged agreement could not have been honored. Using Internet searches, within a single workday, he also demonstrated that the documents themselves were obvious forgeries.

Among the anomalies the IAEA found were discontinued letterheads, wrong dates, and forged signatures. One letter referred to the 1965 constitution of Niger where a new constitution had been in force since August 9, 1999. A letter dated October 2000 bore the signature of the man who had been foreign minister of Niger in 1988. A legal ordinance was cited that had been enacted in 1974 rather than the date in the letter, July 2000. Jacques Baute went back to the U.S. mission and asked for any other evidence the Americans or British might have, anything that might bear on authenticity. Nothing came.

(The fact that British intelligence also had the opportunity to present evidence on the accuracy of the Niger story but chose not to dispute the IAEA's findings of forgery is a telling comment on continued claims in Britain that SIS stands behind the Niger story.)

Mohammed ElBaradei reported his findings to the Security Council on March 7: "Based on thorough analysis, the IAEA has concluded, with the concurrence of outside experts, that these documents—which formed the basis for the recent reports of uranium transactions between Iraq and Niger—are in fact not authentic." The IAEA had also discussed the issue with both Iraq and Niger, and Saddam's government had given the inspectors "a comprehensive explanation of its relations with Niger," including the 1999 trip by its ambassador to Italy. ElBaradei further reported his agency's overall conclusion that "there is no indication that Iraq has attempted to import uranium since 1990."

The Bush administration rejoinder came from Vice President Cheney on March 16. During a television appearance Cheney dismissed the work of this UN inspection agency, saying, "I think Mr. ElBaradei frankly is wrong." Cheney then swung into a savage denunciation: "If you look at the track record of the International Atomic Energy Agency and this kind of issue, especially where Iraq is concerned, they have consistently underestimated or missed what it was Saddam Hussein was doing. I don't have any reason to believe they're any more valid this time than they've been in the past. We believe he has, in fact, reconstituted nuclear weapons."

This exchange shows in sharp relief the essential tactic of the Bush administration: as each of its claims disintegrated, they would brand those who demolished the charges as fools, dupes, victims of disinformation, or worse.

On March 19, the day America went to war, the IAEA struck back with further commentary in a document presenting the work program it would have followed had there been no conflict. ElBaradei's paper noted that there had been no outstanding issues with respect to Iraq's nuclear programs as of December 1998—all nuclear materials were accounted for, there were no signs of successful efforts to make nuclear weapons, Iraqi indigenous production of fissile material had amounted to only a few grams, Baghdad's progress in its main areas of effort (electromagnetic separation and centrifuge enrichment) had been stopped to the point where Iraq had no physical capability for production of significant quantities of weapons-grade material, and Iraqi weaponization still faced hurdles. The IAEA now argued that Baghdad could have achieved little in the intervening years, reiterating that its monitors had found nothing in the new round of inspections to indicate Iraq was any further along than before.

The collapse of the Niger story still did not incline the Bush people to stop making claims about Iraqi imports of uranium ore, even after the war, when U.S. military and intelligence officers could range all over the country themselves and yet found none of these materials. A California congressman, Henry A. Waxman, played a key role in pressing the Bush administration to explain its use of the Niger story, as well as other aspects of the prewar intelligence, repeatedly sending letters to President Bush, Condoleezza Rice, Colin Powell, and others. By early July 2003 the administration had come under increasing pressure to explain its basis for the uranium charges. This time officials shifted to argue that Bush did not need the Niger allegations to make the charge that had been in the "Sixteen Words." As National Security Council spokesman Michael N. Anton put it on July 8, "The documents alleging a transaction between Iraq and Niger were not the sole basis for the line in the President's State of the Union speech."

The new version was a reference to two other African countries that had been mentioned in the NIE of 2002, Somalia and the Democratic Republic of the Congo. But the intelligence grounds for that contention were dubious at best. The Democratic Republic of the Congo (formerly Zaire) had been known as a uranium source since its days as a Belgian colony. But that nation was emerging from, or perhaps still embroiled in, civil war. The government had minimal control over the part of the country where the mines were located, the rebels had no control over the means of transportation and ports required to ship uranium ore, and all hands were busy competing for power in desultory negotiations. A UN mission being installed in the Congo along with international peacekeeping forces could be expected to take a dim view of uranium exports to Iraq.

As for Somalia, even more than the Congo its government had fallen into decrepitude. The warlords who had bedeviled the U.S. humanitarian intervention of the early 1990s remained in place and were essentially as strong as ever, with an interim national government formed several years ago possessing only nominal authority. Uranium shipments required security and stability of which Somalia had little. Uranium deposits have been known to exist in Somalia at least since the 1970s, but that impoverished land invested little in development even before the warlord period, and even less now. Standard references note that Somalia's mineral wealth remains unexploited. The 2001 edition of the CIA's own reference, *The World Factbook*, notes Somalia's principal exports as bananas and livestock, with the latter alone accounting for 65 percent of export earnings. There are no mineral exports at all. The industrial sector, actually focused on processing of agricultural products, is mostly shut down, companies are printing their own money, and the telecommunications system was completely destroyed in the civil war. In the 1970s, foreign corporations had licenses to explore for oil; in 2001 the petroleum refining industry is recorded as mostly shut down. The idea that Saddam Hussein could be buying uranium in Somalia is laughable. Moreover, not a shred of evidence has been presented to support allegations of Iraqi uranium purchases in either country.

Press accounts of later testimony to Congress by Dr. David Kay, technical director of the American weapons experts who scoured Iraq for weapons of mass destruction after the war, indicate not only that searchers found no evidence of any Iraqi uranium ore deal with Niger, but that Baghdad *rejected* an offer of ore from another, as yet unidentified, country.

With the collapse of the Niger story, George Bush's deception on the Iraqi threat began to unravel, a part of the tale reserved for our final chapter. But there is still one piece that needs mention here, one which goes back to the Wilson mission. Ambassador Joseph Wilson went public with his knowledge in early July 2003. Only a short time afterward, on July 14 to be precise, Robert Novak's column, already briefly cited here, publicly identified Valerie Plame as a member of the CIA's clandestine service. Plame's ability to take on overseas covert assignments, and perhaps even her safety, were thereby compromised. Under the Intelligence Identities Protection Act of 1982 it is a federal crime for an official to reveal the identity of a serving covert officer of the CIA. If the official holds current security clearances, such revelation may entail additional crimes. In his original column Novak reported that two senior members of the Bush administration called him up to encourage him to tell what they termed the real story, which they saw as the connection of the CIA's Plame with Wilson and the Niger mission, as if that set up a predetermined conclusion. The Novak column essentially documented a crime—revelation of a CIA covert officer's name. It has since been reported that the two officials shopped this story to six different journalists before Novak wrote his piece, which used Plame's name, although he did not accept the spin the leakers wished to put on the Niger business. Clearly the Bush people wanted their version of the Iraq intelligence story to dominate the public debate and were ready to play hardball to intimidate anyone who felt tempted to blow the whistle.

Within days of the Novak column the Central Intelligence Agency had referred the incident to the Justice Department for investigation into the leak of Plame's name, and had begun its own internal inquiry as to whether any of its sources abroad were endangered by the revelation. In late September 2003 it emerged that the Justice Department is actively investigating the White House in connection with this crime. At this writing the investigation is ongoing.

6

The Sting

The Bush administration wasted no time after the State of the Union, preparing its right uppercut, the third punch in its plan to reverse the growing opposition to a war with Iraq. There are reports that President Bush actually made his final decision to invade in late January 2003, but as yet there is no confirmation. The timing is reported to have been for late February, but was delayed at the request of the British. What is demonstrable is that the Bush people worked feverishly to lay the groundwork for that invasion. Unfortunately for Bush, his haphazard diplomacy the previous year required him to return to the UN Security Council to secure a new resolution freeing him to conduct war. Bush needed the Council to judge Iraq as in violation of the resolution governing the new weapons inspections, thus activating the punishments promised for that eventuality: The road to Baghdad lay through New York.

Especially tragic from this period is George Bush's refusal to hear the steadily rising expressions of opposition to the war, and the numerous foreign contacts warning they could not support an Iraqi war. Unwilling to grant a longer timetable for UN weapons inspectors, Bush was rushing to war. It is clear that additional inspections would have established there was no Iraqi threat. Instead Bush wanted to hurry in order to invade Iraq before the high summer heat made military action much more difficult.

This punch utilized Secretary of State Colin L. Powell, the most credible Bush administration official. Reports are that the Powell presentation was originally suggested by State's then-policy planning chief, Richard N. Haass. Powell, the general who had masterminded the confrontation with Saddam in the first Gulf War, could hardly be questioned on his warcraft. Powell had previously sat in the Reagan White House during the so-called "tanker war," a part of the Iran-Iraq war of the 1980s, when Iraq had tried to interdict oil exports from Iran by attacking shipping in the Persian Gulf. General Powell's experience as chairman of the Joint Chiefs of Staff in the Gulf War, and as deputy national security adviser for Ronald Reagan, had taught him the importance of international cooperation and alliances. He had deliberately sought out the opportunity to assume the helm of America's diplomatic ship at the State Department. Widely regarded as the level-headed one among Bush's advisers, Powell had traction. The president bet that if Colin Powell went to the Security Council with a tale of Iraqi perfidy, people would listen and decide it must be true. The Americans could move for their UN resolution immediately afterward, again using Great Britain to table the actual motion, avoiding whatever antipathy there might be for a military action directly fostered by the United States.

For Secretary Powell to have maximum impact at the UN Security Council, he not only had to have a bill of particulars to present, he had also to believe in what he was saying. The contents of the speech draft therefore had to satisfy Powell first. Thus, preparations for the speech went far beyond the usual vetting process. Powell wanted to be personally satisfied about each charge he made, while the Bush administration had to be comfortable with Powell's making them. The desire for new intelligence to spark Powell's rhetoric also led to an intense push to declassify recent items for the speech.

Preparations went on in tandem with those for the State of the Union. For example, on January 25, as Bush's speechwriters entered the home stretch, Condi Rice held an important session at the White House where officials bandied about items they wanted included in the Powell speech. The most important presentation heard in the Situation Room that day would come from I. Lewis ("Scooter") Libby, Vice President Cheney's chief of staff and de facto national security adviser, who offered up a smorgasbord of charges against Iraq from which Powell could pick and choose. Stephen Hadley participated and said later that Libby had so much on his plate he could not get through all the material in the time allotted. Among Libby's biggest concerns was to make sure Powell insist there had been a connection between Saddam and the September 11 attacks. Following the meeting, a forty-five-page summary of Libby's menu was written up and sent to Powell for his own speechwriters. There were also thirty-eight pages on alleged links to terrorism and another sixteen on Iraqi human rights abuses.

The next stop was CIA headquarters in Langley, Virginia. In a conference room next door to director Tenet's office, an array of people gathered on January 31 to begin reviewing the intelligence that would go into Powell's speech. Secretary Powell himself would wade through the whole morass. This was a "murder board," an exercise in which the object is to pick holes in a briefing or plan, a common military practice that Powell here adapted to diplomacy. Condoleezza Rice attended the first day, and later dipped in when she could, especially for the speech rehearsals. The NSC staff would be in constant attendance. Cheney and Donald Rumsfeld were also represented. George Tenet and John McLaughlin headed the CIA contingent.

Powell knew he had a problem. A month earlier, in December, Powell's INR staff had briefed to him the results of a major review on intelligence on possible Iraqi weapons of mass destruction that had concluded, essentially, that there weren't any. The secretary had already gone beyond his intelligence experts in public claims about Iraqi nuclear weapons. Then, the day before meetings began on the speech draft, Colin Powell learned from his chief of staff that his own people were saying the intelligence community lacked data to back up various assertions the administration wanted to make. Powell, who was also determined to make his Security Council presentation visual, had another problem too—no overhead photography existed for some of the things he wanted to show, while the best satellite pictures in every case were highly classified.

By Secretary Powell's own account, he worked until midnight three nights and stayed late a fourth to get through all the issues. There were six days of meetings in all, including five dress rehearsals. One evening, February 2, the group ordered in pizza to fuel their debates. Part of the time the issue fell between Powell and the CIA people. He would call out an issue and Tenet or McLaughlin would give the CIA's position. If they did not know the material well enough, other analysts walked the senior officials through their collected evidence. As Powell recalled, "There were a lot of cigars lit. I didn't want any going off in my face or the president's face." Another time Powell put the same thought more formally: "I knew that it was the credibility of the United States that was going to be on the line on the fifth of February. The credibility of the President of the United States and my credibility." Powell's task proved formidable in every way.

Among the more obstinate helpers, Dick Cheney's staff fought hard to retain every item on their list. Scooter Libby clung like a bulldog. The nickname, bestowed by a doting father watching the toddler crawl away from his crib, captures Libby's qualities as an operator quite well. A conservative lawyer, Libby and his deputy on the Cheney staff were the counsellors to the Cox Commission of the late 1990s, a congressionally appointed panel that made the case that China had been systematically looting U.S. technology. Certain aerospace corporations were the poster children for these claims, but other times corporations were beneficiaries of Libby's skills. As a lawyer he was known as a protégé of Leonard P. Garment, prominent as Richard Nixon's attorney in the Watergate scandal.

Scooter joined Cheney's vice presidential staff at fifty, but he was no stranger to the VP, nor to national security, probably Libby's main interest. A decade earlier he had been with Cheney at the Pentagon. He and Paul Wolfowitz collaborated on a notorious policy paper in 1992 that prescribed a national security strategy of U.S. preeminence, a close foreshadowing of what became George W. Bush's strategy. Libby had also long advocated the overthrow of Saddam Hussein, being among the signatories of the 1998 open letter to Clinton that served partly as a neo-con manifesto. From his office suite on the second floor of the Eisenhower Executive Office Building, Libby sat only steps away from his boss in the West Wing, and in a good place to pop in on Condi Rice or Stephen Hadley to push a point. And push he did.

Sources who worked on the Powell Security Council speech later told reporters that the menu Libby presented on January 25, though given in the spirit of a contribution, in actuality served the Cheney staff as a catechism: "Every piece offered . . . they fought tooth and nail to keep it in." By the end of the first day Powell had had so many problems with the Libby menu he rejected it, afterwards working from the NIE.

Iraqi unmanned aerial vehicles became one focus of the fight over the speech. The National Intelligence Estimate had postulated these drones could be used to attack the American homeland, and Cheney's staff wanted the drones to be a big feature in the speech. They centered their arguments on guidance software Iraq had attempted to procure, which contained built-in terrain maps of the United States—a bit of intelligence that had also been used in the estimate. The Air Force, however, had been aware of the computer software and still dissented on this aspect of the NIE. Air Force analysts pointed out that these kinds of terrain maps are automatically prepackaged in most commercially available guidance software, so no particular intent could be associated with the U.S. maps bundled into the equipment Iraq had bought. The issue surfaced again during the Powell speech preparations. When Powell checked the evidence, not only did it become clear the software was much less sophisticated than required for accurate cruise missiles, the CIA proved unable to verify that the Australian manufacturers had delivered any equipment to Baghdad. The Australian company had offered the equipment to Iraq, Baghdad had not sought out this capability. And the Air Force remained correct that intentions could not be divined merely from the fact of this procurement.

Colin Powell would comment on Iraqi drones at the Security Council, but he made no mention of the guidance software evidence. The extent to which the secretary of state was willing to go to accommodate the Bush White House, however, is illustrated by the fact that he left in the assertion that these drones could attack the United States in the face of evidence to the contrary.

A second point at issue was the contention—made repeatedly by Dick Cheney—that Saddam Hussein had been involved in the September 11 attacks. This went back to the allegation that one of the plotters had met with Iraqi agents in Prague months before the attacks, a meeting that by January 2003 was given little credence even within the Bush White House. Scooter Libby demanded the inclusion of this charge. Reports are that Stephen Hadley did also, as did Pentagon representatives. Colin Powell turned them down. It is reported that he physically flung away some pages concerning the alleged Al Qaeda connections of Saddam, exclaiming, "I'm not reading this bull–!" Ultimately though, Powell would keep the broad allegation that Saddam somehow was aligned with or coddling terrorists, while not making a direct connection between Saddam and 9/11 (a major analysis of Saddam's links to terrorism follows the Powell speech below).

On the question of Iraqi nuclear weapons, the main Bush administration evidence rested on the aluminum tubes and the alleged Niger uranium deal. As the group reviewed the draft language, Powell, Tenet, Rice, and other participants rolled one of the tubes across the table, making a little game out of the exercise. Powell inserted some qualifiers but kept the aluminum tubes in his speech *knowing* that the intelligence was disputed, but he threw out the Niger uranium. Aides wanted to dramatize one other shard of evidence, a cadre of Iraqi scientists to whom President Bush had referred in his Veterans of Foreign Wars speech in Cincinnati, by showing a photograph of a group of Iraqi scientists meeting with Saddam. Such a picture had been published in an Iraqi newspaper a couple of years earlier.

"Now tell me who these guys are," Colin Powell asked.

Analysts reassured the secretary: "Oh, we're quite sure this is his nuclear crowd."

"How do you know? Prove it. Who are they?" Powell shot back.

The agency was not only unable to say who the scientists were, they were unable to state as a fact that the persons in the photograph were even scientists, much less nuclear experts. Once more Powell retained the general reference to the scientists but threw out the picture. Though Colin Powell deliberately made himself the judge and jury on what to include in his Security Council presentation and took pains to satisfy himself on the underlying intelligence, more often than not he watered down items rather than eliminating them.

Giving the speech the desired impact meant releasing to the public at least some classified information. Stephen Hadley led a special group making determinations on what new material to open. Possibly the most notable instance would come in the case of the alleged Iraqi mobile biological and chemical warfare laboratories, previously mentioned to the public numerous times but never detailed. National Security Agency intercepts of Iraqi communications traffic from November 2002 commenting on the UN inspections were other examples of absolutely fresh intelligence, which George Bush himself had first heard only weeks before. Satellite photos Powell used to illustrate Iraqi deception activity—assuming the pictures were actually taken by spy satellites, and at the places, dates, and times the United States would assert—were also new, as was an overhead image of the Iraqi air experimental facility of Samarra. The close-up image of one of the aluminum tubes was a first. But the illustrations would be a mixed bag. Many photographs used in the Security Council speech were recycled. A few of the pictures were merely generic, such as one of a U-2 spyplane. Some photographs had appeared first in the CIA white paper, some in the British Iraq dossier, others in White House (WHIG) publications, still others in a public briefing on Iraqi deception techniques the Defense Intelligence Agency had presented in October. For some things, there were no photographs, in particular the mobile weapons labs, so the CIA prepared artists' conceptions and those were used at the UN Security Council.

The Bush administration deliberately built public expectations for the Powell presentation. Pieces began to appear in the media days ahead of time based on claims put out at the White House and State Department that the upcoming address would go farther, hit harder, than anything to date. A top aide to Powell, Richard L. Armitage, told a Senate committee even as the secretary of state convened his murder board that the speech would feature the mobile weapons labs, data on Iraqi purchases for nuclear, chemical, and biological weapons, and Saddam's terrorist links. Communications intelligence would be mentioned in some of the buildups. By the day before the speech, the hype had gone too far—reporters had been given the impression Powell would present spy photos of Iraqi mobile weapons laboratories.

By then Colin Powell had gone to New York and holed up at the Waldorf-Astoria Hotel. To make sure there were no misimpressions regarding whether this represented the view of U.S. intelligence, the secretary of state collared the director of central intelligence and brought him along to New York. The U.S. administration rented a big meeting room at the Waldorf and staged their final two rehearsals of the speech there. The dice were in play. The following morning, Wednesday, February 5, 2003, secretary of state Colin L. Powell went to the UN and took the right front seat at the U.S. place at the Security Council conference table. Director George Tenet sat immediately behind him. The dice had begun to roll.

document 6. *Colin Powell's Remarks to the UN Security Council, February 5, 2003.*

U.S. DEPARTMENT *of* STATE

Remarks to the United Nations Security Council

Secretary Colin L. Powell
New York City
February 5, 2003

SECRETARY POWELL: Thank you, Mr. President. Mr. President and Mr. Secretary General, distinguished colleagues, I would like to begin by expressing my thanks for the special effort that each of you made to be here today. This is an important day for us all as we review the situation with respect to Iraq and its disarmament obligations under UN Security Council Resolution 1441.

1.

Last November 8, this Council passed Resolution 1441 by a unanimous vote. The purpose of that resolution was to disarm Iraq of its weapons of mass destruction. Iraq had already been found guilty of material breach of its obligations stretching back over 16 previous resolutions and 12 years.

Resolution 1441 was not dealing with an innocent party, but a regime this Council has repeatedly convicted over the years.

Resolution 1441 gave Iraq one last chance, one last chance to come into compliance or to face serious consequences. No Council member present and voting on that day had

any illusions about the nature and intent of the resolution or what serious consequences meant if Iraq did not comply.

And to assist in its disarmament, we called on Iraq to cooperate with returning inspectors from UNMOVIC and IAEA. We laid down tough standards for Iraq to meet to allow the inspectors to do their job.

This Council placed the burden on Iraq to comply and disarm, and not on the inspectors to find that which Iraq has gone out of its way to conceal for so long. Inspectors are inspectors; they are not detectives.

2.

I asked for this session today for two purposes. First, to support the core assessments made by Dr. Blix and Dr. ElBaradei. As Dr. Blix reported to this Council on January 27, "Iraq appears not to have come to a genuine acceptance, not even today, of the disarmament which was demanded of it."

And as Dr. ElBaradei reported, Iraq's declaration of December 7 "did not provide any new information relevant to certain questions that have been outstanding since 1998."

My second purpose today is to provide you with additional information, to share with you what the United States knows about Iraq's weapons of mass destruction, as well as Iraq's involvement in terrorism, which is also the subject of Resolution 1441 and other earlier resolutions.

I might add at this point that we are providing all relevant information we can to the inspection teams for them to do their work.

The material I will present to you comes from a variety of sources. Some are U.S. sources and some are those of other countries. Some are the sources are technical, such as intercepted telephone conversations and photos taken by satellites. Other sources are people who have risked their lives to let the world know what Saddam Hussein is really up to.

I cannot tell you everything that we know, but what I can share with you, when combined with what all of us have learned over the years, is deeply troubling. What you will see is an accumulation of facts and disturbing patterns of behavior. The facts and Iraqis' behavior, Iraq's behavior, demonstrate that Saddam <u>Hussein and his regime have</u>

3. <u>made no effort, no effort, to disarm,</u> as required by the international community.

Indeed, the facts and Iraq's behavior show that Saddam Hussein and his regime are concealing their efforts to produce more weapons of mass destruction.

Let me begin by playing a tape for you. What you're about to hear is a conversation that my government monitored. It takes place on November 26th of last year, on the day before United Nations teams resumed inspections in Iraq. The conversation involves two senior officers, a colonel and a brigadier general from Iraq's elite military unit, the Republican Guard.

[The tape is played.] <u>AUDIO</u>

SECRETARY POWELL: Let me pause and review some of the key elements of this conversation that you just heard between these two officers.

First, they acknowledge that our colleague, Mohammed ElBaradei is coming, and they know what he's coming for and they know he's coming the next day. He's coming to look for things that are prohibited. He is expecting these gentlemen to cooperate with him and not hide things.

But they're worried. We have this modified vehicle. What do we say if one of them sees it? What is their concern? Their concern is that it's something they should not have, something that should not be seen.

The general was incredulous: "You didn't get it modified. You don't have one of those, do you?"

"I have one."

"Which? From where?"

"From the workshop. From the Al-Kindi Company."

"What?"

"From Al-Kindi."

"I'll come to see you in the morning. I'm worried you all have something left."

"We evacuated everything. We don't have anything left."

Note what he says: "We evacuated everything." We didn't destroy it. We didn't line it up for inspection. We didn't turn it into the inspectors. We evacuated it to make sure it was not around when the inspectors showed up. "I will come to you tomorrow."

GEN: Yeah, yeah. I'll come to you in the morning. I have some comments. I'm worried you all have something left.
COL: We evacuated everything. We don't have anything left.
GEN: I will come to you tomorrow.
COL: Okay.

4. The Al-Kindi Company. This is a company that is well known to have been involved in prohibited weapons systems activity.

Let me play another tape for you. As you will recall, the inspectors found 12 empty chemical warheads on January 16th. On January 20th, four days later, Iraq promised the inspectors it would search for more. You will now hear an officer from Republican Guard headquarters issuing an instruction to an officer in the field. Their conversation took place just last week, on January 30.

[The tape was played.] AUDIO

SECRETARY POWELL: Let me pause again and review the elements of this message.

HQ: Sir...
Field: Yes.
HQ: There is a directive of the [Republican] Guard Chief of Staff at the conference today.
Field: Yes.
HQ: They are inspecting the ammunition you have.
Field: Yes.

"They are inspecting the ammunition you have, yes?"

"Yes. For the possibility there are forbidden ammo."

"For the possibility there is, by chance, forbidden ammo?"

"Yes.

"And we sent you a message yesterday to clean out all the areas, the scrap areas, the abandoned areas. Make sure there is nothing there. Remember the first message: evacuate it."

This is all part of a system of hiding things and moving things out of the way and making sure they have left nothing behind.

HQ: ...for the possibility there are forbidden ammo.
Field: Yes?
HQ: For the possibility there is by chance, forbidden ammo.
Field: Yes.
HQ: And we sent you a message to inspect the scrap areas and the abandoned areas.

Field: Yes.
HQ: After you have carried out what is contained in the message... destroy the message.
Field: Yes.
HQ: Because I don't want anyone to see this message.
Field: Okay okay.

You go a little further into this message and you see the specific instructions from headquarters: "After you have carried out what is contained in this message, destroy the message because I don't want anyone to see this message."

"Okay."

"Okay."

5. Why? Why? This message would have verified to the inspectors that they have been trying to turn over things. They were looking for things, but they don't want that message seen because they were trying to clean up the area, to leave no evidence behind of the presence of weapons of mass destruction. And they can claim that nothing was there and the inspectors can look all they want and they will find nothing.

This effort to hide things from the inspectors is not one or two isolated events. Quite the contrary, this is part and parcel of a policy of evasion and deception that goes back 12 years, a policy set at the highest levels of the Iraqi regime.

We know that Saddam Hussein has what is called "a Higher Committee for Monitoring the Inspection Teams." Think about that. Iraq has a high-level committee to monitor the inspectors who were sent in to monitor Iraq's disarmament -- not to cooperate with them, not to assist them, but to spy on them and keep them from doing their jobs.

6. The committee reports directly to Saddam Hussein. It is headed by Iraq's Vice President, Taha Yasin Ramadan. Its members include Saddam Hussein's son, Qusay.

This committee also includes Lieutenant General Amir al-Sa'di, an advisor to Saddam. In case that name isn't immediately familiar to you, General Sa'di has been the Iraqi regime's primary point of contact for Dr. Blix and Dr. ElBaradei. It was General Sa'di who last fall publicly pledged that Iraq was prepared to cooperate unconditionally with inspectors. Quite the contrary, Sa'di's job is not to cooperate; it is to deceive, not to disarm, but to undermine the inspectors; not to support them, but to frustrate them and to make sure they learn nothing.

We have learned a lot about the work of this special committee. We learned that just prior to the return of inspectors last November, the regime had decided to resume what we heard called "the old game of cat-and-mouse."

For example, let me focus on the now famous declaration that Iraq submitted to this Council on December 7th. Iraq never had any intention of complying with this Council's mandate. Instead, Iraq planned to use the declaration to overwhelm us and to overwhelm the inspectors with useless information about Iraq's permitted weapons so that we would not have time to pursue Iraq's prohibited weapons. Iraq's goal was to give us in this room, to give those of us on this Council, the false impression that the inspection process was working.

You saw the result. Dr. Blix pronounced the 12,200-page declaration "rich in volume" but "poor in information and practically devoid of new evidence." Could any member of this Council honestly rise in defense of this false declaration?

Everything we have seen and heard indicates that instead of cooperating actively with the inspectors to ensure the success of their mission, Saddam Hussein and his regime are busy doing all they possibly can to ensure that inspectors succeed in finding absolutely nothing.

7. My colleagues, every statement I make today is backed up by sources, solid sources. These are not assertions. What we are giving you are facts and conclusions based on solid intelligence. I will cite some examples, and these are from human sources.

Orders were issued to Iraq's security organizations, as well as to Saddam Hussein's own office, to hide all correspondence with the Organization of Military Industrialization. This is the organization that oversees Iraq's weapons of mass destruction activities. Make sure there are no documents left which would connect you to the OMI.

We know that Saddam's son, Qusay, ordered the removal of all prohibited weapons from Saddam's numerous palace complexes. We know that Iraqi government officials, members of the ruling Ba'ath Party and scientists have hidden prohibited items in their homes. Other key files from military and scientific establishments have been placed in cars that are being driven around the countryside by Iraqi intelligence agents to avoid detection.

Thanks to intelligence they were provided, the inspectors recently found dramatic confirmation of these reports. When they searched the homes of an Iraqi nuclear scientist, they uncovered roughly 2,000 pages of documents. You see them here being brought out of the home and placed in UN hands. Some of the material is classified and related to Iraq's nuclear program.

Tell me, answer me: Are the inspectors to search the house of every government official, every Ba'ath Party member and every scientist in the country to find the truth, to get the information they need to satisfy the demands of our Council?

Our sources tell us that in some cases the hard drives of computers at Iraqi weapons facilities were replaced. Who took the hard drives? Where did they go? What is being hidden? Why?

There is only one answer to the why: to deceive, to hide, to keep from the inspectors.

8. Numerous human sources tell us that the Iraqis are moving not just documents and hard drives, but weapons of mass destruction, to keep them from being found by inspectors. While we were here in this Council chamber debating Resolution 1441 last fall, we know, we know from sources that a missile brigade outside Baghdad was dispersing rocket launchers and warheads containing biological warfare agent to various locations, distributing them to various locations in western Iraq.

Most of the launchers and warheads had been hidden in large groves of palm trees and were to be moved every one to four weeks to escape detection.

We also have satellite photos that indicate that banned materials have recently been moved from a number of Iraqi weapons of mass destruction facilities.

Let me say a word about satellite images before I show a couple. The photos that I am about to show you are sometimes hard for the average person to interpret, hard for me. The painstaking work of photo analysis takes experts with years and years of experience, poring for hours and hours over light tables. But as I show you these images, I will try to capture and explain what they mean, what they indicate, to our imagery specialists.

Let's look at one. This one is about a weapons munition facility, a facility that holds ammunition at a place called Taji. This is one of about 65 such facilities in Iraq. We know that this one has housed chemical munitions. In fact, this is where the Iraqis recently came up with the additional four chemical weapons shells.

Here you see 15 munitions bunkers in yellow and red outlines. The four that are in red squares represent active chemical munitions bunkers.

9. How do I know that? How can I say that? Let me give you a closer look. Look at the image on the left. On the left is a close-up of one of the four chemical bunkers. The two arrows indicate the presence of sure signs that the bunkers are storing chemical munitions. The arrow at the top that says "security" points to a facility that is a signature item for this kind of bunker. Inside that facility are special guards and special equipment to monitor any leakage that might come out of the bunker. The truck you also see is a signature item. It's a decontamination vehicle in case something goes wrong. This is characteristic of those four bunkers. The special security facility and the decontamination vehicle will be in the area, if not at any one of them or one of the other, it is moving around those four and it moves as needed to move as people are working in the different bunkers.

Now look at the picture on the right. You are now looking at two of those sanitized bunkers. The signature vehicles are gone, the tents are gone. It's been cleaned up. And it was done on the 22nd of December as the UN inspection team is arriving, and you can see the inspection vehicles arriving in the lower portion of the picture on the right.

The bunkers are clean when the inspectors get there. They found nothing.

10. This sequence of events raises the worrisome suspicion that Iraq had been tipped off to the forthcoming inspections at Taji. As it did throughout the 1990s, we know that Iraq today is actively using its considerable intelligence capabilities to hide its illicit activities. From our sources, we know that inspectors are under constant surveillance by an army of Iraqi intelligence operatives. Iraq is relentlessly attempting to tap all of their communications, both voice and electronics. I would call my colleagues' attention to the fine paper that the United Kingdom distributed yesterday which describes in exquisite detail Iraqi deception activities.

In this next example, you will see the type of concealment activity Iraq has undertaken in response to the resumption of inspections. Indeed, in November of 2002, just when the inspections were about to resume, this type of activity spiked. Here are three examples.

At this ballistic missile site on November 10th, we saw a cargo truck preparing to move ballistic missile components.

At this biological weapons-related facility on November 25th, just two days before inspections resumed, this truck caravan appeared -- something we almost never see at this facility and we monitor it carefully and regularly.

At this ballistic missile facility, again, two days before inspections began, five large cargo trucks appeared, along with a truck-mounted crane, to move missiles.

We saw this kind of housecleaning at close to 30 sites. Days after this activity, the vehicles and the equipment that I've just highlighted disappear and the site returns to patterns of normalcy. We don't know precisely what Iraq was moving, but the inspectors already knew about these sites so Iraq knew that they would be coming.

We must ask ourselves: Why would Iraq suddenly move equipment of this nature before inspections if they were anxious to demonstrate what they had or did not have?

Remember the first intercept in which two Iraqis talked about the need to hide a modified vehicle from the inspectors. Where did Iraq take all of this equipment? Why wasn't it presented to the inspectors?

11.

Iraq also has refused to permit any U-2 reconnaissance flights that would give the inspectors a better sense of what's being moved before, during and after inspections. This refusal to allow this kind of reconnaissance is in direct, specific violation of operative paragraph seven of our Resolution 1441.

Saddam Hussein and his regime are not just trying to conceal weapons; they are also trying to hide people. You know the basic facts. Iraq has not complied with its obligation to allow immediate, unimpeded, unrestricted and private access to all officials and other persons, as required by Resolution 1441. The regime only allows interviews with inspectors in the presence of an

12.

Iraqi official, a minder. The official Iraqi organization charged with facilitating inspections announced publicly and announced ominously, that, "Nobody is ready" to leave Iraq to be interviewed.

Iraqi Vice President Ramadan accused the inspectors of conducting espionage, a veiled threat that anyone cooperating with UN inspectors was committing treason.

Iraq did not meet its obligations under 1441 to provide a comprehensive list of scientists associated with its weapons of mass destruction programs. Iraq's list was out of date and contained only about 500 names despite the fact that UNSCOM had earlier put together a list of about 3,500 names.

Let me just tell you what a number of human sources have told us. Saddam Hussein has directly participated in the effort to prevent interviews. In early December, Saddam Hussein had all Iraqi scientists warned of the serious consequences that they and their families would face if they revealed any sensitive information to the inspectors. They were forced to sign documents acknowledging that divulging information is punishable by death.

Saddam Hussein also said that scientists should be told not to agree to leave Iraq; anyone who agreed to be interviewed outside Iraq would be treated as a spy. This violates 1441.

In mid-November, just before the inspectors returned, Iraqi experts were ordered to report to the headquarters of the Special Security Organization to receive counter-intelligence training. The training focused on evasion methods, interrogation resistance techniques, and how to mislead inspectors.

13. Ladies and gentlemen, these are not assertions. These are facts corroborated by many sources, some of them sources of the intelligence services of other countries.

For example, in mid-December, weapons experts at one facility were replaced by Iraqi intelligence agents who were to deceive inspectors about the work that was being done there. On orders from Saddam Hussein, Iraqi officials issued a false death certificate for one scientist and he was sent into hiding.

In the middle of January, experts at one facility that was related to weapons of mass destruction, those experts had been ordered to stay home from work to avoid the inspectors. Workers from other Iraqi military facilities not engaged in illicit weapons projects were to replace the workers who had been sent home. A dozen experts have been placed under house arrest -- not in their own houses, but as a group at one of Saddam Hussein's guest houses.

It goes on and on and on. As the examples I have just presented show, the information and intelligence we have gathered point to an active and systematic effort on the part of the Iraqi regime to keep key materials and people from the inspectors, in direct violation of Resolution 1441.

The pattern is not just one of reluctant cooperation, nor is it merely a lack of cooperation. What we see is a deliberate campaign to prevent any meaningful inspection work.

My colleagues, Operative Paragraph 4 of UN Resolution 1441, which we lingered over so long last fall, clearly states that false statements and omissions in the declaration and a failure by Iraq at any time to comply with and cooperate fully in the implementation of this resolution shall constitute -- the facts speak for themselves -- shall constitute a further material breach of its obligation.

We wrote it this way to give Iraq an early test, to give Iraq an early test. Would they give an honest declaration and would they, early on, indicate a willingness to cooperate with the inspectors? It was designed to be an early test. They failed that test.

14. By this standard, the standard of this Operative Paragraph, I believe that Iraq is now in further material breach of its obligations. I believe this conclusion is irrefutable and undeniable.

Iraq has now placed itself in danger of the serious consequences called for in UN Resolution 1441. And this body places itself in danger of irrelevance if it allows Iraq to continue to defy its will without responding effectively and immediately.

This issue before us is not how much time we are willing to give the inspectors to be frustrated by Iraqi obstruction. But how much longer are we willing to put up with Iraq's non-compliance before we, as a Council, we as the United Nations say, "Enough. Enough."

The gravity of this moment is matched by the gravity of the threat that Iraq's weapons of mass destruction pose to the world. Let me now turn to those deadly weapons programs and describe why they are real and present dangers to the region and to the world.

First, biological weapons. We have talked frequently here about biological weapons. By way of introduction and history, I think there are just three quick points I need to make. First, you will recall that it took UNSCOM four long and frustrating years to pry, to pry an admission out of Iraq that it had biological weapons. Second, when Iraq finally admitted having these weapons in 1995, the quantities were vast. Less than a teaspoon of dry anthrax, a little bit -- about this amount. This is just about the amount of a teaspoon. Less than a teaspoonful of dry anthrax in an envelope shut down the United States Senate in the fall of 2001.

This forced several hundred people to undergo emergency medical treatment and killed two postal workers just from an amount, just about this quantity that was inside of an envelope.

15. Iraq declared 8500 liters of anthrax. But UNSCOM estimates that Saddam Hussein could have produced 25,000 liters. If concentrated into this dry form, this amount would be enough to fill tens upon tens upon tens of thousands of teaspoons. And Saddam Hussein has not verifiably accounted for even one teaspoonful of this deadly material. And that is my third point. And it is key. The Iraqis have never accounted for all of the biological weapons they admitted they had and we know they had.

They have never accounted for all the organic material used to make them. And they have not accounted for many of the weapons filled with these agents such as their R-400 bombs. This is evidence, not conjecture. This is true. This is all well documented.

Dr. Blix told this Council that Iraq has provided little evidence to verify anthrax production and no convincing evidence of its destruction. It should come as no shock then that since Saddam Hussein forced out the last
16. inspectors in 1998, we have amassed much intelligence indicating that Iraq is continuing to make these weapons.

One of the most worrisome things that emerges from the thick intelligence file we have on Iraq's biological weapons
17. is the existence of mobile production facilities used to make biological agents.

Let me take you inside that intelligence file and share with you what we know from eyewitness accounts. We have first-hand descriptions of biological weapons factories on wheels and on rails.

18. The trucks and train cars are easily moved and are designed to evade detection by inspectors. In a matter of months, they can produce a quantity of biological poison equal to the entire amount that Iraq claimed to have produced in the years prior to the Gulf War.

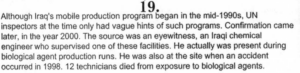

19.
Although Iraq's mobile production program began in the mid-1990s, UN inspectors at the time only had vague hints of such programs. Confirmation came later, in the year 2000. The source was an eyewitness, an Iraqi chemical engineer who supervised one of these facilities. He actually was present during biological agent production runs. He was also at the site when an accident occurred in 1998. 12 technicians died from exposure to biological agents.

He reported that when UNSCOM was in country and inspecting, the biological weapons agent production always began on Thursdays at midnight, because Iraq thought UNSCOM would not inspect on the Muslim holy day, Thursday night through Friday.

He added that this was important because the units could not be broken down in the middle of a production run, which had to be completed by Friday evening before the inspectors might arrive again.

This defector is currently hiding in another country with the certain knowledge that Saddam Hussein will kill him if he finds him. His eyewitness account of these mobile production facilities has been corroborated by other sources.

A second source. An Iraqi civil engineer in a position to know the details of the program confirmed the existence of transportable facilities moving on trailers.

A third source, also in a position to know, reported in summer, 2002, that Iraq had manufactured mobile production systems mounted on road-trailer units and on rail cars.

Finally, a fourth source. An Iraqi major who defected confirmed that Iraq has mobile biological research laboratories in addition to the production facilities I mentioned earlier.

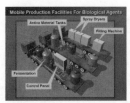

We have diagrammed what our sources reported about these mobile facilities. Here you see both truck and rail-car mounted mobile factories. The description our sources gave us of the technical features required by such facilities is highly detailed and extremely accurate.

As these drawings, based on their description show, we know what the fermentors look like. We know what the tanks, pumps, compressors and other parts look like. We know how they fit together, we know how they work, and we know a great deal about the platforms on which they are mounted.

As shown in this diagram, these factories can be concealed easily -- either by moving ordinary looking trucks and rail-cars along Iraq's thousands of miles of highway or track or by parking them in a garage or a warehouse or somewhere in Iraq's extensive system of underground tunnels and bunkers.

We know that Iraq has at least seven of these mobile, biological agent factories. The truck-mounted ones have at least two or three trucks each. That means that the mobile production facilities are very few -- perhaps 18 trucks that we know of. There may be more. But perhaps 18 that we know of. Just imagine trying to find 18 trucks among the thousands and thousands of trucks that travel the roads of Iraq every single day.

It took the inspectors four years to find out that Iraq was making biological agents. How long do you think it will take the inspectors to find even one of these 18 trucks without Iraq coming forward as they are supposed to with the information about these kinds of capabilities.

Ladies and gentlemen, these are sophisticated facilities. For example, they can produce anthrax and botulinum toxin. In fact, they can produce enough dry, biological agent in a single month to kill thousands upon thousands of people. A dry agent of this type is the most lethal form for human beings.

By 1998, UN experts agreed that the Iraqis had perfected drying techniques for their biological weapons programs. Now Iraq has incorporated this drying expertise into these mobile production facilities.

We know from Iraq's past admissions that it has successfully weaponized not only anthrax, but also other biological agents including botulinum toxin, aflatoxin and ricin. But Iraq's research efforts did not stop there.

Saddam Hussein has investigated dozens of biological agents causing diseases such as gas gangrene, plague, typhus, tetanus, cholera, camelpox, and hemorrhagic fever. And he also has the wherewithal to develop smallpox.

The Iraqi regime has also developed ways to disperse lethal biological agents widely, indiscriminately into the water supply, into the air. For example, Iraq had a program to modify aerial fuel tanks for Mirage jets. This video of an Iraqi test flight obtained by UNSCOM some years ago shows an Iraqi F-1 Mirage jet aircraft. Note the spray coming from beneath the Mirage. That is 2,000 liters of simulated anthrax that a jet is spraying.
(VIDEO)

In 1995, an Iraqi military officer, Mujahid Saleh Abdul Latif told inspectors that Iraq intended the spray tanks to be mounted onto a MiG-21 that had been converted into an unmanned aerial vehicle, or UAV. UAVs outfitted with spray tanks constitute an ideal method for launching a terrorist attack using biological weapons.

20.

Iraq admitted to producing four spray tanks, but to this day, it has provided no credible evidence that they were destroyed, evidence that was required by the international community.

There can be no doubt that Saddam Hussein has biological weapons and the capability to rapidly produce more, many more. And he has the ability to dispense these lethal poisons and diseases in ways that can cause massive death and destruction.

If biological weapons seem too terrible to contemplate, chemical weapons are equally chilling. UNMOVIC already laid out much of this and it is documented for all of us to read in UNSCOM's 1999 report on the subject. Let me set the stage with three key points that all of us need to keep in mind. First, Saddam Hussein has used these horrific weapons on another country and on his own people. In fact, in the history of chemical warfare, no country has had more battlefield experience with chemical weapons since World War I than Saddam Hussein's Iraq.

21. Second, as with biological weapons, Saddam Hussein has never accounted for vast amounts of chemical weaponry: 550 artillery shells with mustard, 30,000 empty munitions and enough precursors to increase his stockpile to as much as 500 tons of chemical agents.

22. If we consider just one category of missing weaponry, 6500 bombs from the Iran-Iraq War, UNMOVIC says the amount of chemical agent in them would be on the order of a thousand tons.

These quantities of chemical weapons are now unaccounted for. Dr. Blix has quipped that, "Mustard gas is not marmalade. You are supposed to know what you did with it." We believe Saddam Hussein knows what he did with it and he has not come clean with the international community.

We have evidence these weapons existed. What we don't have is evidence from Iraq that they have been destroyed or where they are. That is what we are still waiting for.

23. Third point, Iraq's record on chemical weapons is replete with lies. It took years for Iraq to finally admit that it had produced four tons of the deadly nerve agent VX. A single drop of VX on the skin will kill in minutes. Four tons. The admission only came out after inspectors collected documentation as a result of the defection of Hussein Kamel, Saddam Hussein's late son-in-law.

UNSCOM also gained forensic evidence that Iraq had produced VX and put it into weapons for delivery, yet to this day Iraq denies it had ever weaponized VX. And on January 27, UNMOVIC told this Council that it has information that conflicts with the Iraqi account of its VX program.

We know that Iraq has embedded key portions of its illicit chemical weapons infrastructure within its legitimate civilian industry. To all outward appearances, even to experts, the infrastructure looks like an ordinary civilian operation. Illicit and legitimate production can go on simultaneously or on a dime. This dual-use infrastructure can turn from clandestine to commercial and then back again.

These inspections would be unlikely, any inspections at such facilities, would be unlikely to turn up anything prohibited, especially if there is any warning that the inspections are coming. Call it ingenious or evil genius, but the Iraqis deliberately designed their chemical weapons programs to be inspected. It is infrastructure with a built in alibi.

Under the guise of dual-use infrastructure, Iraq has undertaken an effort to reconstitute facilities that were closely associated with its past program to develop and produce chemical weapons. For example, Iraq has rebuilt key portions of the Tareq State Establishment. Tareq includes facilities designed specifically for Iraq's chemical weapons program and employs key figures from past programs.

That's the production end of Saddam's chemical weapons business. What about the delivery end? I'm going to show you a small part of a chemical complex called "Al Musayyib", a site that Iraq has used for at least three years to transship chemical weapons from production facilities out to the field. In May 2002, our satellites photographed the unusual activity in this picture.

Chemical Weapons Leaving Al-Musayyib
May 2002
Decontamination Vehicle
Forklift
35-Ton Cargo Trucks

Here we see cargo vehicles are again at this transshipment point, and we can see that they are accompanied by a decontamination vehicle associated with biological or chemical weapons activity. What makes this picture significant is that we have a human source who has corroborated that movement of chemical weapons occurred at this site at that time. So it's not just the photo and it's not an individual seeing the photo. It's the photo and then the knowledge of an individual being brought together to make the case.

24. This photograph of the site taken two months later, in July, shows not only the previous site which is the figure in the middle at the top with the bulldozer sign near it, it shows that this previous site, as well as all of the other sites around the site have been fully bulldozed and graded. The topsoil has been removed. The Iraqis literally removed the crust of the earth from large portions of this site in order to conceal chemical weapons evidence that would be there from years of chemical weapons activity.

Bulldozed and Freshly Graded Earth, Al-Musayyib Chemical Complex
Jul 2002
Bulldozer
Freshly Graded Earth

To support its deadly biological and chemical weapons programs, Iraq procures needed items from around the world using an extensive clandestine network. What we know comes largely from intercepted communications and human sources who are in a position to know the facts.

Iraq's procurement efforts include: equipment that can filter and separate microorganisms and toxins involved in biological weapons; equipment that can be used to concentrate the agent; growth media that can be used to continue producing anthrax and botulinum toxin; sterilization equipment for laboratories; glass-lined reactors and specialty pumps that can handle corrosive chemical weapons agents and precursors; large amounts of thionyl chloride, a precursor for nerve and blister agents; and other chemicals such as sodium sulfide, an important mustard agent precursor.

Now, of course, Iraq will argue that these items can also be used for legitimate purposes. But if that is true, why do we have to learn about them by intercepting communications and risking the lives of human agents?

With Iraq's well-documented history on biological and chemical weapons, why should any of us give Iraq the benefit of the doubt? I don't. And I don't think you will either after you hear this next intercept.

Just a few weeks ago we intercepted communications between two commanders in Iraq's Second Republican Guard Corps. One commander is going to be giving an instruction to the other. You will hear as this unfolds that what he wants to communicate to the other guy, he wants to make sure the other guy hears clearly to the point of repeating it so that it gets written down and completely understood. Listen.

(Transmission.) <u>AUDIO</u>

COL: Captain Ibrahim?
CAPT: I am with you, Sir.
COL: Remove.
CAPT: Remove. [Repeats instructions]
COL: The expression.
CAPT: The expression.
COL: "Nerve agents."

Let's review a few selected items of this conversation. Two officers talking to each other on the radio want to make sure that nothing is misunderstood. "Remove." "Remove." "The expression." "The expression." "The expression. I got it." "Nerve agents." "Nerve agents." "Wherever it comes up." "Got it, wherever it comes up." "In the wireless instructions." "In the instructions." "Correction, no, in the wireless instructions." "Wireless, I got it."

CAPT: "Nerve agents."
COL: Wherever it comes up.
CAPT: Wherever it comes up.
COL: In the wireless instructions.
CAPT: In the instructions.
COL: Wireless.
CAPT: Wireless.

Why does he repeat it that way? Why is he so forceful in making sure this is understood? And why did he focus on wireless instructions? Because the senior officer is concerned that somebody might be listening. Well, somebody was.

"Nerve agents." "Stop talking about it." "They are listening to us" "Don't give any evidence that we have these horrible agents." But we know that they do and this kind of conversation confirms it.

25. Our conservative estimate is that Iraq today has a stockpile of between 100 and 500 tons of chemical weapons agent. That is enough agent to fill 16,000 battlefield rockets. Even the low end of 100 tons of agent would enable Saddam Hussein to cause mass casualties across more than 100 square miles of territory, an area nearly five times the size of Manhattan.

UN Found 122mm Chemical Warhead

Let me remind you that -- of the 122 mm chemical warheads that the UN inspectors found recently. This discovery could very well be, as has been noted, the tip of a submerged iceberg.

The question before us all, my friends, is when will we see the rest of the submerged iceberg?

(VIDEO)

Saddam Hussein has chemical weapons. Saddam Hussein has used such weapons. And Saddam Hussein has no compunction about using them again -- against his neighbors and against his own people. And we have sources who tell us that he recently has authorized his field commanders to use them. He wouldn't be passing out the orders if he didn't have the weapons or the intent to use them.

We also have sources who tell us that since the 1980s, Saddam's regime has been experimenting on human beings to perfect its biological or chemical weapons.

A source said that 1,600 death-row prisoners were transferred in 1995 to a special unit for such experiments. An eyewitness saw prisoners tied down to beds, experiments conducted on them, blood oozing around the victims' mouths, and autopsies performed to confirm the effects on the prisoners.

Saddam Hussein's humanity -- inhumanity has no limits.

26. Let me turn now to nuclear weapons. We have no indication that Saddam Hussein has ever abandoned his nuclear weapons program. On the contrary, we have more than a decade of proof that he remains determined to acquire nuclear weapons.

IRAQ
FAILING TO DISARM
— NUCLEAR WEAPONS —

To fully appreciate the challenge that we face today, remember that in 1991 the inspectors searched Iraq's primary nuclear weapons facilities for the first time, and they found nothing to conclude that Iraq had a nuclear weapons program. But, based on defector information, in May of 1991, Saddam Hussein's lie was exposed. In truth, Saddam Hussein had a massive clandestine nuclear weapons

27. program that covered several different techniques to enrich uranium, including electromagnetic isotope separation, gas centrifuge and gas diffusion.

We estimate that this illicit program cost the Iraqis several billion dollars. Nonetheless, Iraq continued to tell the IAEA that it had no nuclear weapons program. If Saddam had not been stopped, Iraq could have produced a nuclear bomb by 1993, years earlier than most worst case assessments that had been made before the war.

In 1995, as a result of another defector, we find out that, after his invasion of Kuwait, Saddam Hussein had initiated a crash program to build a crude nuclear weapon, in violation of Iraq's UN obligations. Saddam Hussein already possesses two out of the three key components needed to build a nuclear bomb. He has a cadre of nuclear scientists with the expertise and he has a bomb design.

Since 1998, his efforts to reconstitute his nuclear program have been focused on acquiring the third and last component: sufficient fissile material to produce a nuclear explosion. To make the fissile material, he needs to develop an ability to enrich uranium. Saddam Hussein is determined to get his hands on a nuclear bomb.

28.

Aluminum Tube for Uranium Enrichment

He is so determined that has made repeated covert attempts to acquire high-specification <u>aluminum tubes</u> from 11 different countries, even after inspections resumed. These tubes are controlled by the Nuclear Suppliers Group precisely because they can be used as centrifuges for enriching uranium.

By now, just about everyone has heard of these tubes and we all know that there are differences of opinion. There is controversy about what these tubes are for. Most U.S. experts think they are intended to serve as rotors in centrifuges used to enrich uranium. Other experts, and the Iraqis themselves, argue that they are really to produce the rocket bodies for a conventional weapon, a multiple rocket launcher.

29.

Let me tell you what is not controversial about these tubes. <u>First, all the experts who have analyzed the tubes in our possession agree that they can be adapted for centrifuge use.</u>

Second, Iraq had no business buying them for any purpose. They are banned for Iraq.

I am no expert on centrifuge tubes, but this is an old army trooper. I can tell you a couple things.

First, it strikes me as quite odd that these tubes are manufactured to a tolerance that far exceeds U.S. requirements for comparable rockets. Maybe Iraqis just manufacture their conventional weapons to a higher standard than we do, but I don't think so.

Second, we actually have examined tubes from several different batches that were seized clandestinely before they reached Baghdad. What we notice in these different batches is a progression to higher and higher levels of specification, including in the latest batch an anodized coating on extremely smooth inner and outer surfaces.

Intercepted Aluminum Tubes

Why would they continue refining the specifications? Why would they continuing refining the specification, go to all that trouble for something that, if it was a rocket, would soon be blown into shrapnel when it went off?

The high-tolerance aluminum tubes are only part of the story. We also have intelligence from multiple sources that Iraq is attempting to acquire magnets and high-speed balancing machines. Both items can be used in a gas centrifuge program to enrich uranium.

30.

In 1999 and 2000, Iraqi officials negotiated with firms in Romania, India, Russia and Slovenia for the purchase of a <u>magnet production plant</u>. Iraq wanted the plant to produce magnets weighing 20 to 30 grams. That's the same weight as the magnets used in Iraq's gas centrifuge program before the Gulf War.

This incident, linked with the tubes, is another indicator of Iraq's attempt to reconstitute its nuclear weapons program.

Intercepted communications from mid-2000 through last summer showed that Iraq front companies sought to buy machines that can be used to balance gas centrifuge rotors. One of these companies also had been involved in a failed effort in 2001 to smuggle aluminum tubes into Iraq.

People will continue to debate this issue, but there is no doubt in my mind. These illicit procurement efforts show that Saddam Hussein is very much focused on putting in place the key missing piece from his nuclear weapons program, the ability to produce fissile material.

He also has been busy trying to maintain the other key parts of his nuclear program, particularly his cadre of key nuclear scientists. It is noteworthy that over the last 18 months Saddam Hussein has paid increasing personal attention to Iraq's top nuclear scientists, a group that the government-controlled press calls openly his "nuclear mujaheddin." He regularly exhorts them and praises their progress. Progress toward what end?

IRAQ

FAILING TO DISARM

— DELIVERY SYSTEMS —

Long ago, the Security Council, this Council, required Iraq to halt all nuclear activities of any kind.

Let me talk now about the systems Iraq is developing to deliver weapons of mass destruction, in particular Iraq's ballistic missiles and unmanned aerial vehicles, UAVs.

First, missiles. We all remember that before the Gulf War Saddam Hussein's goal was missiles that flew not just hundreds, but thousands, of kilometers. He wanted to strike not only his neighbors, but also nations far beyond his borders.

While inspectors destroyed most of the prohibited ballistic missiles, numerous intelligence reports over the past decade from sources inside Iraq indicate that Saddam Hussein retains a covert force of up to a few dozen Scud-variant ballistic missiles. These are missiles with a range of 650 to 900 kilometers.

31.

We know from intelligence and Iraq's own admissions that Iraq's alleged permitted ballistic missiles, the al-Samoud II and the Al-Fatah, violate the 150-kilometer limit established by this Council in Resolution 687. These are prohibited systems.

UNMOVIC has also reported that Iraq has illegally imported 380 SA-2 rocket engines. These are likely for use in the al-Samoud II. Their import was illegal on three counts: Resolution 687 prohibited all military shipments into Iraq; UNSCOM specifically prohibited use of these engines in surface-to-surface missiles; and finally, as we have just noted, they are for a system that exceeds the 150-kilometer range limit. Worst of all, some of these engines were acquired as late as December, after this Council passed Resolution 1441.

32.

What I want you to know today is that Iraq has programs that are intended to produce ballistic missiles that fly over 1,000 kilometers. One program is pursuing a liquid fuel missile that would be able to fly more than 1,200 kilometers. And you can see from this map, as well as I can, who will be in danger of these missiles.

As part of this effort, another little piece of evidence, Iraq has built an engine test stand that is larger than anything it has ever had. Notice the dramatic difference in size between the test stand on the left, the old one, and the new one on the right. Note the large exhaust vent. This is where the flame from the engine comes out. The exhaust vent on the right test stand is five times longer than the one on the left. The one of the left is used for short-range missiles. The one on the right is clearly intended for long-range missiles that can fly 1,200 kilometers.

This photograph was taken in April of 2002. Since then, the test stand has been finished and a roof has been put over it so it will be harder for satellites to see what's going on underneath the test stand.

Saddam Hussein's intentions have never changed. He is not developing the missiles for self-defense. These are missiles that Iraq wants in order to project power, to threaten and to deliver chemical, biological -- and if we let him -- nuclear warheads.

Now, unmanned aerial vehicles, UAVs. Iraq has been working on a variety of UAVs for more than a decade. This is just illustrative of what a UAV would look like. This effort has included attempts to modify for unmanned flight the MiG-21 and, with greater success, an aircraft called the L-29.

33.

However, Iraq is now concentrating not on these airplanes but on developing and testing smaller UAVs such as this. UAVs are well suited for dispensing chemical and biological weapons. There is ample evidence that Iraq has dedicated much effort to developing and testing spray devices that could be adapted for UAVs.

34. And in the little that Saddam Hussein told us about <u>UAVs, he</u> has not told the truth. One of these lies is graphically and indisputably demonstrated by <u>intelligence we collected on June 27th last year.</u>

According to Iraq's December 7th declaration, its UAVs have a range of only 80 kilometers. But we detected one of Iraq's newest UAVs in a test flight that went 500 kilometers nonstop on autopilot in the racetrack pattern depicted here.

Not only is this test well in excess of the 150 kilometers that the United Nations permits, the test was left out of Iraq's December 7th declaration. The UAV was flown around and around and around in this circle and so that its 80-kilometer limit really was 500 kilometers, unrefueled and on autopilot -- violative of all of its obligations under 1441.

The linkages over the past ten years between Iraq's UAV program and biological and chemical warfare agents are of deep concern to us. Iraq could use these small UAVs which have a wingspan of only a few meters to deliver biological agents to its neighbors or, if transported, to other countries, including the United States.

My friends, the information I have presented to you about these terrible weapons and about Iraq's continued flaunting of its obligations under Security Council Resolution 1441 links to a subject I now want to spend a little bit of time on, and that has to do with terrorism.

35. Our concern is not just about these illicit weapons; it's the way that these illicit <u>weapons can be connected to terrorists and terrorist organizations</u> that have no compunction about using such devices against innocent people around the world.

Iraq and terrorism go back decades. Baghdad trains Palestine Liberation Front members in small arms and explosives. Saddam uses the Arab Liberation Front to funnel money to the families of Palestinian suicide bombers in order to prolong the Intifadah. And it's no secret that Saddam's own intelligence service was involved in dozens of attacks or attempted assassinations in the 1990s.

But what I want to bring to your attention today is the potentially much more sinister nexus between Iraq and the al-Qaida terrorist network, a nexus that combines classic terrorist organizations and modern methods of murder. Iraq today harbors a deadly terrorist network headed by Abu Musab al-Zarqawi an associate and collaborator of Usama bin Laden and his al-Qaida lieutenants.

Zarqawi, Palestinian born in Jordan, fought in the Afghan war more than a decade ago. Returning to Afghanistan in 2000, he oversaw a terrorist training camp. One of his specialties, and one of the specialties of this camp, is poisons.

When our coalition ousted the Taliban, the Zarqawi network helped establish another poison and explosive training center camp, and this camp is located in northeastern Iraq. You see a picture of this camp.

The network is teaching its operatives how to produce ricin and other poisons. Let me remind you how ricin works. Less than a pinch -- imagine a pinch of salt -- less than a pinch of ricin, eating just this amount in your food, would cause shock, followed by circulatory failure. Death comes within 72 hours and there is no antidote. There is no cure. It is fatal.

Those helping to run this camp are Zarqawi lieutenants operating in northern Kurdish areas outside Saddam Hussein's controlled Iraq. But Baghdad has an agent in the most senior levels of the radical organization Ansar al-Islam that controls this corner of Iraq. In 2000, this agent offered al-Qaida safe haven in the region.

After we swept al-Qaida from Afghanistan, some of those members accepted this safe haven. They remain there today.

Zarqawi's activities are not confined to this small corner of northeast Iraq. He traveled to Baghdad in May of 2002 for medical treatment, staying in the capital of Iraq for two months while he recuperated to fight another day.

During his stay, nearly two dozen extremists converged on Baghdad and established a base of operations there. These al-Qaida affiliates based in Baghdad now coordinate the movement of people, money and supplies into and throughout Iraq for his network, and they have now been operating freely in the capital for more than eight months.

Iraqi officials deny accusations of ties with al-Qaida. These denials are simply not credible. Last year, an al-Qaida associate bragged that the situation in Iraq was "good," that Baghdad could be transited quickly.

We know these affiliates are connected to Zarqawi because they remain, even today, in regular contact with his direct subordinates, include the poison cell plotters. And they are involved in moving more than money and materiel. Last year, two suspected al-Qaida operatives were arrested crossing from Iraq into Saudi Arabia. They were linked to associates of the Baghdad cell and one of them received training in Afghanistan on how to use cyanide.

From his terrorist network in Iraq, Zarqawi can direct his network in the Middle East and beyond. We in the United States, all of us, the State Department and the Agency for International Development, we all lost a dear friend with the cold-blooded murder of Mr. Laurence Foley in Amman, Jordan, last October. A despicable act was committed that day, the assassination of an individual whose sole mission was to assist the people of Jordan. The captured assassin says his cell received money and weapons from Zarqawi for that murder. After the attack, an associate of the assassin left Jordan to go to Iraq to obtain weapons and explosives for further operations. Iraqi officials protest that they are not aware of the whereabouts of Zarqawi or of any of his associates. Again, these protests are not credible. We know of Zarqawi's activities in Baghdad. I described them earlier.

Now let me add one other fact. We asked a friendly security service to approach Baghdad about extraditing Zarqawi and providing information about him and his close associates. This service contacted Iraqi officials twice and we passed details that should have made it easy to find Zarqawi. The network remains in Baghdad. Zarqawi still remains at large, to come and go.

As my colleagues around this table and as the citizens they represent in Europe know, Zarqawi's terrorism is not confined to the Middle East. Zarqawi and his network have plotted terrorist actions against countries including France, Britain, Spain, Italy, Germany and Russia. According to detainees Abu Atiya, who graduated from Zarqawi's terrorist camp in Afghanistan, tasked at least nine North African extremists in 2001 to travel to Europe to conduct poison and explosive attacks.

Since last year, members of this network have been apprehended in France, Britain, Spain

and Italy. By our last count, 116 operatives connected to this global web have been arrested. The chart you are seeing shows the network in Europe.

We know about this European network and we know about its links to Zarqawi because the detainees who provided the information about the targets also provided the names of members of the network. Three of those he identified by name were arrested in France last December. In the apartments of the terrorists, authorities found circuits for explosive devices and a list of ingredients to make toxins.

The detainee who helped piece this together says the plot also targeted Britain. Later evidence again proved him right. When the British unearthed the cell there just last month, one British police officer was murdered during the destruction of the cell.

We also know that Zarqawi's colleagues have been active in the Pankisi Gorge, Georgia, and in Chechnya, Russia. The plotting to which they are linked is not mere chatter. Members of Zarqawi's network say their goal was to kill Russians with toxins.

We are not surprised that Iraq is harboring Zarqawi and his subordinates. This understanding builds on decades-long experience with respect to ties between Iraq and al-Qaida. Going back to the early and mid-1990s when bin Laden was based in Sudan, an al-Qaida source tells us that Saddam and bin Laden reached an understanding that al-Qaida would no longer support activities against Baghdad. Early al-Qaida ties were forged by secret high-level intelligence service contacts with al-Qaida, secret Iraqi intelligence high-level contacts with al-Qaida.

We know members of both organizations met repeatedly and have met at least eight times at very senior levels since the early 1990s. In 1996, a foreign security service tells us that bin Laden met with a senior Iraqi intelligence official in Khartoum and later met the director of the Iraqi intelligence service.

Saddam became more interested as he saw al-Qaida's appalling attacks. A detained al-Qaida member tells us that Saddam was more willing to assist al-Qaida after the 1998 bombings of our embassies in Kenya and Tanzania. Saddam was also impressed by al-Qaida's attacks on the *USS Cole* in Yemen in October 2000.

Iraqis continue to visit bin Laden in his new home in Afghanistan. A senior defector, one of Saddam's former intelligence chiefs in Europe, says Saddam sent his agents to Afghanistan sometime in the mid-1990s to provide training to al-Qaida members on document forgery.

From the late 1990s until 2001, the Iraqi Embassy in Pakistan played the role of liaison to the al-Qaida organization.

Some believe, some claim, these contacts do not amount to much. They say Saddam Hussein's secular tyranny and al-Qaida's religious tyranny do not mix. I am not comforted by this thought. Ambition and hatred are enough to bring Iraq and al-Qaida together, enough so al-Qaida could learn how to build more sophisticated bombs and learn how to forge documents, and enough so that al-Qaida could turn to Iraq for help in acquiring expertise on weapons of mass destruction.

And the record of Saddam Hussein's cooperation with other Islamist terrorist organizations is clear. Hamas, for example, opened an office in Baghdad in 1999 and Iraq has hosted conferences attended by Palestine Islamic Jihad. These groups are at the forefront of sponsoring suicide attacks against Israel.

Al-Qaida continues to have a deep interest in acquiring weapons of mass destruction. As with the story of Zarqawi and his network, I can trace the story of a senior terrorist operative telling how Iraq provided training in these weapons to al-Qaida. Fortunately, this operative is now detained and he has told his story. I will relate it to you now as he, himself, described it.

This senior al-Qaida terrorist was responsible for one of al-Qaida's training camps in Afghanistan. His information comes firsthand from his personal involvement at senior levels of al-Qaida. He says bin Laden and his top deputy in Afghanistan, deceased al-Qaida leader Muhammad Atif, did not believe that al-Qaida labs in Afghanistan were capable enough to manufacture these chemical or biological agents. They needed to go somewhere else. They had to look outside of Afghanistan for help.

Where did they go? Where did they look? They went to Iraq. The support that this detainee describes included Iraq offering chemical or biological weapons training for two al-Qaida associates beginning in December 2000. He says that a militant known as Abdallah al-Iraqi had been sent to Iraq several times between 1997 and 2000 for help in acquiring poisons and gasses. Abdallah al-Iraqi characterized the relationship he forged with Iraqi officials as successful.

As I said at the outset, none of this should come as a surprise to any of us. Terrorism has been a tool used by Saddam for decades. Saddam was a supporter of terrorism long before these terrorist networks had a name, and this support continues. The nexus of poisons and terror is new. The nexus of Iraq and terror is old. The combination is lethal.

With this track record, Iraqi denials of supporting terrorism take their place alongside the other Iraqi denials of weapons of mass destruction. It is all a web of lies.

When we confront a regime that harbors ambitions for regional domination, hides weapons of mass destruction, and provides haven and active support for terrorists, we are not confronting the past; we are confronting the present. And unless we act, we are confronting an even more frightening future.

And, friends, this has been a long and a detailed presentation and I thank you for your patience, but there is one more subject that I would like to touch on briefly, and it should be a subject of deep and continuing concern to this Council: Saddam Hussein's violations of human rights.

Underlying all that I have said, underlying all the facts and the patterns of behavior that I have identified, is Saddam Hussein's contempt for the will of this Council, his contempt for the truth, and, most damning of all, his utter contempt for human life. Saddam Hussein's use of mustard and nerve gas against the Kurds in 1988 was one of the 20th century's most horrible atrocities. Five thousand men, women and children died. His campaign against the Kurds from 1987 to '89 included mass summary executions, disappearances, arbitrary jailing and ethnic cleansing, and the destruction of some 2,000 villages.

He has also conducted ethnic cleansing against the Shia Iraqis and the Marsh Arabs whose culture has flourished for more than a millennium. Saddam Hussein's police state ruthlessly eliminates anyone who dares to dissent. Iraq has more forced disappearance cases than any other country -- tens of thousands of people reported missing in the past decade.

Nothing points more clearly to Saddam Hussein's dangerous intentions and the threat he poses to all of us than his calculated cruelty to his own citizens and to his neighbors. Clearly, Saddam Hussein and his regime will stop at nothing until something stops him.

For more than 20 years, by word and by deed, Saddam Hussein has pursued his ambition to dominate Iraq and the broader Middle East using the only means he knows: intimidation, coercion and annihilation of all those who might stand in his way. For Saddam Hussein, possession of the world's most deadly weapons is the ultimate trump card, the one he must hold to fulfill his ambition.

We know that Saddam Hussein is determined to keep his weapons of mass destruction, is determined to make more. Given Saddam Hussein's history of aggression, given what we know of his grandiose plans, given what we know of his terrorist associations, and given his determination to exact revenge on those who oppose him, should we take the risk that he will not someday use these weapons at a time and a place and in a manner of his choosing, at a time when the world is in a much weaker position to respond?

The United States will not and cannot run that risk for the American people. Leaving Saddam Hussein in possession of weapons of mass destruction for a few more months or years is not an option, not in a post-September 11th world.

My colleagues, over three months ago, this Council recognized that Iraq continued to pose a threat to international peace and security, and that Iraq had been and remained in material breach of its disarmament obligations.

Today, Iraq still poses a threat and Iraq still remains in material breach. Indeed, by its failure to seize on its one last opportunity to come clean and disarm, Iraq has put itself in deeper material breach and closer to the day when it will face serious consequences for its continue defiance of this Council.

My colleagues, we have an obligation to our citizens. We have an obligation to this body to see that our resolutions are complied with. We wrote 1441 not in order to go to war. We wrote 1441 to try to preserve the peace. We wrote 1441 to give Iraq one last chance.

Iraq is not, so far, taking that one last chance.

We must not shrink from whatever is ahead of us. We must not fail in our duty and our responsibility to the citizens of the countries that are represented by this body.

Thank you, Mr. President.

[End]

Released on February 5, 2003

Powell Speech Comments

1. As did George Bush in the State of the Union, Powell here takes the period
   twelve years, not eleven, as the elapsed interval since Iraq had been subject to
   this disarmament regime. The twelve-year mark would actually be reached on
   April 3, 2003, a day on which U.S. troops neared Baghdad after invading Iraq.
   Obviously this is not a major error, but it illustrates the willingness of the administration to exploit every conceivable way of magnifying its case against Iraq.

2. Here Powell mischaracterizes the "core assessments" of Hans Blix and Mohammed ElBaradei. The Blix quote Powell cites pertained to Iraqi cooperation with
   the inspection process—which Blix wanted to improve—not his core conclusion.
   Rather, Blix on January 27 presented data on several disarmament areas (chemical weapons, biological weapons, and missiles) that summarized his uncertainties.
   Blix did not present a core assessment. Secretary Powell does not mention that the very
   next day Hans Blix gave an interview at which he said he had seen nothing thus
   far to justify a war. Blix took that position despite U.S. pressure, including visits
   to him from Condoleezza Rice. Since the Iraq war, Hans Blix (on numerous
   occasions) has said that he had been trying to express doubts on the Iraqi records.
   But that meant equally that Iraq might have no weapons as that it did. Blix
   believes the U.S. "overinterpreted" its intelligence and assumed the existence of
   every weapon for which there was no positive evidence of destruction. This
   increasingly appears to be the truth.

   As for Mohammed ElBaradei and the International Atomic Energy Agency,
   what secretary Powell chose to quote is highly significant—it is *not* IAEA's core
   assessment at all, but a point about desires for greater certainty, which ElBaradei
   specifically noted, "do not constitute unresolved disarmament issues." What the
   IAEA report *does* conclude—in a section labeled "conclusion"—is: "We have to
   date found no evidence that Iraq has revived its nuclear weapons program since
   the elimination of the program in the 1990s." The IAEA report's actual conclusions *could not have been quoted by Powell without undercutting the U.S. case for a war
   authority resolution from the UN.* The IAEA position was deliberately misrepresented,
   the UNMOVIC view somewhat distorted.

3. Although this point probably is accurate for the most recent period (1998–02),
   there is no dispute that Saddam ordered the destruction of large numbers of
   weapons, including munitions, missiles, rocket motors, and more during 1991–
   92. One of the CIA's own declassified intelligence reports of February 1992

states: "Iraq has currently stopped its biological warfare (BW) program and as of early February 1992, has no specific plans to restart the program."

Poor Iraqi record keeping in the aftermath of the Gulf War lay at the root of many disputes, such as whether there remained a "covert force" of Iraqi SCUD missiles, how many chemical shells Iraq possessed, and the like. The existence of these disputes ought to have reminded the drafters of this speech that this passage was not accurate. In addition, Iraqi defector Hussein Kamel in 1995 explicitly told the UN inspectors, and through them the CIA, that Saddam had in that year ordered the destruction of stocks of Iraqi chemical and biological weapons. Whether or not the United States had access to these records, by definition these Iraqi actions *were* efforts to disarm. Postwar analyses are increasingly concluding that Saddam divested himself of remaining chemical and biological stocks in three waves, 1991–92, 1995, and 1998. If accurate, this view corresponds to what was already known (except for 1998) and makes the text here misleading.

4. The Al Kindi Veterinary Vaccine Production Plant, located sixteen miles west of Baghdad, had been scrutinized by UN inspectors since 1991. An early detection team led by David Kay concluded that Al Kindi had had the capability to produce biological warfare agents, but no evidence was ever found that Iraq had actually used it for that purpose. Neither the CIA white paper on Iraqi weapons of mass destruction nor the British Iraq dossier made any mention of Al Kindi whatever.

5. Clearly the communications intercepts are secretary Powell's best cards in this speech. This evidence is suggestive rather than definitive, however, in the absence of recovery of actual stocks of chemical and biological agent. There are reports that Saddam's deception measures aimed at *creating* rather than eliminating the impression he possessed these kinds of weapons, and the messages would fit that purpose well. They would also fit a scenario of moving Iraqi chemical and biological agents and unilaterally destroying them so as to deny the United States evidence such weapons had ever existed.

6. Vice President Ramadan would be captured by the Kurds after the war and was turned over to U.S. occupation forces on August 19, 2003. General Al Sa'adi, in addition to this committee, also sat on the committee liaising with UN weapons inspectors, and is also in U.S. custody, as are, by now, many of the senior scientists previously heading Iraq's chemical, biological, and nuclear weapons programs. All of them have denied Saddam had any weapons of mass destruction.

Some have given evidence that supports deception theories. Any deception program (including American ones) needs coordination by a senior official body, so that the mere existence of such a committee is not in itself evidence of existence of offensive weapons. Whether or not Saddam conducted deception operations, and was attempting to maintain a tool kit for reconstituting weapons production in the future, the case for war Colin Powell made on February 5 had been based on a *current* Iraqi threat, not a hypothetical future one.

7. Here Secretary Powell demands too much of intelligence. Estimating and projection are the province of intelligence, which almost never deals in facts. The "facts and conclusions based on solid evidence" claimed here are really impressions and speculations based on available evidence. The Kerr panel within the CIA as well as a postwar investigation by the House Permanent Select Committee on Intelligence both observed that U.S. intelligence suffered from a dearth of fresh data once the UN inspectors left Iraq in 1998.

The United States had the communications intercepts the secretary cites indicating some kind of Iraqi activity. Previously and later he will show certain satellite imagery that indicates the Iraqis did something at certain sites. What they actually moved Powell himself has to admit the U.S. does not know. In one case U.S. intelligence does know what happened—the Iraqis took a site and cleaned it up. Why is not known. Powell's commentary that these things were done to hide weapons and evidence that the site had contained weapons is value-added; i.e., intelligence analysts made assumptions and concluded that certain things had occurred. That is not the same as "fact." Secretary Powell, clearly conscious of this objection, then cites human intelligence, for it is the agent on the ground who can observe things and hear words that explain the reasons for things overhead that reconnaissance merely observes. The problem with that is the quality of the spies. By late summer 2003, frustrated at the continued inability of its Iraq Survey Group to find any weapons of mass destruction, the Defense Intelligence Agency initiated an internal inquiry on whether the defectors provided by Iraqi exile groups had provided genuine information or reported what they thought the Americans wanted to hear.

8. The report on this missile brigade is a good example of the human source problem just referred to. The United States captured Iraq, including the western part of the country, and had complete and unfettered ability to scour the countryside. In nine months as of this writing, no such rocket launchers or biological warheads have been found. The human reports look good in Colin Powell's address to the Security Council, but they add up to much less than he claims for them.

9. Fenced compounds and security buildings are suggestive but not definitive evidence of the purpose of a facility. Powell uses that here as the decisive signature of the purpose of the compound, as was done on other occasions during the prewar hyping of the Iraq intelligence (notably an October 7, 2002, presentation by DIA on Iraqi deception methods). But there is *no* evidence to support secretary Powell's assertion as to what the building contains ("special guards and special equipment to monitor any leakage"). Other experience indicates that during the Saddam era in Iraq, many kinds of plants and storage facilities were surrounded by fences and features similar to this one. This particular inspection was one of five that the inspectors carried out on December 22 (three by UNMOVIC, two by the IAEA), and it was commented upon specifically by Hans Blix in a follow-up report he made on February 14: "This was a declared site and it was certainly one of the sites Iraq would have expected to be to inspect—us to inspect [sic]. We have noted that the two satellite images of the site were taken several weeks apart. The report of movement of munitions at the site could just as easily have been a routine activity as a movement of proscribed munitions in anticipation of imminent inspection."

10. Secretary Powell's citation of the "fine paper" that British authorities had prepared on Iraqi deception activity became one of the most embarrassing parts of this presentation. The paper turned out to have been partly plagiarized from the work of a private citizen and based on thin material, some of it more than a decade old. The British deception dossier, unlike their Iraq intelligence dossier, was assembled entirely within 10 Downing Street, under the direction of the Iraq Communications Group, formed in December 2002, a unit similar to President Bush's WHIG and headed by Alastair Campbell, the same individual who had sought to shape the September dossier. The SIS representative on the group offered to furnish a briefing note on Iraqi deception techniques. (John Scarlett attended the four meetings of the communications group that dealt with creation of this document, but it is not clear whether he sat at the table as SIS representative or chairman of the Joint Intelligence Committee.) That contribution appears to have been a sort of orientation paper for UN inspectors on what to anticipate in Iraq, what to look for in the street, warning of Iraqi "helpers" with microphones, and the like. The SIS paper was then used by a Coalition Information Center (a British propaganda unit originally created during the Kosovo war of 1999), and points from it were melded into the work of Ibrahim Al-Marashi, a research associate of the Center for Nonproliferation Studies of the Monterrey Institute of International Studies, who had recently published a paper on Iraqi intelligence in the journal *Middle East Review of International Affairs*. More than 60 percent of the British government's supposed inside story of Iraqi intelli-

gence was directly copied from Al-Marashi's work, without permission or attribution. Although under the British system the Joint Intelligence Committee had to approve any public use of SIS material, John Scarlett never saw the completed paper, which was given to the press in England at the beginning of February 2003 and distributed at the UN on February 4. Sources in British intelligence soon complained through the press that the document did not reflect their views, the plagiarism was noticed by scholar Glen Rangwala, and the British paper was discredited as an authoritative source. Actually the British media dubbed it the "dodgy dossier." Once it had been issued, on February 3 Tony Blair rose in Parliament to declare, "We issued further intelligence over the weekend about the infrastructure of concealment." In fact the material did not qualify as an intelligence product. Its use by Colin Powell at the Security Council undercut his own claim to be presenting only the best, and best-scrubbed, intelligence.

11. Iraq had been refusing to guarantee the safety of U-2 flights on the grounds it could not ensure its air defenses could be prevented from firing on the spy planes, not rejecting the flights altogether. Since a fairly intense air campaign continued in which the Americans and British were suppressing Iraqi command control systems and air defenses in the guise of enforcing no-fly zones, the proposition that Iraqi air defense crews might respond to detecting a UN aircraft by assuming it to be part of a coalition protective reaction strike had some merit. The problem as posed by Powell was a real one, as well as Iraqi intransigence, something that Hans Blix complained of repeatedly. But what Powell did not say, however, was that the difficulty had been exacerbated by U.S. military actions. He also neglected to mention that the problem had already begun to move toward resolution. UN helicopters had been flying missions in Iraq since early January, and the Iraqis were moving to acquiesce in the U-2 flights, which the UN would begin during the third week of February. Not only that, but Blix would soon have available assets over and above the U-2s, including French-supplied Mirage jets, German drone aircraft, and a Russian-built Antonov transport with night-vision capability. In short, Powell referred to a diminishing problem.

12. Nothing in the UN resolutions or the inspection scheme obliged Iraq to permit interviews with its personnel without "minders." This is an angle Washington had been pushing since early December at least, based on an expectation that Iraqi scientists without government attendants might say what the United States wanted to hear. There was no particular reason to believe that, other than an assumption (troublesome U.S. assumptions are rife throughout the Iraq affair) that all the Iraqis except the defectors talking to U.S. intelligence were lying (the opposite assumption might have been equally accurate). The demand failed to

take into account the interests of the Baghdad regime, which the United States well knew Saddam Hussein would do. In fact, the Bush administration itself used "minders" in precisely the same way. All intelligence community, White House, and State Department personnel called before the U.S. congressional committee investigating the September 11 attacks, and then the national commission doing the same thing, were accompanied by Bush administration attendants. This was not unusual either. The same practice had been adopted by the Reagan and (first) Bush administrations during Iran-Contra, the Ford administration during the 1975 investigations of the intelligence community, and on other occasions. To raise the matter of Iraqi "minders" to that of a *casus belli* amounts to imposition of a double standard.

13. Information culled from liaison relationships with foreign intelligence services is a mainstay for the United States, but can be a double-edged sword. The data provided can be good, or not, while the foreign service acts as an additional filter. In the matter of the Niger uranium claims, for example, the Italian service SISME seems to have exercised insufficient care for ensuring the accuracy of reports it passed along to the CIA, which in the American political setting opened up a wedge for a fresh distortion of the Iraq intelligence (see pp. 186–87).

14. These paragraphs constitute secretary Powell's call for the Security Council to approve war with Iraq.

15. This figure of 25,000 liters, used in almost all the Bush people's sallies on Iraq that endeavor to detail the clear and present threat, actually does not come from UNSCOM, as Colin Powell here asserts. The final UNSCOM report (1998) came near to being suppressed owing to complaints from Russia, which held a dim view of then-chief inspector Richard Butler. The report had almost no circulation, even among Security Council members. A review panel under an Indian diplomat examined the report and finally released a modified version in the spring of 1999. In the interval the *British* government got hold of the UNSCOM report and issued a white paper that was an interpretation of the UN document. The UNSCOM report said Iraq had retained about 17 tons of precursor material for anthrax. It also noted Baghdad admitted making 8,500 liters of the agent. It was the British white paper that estimated the amount of precursor as sufficient to fabricate three times the amount that Iraq had admitted to manufacturing.

16. The Defense Intelligence Agency in September 2002 included in one of its reports the statement that although Iraq was assumed to have biological weapons stockpiles that might be loaded into weapons and ready for use, the extent of the stock was not certain and *was* subject to debate.

17. An analysis of the CIA's mobile weapons laboratory report appears in the next chapter.

18. Although we shall defer most of this discussion, an extended discussion of mobile labs appears in the next chapter. On the discreet subject of laboratories on rail cars, it is key to note that a railmobile system is inherently less flexible than a roadmobile version for a mobile weapons laboratory, assuming the alleged lab exists. Iraq has more than 27,000 miles of roadway, 85 percent of which is paved. Vehicles, if one were desperate to hide them, could even be driven off the roads. By contrast there are just 1,220 miles of railroad in Iraq and rail cars are strictly confined to the tracks. It is impossible that in more than nine months of actual occupation of Iraq American search teams would not have found a railmobile laboratory if one existed.

19. Manufacturing rates of mobile laboratories would necessarily be considerably less than those of large fixed plants. This is especially true for the situation secretary Powell proceeds to describe—a surreptitious production effort that displaces constantly and is restricted to the one time of the week (the Muslim holy day) when operators are sure that UN inspections will be stood down. Under these circumstances, the notion that the biological agent stock Iraq had possessed at the time of the Gulf War could be replicated in a matter of months—the National Intelligence Estimate puts the interval at three to six months—stretches credulity. The DIA report cited just above found that without outside help Iraq would likely have trouble reaching the production rates that had prevailed before the Gulf War, and this observation would seem to apply doubly to mobile production of biological warfare agents.

20. UN inspectors would eventually confirm Iraq's contention that its effort to modify the tanks was successful, but the attempt to convert the aircraft was not. In March 2003 the inspectors found one of the modified spray tanks at an Iraqi base. Perhaps Iraq had not said the tanks were destroyed because they had not been.

21. Note that Secretary Powell stops short of claiming any particular number of tons of chemical agents in the Iraqi stockpile, though it could be "up to" 500 tons. A few moments later Powell would come back to the subject and quantify the range as between 100 and 500 tons. See the comment at that point in the text.

22. On January 27 Hans Blix had used the example of 6,500 bombs, a number drawn from a discrepancy in the so-called "Air Force Document" (an Iraqi air force paper that listed munitions expenditures in the Iran-Iraq and Gulf wars against an inventory of stocks was found by UN inspectors in 1998; Baghdad

tried to protect the document, leading to an earlier crisis on inspections), to illustrate suspicions that could be drawn from Iraq's lack of responsiveness to inspectors. Here Powell takes suspicions and concretizes them, making the 1,000 tons of chemical weapons capacity in the munitions into a real, unaccounted-for agent.

23. Note the reference to Iraqi defector Hussein Kamel in a context favorable to what the Bush people sought to achieve. In the light of postwar failure to discover any Iraqi gases, including VX, the late 1990s laboratory detections of trace residues of VX in Iraqi artillery shells raise questions equally about the disposition of the Iraqi stocks and the lab test methods.

24. Between May and July of 2002 there was no UN Security Council Resolution 1441, no UN inspection program, and no reason for the Iraqis to engage in deception activity. The Defense Intelligence Agency in a September 2002 report noted there had been a flurry of Iraqi munitions movement activity during the summer, which it associated with an effort to distribute munitions to cope with an American attack. It is equally possible that munitions movements formed part of a consolidation effort. The movement of material and removal of topsoil are consistent with standard procedures in deactivating a facility handling hazardous materials. Such measures do not necessarily mean that a deception operation is underway, though they may, but again at this point in time Baghdad had no need to deceive inspectors. The same kinds of site clean-up activity have occurred in many instances of base closure within the United States itself.

25. Here Secretary Powell misrepresents U.S. intelligence on the size of Iraq's chemical weapons stockpile. In the 2002 National Intelligence Estimate, the high end of the range projecting Saddam's stockpile was 500 tons, an amount in which U.S. intelligence had less confidence than its mainline estimate. The lower end of the projection came in at 100 tons, of which the CIA was confident, using the rating "probably." Powell's use of the word "conservative" here in intelligence usage denotes "at least," which amounts to a claim that Iraq possesses a greater quantity than the amount mentioned. That is misleading.

26. Here the National Intelligence Estimate contained important disagreements on whether an Iraqi nuclear program continued and on the extent of its progress. Within the State Department, Powell's own Bureau of Intelligence and Research believed Saddam's nuclear scientists were not getting anywhere fast. Senior analyst Greg Thielmann retired shortly before these events and recalled two major INR analytical reports were sent to the secretary of state concluding that there

was no reliable evidence to support the assertion that Saddam had restarted his
nuclear program at all. Thielmann would later say of the reports to Powell,
"These were not weaselly worded, they were as definitive as these things go." At
the Security Council on February 5, Secretary Powell differed markedly, on this
and other issues, with the intelligence staff of his own department.

27. Note that Secretary Powell here steps back from President Bush's extravagant
declaration in the State of the Union that Saddam had pressed ahead on uranium
enrichment using five different methods. Powell cites only three.

28. For a discussion of the now-notorious (as Powell himself concedes) aluminum
tubes see pp. 93–104.

29. Secretary Powell's language here obscures the extent of disagreement within U.S.
intelligence on the tubes and makes no effort to distinguish a range of general
opinion from the dissenting experts who considered the centrifuge theory inaccurate. There simply was not the degree of unity within U.S. intelligence Powell
suggests, again trampling on the views of his own State Department analysts.
Equally important are the findings of the International Atomic Energy Agency
(IAEA). In any case, Powell was talking about the theoretical ability to adapt (i.e.,
remanufacture) the tubes. In its investigations of Iraq, the IAEA found that Baghdad lacked the necessary flow-forming capabilities, which made it, in the words
of Mohammed ElBaradei's March 7 report, "highly unlikely that it [Iraq] is currently able to produce aluminum cylinders consistently to the tolerances required
for centrifuge enrichment." In nontechnical terms, the tubes Iraq imported were
of the wrong dimensions for centrifuges, and the country itself lacked the manufacturing capability to produce ones that could have been suitable.

30. The magnets also figured in the discussion of a possible Iraqi nuclear weapons
program in the 2002 National Intelligence Estimate, where State Department
analysts rejected the contention that Iraq's purchases proved the weapons effort
to be underway. The IAEA reached the same conclusion. Imports of magnets
were unnecessary for a nuclear program, the inspectors found, because Iraq had
sufficient expertise from the pre-1991 period to design its own magnets for centrifuges. Iraqi imports of magnets had begun in 1998, not the following year,
and included twelve different designs. The plant Colin Powell refers to had been
contracted for in June 2001 for installation in 2003, and no delivery took place
before the coalition invasion of Iraq. The IAEA reviewed the plans for a magnet
plant and observed: "the replacement of foreign procurement with domestic magnet production seems reasonable from an economic point of view."

31. The "numerous intelligence reports" that Secretary Powell cites here are a prime
    example of the weaknesses in the intelligence on Iraq. On the one hand, there
    were numerous *analytical* reports that referred to a covert SCUD force, but that
    intelligence was in the nature of common wisdom, simply repeating what was
    thought to be true. On the other hand, there were intelligence *field* reports, *from
    before 1998*, that expressed doubts about Iraq's account that it had destroyed all
    missiles of this type. There was *no* physical evidence for the covert missile force,
    and the only concrete evidence lay in the discrepancies in accounting among lists
    of the numbers of SCUD-type missiles Iraq had imported, and the numbers var-
    iously expended, whether in testing, the Iran-Iraq war, or the Gulf War. During
    its invasion of Iraq and afterward, the coalition captured or detained many senior
    Iraqi leaders, including the military commanders, weapons scientists, and indus-
    trial managers responsible for Saddam's missile forces. According to the interim
    report of the Iraq Survey Mission, only one official made any claim regarding
    the existence of this alleged missile force, and he recanted that statement almost
    immediately, suggesting that coalition interrogators were asking leading questions.

32. Powell is correct to note evidence that Iraq continued efforts to develop long-
    range missiles. But in 2002–03, Baghdad stood far from that goal. The necessary
    missiles had not even reached the hardware stage; rocket motors had yet to be
    engineered, static-tested, or married to an air frame. In essence Iraq remained at
    the blueprint stage except for certain necessary preparatory facilities (engine test
    stands, solid fuel casting chambers) already under construction. But those were
    under observation, as Powell demonstrates with his satellite photograph here, and
    Iraq could not flight test such a missile without U.S. intelligence knowing about
    it. Long-range Iraqi missiles were projected by the United States in the foreign
    ballistic missile NIEs of both 1995 and 1999, in other intelligence reports prior
    to that time, as well as in the periodic reports to Congress on weapons of mass
    destruction of 2000–03. This intelligence does not meet the test of clear and
    present danger, or strengthen the Bush administration contention that Saddam
    Hussein posed a current threat to the United States.

33. The smaller unmanned aerial vehicles Secretary Powell refers to, even if designed
    as weapons carriers, would necessarily have had very restricted abilities as aerosol
    dispensers. UN inspectors found some of these UAVs before the war, and U.S.
    troops captured some others during the war; they had design features and fittings
    that seem clearly to have been intended for overhead surveillance purposes.

34. Intelligence on an Iraqi UAV test of June 27, 2002, is one of the pieces of fresh
    intelligence that Colin Powell unveiled in his Security Council address. The test

took place at the Iraqi range at Ibn Fernas air base, and the drone, a vehicle apparently known as the RPV-20, flew for 300 miles. The system had been declared to UN inspectors, and Iraq had maintained its range met the restriction (90 miles) contained in UN resolutions. This is a "material breach" in the sense of Resolution 1441, but it concerned a system that lacked offensive aerial capability owing to its lack of payload capacity and fittings for surveillance rather than agent dispersal.

Another aspect of the Iraqi drone program that remains untouched in all the discussion of ranges and dispenser tanks is control features. The long-range test of 2002 involved a drone on autopilot, which simply flew in a racetrack pattern. It is quite likely that a limiting factor in Iraqi UAV efforts throughout was lack of the ability to command the drones to respond to remote piloting. The communications and avionics requirements for remote piloting, particularly radio range limitations, imposed unavoidable obstacles to any Iraqi UAV program but *especially* to any effort at drones with offensive military capability. This is additional reason to believe the drones lacked a practical military capability against the U.S. homeland, and that they contributed little to an Iraqi current threat to the United States.

35. Questions of Saddam's links with terrorism are treated as a major subject in the following section.

Iraq's Alleged Connections to Terrorism

Secretary of State Colin L. Powell made Iraq's links to terrorism a major theme in his presentation to the UN Security Council. Most disturbingly, he alleged a connection with Osama bin Laden's Al Qaeda group. As the speech shows, Powell began with his charge that "Iraq and terrorism go back decades," through a few general charges, to a series of claims regarding the "more sinister nexus between Iraq and the al-Qaida terrorist network," as personified by one militant leader, Abu Musab al-Zarqawi. Powell then moved from the particular to the global, charging Saddam with major ties to Al Qaeda. In a striking claim picked up and repeated the next day by George W. Bush, Powell asserted there had been at least eight meetings of senior Iraqi intelligence agents and Al Qaeda figures since the early 1990s. "This [American] understanding," the secretary intoned, "builds on decades-long experience with respect to ties between Iraq and al-Qaida." As for Iraq's denial of this, "It is all a web of lies." Powell turned to Saddam's support for the Palestinian fight with Israel, then finished with a condemnation of Iraq's internal repression and violations of human rights.

Al Qaeda did not exist before 1989, so there is no possibility that the United States could have had "decades" of experience observing its relationship with Saddam Hussein, but that is a minor point. A key question is what Colin Powell did *not* speak about at the Security Council. Since the Powell speech by his own account represented the authoritative distillation of the U.S. case against Saddam, and the claim that Saddam had participated in the September 11 attacks against America appeared nowhere in it, the conclusion is that this allegation did not pass muster. Cheney aide Scooter Libby and Pentagon representatives had pushed hard for inclusion of the charge but failed. That charge remained at the heart of Bush administration justifications for war, however, and would be repeated again.

The case against Saddam on terrorism grounds exists on a number of levels and needs to be examined at each one. There are two stories at the highest level, the first being the record of the Bush administration's use of this issue, the second whether a strategic link between Saddam and bin Laden actually existed. Several matters of substance underlie the overarching issues starting with the September 11 charge. Also involved here are whether an Al Qaeda network existed in Iraq, whether weapons of mass destruction were involved, and what Saddam's stance on Palestine has to do with the war. Finally, there are questions of evidence. Each of these will be treated in turn.

Just a few days after the September 11, 2001, attacks, Vice President Cheney was asked in a television interview whether Saddam Hussein had had anything to do with the tragedy. The question was understandable. Americans were desperately searching for meaning and reason, explanations of why and how. Many, including this analyst, briefly toyed with the notion that Saddam had been involved. Cheney's stand at the time clarified the question and amounted to a public service: he denied any connection while acknowledging that Saddam had had links to terrorism in the past. But his stance soon wavered. Two months later, in November, during a similar tele-

vision appearance, Cheney indicated he believed that one of the September
11 hijackers had met Iraqi agents in Prague five months before the attacks.
In a third television appearance on National Broadcasting Network's *Meet the
Press* on December 9, the vice president said of the alleged Prague meeting,
"It's been pretty well confirmed." Before the Council on Foreign Relations
in February 2002, Cheney appeared to soften, citing Saddam's past relations
with terrorists but not claiming a specific connection to September 11. But
about the time of Vice President Cheney's trip to Europe and the Middle
East to drum up international support for a war, his line hardened and afterward did not budge. Right through the fall of 2003, after the invasion had
turned up no new evidence, Cheney continued to assert the reality of Saddam's Al Qaeda links, including the Prague meeting (about which more presently). A first-order question is, What changed the vice president's mind?

Prominent figures among the neo-con movement, including Richard
Perle on the Defense Policy Board and former CIA director R. James Woolsey, insisted there had to be a link between Saddam and the 9/11 attacks.
Woolsey went out of his way to draw attention to theories advanced by
conservative scholar Laurie Mylroie, which purported to connect Saddam to
such diverse terrorist strikes as the 1993 truck bombing at New York's
World Trade Center and an abortive plot in the Philippines two years afterward. The Policy Board recommended, and deputy secretary of defense Paul
Wolfowitz approved, a mission to Britain by Woolsey in search of evidence
to back up the Mylroie thesis. Woolsey's search proved fruitless except for
assorted details on the lives of certain terrorists, plotters who moved in circles
that would later be identified with Al Qaeda, not with Saddam.

Another set of events reflecting the kind of hysteria engulfing many
Americans during that time followed in October, when attacks using a biological warfare agent (anthrax) through the mail occurred in the United
States. Widespread claims that the anthrax was Iraqi in origin put U.S. authorities under some pressure to jump to conclusions, but were met judi-
ciously. Investigation eventually established the strain of anthrax involved to
have come from a U.S. weapons laboratory (the perpetrators of the anthrax

mail attacks have yet to be discovered but the incidents are now regarded as domestic acts).

Meanwhile, assertions of Saddam's links to 9/11 did not match U.S. intelligence reporting. The State Department is responsible for annual reports on terror through its coordinator for counterterrorism. The report for the year 2000, which appeared in April 2001, maintained that Iraq "planned and coordinated international terrorism," but that its targets were Iraqi exiles overseas. The official report specifically said, "The regime has not attempted an anti-Western terrorist attack since its failed plot to assassinate former President Bush in 1993 in Kuwait." A State Department list of forty-five nations where Al Qaeda had operated that was also produced at around this time did not include Iraq. Even after months of dispute over whether 9/11 ringleader Mohamed Atta had met with an Iraqi agent in Prague, the annual worldwide threat briefing that Carl Ford of State's Bureau of Intelligence and Research (INR) presented to the Senate select committee in February 2002 did not endorse the allegations. Answering questions for the record Ford noted, "This contact concerns us and remains under investigation but it does not definitively link Iraq to the September 11 attacks." The INR responses detailed a number of Iraqi contacts with terror groups, mostly Palestinian or anti-Iranian, none of them Al Qaeda. The INR view closely paralleled that at the CIA. George Tenet's comments at the same global threat briefing also noted that Iraq had not attempted anything against the United States since the attempted assassination. A broader community inquiry coordinated by National Intelligence Officer Paul Pillar appeared in the spring of 2002 titled "Iraq and Al Qaeda: A Murky Relationship."

Over the following months, various developments weakened the claim about the Prague meeting between an Iraqi agent and an Al Qaeda plotter. Virtually all other allegations bearing on the question of Baghdad's relationship with Al Qaeda had emerged in 2001 or earlier. Suddenly in August, the same month the Bush White House created its Iraq information group (WHIG) and the Pentagon a similar entity, the administration took measures to clear its path to allegations about Saddam and Al Qaeda.

One crucial move took place within the intelligence community. Most analysts at the CIA agreed there was no such relationship. The key confrontation took place in August between a Pentagon group led by Douglas Feith, undersecretary for policy, and a CIA contingent of as many as twenty led by George Tenet. Feith brought along a pair of gunslingers from his office, Tina Shelton of DIA and Christopher Carney, a Navy intelligence specialist, who were with a unit formed to reassess intelligence data. They had been engaged in a novel exercise, taking a hypothesis (that Saddam and bin Laden were allied) and seeing if the data fit it, rather than taking the data and adding it up to form their conclusion.

Shelton and Carney told the audience they thought Saddam's links to Bin Laden were extensive and appear to have begun when Bin Laden lived in the Sudan during the early 1990s. They regaled the group with stories of visits to the Sudan by Iraqi intelligence operatives, and exchanges of visits between Iraq and Afghanistan later, where requests for assistance were allegedly made. According to Jeffrey Goldberg, author of the best account of this episode, the Feith group "expected resistance from CIA officials, but, to the surprise of many in the room, Tenet was open to the Pentagon analysis." Apparently the CIA director had commissioned his own alternative analysis along similar lines previously and had come to share this view. The Counterterrorism Center at Langley agreed. The intelligence directorate's Near East and South Asia division did not. Tenet sided with the Counterterrorism Center analysts.

The red team exercise Tenet relied upon for his recasting of intelligence views on Saddam and Al Qaeda utilized a technique increasingly popular since the 1980s of turning the glass upside down to look at a situation from a different point of view. In 1998, during the second term of the Clinton administration, the National Security Council staff had carried out the same kind of exercise. Says Daniel Benjamin, a participant in the 1998 study, "We looked at this as an opportunity to disprove the conventional wisdom, and basically we came to the conclusion that the CIA had this one right." Not much in the way of fresh evidence appeared between then and the summer of 2002, when Tenet changed his view, if not the agency's, particularly with

regard to the necessary high-level contacts between Saddam and Al Qaeda
that would have been necessary to create this unholy alliance.

Tenet's red team and Feith's intelligence unit had both relied upon in-
ductive, rather than deductive, analysis in constructing their intelligence picture. This approach magnifies the role of assumptions, which in this method
substitute for conclusions, becoming the starting point for marshaling the
intelligence reporting. Bush administration assumptions about Iraq, which we
have seen as flawed in several other cases, had suddenly become the central
driver for fresh intelligence summaries showing Saddam in a harsh light.

Early in September Paul Wolfowitz met with FBI assistant director for
counterterrorism Paul D'Amuro to go over the Prague ground one more
time. D'Amuro would not agree that the data was hard enough to say with
assurance there had been an Iraq–Al Qaeda confab, but the Bureau retreated
enough to acknowledge that such an encounter was a possibility. Referring
to the whole state of play on the Iraqi connection to terrorism, a senior official
told a reporter, "It's a thin reed."

Aside from Dick Cheney's verbal sallies in the spring, there had been
few references to Saddam and Al Qaeda until the very moment in August
and September when it became important in the Bush White House to sell
the notion of an Iraqi threat. This is what raises the Saddam–Al Qaeda alliance allegation from a simple mistake to the level of an element in the plot
to hoodwink America, taking shameless advantage of the same hysteria that
had engulfed the nation after September 11, 2001. The change can be dated
closely—on September 8, 2002, President Bush told the Canadian prime minister that the United States was focused on weapons of mass destruction, not
Iraqi links to Al Qaeda. But beginning on September 25 came another of
those coordinated message offensives so appealing to the president.

This spin campaign began, like many other things, with Condoleezza
Rice. Just the day before, the CIA had secretly presented Congress with some
of its intelligence on Iraqi weapons of mass destruction. Rice kicked off the
visible part of the effort. The national security adviser in a television appearance accused Iraq of providing training to Al Qaeda militants in chemical

weapons development and Baghdad of providing refuge for militants fleeing the fall of Afghanistan. Rice said her reports were from high-level former Al Qaeda militants in U.S. custody. Press spokesmen Ari Fleischer followed up the next day: "We have solid evidence of the presence in Iraq of Al Qaeda members, including some who have been in Baghdad. We have solid reporting of senior-level contacts between Al Qaeda and Iraqi officials going back a decade and, as Condi said, of chemical and biological agent training." At that moment Donald Rumsfeld was on his way back from Warsaw, where he had been for a conference among NATO ministers, and where CIA deputy director John McLaughlin had briefed the assemblage on the Iraqi threat. Back in Washington Rumsfeld told a press conference at the Pentagon that he had "bulletproof" evidence of Saddam's relationship with Osama bin Laden: "We have what we consider to be very reliable reporting of senior-level contacts going back a decade, and of possible chemical and biological agent training." President Bush capped the offensive with his October 7 address to the Veterans of Foreign Wars in Cincinnati, where he said that Saddam was hiding terrorists.

This was the moment George Tenet chose to send his letter to Congress amplifying the National Intelligence Estimate (see Chapter 3). In it, Tenet first raised the fear of Iraqi direct attacks on the United States by asserting the opposite, that Saddam "for now" appeared to have drawn a line short of terrorist attacks either conventional or with chemical and biological weapons. Tenet never said that Iraq was not at war with the United States and, even by U.S. data, had not made any move against the United States for a decade. He implied the struggle was current and that Iraqi forbearance a mere matter of tactics.

Even more striking, and most likely the result of the Pentagon reanalysis of the intelligence, were the points directly on the Saddam–Al Qaeda ties. Tenet repeated secretary Rumsfeld's "bulletproof" assertion that there had been senior-level contacts between Saddam and bin Laden going back a decade. He also asserted other points made by both Rumsfeld and Rice, among others that Al Qaeda members had been in Iraq since the Afghan war, including in Baghdad; that Al Qaeda had sought training in the making of

poisons and bombs; and that the sides had discussed safe haven and reciprocal nonaggression. In essence, Tenet's October 7 letter used much of the
bill of particulars that Douglas Feith's office had produced and that Colin
Powell would present to the UN Security Council the following February.

As had Condi Rice, CIA director Tenet sourced some of his key allegations to detainees, including some of high rank. Elsewhere these sources
are reported to have been Abu Zubaydah, former Al Qaeda chief of operations, and Ibn Al-Shaykh Al-Libi, a Libyan and former commander of one
of the Afghan training camps. Zubaydah is the same individual who, also in
2002, had the Americans tied up in knots after telling them that Al Qaeda
planned to blow up the Brooklyn Bridge on Memorial Day, and caused much
additional anguish with his mention of bombs at apartment buildings and
shopping malls. On September 3, 2002, Zubaydah told interrogators that
Bin Laden *opposed* any formal alliance with Baghdad as threatening to Al
Qaeda's independence. Informal cooperation was not ruled out, but it was
Zubaydah, not Bin Laden, who favored alliance. If Zubaydah is to be believed
on his contentions about warnings, what he said about alliances must also
be respected.

A year later Zubaydah plus another, equally senior former militant,
Khalid Sheik Mohammed, were each reported to have told their interrogators
that Al Qaeda leaders talked about but rejected the idea of working with
Saddam Hussein. Mohammed, who replaced Zubaydah as operations chief
until his capture in March 2003, was in some ways an even more significant
figure owing to his role in organizing the actual September 11 plot. If there
had been a Saddam role in the 9/11 attacks, Sheik Mohammed had no reason
to deny it.

Ibn Al-Shaykh Al-Libi told interrogators that a comrade had talked to
him about being asked to go to Baghdad in 1998 and arrange for training
in poisons and gases. According to Al-Libi, two terrorists actually went for
the training in December 2000. This was hearsay information, not hard
intelligence. Administration public statements misconstrued both terrorists'
interrogations.

Like every other aspect of the hoodwinking of America, the problem here was about the evidence. Reconstructing the 9/11 plot and the alleged Saddam link was difficult. As another of those ubiquitous "senior officials" said in *Newsweek* in early October 2002, "It's like a jigsaw puzzle . . . you have a little fragment here and another fragment there. But you don't know whether you're looking at a face or a monkey's ass." Shortly after the Bush Cincinnati speech, British newspapers reported both MI-6 and MI-5 as being deeply concerned at the "unsubstantiated claims" being made in the United States regarding links between Saddam and Bin Laden.

Assertions of the Al Qaeda link to Saddam that appeared in the National Intelligence Estimate drew footnotes just like the ones about Iraqi nuclear programs. The NIE assessment on the Iraqis training Al Qaeda militants on bombmaking and chemical weapons is reportedly that the evidence remained insufficient to prove the case. It was at this time, out of frustration, that senior State Department intelligence analyst Greg Thielmann chose to retire, complaining later of pressure put on analysts by Bush administration political appointees to render specific judgments. Of the Iraqi terrorism judgments themselves, Thielmann would later say that the administration was "misleading the public in implying there was a close connection." Moreover, as Thielmann told the *Boston Globe*, "Based on the terrorism experts I met with during my period of government, I never heard anyone make the claim there was a significant tie between Al Qaeda and Saddam Hussein."

What do we know publicly about high-level contacts between Saddam's Iraq and Al Qaeda? News media have cited two CIA reports, from 1993 and 1996, respectively, the first that Saddam had forged a nonaggression pact, the second that Iraq had provided Bin Laden with a bomb-making expert to train Al Qaeda people. Both of these reports, in substance, figure in the Tenet letter of October 2002 and the Powell UN presentation in February 2003. However, Tenet steps back from the assertion that there was a pact, to claim only that such an agreement was discussed. Powell went full-bore to the statement that the sides reached agreement.

The truth here is not in the public domain, but the leak in the fall of 2003 of a memorandum of information from Douglas Feith's office revealed a number of the reports that undoubtedly furnished the basis for the administration's claims a year earlier. Among these were items alleging that Brigadier General Salim al-Ahmed, the Iraqi intelligence service's principal expert on explosives, was observed at Bin Laden's Khartoum farm in September-October 1995 and again in July 1996, on the latter occasion in company with Iraqi intelligence chief Mani Abd-al-Rashid al-Tikriti, supposedly to discuss making letter bombs as well as explosive devices to be placed aboard aircraft. Al-Tikriti allegedly used the visit to the Sudan of an Iraqi commercial delegation to cover his own travel. Unfortunately for the "well-placed source" (Feith's office's description) who originated these reports, the Sudan had deported Osama bin Laden to Afghanistan on May 18, 1996, making a July 1996 meeting in Khartoum impossible. A number of other items record two Iraqi intelligence officers meeting with Bin Laden and his Egyptian ally, Ayman al-Zawahiri, in Afghanistan in late 1998.

There are a number of known facts that bear on the question. First, among the early Osama bin Laden initiatives was his effort (rejected by Saudi Arabia) at the time of the Gulf War to form a legion of fighters who would expel Iraq from Kuwait without the need for intervention by the American "crusaders." That was hardly the act of a man ready to make a deal with Saddam. Bin Laden moved to the Sudan in 1991, his way facilitated by Sudanese religious and political leader Mullah Hassan al-Turabi, whose National Islamic Front had seized power in a 1989 coup. It is Turabi who is supposed to have served as intermediary in setting up talks between Bin Laden and Saddam (and he is mentioned in some of these intelligence reports). It is true that Sudan took the Iraqi side in the Gulf War, but in the early 1990s its warm relations were with Islamic Iran, not secular Iraq. There is little evidence other than that produced in Feith's office that Turabi had any relationship with Saddam, and little reason to think he would have set up these high-level meetings. Equally important, in 1991 Al Qaeda was in its infancy. There is no reason to believe Saddam would have seen Bin Laden as important enough to be worth paying attention to. There is also the standard interest of intelligence services in evaluating the playing field, which could have led to contacts whose true purpose was to keep an eye on Al Qaeda.

Media reports about Iraq–Al Qaeda meetings in 1996 are confirmed by
Colin Powell, who told the Security Council that a foreign security service
had passed the CIA information that Bin Laden met with a senior Iraqi
intelligence official in Khartoum. This was presumably either Al-Tikriti or
his deputy, Faruq Hijazi, whom we shall see again in a moment. The wording
here reads as if Bin Laden could sit back planning some terror campaign and
ask Saddam to help him. The real situation at the time was quite different.
Powell's foreign agency is likely a reference to Sudanese intelligence, for that
country at that time had determined to attempt a rapprochement with the
United States. It is known that the Sudanese gave sensitive intelligence on
terrorists tracked through Khartoum to an intermediary for transmission to
the United States in October 1996. A few months earlier Sudan quietly gave
the CIA permission to photograph militant training camps, the likely sources
for the information. The problem with 1996 is that Bin Laden's good relations with the Sudanese had disintegrated. In fact, that spring the Sudanese
tried to hand Bin Laden over to the United States, or failing that, to Saudi
Arabia. Both refused and Sudan expelled Bin Laden instead. The Bin Laden
training camps closed (some months later Turabi was put under house arrest,
not to be released until October 2003). It was no time for Saddam to be
sending people to Khartoum to discuss joint ventures, and Bin Laden was
not even in the Sudan.

The Afghan move also puts the nix to another of Powell's allegations,
that a senior defector from Saddam's Mukhabarat reports Iraq sent agents to
Afghanistan in the mid-1990s to train Al Qaeda militants. Bin Laden only
arrived on the Afghan scene in 1996 and needed time to set up his operation.
It would be the spring of 1997 before Al Qaeda became a going concern at
Kandahar, and another year still until its training camp system was up and
running.

Most intriguing of all is a claim that attracted considerable attention
among the media and those cheerleaders who wanted to build support for
the invasion. This allegation is that the Egyptian Ayman al-Zawahiri visited
Baghdad for direct talks in early 1998. This is supposedly attested by a
former Zawahiri bodyguard held by the Kurds in northern Iraq and a British

newsman, who reported finding a document (dated February 19, 1998) dealing with plans to receive the envoy, coming from Khartoum. The visit is
supposed to have been so successful it was extended by a week. One problem
with this report is dates. On February 23 Zawahiri was in Afghanistan where
his then-independent *Egyptian* jihadist group made its own alliance with Bin
Laden. Until then Zawahiri could not have represented Al Qaeda. A different
report has the Baghdad visit beginning April 25 for Saddam's birthday cel-
ebration three days later, meeting with vice president Taha Yasin Ramadan.
By then Zawahiri would not have been coming from Khartoum but from
Afghanistan. *Neither* George Tenet nor Colin Powell made use of this allegation in their cases against Iraq, suggesting that U.S. intelligence could not
verify these claims.

Powell did allude to another visit story, one that has Colonel Faruk al-
Hijazi, an Iraqi intelligence branch chief, later appointed ambassador to Turkey, traveling to Afghanistan to meet there with Osama bin Laden. Al-Hijazi
had previously seen Bin Laden in Khartoum in 1994, when the Al Qaeda
leader supposedly asked for help acquiring limpet mines. On the 1998 visit,
the report was that the Iraqi officer offered asylum to Bin Laden. Other
accounts discount the Al-Hijazi visit to Afghanistan, noting that Turkish intelligence sources had no record of Al-Hijazi going there.

In fact, at the Security Council, Colin Powell declared there had been
at least eight of these high-level visits between senior Iraqi and Al Qaeda
officials. If confirmation for these stories were available, the Bush administration would long since have publicized it. Instead, in October 2003 Douglas
Feith's office produced a memorandum for the Congress on Iraq–Al Qaeda
contacts that relied upon lower-level intelligence reports to document the
alleged meetings, offers, and agreements. Both Taha Yasin Ramadan and
Faruk Al-Hijazi gave themselves up or were apprehended by American troops
after the fall of Baghdad. Both were subjected to "custodial interviews," the
latest euphemism for interrogations. Neither is recorded as confirming the
alleged visits, and another Iraqi intelligence official whose conversations with
U.S. interrogators are cited maintained the last contact between Iraq and Al
Qaeda had taken place in July 1999. In the case of Faruk Al-Hijazi, regarded

so favorably by American officials that he has been mentioned as possible head of a new post-Saddam Iraqi intelligence service, the absence of reports that he confirms ties between Hussein and Al Qaeda must be seen as especially significant.

Of all the visit stories, the most controversial would be Prague. It too did not make the cut for Colin Powell's speech, despite having come direct to the secretary in the first place. The essential allegation is that between April 8 and 11, 2001, five months before 9/11, Al Qaeda ringleader Mohamed Atta went to the Czech Republic to meet Iraqi intelligence officer Ahmed Khalil Ibrahim Samir Al-Ani, a functionary of the Iraqi embassy. Al-Ani was actually expelled from the Czech Republic for activities incompatible with his diplomatic status a few weeks later. The provenance of this account is what gave it wings, for the information came from the Czech government based on reports by the Czech intelligence service. The information was so suggestive that, regardless of ignorance as to what these individuals might have discussed if they had met, the story instantly became the foundation for charges that Saddam was implicated in the September 11 attacks.

The outlines of the Prague story first emerged in press reporting of the movements of conspirator Atta and were sourced to federal law enforcement officials, but the Czech side came up in early November 2001, when the Czech prime minister stopped by Washington on his way to the opening of the UN General Assembly. Milos Zeman told Powell that Atta and Al-Ani had discussed attacking the Radio Free Europe headquarters, which is located in Prague. Zeman told most of this story to reporters before he left for New York. A month later Czech interior minister Stanislav Gross added the imprimatur of Czech intelligence. Juicy details included the fact that Iraqi spy Al-Ani had been seen on surveillance tapes from Radio Free Europe cameras, apparently casing the target, that he and Atta had been identified by a Czech intelligence source having lunch or, in another version, at the Iraqi embassy.

The story began to evaporate after public disagreement by Czech president Vaclav Havel. It would soon be reported that the Czechs were only 70 percent sure of their information. It emerged that the informant, an Arab student in Prague, apparently not considered particularly reliable, had reported only after September 11, when the face of Atta had been flashed all over the world. The Czechs knew about Al-Ani and Radio Free Europe (RFE)—the RFE offices contained the exile station Radio Free Iraq and had long been thought threatened, hence regular surveillance had been in place. But that did not automatically implicate Atta. The FBI traced Atta's movements through the months before 9/11 and established that at this time he had been living in Virginia Beach. Credit card receipts showed him there on April 2, and in Florida renting a car on the 11th. The CIA could find no information that Atta had entered the Czech Republic, under either his own name or any known alias, during this period, and no expense records, travel reservations, or anything else confirm the trip. Since it would be established that the 9/11 hijackers commonly used their own names, this became a telling point. Investigation apparently also found that Al-Ani had a side business selling cars and often used a German Muslim used-car dealer from Nuremburg who bore a striking resemblance to Mohamed Atta. Exile sources identified Al-Ani as a specialist in recruiting among the Iraqi expatriate community, not a paramilitary type. Ahmad Khalil Ibrahim Samir Al-Ani would be captured by U.S. forces in Iraq in early July 2003, as would his section chief in Iraqi intelligence, who would also have had knowledge of this Prague plot if it were real. No confirmation has been forthcoming.

As troubling as the Prague plot that did not materialize is another charge Powell did use at the UN—that Iraq had a terrorist chemical and biological weapons laboratory in a village in northern Iraq. The secretary of state showed a photo of the village at the Security Council. The whole thing formed part of a Bush administration attempt to show that Saddam was in league with Al Qaeda by supporting, even commanding, a terrorist group that sheltered Al Qaeda militants. The movement, called Ansar al-Islam, formed in September 2001 from several smaller groups that had been around since the 1990s. It represented a Muslim fundamentalist reaction to Kurdish secularism. Ansar fought the Kurds and was so well equipped that Kurdish authorities decided it had to be trained and supplied from Baghdad. Ansar did open its doors to Muslim militants, but these were more allies of Al Qaeda than Bin Laden fighters. As for the supplies, Iran was the more likely source. Days ahead of the Powell speech Ansar's leader denounced the U.S. suspicions. When the speech occurred, he repeated that his movement had no ties to Saddam and indeed that Saddam was his enemy.

The village existed, but it was a lot different than advertised. Ansar immediately invited a group of perhaps twenty journalists to visit the place, Sarget, which proved to be a small hamlet with no laboratory or industrial equipment, and buildings that had clearly been homes until taken over for the headquarters of what Ansar called its Victory Brigade. On Capitol Hill at a hearing after returning from New York, Powell himself admitted the camp had not even been continuously occupied over the previous six months. Kurdish officials were separately quoted as knowing nothing about the alleged weapons laboratory.

The weapons laboratory charge formed the capstone of Powell's discussion of Al Qaeda terrorists, text that consumed about half of the entire U.S. presentation on Saddam and terrorism. Much of this discussion focused on a single terrorist and his networks. That individual, Abu Musab al-Zarqawi, was a Palestinian and Jordanian national, and another of those Arab Afghans who had gotten their start, like Osama bin Laden himself, fighting the Russian occupiers of Afghanistan in the 1980s. Al-Zarqawi first gained notoriety when he was linked to the Millenium plots in Jordan, abortive attempts to bomb hotels and movie theaters in Amman on the eve of the millennium in 1999.

As additional information about Zarqawi appeared, it showed that, while he knew Bin Laden, he could hardly be described as an Al Qaeda lieutenant. Given financial backing by a member of the Qatari royal family, Zarqawi had utilized the funds for his own activities and sent none of it on to Al Qaeda. Other reports had his network receiving money from Iran, and Zarqawi had been in that country before his visit to Baghdad. Al-Zarqawi did have networks in western Europe—as many as 119 alleged terrorists have been linked to him, and cells broken up in Britain, France, and Italy—and these cells did prepare to use chemical weapons. But the only known attack carried out by the Zarqawi network was the murder of American Agency for International Development official Lawrence Foley in Jordan in October

2002. Two militants who participated in the assassination, along with Zarqawi's deputy, were arrested and interrogated, furnishing much of the information showcased by Colin Powell at the UN and permitting police in Britain and France to break up cells in their countries.

There is no known evidence that Bin Laden issued orders or tasked Zarqawi to hit any particular targets. It would be more accurate to describe Al-Zarqawi's network as fighting a parallel war to Al Qaeda's. Al-Zarqawi fought alongside Bin Laden when the United States and other nations attacked Afghanistan to overthrow Taliban rule and end the Al Qaeda sanctuary there, and he was badly wounded in the leg. By August 2002 Al-Zarqawi had escaped to Baghdad, where his leg had to be amputated and a prosthesis fitted. During this time Jordanian intelligence learned of his presence and passed that knowledge to the CIA. Colin Powell's reference in the speech to a friendly service asking the Iraqis to go after Al-Zarqawi is to the Jordanians. At that point the Jordanian terrorist disappeared from Baghdad. Powell implies that the Zarqawi network controlled Ansar al-Islam, which is not correct. To describe Al-Zarqawi as a senior Al Qaeda official is also misleading.

By contrast, Secretary Powell's charge that Iraq trained Palestinians in use of small arms and explosives was largely correct. For some years there had been a training camp at Salman Pak that could handle forty to fifty militants at a time. Saddam for years had also paid indemnities to the families of Palestinians killed in the intifada as well as sums to those whose homes were destroyed by Israeli incursions into the West Bank and Gaza Strip. In January 2001 the Iraqis received George Habash, former head of the Popular Front for the Liberation of Palestine (PFLP), and a PFLP delegation visited Baghdad that September. The terrorist Sabri al-Banna (Abu Nidal) had lived in Baghdad since being expelled from Libya, and then Egypt, but he died in the summer of 2002. The Abu Nidal network, often held out as a prime example of Saddam's support for terror, for example by President Bush in his Cincinnati speech, had not carried out an attack since January 1994. Banna had basically retired. The same was true of the *Achille Lauro* hijacker, Mohammed Abdul Abbas, also resident in Baghdad. Saddam *was* serious

about the Palestinian cause. In fact, to the degree there was any real cooperation between Iraqis and the Zarqawi network, this probably followed from
its Palestinian political objectives, not any Muslim fundamentalist interest.
Support for the Palestinian cause nevertheless did not make Saddam's Iraq
a clear and present threat to the United States.

Now a word about evidence. Unlike Colin Powell's presentations on
Iraqi weapons and deception, the terrorism material was based largely on
information from foreign intelligence services, like the Czechs, the Sudanese,
and the Jordanians, or on data from defectors brought to American attention.
Many of the latter, possibly all of them, were shopped to the United States
from two sources, the exiles of the Iraqi National Congress and the Kurds
of northern Iraq. Both groups had agendas of their own. The Iraqi National
Congress wanted a war, since that was its main chance to return to Iraq and
make a bid for power in a post-Saddam nation. Among the defectors they
produced on issues Colin Powell took up at the UN were people who testified
to alleged high-level meetings of Iraqis with Al Qaeda—particularly the Prague
story and the allegation that the Iraqi ambassador in Turkey had gone to
Afghanistan—who claimed Saddam had sent agents to train militants, who
took pictures of terrorists, reported on the training camp at Salman Pak, and,
we shall see later, were active in the story of alleged Iraqi mobile weapons
laboratories (exile leader Ahmad Chalabi, after the war, when the mobile
labs became controversial, denied that his group had had anything to do with
intelligence on this subject).

The Kurds produced defectors and alleged prisoners who told outsiders
of Iraqi intelligence agents running the Ansar al-Islam group, alleged Saddam
plans for terrorist attacks in the Persian Gulf area, reported on the Saddam
birthday visit of a top Egyptian terrorist, and linked Saddam and Al Qaeda
in the Ansar villages. A lot of this information proved highly convenient for
the case the Bush administration needed to make, and clearly the purveyors
had a good idea what the Bush people wanted. One hopes that the defector
information was checked and scrubbed carefully before use was made of it.

On October 27, 2003, undersecretary of defense Douglas Feith sent a
memorandum to the Senate Intelligence Committee designed to amplify for

the record testimony he had given that July, when Feith had continued to maintain Saddam had had a strong connection with Al Qaeda. The memorandum covered a paper that cited some fifty items of intelligence on this connection, sourced to the intelligence agency or collection channel from which the information had appeared. Very quickly the memorandum leaked to reporter Stephen F. Hayes of a conservative political magazine, *The Weekly Standard*, and he used it to write an article titled "Case Closed" that purported to demonstrate that the Saddam–Bin Laden charges were exactly right. In actuality, the leak showed several things, all of them different than what the reporter supposed. Most important, the intelligence paper amounted to a summary of the case Feith's officers had made at the CIA in August 2002. The same people, and their successors, responsible for massaging the intelligence with their hypothesis-driven "alternative analysis," were suddenly being cited as the chapter and verse that "proved" the terrorism case. Many CIA analysts had not been happy with those claims then or now.

Second, a review of the actual sourcing confirms the points here about how Feith's intelligence office used Iraqi exile information. While the original Pentagon memorandum has not been made completely available to the public, *The Weekly Standard* reprinted almost half of its fifty items. Of the reprinted items, sources for four are not specified, and of the remainder, the overwhelming majority, about a dozen, are attributed either to "sensitive reporting" or to a "well-placed source," both euphemisms for Iraqi exiles, defectors, and the Kurds. These include the most lurid charges, such as alleged non-aggression pacts, cooperation agreements, Iraqi explosives training, and alleged support with passports and money. Only a handful of the items are attributed to CIA reports or to foreign intelligence services, the latter primarily concerning the alleged Atta visit to Prague and the Faruk al-Hijazi trip to Afghanistan. Several items in the October 2003 paper were collected postwar from former Iraqi officials or intelligence officers, and these contributions tend to undercut other charges in the paper. In addition, citation of these sources makes it remarkable that there are in this paper *no* confirmations by themselves of key actions that Iraqi intelligence officers allegedly took (such as Faruk al-Hijazi or Ahmed Khalil Ibrahim Samir al-Ani). Further, the several citations the Feith intelligence paper sources to interrogations of former terrorists (like Abu Zubaydah and Ibn al-Shaykh al-Libi) can either be read two ways (Zubaydah) or represent hearsay (Al-Libi). In short, this intelligence does not add up the way its purveyors suppose.

Finally, review of the actual content of the intelligence items reveals a very close correspondence between a number of the items and leaks that appeared in the U.S. press over the months before the Iraq war. This correspondance confirms the suspicion that the Bush administration engaged in a pattern of leaking secret intelligence information in hopes of scaring the public about Saddam's alleged plotting. The hoodwinking of America proceeded on many fronts.

Saddam Hussein's interests were and remained very different from those of Osama bin Laden. Hussein sought to protect his power over a nation. His state had to be a secular one because his confessional group remained a minority in Iraq. Bin Laden sought to overthrow secularism, and ultimately that meant Hussein too. Secretary Powell dismissed this objection. In his speech Powell said the thought did not comfort him. Just ten days after Powell's speech an audiotape from Bin Laden would be broadcast on Middle Eastern television and radio stations, calling on Iraqis to rise up against an American invasion. The Bush administration seized on the tape as evidence of collusion between Bin Laden and Saddam. But the tape had had nothing but contempt for Saddam Hussein, branding the Saddam regime an "infidel." Bin Laden's message was of solidarity among Muslim peoples, not of assistance to a government. *After* the fall of Iraq to the invasion, Al Qaeda militants began to show up in Iraq to fight alongside Saddamist guerrillas against the coalition occupation. Those who had warned that attacking Iraq might be the thing to drive together Saddam Hussein and the terrorists had been exactly right.

Almost three months after the fall of Baghdad, the UN study group charged with monitoring the activities of Al Qaeda rendered the latest in its series of periodic reports. Their investigation found no evidence of alliance between Saddam and Al Qaeda. In the U.S. Congress, the preliminary findings of the House Permanent Select Committee on Intelligence, as put in a letter to George Tenet on September 25, 2003, and based on three volumes of CIA reports, were that there had been substantial gaps in CIA's intelligence collection and "either a 'low threshold' or 'no threshold' " on presenting new data as vetted information. George Tenet rejects these charges. In the meantime the United States, having occupied Iraq, at least initially left at least one terrorist group, Al Daawa al Islamiyah ("Islamic Call"), armed, though there have been reports of its disarming since. The Al Daawa was responsible for a notorious bombing of the U.S. embassy in Kuwait (and the French one as well) in 1983, and liberation of Daawa prisoners held in Kuwait later became the rationale for the seizure of American hostages in Lebanon. A major terrorist enemy during the Reagan years, Al Daawa's enmity against Saddam suddenly made it a U.S. ally. That all terrorist groups in Iraq were not instantly disarmed by the occupation forces is further evidence that the Iraq invasion was not about defeating terrorism.

In the days and hours after Secretary of State Powell addressed the Security Council, the United States would need the help of not one but many governments, to pass the UN resolution that would put a legal base under its planned invasion of Iraq. Powell had taken his best shot at laying a foundation of evidence for action. He had a few good hits, a lot of hyperbole, and some outright errors, doubtless ones the United States hoped no one would notice. Now the dice were rolling. The result would be tragedy for everyone.

7

The Reckoning

With the Security Council speech, Secretary of State Colin Powell had gone as far as he could to muster the intelligence in favor of war. That the United Nations went against U.S. desires would be a measure of the Bush people's inflated sense of their diplomatic prowess. Powell was joined out on the limb by secretary of defense Donald Rumsfeld, who said shortly after President Bush's State of the Union address not only that Saddam had sought uranium from Africa, but that the Iraqis had a design for a nuclear bomb and several effective means of enriching fissile materials. They would be joined soon by CIA director George Tenet. At Powell's speech, the spy chieftain had simply been a presence, sitting behind Powell as the nation's chief diplomat explained why the UN should acquiesce in an end to diplomacy. On February 11, it was Tenet himself at the witness table on Capitol Hill, as he presented the CIA's annual worldwide threat briefing. Between the Powell speech and the Tenet briefing, the administration raised its terrorist threat index to its next-to-highest level, for no apparent reason other than to heighten public fears, which were exploited by new threat talk.

The lead threat remained Al Qaeda, but Iraq was up second, and Tenet's description echoed Colin Powell's. Some of the language was nearly identical, as in the CIA director's invocation of "the aluminum tubes you have heard so much about." Tenet's testimony went down the list, starting with Iraq's deception efforts, then to biological weapons programs—alleged to include mobile laboratories; clandestine procurement, missiles flight-tested to beyond 90 miles—and development of a 600+ mile-range rocket; unmanned aerial vehicles; and so on. Tenet made two points on Saddam and Al Qaeda: he pictured Abu Musab al-Zarqawi as "a close associate" of Osama bin Laden; and he asserted that Iraq had trained Al Qaeda in poisons, gases, and document forgery. Tenet declared his information was "based on a solid foundation of intelligence" from "credible and reliable sources." Asked where Zarqawi might be, Tenet said in Baghdad (other CIA officials answered the same question by saying they had no idea). As for the increased terrorist alert level, Tenet claimed to be responding to intelligence he characterized as "the most specific we have seen," including "poisons and chemicals" and "the use of a radiological dispersion device." It is difficult to believe Tenet credited all these allegations or thought their sources unimpeachable. Nothing at all happened. Hopefully the assessed reliability of the sources was downgraded afterward.

On a certain level the administration's tactics worked. Support for war, as measured by a *Washington Post*/ABC News poll taken just after Powell's UN appearance, grew to 66 percent. But the heated rhetoric also inflamed the opposition. Days after Tenet testified on Capitol Hill, over 300,000 Americans turned out in New York City to oppose the conflict. And in England more than a million marched against war in London, the largest public demonstration in British history. Worldwide more than 11 million protesters participated in actions in ninety cities, again unprecedented. There would also be an explosion of state and municipal legislation rejecting war with Iraq. Several states and more than 120 cities and towns passed official resolutions condemning war. Antiwar organizers mounted a massive e-mail lobbying effort with Congress and carried out innumerable local actions as well. Opposition to a war with Iraq remained at a high level right through the war.

In the Persian Gulf the necessary military buildup proceeded apace. Air bases in Qatar, Kuwait, and Oman filled to capacity. Three of the U.S. Navy's aircraft carriers were in the Gulf by early February and that number would double. Deployments Rumsfeld had ordered just after Christmas soon led to troops in marshalling areas in Kuwait. That nation declared its northern half a restricted military zone. Very quickly the entire part of Kuwait fronting the Iraqi border bristled with coalition military bases. The day of Powell's presentation at the Security Council, 113,000 American troops were in the Gulf. The main force was the 3rd Infantry Division. Already slated for the Central Command theater were 150,000 servicewomen and men, and another 20,000 were ordered to deploy on February 14, including the 3rd Armored Cavalry Regiment, which turned out to be one of the most important units among coalition forces. The 3rd Armored Division and a U.S. Marine task force of division size were deploying. Great Britain committed about 20,000 of its forces and Australia roughly 1,800. There were also tiny contingents from New Zealand, Poland, the Czech Republic, and a few other nations. In early March, work began on cutting through the wire barriers and other obstacles that blocked the Kuwaiti border. By then coalition forces numbered 225,000 and the 101st Airborne Division (Airmobile) was en route to the theater. That essentially completed the troop list, which topped out at about 240,000.

Ham-fisted diplomacy bedeviled the Bush administration war plans. A major feature of the concept was to hit Saddam from different directions simultaneously. Jordan's refusal to participate ruled out any attack from the west. At a minimum Bush strategists wanted a big strike from the north, and they slated the 4th Infantry Division to move through Turkey and assault Iraq across its northern border. But American intervention was enormously unpopular in Turkey, with polls running eight-to-one or higher against joining, plus controversy over NATO's reluctance to furnish combat support to Turkey. Even a simple permission for American forces to transit the country and use Turkish bases to supply an American expeditionary unit was in doubt. The Bush administration offered huge foreign aid ($26 billion in grants and loans) as an incentive and confidently sent ships full of the 4th Division's equipment to Turkish ports. The Turks held out for a lot more, twice rejecting participation in parliamentary votes as the government, newly taken over by a Muslim religious party, denied cooperation to Washington.

In any event, the 4th Division's ships sat in Turkish ports for days, then were sent back to sea and rerouted to the Persian Gulf, thence Kuwait, a movement that consumed weeks. The unit ultimately deployed through Kuwait and did not arrive at the front until the war had ended. As for the northern expedition, CENTCOM cobbled together an ersatz version of the northern pincer, using small Special Forces units eventually backed by the 173rd Airborne Brigade, diverted from its NATO southern region reserve role. The force staged through Rumania, and the Turks at least permitted American aircraft to cross their airspace in delivering the force to the Kurdish region of Iraq. The northern pincer would have little offensive capability and never attempted any assault toward Baghdad.

Washington's myopic overconfidence in its diplomacy with Turkey was based on the series of visits Paul Wolfowitz had made there the previous year. The Turks had frankly told Wolfowitz of their disdain for the Iraq plan, but the Americans had not listened. The story would be replicated on the main diplomatic front at the UN Security Council.

The Bush administration had known for at least a year that there would be significant international opposition to a U.S. war against Iraq. Through 2002 there had been a succession of setbacks for the diplomacy of war, not least Washington's failure to secure a UN resolution permitting immediate resort to force. A few nations lined up with the Americans and British—the troop-contributing countries have already been mentioned—also including Spain, Portugal, Denmark, and Hungary. In Italy, prime minister Silvio Berlusconi favored the war, but much of his country did not. Germany and France continued their opposition. Despite some individual countries' support for the U.S. position, the fifteen nations of the European Union insisted war need not occur. Russia wavered but basically opposed the U.S. enterprise. China kept its own counsel but expressed little support for the view of the Iraqi threat Colin Powell presented at the Security Council. Japan took the U.S. side but only at the last moment. More than half the members of the 114-nation strong Non-Aligned Movement voted in favor of a summit resolution opposing the Iraq war. Kuwait and the small Gulf states were the only Arab countries to support the war, with Egypt, Syria, Iran, Jordan, Tunisia, Libya, and Yemen solidly opposed to the conflict, and Saudi Arabia torn between a stance of opposition and its friendship for the United States.

Thus President Bush's pursuit of a Security Council resolution authorizing war faced strong resistance. Washington and London lobbied the member states on the Council intensely. Special problems were obtained there as well. Any of the five permanent members (the United States, Britain, France, China, Russia), by voting against the resolution, would veto it. Among the other members (selected by the UN General Assembly for two-year terms on the Security Council), Mexico had had excellent relations with George W. Bush going into his presidency, but Bush then reneged on commitments made to Mexican leaders. Chile, once a darling of American administrations, had been largely neglected by the Bush presidency. The African nations Cameroon, Guinea, and Angola had been almost completely ignored. Suddenly their votes were of crucial importance to Washington. Besides the British, Spain offered the only secure vote for Bush on the Security Council, since these two nations, plus the United States, were the cosponsors of the war resolution. Pakistan, though an ally in the war on terrorism, had a majority Muslim religious party and would abstain on a demand for war with a Muslim country. Germany and Syria were sure to vote against the resolution. Bush needed nine votes including all five permanent members to pass the mandate for war.

Supervised by the State Department, lobbying would be extensive and sustained. President Bush and Vice President Cheney made telephone calls, with Bush and England's Tony Blair coordinating their approaches to the member nations. Secretary of state Colin Powell worked on a lower level and passed problem cases up the ladder to Bush. Invitations to the White House, trade favors, bits and pieces of foreign aid, and immigration action were all on offer. Cameroon was offered a presidential visit. Guinea seemed like Italy, with the government leaning toward the Bush administration but the public opposed to any war. Chile resented the American lobbying. The lesson was again that the international organization did not behave in the fashion of the U.S. Congress, and the Bush administration could not so easily buy support, especially for the parsimonious items that were offered (the $26 billion offer to Turkey would be exceptional, and was made only after Ankara flatly rejected an initial bid of $2 billion to a country that considered it had lost $50 billion as a result of the 1990–91 Gulf War). Bush also complicated his case by setting the goalposts on Iraq yet higher at the beginning of March, insisting that mere disarmament of Iraq was insufficient to avert war, that Saddam Hussein would have to step down as well. This latter was the proof of Bush's real goals in the Iraq war.

Hans Blix and Mohammed ElBaradei were again scheduled to report on their weapons inspections of Iraq on March 7. President Bush personally put pressure on the monitors the previous night with a full-scale press conference, only the second of his presidency. Once more Bush sold the war based on the present Iraqi threat: "Saddam Hussein . . . possesses weapons of terror. He provides funding and safe haven to terrorists, terrorists who would willingly use weapons of mass destruction against America." Bush knew what he knew "from multiple intelligence sources," and Iraq's camouflage of its weapons could not be tolerated: "Inspection teams do not need more time or more personnel. All they need is what they have never received, the full cooperation of the Iraqi government." Iraq, Bush said, "is a part of the war on terror." The president also said several times that the world had reached "the last phase of diplomacy."

Bush would be asked quite directly about the intelligence. Rumsfeld had once said that any nation with an intelligence service knew that Saddam had weapons of mass destruction; now Bush was asked why so many countries with such services did not seem to agree that Iraq posed any threat. The president changed the subject. Bush used the word "disarm" six times in that response.

Elsewhere Bush returned to that theme. He would be quite plain as to his purposes in Iraq: "Should we have to go in, our mission is very clear: disarmament. And in order to disarm it will mean regime change." In other words, the rationale for this war hinged *directly* on the existence of an arsenal of Iraqi weapons of mass destruction, which President Bush deemed to require the simultaneous overthrow of Saddam Hussein.

The UN resolution and Washington's desperate push for the votes to pass it was an inevitable question that evening. A reporter asked President Bush if he would go for a vote even if the United States lacked enough commitments to ensure passage.

"No matter what the whip count is," George Bush shot back, "we're calling for the vote."

Despite that bravado, talk of wanting people to stand up and "say what their opinion is about Saddam Hussein and the utility of the United Nations," as Bush also said at his press conference, his administration did just the opposite. On March 7, Blix and ElBaradei presented their reports to the Security Council. Their updates essentially said that the inspection system had attained a critical mass, achieved some real results, ironed out most cooperation difficulties with the Iraqis, and stood to attain its goals given time to accomplish the task. Given the choice between a functioning weapons inspection system that could keep Iraq from a weapons arsenal or a U.S.-inspired war, support for the Security Council resolution wavered. France and Russia were already threatening to use their vetoes at the Council, and by March 10 it appeared that the majority vote, not even counting the vetoes, would be *against* the war resolution. The British made an eleventh-hour bid to rescue the mandate by revising the draft to include intermediate benchmarks for Iraqi compliance, but the Americans rejected several countries' requests for extensions of the final deadline for Iraq's disarmament to after March 17. It is equally possible that the Bush people feared delays that would lead to more postponements, or that they had by now locked in the military timetable for the invasion of Iraq. In either case, at this point, France announced that it would definitely use its veto in the Security Council to kill the war mandate.

The UN resolution that George Bush had promised he would call for "no matter what the whip count" quietly went into the round file. *No* resolution passed the Security Council, there was *no* mandate for war under Security Council Resolution 1441. United Nations Secretary General Kofi Annan drew the implications of those facts quite directly, telling a group that the UN charter "is very clear on circumstances under which force can be used." Annan went on to declare, "If the U.S. and others were to go outside the Council and take military action on their own, it would not be in conformity with the charter."

On March 16 President Bush held a hastily arranged summit conference of only a few hours' duration for the cosmetic purpose of endowing Iraq action with some multilateral flavor. The next day he issued an ultimatum to Saddam Hussein. The war began two days later with powerful air strikes on a Baghdad compound where the Iraqi leader was believed to be meeting with associates.

Chutes and Ladders

Allied troops crossed their lines of departure for the invasion of Iraq wearing protective suits and bearing gear to defend against chemical weapons. The suits came off a few days into the campaign when no chemical weapons materialized. Varying suppositions were made during the month or so that active operations predominated. The Iraqis would use their chemicals at the outset; then it was supposed the Iraqis might use them in key battles, like those for Basra and Nasiriyah, then that the weapons would come out when coalition forces crossed an imaginary "red line" surrounding Baghdad—secretary Rumsfeld even told the world he *knew* where Saddam's weapons of mass destruction were, around Baghdad and Tikrit. When Baghdad fell during the first week of April 2003 no chemical weapons had yet been used, only a few of the battlefield rockets had been launched—with conventional warheads only—none of the claimed covert force of longer-range missiles had materialized, to be used either against Israel or anywhere else, and Iraqi forces had made no use of biological agents.

The Iraqi forces were obviously in extremis. Recall that the CIA's analysis in both the National Intelligence Estimate and director Tenet's letter to Senator Graham stated that these were the precise circumstances under which there was a high probability Iraq would resort to its exotic weapons. That had actually been a reasonable assumption, and it was the same one Rumsfeld made in supposing the Iraqis would unleash their chemicals in a last-ditch defense. But nothing happened at all, and not only because the Iraqi army largely disintegrated. Saddam retained substantial enough control over his forces that he was able to take some of the best of them with him, converting regular forces to a guerrilla command. That meant he retained sufficient command capacity to unleash chemical and biological weapons too, if he had had them. When President Bush made his flight to the aircraft carrier *Abraham Lincoln* on May 1 to declare that the war was over, no weapons of mass destruction had been used against Americans or anyone else.

The coalition did not merely wait to be hit with Saddam's exotic weaponry. Instead the forces made preparations to seek out and neutralize Iraqi weapons of mass destruction. The equivalent search during the Afghan campaign of 2001–02 had been beset by problems of coordination and competition, so advance preparation for a new attempt certainly seemed necessary. Nevertheless, the final draft of the Joint Chiefs of Staff postmortem on lessons learned from the Iraqi war concludes that the planning for the weapons search was completed so close to the invasion that it was impossible for CENTCOM to carry out the mission effectively. Reports suggest the search plan received approval at the White House late in January, at the same time Bush conducted his "Sixteen Words" propaganda offensive, too late to procure specialized equipment, train additional experts, or develop a robust search organization, in the military's view. This is yet another bit of evidence suggesting the Iraqi weapons were less important to the Bush administration in fact than they were to its public relations posture.

In spite of the late plans, an elaborate scheme was put in place, involving several levels of activity. The search for exotics became a priority for the commandos of Task Force 20, who moved ahead of advancing forces, operating behind enemy lines. The Special Forces, Delta Force, Navy Seal, Air Force Special Operations, British Special Air Service, and other foreign experts comprising the task force were supposed to look for Iraqi SCUDs, neutralize key targets, and try to paralyze the Iraqi high command. But they had also attached experts on weapons of mass destruction, had trained to spot them, were equipped to test for them, and had separate intelligence and reporting channels to get data on this subject up to senior leaders. Task Force 20 also had its own sensor equipment, helicopters, and a portable biological laboratory that set up in a tent and traveled in a Humvee. The special unit received its greatest acclaim for a night raid that freed U.S. prisoner Jessica Lynch, but the weapons search was its bread and butter.

By every contemporary account, the hunt for Iraqi weapons of mass destruction was a top priority not only of the special forces, but of the CENT-COM army as a whole, particularly for its intelligence staffs. In Washington, the Defense Threat Reduction Agency had prepared 9,000 copies of a recognition manual, the *WMD Facility, Equipment and Munitions Identification Handbook*, which frontline forces used to decide whether facilities, machinery, substances, or equipment might be suspicious. The Central Intelligence Agency (CIA) and Defense Intelligence Agency (DIA) had prepared lists with 578 sites ranked with priorities for search. Instant secure communications channels had been arranged so that questions could be passed to the units back home with the big national databases, while the CENTCOM forces themselves already had a set of computerized files containing a high proportion of the data holdings. There were twice-daily global teleconferences to handle breaking developments. General Franks' staff maintained daily a priority list of the top 19 sites to be checked that day for weapons of mass destruction, along with a second list of 68 places to be checked for other reasons. The CENTCOM staff also had top priority for literally all U.S. reconnaissance and intelligence collection assets, under procedures worked out months in advance.

The frontline troops of the field forces would be the first detectors for possible discoveries of weapons of mass destruction. Intelligence staffs of those units provided somewhat greater expertise in identification, enough to rule out obviously innocent finds and summon specialists for the more suspicious ones. Special site survey teams of the 75th Exploitation Task Force (the acronym-happy military called this the XTF), under Colonel Richard R. McPhee, would then check the suspicious items. McPhee had several hundred personnel, primarily military, but with a sprinkling of CIA and even some FBI experts on board. On the other hand, he lacked reliable communications equipment and Arabic linguists. Where Task Force 20 had its own information folders on each prime target, the 75th had to request intelligence from higher commanders. When the Mobile Exploitation Teams (METS) needed helicopters or other specialized gear, he had to ask superiors and await the results. He also lacked authority to take Iraqis into custody for interrogation. In short, there were still practical impediments to accomplishing the mission.

At the last moment, just a few weeks before the war began, the Bush administration decided to include in the weapons hunt some of the Americans who had formerly worked with UN inspectors in the 1990s, though only a handful made it to the war zone in time to be of use. McPhee also had his own specialized labs for both chemical and biological agents plus photographic equipment. These mobile labs arrived so late they would be assembled just ten days before the invasion, too late for familiarization, calibration, and practice to hone test skills.

The 75th had four METs to do more detailed analyses. Each had about twenty-five specialists. For the most subtle work, the DIA had sent its Chemical Biological Intelligence Support Team. The METs and other surveyors would take samples that could then be analyzed in detail. It is reported that McPhee's labs could do an analysis with 90 percent accuracy within a few hours. Significant samples would also be returned to the United States, where the Army's highly sophisticated laboratories at Edgewood Arsenal and Fort Detrich, or the Navy's Biological Defense Research Directorate, would do even more minute examinations.

As the war kicked off, the site survey teams itched to get into the action. But they were repeatedly stymied. Planned searches would be scrubbed when advancing combat units reached a place and reported it empty. Other times the survey team reached a site only to discover Task Force 20 had been there already and done the necessary sampling. At least once a Task Force 20 unit was still at work when a site team arrived on location. The Special Forces commander ordered the weapons searchers to clear out.

Nevertheless, whoever made the effort, the work got done. Task Force 20 sent hundreds of samples home for further analysis. The 75th Exploitation Task Force, for its part, checked out 350 sites, including many of the top hundred on the big list from Washington, which were visited by its Mobile Exploitation Teams or Site Survey Teams. Typical would be the experience of Survey Team 3, in which *Washington Post* reporter Barton Gellman was embedded. The group arrived in theater on February 22 and executed its first mission on March 22, three days into the war. That run, near Basra, found harmless powder plus a student's report for a high school chemistry class. A week later the team went to Nasiriyah, not long after the town was taken (and Jessica Lynch captured by the Iraqis) to check a site reputed to hold chemical and biological weapons. That place proved looted and empty. Several visits to facilities on the approaches to Baghdad resulted in a fruitless search for chemicals supposedly buried in the yard of a girls' school, and a pair of depots whose allegedly chemical warheads for missiles turned out to be mere high explosives. Team 3 moved into Baghdad the day after its capture, and on April 10 visited the key nuclear weapons complex at Tuwaitha. The International Atomic Energy Agency records showed Tuwaitha to have had just under two tons of enriched uranium before the war, along with over 94 tons of uranium ore, about a fifth of Iraq's full supply. Tuwaitha proved deserted, unguarded, and the looting there continued for weeks. (The Bush administration refused to allow Hans Blix's UN weapons inspectors to return to Iraq but made an exception for the IAEA's nuclear experts, at least to the extent of permitting them to check inventories of Iraqi fissile materials. That material, for Iraqi research programs, was the only radioactive material in the country. The IAEA visited Tuwaitha on June 7 and found all materials accounted for.) Looters dumped the uranium before making off with the canisters in which it had been stored. *There was no missing enriched uranium from which Saddam could have built a nuclear bomb.*

Over the next month Lieutenant Colonel Charles Allison led his Site Survey Team 3 on almost two dozen missions to supposed key weapons of mass destruction facilities all around the Baghdad area. One of them was to the Salman Pak training camp where Iraq had trained Palestinian guerrillas. Cheerleaders for the war claimed Al Qaeda had learned the terror trade in a compound at the camp. There was no trace of the chemical and biological agents that had supposedly been demonstrated for Al Qaeda. Salman Pak training camp had been among CENTCOM's top nineteen priorities for a visit.

The only uranium Team 3 found would be in the depleted uranium shells of a destroyed M-1 Abrams. An alleged chemical storage area at one facility turned out to be an Olympic-size swimming pool, a production plant had actually been a distillery making whiskey, another chemical storage site was a plant making car license plates, a cache of documents on chemical weapons a graduate student's master's thesis. These findings were not the exceptions; they were the day-to-day experience. The low point probably came on May 1, when the weapons searchers went to an alleged key facility of the Special Security Organization, the intelligence service known to be in direct charge of Iraq's effort to hide its weapons programs. There they found a building whose door had to be broken down to get inside. Trudging through the dark interior the searchers came to another locked door. When they broke in, the room on the other side turned out to be full of vacuum cleaners. In another example, Team 3's deputy commander, Major Kenneth Deal, called out "smoking gun" when, during a visit to a Baath Party head-quarters that turned out to be a library and recreation center, he encountered a document—which turned out to be an Arabic translation of a passage from historian A.J.P. Taylor's *The Struggle for Mastery in Europe*. In a dispatch, re-porter Gellman noted, "Smoking gun is now a term of dark irony here."

A senior officer, quoted by *New York Times* reporter Judith Miller, who was embedded with Mobile Exploitation Team Alpha, put the reality of the weapons search this way: "The teams would be given a packet, with pictures and a tentative grid. . . . They would be told: 'Go to this place. You will find a McDonald's there. Look in the fridge. You will find French fries, cheese-burger and Cokes.' And they would go there, and not only was there no fridge and no McDonald's, there was never even a thought of putting a McDonald's there. Day after day it was like that."

Realities were soon reflected in operational method. Before the end of April, half the 75th's mobile exploitation teams were taken off the weapons-of-mass-destruction mission and put on other tasks. The British officer who served as chief exploitation planner, Wing Commander Sebastian Kendall, explained to Gellman, "There has been no conscious decision to reduce the number of teams devoted to weapons of mass destruction . . . it's true to say that the environment is changing based on reality." Similarly the unit's night operations director, Lieutenant Colonel Michael Slifka, remarked, "There's just not much just now for the METs to do." Before the end of April, barely one month after the start of the weapons hunt, Colonel McPhee's unit had taken mobile exploitation teams off the line and was replacing nuclear and chemical specialists with fresh personnel, many deployed from the Utah National Guard, who were given different assignments. Within a couple more weeks the withdrawal from the theater of the 75th Exploitation Task Force would be announced.

Frontline troops made most of the actual discoveries during the war. At an Iraqi depot they found protective suits against chemical weapons and drugs to counteract biological agents. At another place were drums containing chemicals, at yet another an unknown powder substance. The suits were defensive gear, not weapons of mass destruction, the drums held pesticides, the powder proved inoffensive. Washington officials who started out promising the big discovery was yet to come fell back to relying upon Saddam's own deception programs, arguing that after so many years of being hidden, weapons of mass destruction would not be found so quickly, and ended up asserting that more sophisticated lab tests would show the samples to be the advertised weapons. Nothing materialized.

Until late April, that is. On April 19 Kurdish peshmerga fighters near Erbil found a trailer that had been stolen, stripped, and reportedly washed down with ammonia. It seemed similar to the mobile biological weapons laboratories that Colin Powell and others had accused Saddam of using. Near Baghdad late in April U.S. troops found a van (not a trailer truck) apparently outfitted as a toxicology laboratory. Americans from the 101st Airborne Division began more intensive searches that revealed a second "mobile facility" early in May. Parked only about fifty feet outside the entrance to Iraq's major rocket-testing complex at Mosul, called Al Kindi, it had been stripped of its wheels and looted. American soldiers, standing guard at the gate for several

weeks now, had never noticed the trailer. On May 9 the United States announced the discovery. When Maj. Paul Handelman, the airborne division's
chemical warfare officer, took a team to examine this trailer they found it
had an air compressor, refrigerator, fermenter, and dryer. Handelman found
no trace of chemical weapons. A team from the 75th Exploitation Task Force
came up from Baghdad for more sophisticated tests. The truck was quite
similar to the stolen trailer the Kurds had found near Erbil a few weeks
earlier.

Iraqi scientists at Al Kindi told the Americans the trailer was a mobile
unit for separating water into hydrogen, which could then be used for
weather balloons.

Colonel McPhee sent Chemical Biological Intelligence Support Team
Charlie to Mosul. This was a three-person element of his DIA special group,
which had won awards from the CIA for its work in Afghanistan. British
officers tagged along to assist. Charlie did a four-day preliminary investigation. The team leader was a twenty-year veteran of Special Forces, an explosives specialist become nuclear expert. His chemical man was a former
Marine. They made tests, then carefully shipped the entire trailer to the U.S.
base at Baghdad International Airport, where all three Iraqi trucks would be
moved for detailed examination. Team Charlie checked the results of the
tests administered by the Americans of the 101st Airborne and made a visual
inspection. They found plates on equipment that indicated manufacture between 2000 and 2002, and one, indicating the Al Nasser Company as producer of one item, significant because Al Nasser had helped design a major
Iraqi chemical plant destroyed in the Gulf War. The trailer contained a fermenter, a compressor, a refrigerator, a water circulation system, a cooling
system based on an air-conditioner, and a system for recapturing gases.

The team quickly ruled out a nuclear weapons function for the trailer.
But the chemical expert and biological specialist each thought the trailer was
a production facility for their type weapon. They rejected notions that the
trailer had been a decoy, that its function had been to produce vaccines, or
that it was associated with missile fuel.

The trailer had no protective suits or closet spaces for such equipment to be stored, nor was the system self-contained to prevent escape of biological organisms. Team members thought that meant Saddam had so little regard for the lives of his technicians that Iraq did not bother providing safety equipment. The trailer, rather than a fully enclosed body, had only a metal latticework that could be covered with canvas. It also had no shock absorbers on its axles. Only the fermenter was made of stainless steel, and none of the equipment was glass-lined, meaning that the overall system could not withstand the corrosive toxic chemical precursors used in deriving weapon agents.

At Baghdad a technical group flown in from Washington made a further assessment and compiled engineering drawings of the system. Equipment from the trailers and van was then shipped bodily to the United States for further analysis. In the meantime the other inquiries were fodder for CIA and DIA experts in Washington. By May 20, barely two weeks after the Al Kindi capture, reporters were working up a story about the joint CIA-DIA analysis of the trailer that had begun to make its way around the high levels of the Bush administration. With blinding speed this White House that has been so concerned with secrecy decided to declassify the CIA-DIA report (reproduced below). The paper would be jazzed up with text connecting it to Colin Powell's UN speech, then released on May 28 under the title "Iraqi Mobile Biological Warfare Agent Production Plants."

"You should have seen the smile on my face when one day the intelligence community came in and gave me a photo, and said, 'Look,' " Secretary Powell told reporters once the report had been released.

George W. Bush considered himself vindicated. The president announced to all and sundry on May 30 that America had found the Iraqi *weapons* of mass destruction. The sense of relief in administration pronouncements of the time was palpable, as if they finally had some proof on which to hang their multitudinous allegations. Yet once more there would be less to the evidence than met the eye.

document 7. *CIA/DIA Report, May 28, 2003.*

28 May 2003

Iraqi Mobile Biological Warfare Agent Production Plants

Reported Mobile Plants Compared to Those Found in Iraq

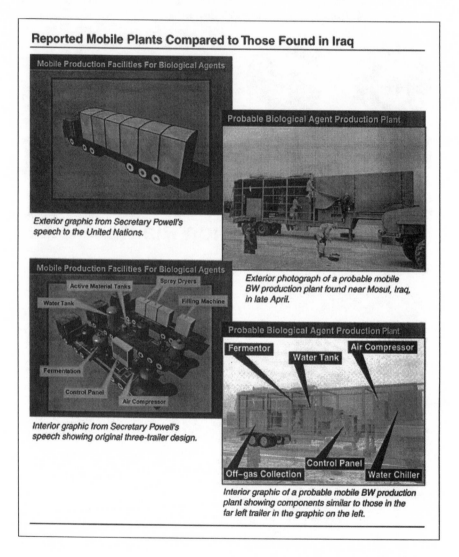

Mobile Production Facilities For Biological Agents

Exterior graphic from Secretary Powell's speech to the United Nations.

Probable Biological Agent Production Plant

Exterior photograph of a probable mobile BW production plant found near Mosul, Iraq, in late April.

Mobile Production Facilities For Biological Agents

Active Material Tanks   Spray Dryers
Water Tank   Filling Machine
Fermentation
Control Panel
Air Compressor

Interior graphic from Secretary Powell's speech showing original three-trailer design.

Probable Biological Agent Production Plant

Fermentor   Water Tank   Air Compressor

Off-gas Collection   Control Panel   Water Chiller

Interior graphic of a probable mobile BW production plant showing components similar to those in the far left trailer in the graphic on the left.

Iraqi Mobile Biological Warfare Agent Production Plants

Overview

Coalition forces have uncovered the strongest evidence to date that Iraq was hiding a biological warfare program.

- Kurdish forces in late April 2003 took into custody a specialized tractor-trailer near Mosul and subsequently turned it over to US military control.

- The US military discovered a second mobile facility equipped to produce BW agent in early May at the al-Kindi Research, Testing, Development, and Engineering facility in Mosul. Although this second trailer appears to have been looted, the remaining equipment, including the fermentor, is in a configuration similar to the first plant.

- US forces in late April also discovered a mobile laboratory truck in Baghdad. The truck is a toxicology laboratory from the 1980s that could be used to support BW or legitimate research.

1. The design, equipment, and layout of the trailer found in late April is strikingly similar to descriptions provided by a source who was a chemical engineer that managed one of the mobile plants. Secretary of State Powell's description of the mobile plants in his speech in February 2003 to the United Nations (see inset below) was based primarily on reporting from this source.

Secretary Powell's Speech to the UN

Secretary Powell's speech to the UN in February 2003 detailed Iraq's mobile BW program, and was primarily based on information from a source who was a chemical engineer that managed one of the mobile plants.

- Iraq's mobile BW program began in the mid-1990s—this is reportedly when the units were being designed.

- Iraq manufactured mobile trailers and railcars to produce biological agents, which were designed to evade UN weapons inspectors. Agent production reportedly occurred Thursday night through Friday when the UN did not conduct inspections in observance of the Muslim holy day.

2.
- An accident occurred in 1998 during a production run, which killed 12 technicians—an indication that Iraq was producing a BW agent at that time.

3. Analysis of the trailers reveals that they probably are second- or possibly third-generation designs of the plants described by the source. The newer version includes system improvements, such as cooling units, apparently engineered to solve production problems described by the source that were encountered with the older design.

- The manufacturer's plates on the fermentors list production dates of 2002 and 2003—suggesting Iraq continued to produce these units as late as this year.

[Table of Contents]

Prewar Assessment

The source reported to us that Iraq in 1995 planned to construct seven sets of mobile production plants—six on semitrailers and one on railroad cars—to conceal BW agent production while appearing to cooperate with UN inspectors. Some of this information was corroborated by another source.

- One of the semitrailer plants reportedly produced BW agents as early as July 1997.

- The design for a more concealable and efficient two-trailer system was reportedly completed in May 1998 to compensate for difficulties in operating the original, three-trailer plant.

4.
- Iraq employed extensive denial and deception in this program, including disguising from its own workers the production process, equipment, and BW agents produced in the trailers.

[Table of Contents]

Plants Consistent With Intelligence Reporting

5. Examination of the trailers reveals that all of the equipment is permanently installed and interconnected, creating an ingeniously simple, self-contained bioprocessing system. Although the equipment on the trailer found in April 2003 was partially damaged by looters, it includes a fermentor capable of producing biological agents and support equipment such as water supply tanks, an air compressor, a water chiller, and a system for collecting exhaust gases.

6. The trailers probably are part of a two- or possibly three-trailer unit. Both trailers we have found probably are designed to produce BW agent in unconcentrated liquid slurry. The missing trailer or trailers from one complete unit would be equipped for growth media preparation and postharvest processing and, we would expect, have equipment such as mixing tanks, centrifuges, and spray dryers.

- These other units that we have not yet found would be needed to prepare and sterilize the media and to concentrate and possibly dry the agent, before the agent is ready for introduction into a delivery system, such as bulk-filled munitions. Before the Gulf war, Iraq bulk filled missile and rocket warheads, aerial bombs, artillery shells, and spray tanks.

Prewar Iraqi Mobile Program Sources

7. The majority of our information on Iraq's mobile program was obtained from a chemical engineer that managed one of the plants. Three other sources, however, corroborated information related to the mobile BW project.

8. • The second source was a civil engineer who reported on the existence of at least one truck-transportable facility in December 2000 at the Karbala ammunition depot.

    • The third source reported in 2002 that Iraq had manufactured mobile systems for the production of single-cell protein on trailers and railcars but admitted that they could be used for BW agent production.

9. • The fourth source, a defector from the Iraq Intelligence Service, reported that Baghdad manufactured mobile facilities that we assess could be used for the research of BW agents, vice production.

Our analysis of the mobile production plant found in April indicates the layout and equipment are consistent with information provided by the chemical engineer, who has direct knowledge of Iraq's mobile BW program.

• The source recognized pictures of this trailer, among photographs of unrelated equipment, as a mobile BW production plant similar to the one that he managed, even pointing out specific pieces of equipment that were installed on his unit.

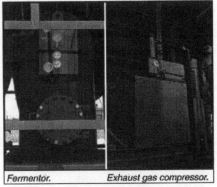

Fermentor.   Exhaust gas compressor.

[Click image to enlarge]

Common elements between the source's description and the trailers include a control panel, fermentor, water tank, holding tank, and two sets of gas cylinders. One set of gas cylinders was reported to provide clean gases

—oxygen and nitrogen—for production, and the other set captured exhaust gases, concealing signatures of BW agent production.

- The discovered trailers also incorporate air-stirred fermentors, which the source reported were part of the second-generation plant design.

- Externally, the trailers have a ribbed superstructure to support a canvas covering that matches the source's description.

- Data plates on the fermentors indicate that they were manufactured at the same plant the source said manufactured equipment for the first generation of mobile plants. The plant also was involved in the production of equipment used in Iraq's pre-Gulf war BW program.

10. Employees of the facility that produced the mobile production plants' fermentor revealed that seven fermentors were produced in 1997, one in 2002 and one in 2003.

Interior view of fermentor, media tank, water supply tanks, and gas cylinders connected by pipes.

[Click image to enlarge]

- The seven fermentors appear to corroborate the source's reporting that Iraq in the mid-1990s planned to produce seven mobile production plants.

- The two fermentors produced in 2002 and 2003 reportedly were sent to the al-Kindi Research, Testing, Development, and Engineering facility in Mosul—the site where the second trailer was found—and probably are the fermentors found on the trailers in US custody.

There are a few inconsistencies between the source's reporting and the trailers, which probably reflect design improvements.

11.
- The original plants were reported to be mounted on flatbed trailers reinforced by nickel-plate flooring and equipped with hydraulic support legs. The discovered plants are mounted on heavy equipment

transporters intended to carry army tanks, obviating the need for reinforced floors and hydraulic legs.

12.
- The trailers have a cooling unit not included in the original plant design, probably to solve overheating problems during the summer months as described by the source.

- The original design had 18 pumps, but the source mentioned an effort to reduce the number to four in the new design. The trailer discovered in late April has three pumps.

[Table of Contents]

Legitimate Uses Unlikely

Coalition experts on fermentation and systems engineering examined the trailer found in late April and have been unable to identify any legitimate industrial use—such as water purification, mobile medical laboratory, vaccine or pharmaceutical production—that would justify the effort and expense of a mobile production capability. We have investigated what other industrial processes may require such equipment—a fermentor, refrigeration, and a gas capture system—and agree with the experts that BW agent production is the only consistent, logical purpose for these vehicles.

13.
- The capability of the system to capture and compress exhaust gases produced during fermentation is not required for legitimate biological processes and strongly indicates attempts to conceal production activity.

- The presence of caustic in the fermentor combined with the recent painting of the plant may indicate an attempt to decontaminate and conceal the plant's purpose.

- Finally, the data plate on the fermentor indicates that this system was manufactured in 2002 and yet it was not declared to the United Nations, as required by Security Council Resolutions.

14. Some coalition analysts assess that the trailer found in late April could be used for bioproduction but believe it may be a newer prototype because the layout is not entirely identical to what the source described.

Manufacturer's data plate on the fermentor.
[Click image to enlarge]

A *New York Times* article on 13 May 2003 reported that an agricultural expert suggests the trailers might have been intended to produce biopesticides near agricultural areas in order to avoid degradation problems. The same article also reported that a former weapons inspector suggests that the trailers may be chemical-processing units intended to refurbish Iraq's antiaircraft missiles.

- Biopesticide production requires the same equipment and technology used for BW agent production; however, the off-gas collection system and the size of the equipment are unnecessary for biopesticide production. There is no need to produce biopesticides near the point of use because biopesticides do not degrade as quickly as most BW agents and would be more economically produced at a large fixed facility. In addition, the color of the trailer found in mid-April is indicative of military rather than civilian use.

15.
- Our missile experts have no explanation for how such a trailer could function to refurbish antiaircraft missiles and judge that such a use is unlikely based on the scale, configuration, and assessed function of the equipment.

- The experts cited in the editorial are not on the scene and probably do not have complete access to information about the trailers.

[Table of Contents]

Hydrogen Production Cover Story

16. Senior Iraqi officials of the al-Kindi Research, Testing, Development, and Engineering facility in Mosul were shown pictures of the mobile production trailers, and they claimed that the trailers were used to chemically produce hydrogen for artillery weather balloons. Hydrogen production would be a plausible cover story for the mobile production units.

- The Iraqis have used sophisticated denial and deception methods that include the use of cover stories that are designed to work. Some of the features of the trailer—a gas collection system and the presence of caustic—are consistent with both bioproduction and hydrogen production.

The plant's design possibly could be used to produce hydrogen using a chemical reaction, but it would be inefficient. The capacity of this trailer is larger than typical units for hydrogen production for weather balloons. Compact, transportable hydrogen generation systems are commercially available, safe, and reliable.

[Table of Contents]

Sample Collection and Analysis

We continue to examine the trailer found in mid-April and are using advanced sample analysis techniques to determine whether BW agent is present, although we do not expect samples to show the presence of BW agent. We suspect that the Iraqis thoroughly decontaminated the vehicle to remove evidence of BW agent production. Despite the lack of confirmatory samples, we nevertheless are confident that this trailer is a mobile BW production plant because of the source's description, equipment, and design.

- The initial set of samples, now in the United States, was taken from sludge from inside the fermentor, liquid that was in the system and wipes from the equipment. A sample set also was provided to a coalition partner for detailed laboratory analysis.

17.
- ·As we expected, preliminary sample analysis results are negative for five standard BW agents, including *Bacillus anthracis*, and for growth media for those agents. In addition, the preliminary results indicate the presence of sodium azide and urea, which do not support Iraqi claims that the trailer was for hydrogen production.

- Additional sample analysis is being conducted to identify growth media, agent degradation products, and decontamination chemicals that could be specific for BW agents, as well as to identify a chemical associated with hydrogen production.

[Table of Contents]

Mobile Production Plant Versus Mobile Laboratory?

Although individuals often interchangeably use the terms production plant and laboratory, they have distinct meanings. The mobile production plants are designed for batch production of biological material and not for laboratory analysis of samples. A truck-mounted mobile laboratory would be equipped for analysis and small-scale laboratory activities. US forces discovered one such laboratory in late April.

- The mobile laboratory—installed in a box-bodied truck—is equipped with standard, dual-use laboratory equipment, including autoclaves, an incubator, centrifuges, and laboratory test tubes and glassware.

- These laboratories could be used to support a mobile BW production plant but serve legitimate functions that are applicable to public heath and environmental monitoring, such as water-quality sampling.

Iraqi mobile laboratory.

[Click image to enlarge]

Interior view of mobile laboratory.

[Click image to enlarge]

Mobile Lab Comments

1. Here the CIA/DIA paper confirms that secretary Powell's February presentation had been based on the single defector source. In August 2003, the German newspaper *Die Zeit* would report that the Iraqi defector had been a source for the German intelligence service BND and was considered unreliable, so much so that problems with the source had been noted when the Germans passed him on to the CIA.

2. "An accident" could be anything. For example, if the trailer had been a hydrogen gas production unit, as claimed by Iraqi scientists at Al Kindi when the trailer was first discovered, it is perfectly possible to postulate an accident triggered by an electrical or other spark that might have killed a dozen people. Alternatively, spores released from a containment failure (if the trailer were a research laboratory) or chemicals leaked in similar fashion (were the trailer a pesticide producer or chemical weapons unit) could have had the identical effect. Without more specific detail, the CIA/DIA report is simply asking readers to take on faith the assertion that biological warfare agents were in production in 1998.

3. This language obscures an acknowledgment by the authors of the CIA/DIA report that *in fact there are discrepancies between what their source told them and the trailers found in 2003.*

4. To take the CIA/DIA report at its word, this passage demands a question: If the Iraqi government concealed from its own workers the production process, equipment, and product of this facility, how does the defector know the trailer is a biological warfare facility producing active weapon agents?

5. Nothing about the equipment on the captured trailers specialized it to biological processing. This accounts for the initial impressions of experts from the 75th Exploitation Task Force that the trailer could have either chemical or biological functions. This point will be important later.

6. In the UN Security Council on February 5, Secretary of State Colin Powell had described the same two- or three-truck unit. In May, having captured two (apparently identically equipped) trailers and a van, U.S. intelligence remains unable to specify the elements of the system. This is disturbing. It is also the case that the trailers the United States *did* find were *not capable* of producing weapons at all. The *other* alleged trailers, none of which were ever seen, much less captured, were the key elements for production of biological agents.

7. Note that U.S. intelligence has relied upon a single source, a defector. None of the other sources mentioned below (also defectors) did anything more than confirm the existence of mobile laboratories. The role of the Iraqi National Congress (INC) in producing defectors who retailed intelligence the United States wanted to hear has already been seen as critical in Bush administration descriptions of an alleged Iraqi alliance with Al Qaeda. Here again it has produced the key information. Ahmed Chalabi, chief of the INC and now a member of the Iraqi governing council, confirmed on television during a U.S. visit in June 2003 that INC had produced the defectors to speak about the mobile labs. The CIA was already leery of INC-provided defector information. The DIA in 2003 decided to conduct its own review of the defectors and their information. That review has been reported as concluding that most of the defector data had been of little or no value.

8. This source is cited as confirming nothing more than the presence of a truck in one single place on one specific date. On February 5, Colin Powell had cited the same source for the much broader claim of confirming "the existence of transportable facilities moving on trailers" (see p. 213). At a minimum, the briefing designed to get the UN to approve a war had exaggerated the scope of this intelligence.

9. Here the defector reports nothing more than that the mobile facilities were manufactured by Iraq. U.S. intelligence is adding its conclusions to the information from the defector, that the facilities were for research of biological agents *instead* of production, but worded to suggest this was information from the defector. On February 5 Powell had said (p. 213) the source had informed the United States that Iraq had mobile laboratories *in addition to* the production plants. The trailer that is the subject of this CIA/DIA report *does not have the equipment to conduct research on biological weapons.* The DIA had actually interviewed this Iraqi officer twice in early 2002 and established that he had no first-hand information and may have been coached by the Chalabi group. In May 2002 DIA issued a notice warning of fabrications by this officer, a warning overlooked both in assembling the Powell UN speech *and* in this CIA/DIA report.

10. To take the CIA/DIA report at its own word, this text indicates that the United States captured *both* of the recent production trailers and *none* of the much more numerous original models, a highly improbable occurrence.

11. This text is much more important than it sounds. Hydraulic legs suggest that stability was a key requirement for safe operation of the equipment. Uneven placement of the trailer, shaking, and the like threatened the activity conducted.

That characteristic would be quite likely for a chemical or biological warfare plant. Yet the trailers the United States captured *did not even have shock absorbers for their wheels.* That alone would have created a danger of damaging the plant. If so, the absence of closets or other provisions for storage of protective gear acquires major import. Lack of platform stability would be less critical for a hydrogen gas production unit than a biological warfare plant. In addition, the lack of shock absorbers indicates the trailer had been designed to be *movable* rather than *mobile.* In that context the location of the trailer only a short distance from the entrance to a key Iraqi missile test facility is particularly significant. Al Kindi would have needed frequent use of weather balloons filled with hydrogen for wind prediction and range instrumentation associated with missile tests.

12. The presence of a cooling unit could also suggest a hydrogen gas separation process, although the explanation given here is plausible as well.

13. The trailers were clearly military issue; the argument here rejecting any "legiti- mate industrial use" is entirely beside the point, and the assertion that "BW agent production is the only consistent, logical purpose" is jumping to the conclusion. The original U.S. site inspection team sent to Al Kindi postulated multiple pos- sible uses (chemical, biological). The Iraqi scientists suggested a third, innocent one. If the trailer was indeed a hydrogen gas plant, the capability of the system to capture and compress gases would have been the *primary output* determinant, rather than a concealment mechanism, as the paper concludes. This represents an attempt to conceptualize how the things actually found could be fit into a preconceived object, the biological warfare plant. Likewise, the statement regard- ing residue in the fermenter, which has been identified elsewhere as aluminum. Aluminum and mineral deposits would be a natural by-product of the separation of water into oxygen and hydrogen. These are examples of the same kind of hypothesis-driven intelligence analysis as was used to conclude there was an al- liance between Saddam and Al Qaeda. As for declaration to the UN, Iraq would not have regarded a gas plant for balloons as requiring such reporting.

The "no legitimate use" argument also presupposes there *was* no other possible use. The 75th Exploitation Task Force itself had vans with even more sophisti- cated equipment. As for commercial use, in the United States the John Morris Corporation produces a BioFlo 5000 fermenter (in two sizes) with even more capabilities than the Iraqi plant. It has an air scrubber system (held in the CIA/ DIA report to be present for concealment), and an optional exhaust gas con- denser. Poland produces similar equipment, which is advertised as a "bioreactor" suitable for producing microbes to consume contaminants in soil, necessary for cleaning hazardous waste from storage, spill, and other sites.

David Albright, of the Institute for Science and International Security, objects to the failure to conduct an objective technical study by qualified nongovernmental experts and adds, "The government's finding is based on eliminating any possible alternative explanations for the trucks, which is a controversial methodology under any circumstances. . . . The selective use or disregarding of information raises questions whether the report was written with a preferred solution in mind."

14. The reference to "coalition analysts" suggests that British intelligence agreed with the U.S. conclusion. Just a few weeks after the CIA/DIA report, the English press noted that the British technical review had concluded the trailers were hydrogen plants. *The Observer* quoted one of the British scientists involved: "They are not mobile germ warfare laboratories. You could not use them for making biological weapons. They do not even look like them. They are exactly what the Iraqis said they were—facilities for the production of hydrogen gas to fill balloons." In 1982, before the Gulf War, Iraq had imported Marconi hydrogen generation equipment. In July 2003, former UN weapons inspector Scott Ritter would report that British officials saw the trailer system as an exact replication of the Marconi equipment.

15. This statement is an example of the way the CIA/DIA report ignores or obscures inconvenient information. "Missile experts" could hardly be unaware of the uses of balloons on rocket test ranges. The statement here is only true within an extremely narrow range of fact: the "scale" (which is ruled in the next section to be too generous for "efficient" hydrogen manufacture) and the "assessed function" (which is indeterminant since the equipment has capabilities in several fields and this report is supposed to be deciding which function applies). "Configuration" of the equipment is arguably *better* suited for a hydrogen plant than for a germ warfare producer.

16. The hydrogen gas plant explanation that is being dismissed here *could not be* a "plausible cover story" unless hydrogen production was a credible function of the trailer. This conflicts with the repeated assertion in the report that U.S. intelligence analysts cannot conceive of a credible function of the trailers other than biological agent production.

17. In this remarkable statement, the *absence* of any trace of five different biological warfare agents is dismissed as being of no importance. Moreover, sodium and urea could be present in mineral deposits from the disaggregation of water, and their presence in the trailer would not be inconsistent with its use as a hydrogen gas plant.

Fingers in the Dike

The claim of Iraqi mobile weapons plants began unraveling almost instantly. The State Department's intelligence unit (INR) prepared a classified memorandum on June 2, 2003, objecting that it was premature to conclude the trailers were mobile weapons facilities. That paper was still secret in mid-June when someone from the British defense establishment broke ranks and leaked the conclusions of the British technical evaluation that the trailers were not weapons facilities but hydrogen gas plants. The INR memo leaked ten days later. By then Colin Powell had used the CIA/DIA report as evidence that his own UN speech had been completely accurate, and George W. Bush had used it to claim that weapons of mass destruction had actually been found. These new assertions were efforts to plug the dikes of misinformation Bush had used to justify the war, which were now, literally and figuratively, springing more and more leaks.

State Department spokesman Richard Boucher made a game effort at covering Powell's flank when the INR memo leak appeared on June 26. Boucher explained that INR was not disputing the CIA/DIA analysis so much as pointing out questions that needed to be looked at. The spokesmen insisted that CIA people had looked more closely at the trailers than INR, had taken their concerns into account, and were still confident in the accuracy of their report. But neither Boucher nor Powell convincingly refuted the impression that INR had dissented from this latest bit of administration bombast.

The CIA stood its ground. Spokesman Bill Harlow opined that others "are entitled to their opinion, of course, but we stand behind the assertions" in the CIA/DIA report. Yet differing opinions piled up quickly in support of the INR folks. William C. Patrick III, who had worked in the U.S. chemical weapons program, pointed out that the trailers had no steam sterilization equipment: "That's a huge minus." The CIA produced a group of three anonymous analysts to defend the paper, contriving a defense for the criticisms. No way to drain germ-impregnated fluids from the processing tank? A small pipe at the bottom. That was too small? The compressors' purpose could be to pump air into the tanks to force them to drain under pressure.

Low production? The plant as they conceived it could produce enough to fill five bombs per month. (For biological weapons, and chemical ones especially, five bombs a month is not that much.)

His agency clearly under fire, shortly after publication of the CIA/DIA paper on the trailers director George Tenet issued an official statement expressing his high confidence in the CIA's intelligence on Iraq, the accuracy of its reporting, and his regard for its analysts. Then it was reported that the CIA had reassigned the chief of its Iraq task force to its personnel office.

The chief of CIA's Iraq Issues Group, an interoffice ad hoc assemblage of key analysts, was sent to Baghdad on extended assignment, usefully out of the way of inquiring congressmen and reporters.

Next it transpired that people at the DIA were not all on board either. The CIA/DIA paper apparently did not reflect the views of the agency's engineering experts. The DIA engineers discussed the evidence in June and again in July. Their report leaked in early August. The consensus was the trailers were hydrogen gas plants. When the intelligence community assembled an interagency group of sixteen analysts to review the evidence, only one held out for the view the trailers were weapons factories.

Simultaneous with the fiasco over the Iraqi trailers, another strand of the Bush administration's embroidery work began to come undone. For months occasional items in the press reported on a shadow CIA at the Pentagon, a tiny unit created to look at intelligence reporting and give the Office of the Secretary of Defense (OSD) a different take on it. The unit had actually come into existence at the initiative of undersecretary of defense for policy Douglas J. Feith soon after the 9/11 attacks. It began work that October. The different-anglers, at first two, later four or five persons (in some reports the number of employees peaked at about a dozen) under Abram Shulsky, resided within OSD's Office of Near East and South Asian Affairs and called themselves "the Cabal." So far, little is known of their contributions to the war in Afghanistan, and they remained below the public's event horizon right through the fall of 2002.

Another of the coterie of neo-conservative national security aides, Abram Shulsky had been an associate of Richard Perle and Elliott Abrams since the 1960s. All three had worked on Capitol Hill for conservative Democrat Henry

("Scoop") Jackson. All were products of the same University of Chicago intellectual hothouse that produced Robert Joseph and Zalmay Khalilzhad. Shulsky
spent some time with the conservative think tank National Strategy Information Center, which had a Consortium for the Study of Intelligence. The strategy center had close links to such figures as William J. Casey and flourished
during the Carter and early Reagan administrations. He then returned to Capitol Hill to become designated professional for Senator Daniel Patrick Moyni-
han on the staff of the Senate Select Committee on Intelligence. Moving on to
the RAND Corporation, Shulsky authored a book, *Silent Warfare: Understanding
the World of Intelligence*, an overview that acquired a certain reputation as a spy
text. It was at RAND that Shulsky met "Scooter" Libby. Together Shulsky and
Libby wrote a policy paper advocating a strategy of American unilateralism,
prefiguring the policy doctrine that Libby and Paul Wolfowitz would later as-
semble for the first Bush administration.

Three points emerge from this recitation. First, Abram Shulsky *did* have
credentials for the intelligence job Doug Feith gave him. Second, Shulsky had
close ties with the hierarchy of neo-conservative operators who were pushing
Bush administration policy on Iraq, including particularly Wolfowitz, Libby,
Feith, and Perle. Third, in terms of substance, Shulsky had committed himself
to the muscular interventionism characteristic of this group. That meant doing what it took to help make the Iraq war happen, which inevitably had an
impact on the objectivity of his Cabal's intelligence review.

What had been distinctive about Shulsky's book was its effort to postulate novel ways to conceptualize in intelligence. Several novel methods, as
well as trendy subjects, had been current in the field during the 1980s when
Shulsky built the intellectual underpinnings of his work. Numerical methods
of probability analysis, heuristic prediction by approximation (testing outcomes by trial and error until assigned values corresponded to results),
hypothesis-driven analysis, psychological profiling of leadership, and Red-
teaming (attempting to replicate the operational code of the adversary) were
increasingly in vogue as methods, and Shulsky paid attention to them. One
trendy subject had been the uses of disinformation and deception. At the
time, the main practitioners of deception had been considered to be the

Russians (then Soviets), but after the Cold War that label could easily have been transferred to the Iraqis, who had been Soviet clients.

The Iraq intelligence work performed by Shulsky's small cell inside the Office of Near East and South Asian Affairs (NESA) utilized one of these methods, essentially reversing the process of deduction. The Pentagon intelligencers took the hypothesis that there had been a deal between Saddam and Al Qaeda, then looked to see if the intelligence reporting matched that notion, instead of adding up the reports to see if they yielded evidence of the deal. This was useful as an intellectual exercise but yielded a conclusion that necessarily had to be speculative. The results had been presented at the CIA in August 2002 when Douglas Feith took Shulsky's lead analysts to rebut the views of those who did not believe in the Iraqi threat. Director Tenet caved, as has already been related.

Afterward the Cabal performed support work for the high-and-mighty at the White House and in the Pentagon. They were rewarded. The NESA shop got an addition in October 2002, the Office of Special Plans (OSP), essentially the Cabal, which, among other things, was given charge of Pentagon planning for the postwar occupation of Iraq. Another Middle East specialist, Karen Kwiatkowski, an Air Force lieutenant colonel who served in Feith's office until retiring in April 2003, has described a free-wheeling process that crossed all bureaucratic lines, as OSP employees not only worked for Feith and secretary Rumsfeld, but were on call for support to Vice President Cheney's office as well. William J. Luti, the NESA director, had been under Dick Cheney in the first Bush administration, where, naturally enough, he'd been an associate of "Scooter" Libby as well. In their work for Cheney's office, the Luti group became, in effect, an analytical extension for the vice president's shadow NSC staff. Colonel Kwiatkowski saw so much happening that went against her sense of good order and discipline that she finally decided the operation added up to a subversion of constitutional limits on executive power.

One of the oddities would be the close relationship between the NESA Cabal and the exiles of the Iraqi National Congress (INC). Outsiders would be given the impression that the Shulsky shop confined itself to taking existing intelligence reports and trying to contrive a fresh way to visualize how they fit together. But the October 2003 Feith intelligence memorandum to Congress establishes clearly that the exiles were the most frequently relied upon sources in constructing their vision of Saddam and Al Qaeda. Feith and Luti would insist the Shulsky cell merely used transcripts of interrogations separately made by DIA's Defense HUMINT Service. But, as journalist Seymour Hersh would report in *The New Yorker*, the INC not only provided intelligence on demand, it furnished defectors to testify. Moreover, the Bush people rejected the results of a summer 2001 Pentagon review of INC's capability and credibility on the grounds the reviewers were anticipating failure, while the administration aimed for success. In effect Bush and his key advisors deliberately tossed away a warning that would have saved them when the Iraq intelligence issue took center stage.

The problematical aspect of reliance upon defectors has been illustrated in several places, but the INC pipeline into the Pentagon would be especially pernicious. Another remarkable feature of this relationship is that the INC connection grew stronger, not weaker, once the Office of Special Plans began work on schemes for an occupation of Iraq. Since the Bush White House continued to shop for that version of the intelligence most suitable for its intentions, and Luti's OSP had an inside view of that policy while crafting its intelligence, the result was self-feeding. Moreover, the Shulsky cell was mixing intelligence collection, reporting, and policy functions all in one place. According to Hersh, "By last fall [2002], the operation rivaled both the CIA and the Pentagon's own Defense Intelligence Agency, the DIA, as President Bush's main source of intelligence regarding Iraq's possible possession of weapons of mass destruction and connection with Al Qaeda."

All these developments remained obscure until the moment when two other reporters revealed the existence of the Shulsky cell in a front-page story in the *New York Times* in October 2002. Secretary of Defense Donald H. Rumsfeld was asked about the unit the same day. By Rumsfeld's account, he knew so little about the Shulsky shop he'd had to ask aides. Rumsfeld declared, "Any suggestion that it's an intelligence-gathering activity or an intelligence unit of some sort, I think, would be a misunderstanding of it."

The secretary went on to deny being unhappy in any way with the intelligence he regularly received from the CIA, DIA, and other agencies. He liked his CIA briefer, said Rumsfeld, and he had only been briefed once by people from the Shulsky cell, whom he knew only as working for Doug Feith.

Of his single briefing, the secretary of defense remarked, "I was so interested in it, I said, gee, why don't you go over and brief George Tenet. So they did."

The single briefing had been the Cabal's Saddam-Al Qaeda presentation, and it was Rumsfeld himself who sent them over to slay those CIA doubters. "There's no mystery about all this," the secretary commented. But, of course, there was. When Rumsfeld went on to say there were no differences between his view and the CIA's on Saddam–Al Qaeda links, and that that was why, a few weeks before, when he had said his intelligence was "bulletproof," the Pentagon chief was referring to Tenet's about-face after the August 2002 meeting with Feith's analysts.

In fact, there were plenty of differences. George Tenet might order his agency to take a certain position, and it is perfectly possible the Saddam–Al Qaeda alliance thesis was acceptable to the CIA Counterterrorism Center. But the line analysts on Iraq, the Middle East, and the other substantive areas involved were not convinced at all. That is precisely why senior CIA people with the Iraq task force and its analytical group were transferred out of those slots not long after the war. CIA officers were restive, dismayed at the disregard for their agency's reporting displayed by the Bush people amid the administration's drive into Iraq. *That*, in turn, was exactly what made the later leak of a covert CIA officer's affiliation so explosive.

The Shulsky shop within Lutti's Office of Special Plans became more controversial itself as well. Bits and pieces of its story surfaced in different places, notably *The New Yorker*, which carried a piece that touched on the subject in February 2003, then the more extensive Seymour Hersh treatment in mid-May. Other reports then multiplied, especially in the foreign media, until by early June the Pentagon decided it had a major public relations problem on its hands. That is the background to the Douglas Feith press conference of June 4, 2003, a transcript of which is reprinted here.

Updated 04 Jun 2003

Presenter: Douglas J. Feith, USD (Policy)   Wednesday, June 4, 2003 - 8:38 a.m. EDT

DoD Briefing on Policy and Intelligence Matters

(Briefing on policy and intelligence matters. Participating were Douglas J. Feith, under secretary of defense for policy, and William J. Luti, deputy under secretary of defense for special plans and Near East and South Asian affairs.)

Feith: Good morning.

Bill, do you want to join me up here?

The reason that we were interested in meeting with you this morning is to help lay to rest some stories that have been circulating about the Defense Department that are not true and are beginning to achieve the status of urban legends. So we thought we would try to help straighten the record out.

There are four issues that I think I'd like to address. One is this so-called, or alleged intelligence cell and its relation to the Special Plans Office. Secondly is the issue of intelligence judgments regarding Iraqi weapons of mass destruction. Third is the department's alleged intent to topple the Iranian regime, about which there have been a number of inaccurate news stories. And finally, our policy and the Defense Department's views on the organization called the MEK, the Mujahedeen e Khalq, an Iranian terrorist group. And I'd like to start with a review of some of these items, and then my colleague, Bill Luti and I will be happy to take some of your questions.

On this so-called intelligence cell, which has been hyped in various publications as a Department of Defense effort to create a unit that would somehow substitute for the CIA, I'd like to give you what actually is the story. After the September 11th attack, I identified a requirement to think through what it means for the Defense Department to be at war with a terrorist network. This was an unusual circumstance -- warfare has traditionally been against nation states -- and we understood that it presents a number of peculiar conceptual challenges to be at war with a network, or as I've described it as a network of networks of terrorist organizations.

So, I asked for some people to think through -- first of all, to review the large amount of intelligence on terrorist networks, and to think through how the various terrorist organizations relate to each other and how they relate to different groups that support them; in particular, state sponsors. And we set up a small team to help digest the intelligence that already existed on this very broad subject. And the so-called cell comprised two full-time people. This is why you see

1.

that I think it's almost comical that people think that this was set up as somehow an alternative -- (Chuckles.) -- to the intelligence community or to the CIA. I mean, it was two full-time people. They drew from time to time on assistance from a few others. I mean, altogether, we're talking about four people, five people, you know, at one time or another, doing the work.

The team began its work in October of 2001. It was not involved in intelligence collection. Rather, it relied on reporting from the CIA and other parts of the intelligence community. Its job was to review this intelligence to help digest it for me and other policymakers, to help us develop Defense Department strategy for the war on terrorism. And as I said, it looked at these interrelationships among terrorist organizations and their state sponsors. It did not confine its review to Iraq or al Qaeda. I mean, it was looking at global terrorist networks and the full range of state sponsors and other sources of support for terrorist groups. <u>Its main conclusion was that</u>
2. <u>groups and states were willing to cooperate across philosophical, ideological lines.</u>

So, it came up with the -- a number of interesting connections of where, for example, Sunni and Shi'a groups cooperated, or religious- based groups cooperated with secular groups or states. And so it showed that we cannot simply assume that the only cooperation that existed in the world among terrorist groups and their sponsors was on some kind of pure ideological or philosophical lines. I mean, this is not that shocking for anybody who remembers that, for example, the Nazis and the Soviets had a strategic alliance also. But it was a very important point, because there was a lot of debate in government circles and in academic circles about whether these different groups do in fact cooperate across these philosophical lines.

I think what has become the focus of a lot of the press stories about this is the fact that in the course of its work, this team, in reviewing the intelligence that was provided to us by the CIA and the intelligence community, came up with some interesting observations about the linkages between Iraq and al Qaeda. And when they did, and they brought those to the attention of top-level officials here in the department, and we arranged for a briefing of these items to Secretary Rumsfeld, he looked at that and said, "That's interesting. Let's share it with George Tenet." And so some members of the team and I went over, I think it was in August of 2002, and shared some of these observations. And these were simply observations of this team based on the intelligence that the intelligence community had given to us, and it was just in the course of their reading it, this was incidental to the purpose of this group. But since they happened to come up with it and since it was an important subject, we went over, shared it with George and people at the CIA. My impression was it was pretty well received, and that was that. It was one meeting.

There have been a number of misperceptions about this team. One of them is that, there have been several press articles that have identified this team with the Special Plans Office in Dr. Luti's organization. Dr. Luti is the deputy under secretary of defense for -- let me get it right --

Luti: Special Plans and Near Eastern/South Asian Affairs.

Feith: Special Plans and Near Eastern/South Asian Affairs.

Luti: Twenty-seven countries.

Feith: And this intelligence cell -- alleged -- which is this team that did this particular project, which was not an intelligence project -- it was a matter of digesting other people's intelligence products -- this team is not -- was not part of that office; wasn't related to it. In fact, the team stopped doing its work -- basically, once we had that meeting with the CIA and the team had given us a report on these terrorist network interconnections, there was no team anymore. And they stopped doing their work before the Special Plans Office, if I have it straight, was actually created within Dr. Luti's organization.

Q: (Off mike.)

Luti: October of 2002. We had -- a decision was made in August of 2002 to reorganize, and Doug will explain to you why. But those are the dates.

Q: And that team stopped in August 2002?

Feith: Roughly. The -- (Chuckling.) -- and the Special Plans Office was called Special Plans, because at the time, calling it Iraq Planning Office might have undercut the -- our diplomatic efforts with regard to Iraq and the U.N. and elsewhere. We set up an office to address the whole range of issues regarding Iraq planning.

Luti: And if I may, it's clear to make a distinction; it's a policy planning office, just like -- in my shop, I have essentially three directorates: A Middle East directorate with a handful of people working, a South Asia directorate with a handful of people working, and I used to have a Northern Gulf directorate, which we expanded to meet the incredibly stepped-up requirements in the summer and fall of last year to deal with Iraq. We needed help, we needed people. So, we expanded it. And that's what I do -- policy planning.

Feith: So, I mean, there have been some people who have kind of concocted a goulash of snippets about this team that was working on the terrorist interconnections and the Special Plans Office, and they mixed them up when there's no basis for the mix.

As I mentioned, this team that was doing the terrorist analysis was not focused on Iraq. I mean, they focused -- they did not have a narrow focus. It was a global -- it was a global exercise, even though this particular report that -- briefing, I should say, that was prepared and given to the CIA focused on Iraq and al Qaeda because, as I said, that kind of fell out incidentally from the work that they were doing on global terrorist networks.

Third, there are some press accounts that have tied the team to what is called the intelligence collection program, which was a program for debriefing Iraqi defectors over recent years. And in fact the team had nothing to do with that program or the transfer of the management of that program from the State Department to the Defense HUMINT [Human Intelligence] Service.

And the -- with regard to this intelligence collection program, the reports that were obtained from the debriefings of these Iraq defectors were disseminated in the same way that other intelligence reporting was disseminated, contrary to one particular journalist account who suggested that the Special Plans Office became a conduit for intelligence reports from the Iraqi National Congress to the White House. That's just flatly not true. And in any event, that was a Defense Intelligence Agency/Defense HUMINT Service function, and not -- it was not anything that was run out of the policy organization. So again, this is part of the goulash of inaccuracies.

And then finally there were some accounts that asserted that the team dealt with the weapons of mass destruction issue, and there have been a number of stories in recent days that suggested that this was a team that somehow developed the case on Iraqi weapons of mass destruction,

3.

and it didn't -- I mean, it -- and that is also flatly not true. The team was focused on terrorist networks; it was not focused on weapons of mass destruction.

Now on this issue of intelligence judgments -- now to get to my second topic, the intelligence judgments on Iraqi weapons of mass destruction, Secretary of State Powell talked about our intelligence sources when he gave his presentation on February 5th to the U.N. Security Council. He played tapes of Iraqis who were discussing -- these were intercepts of Iraqi communications in which there were discussions of the concealing of weapons of mass destruction from U.N. inspectors. Secretary Powell cited the reports of witnesses and informants. He discussed the U.S. government's knowledge of Iraq procurement efforts in the weapons of mass destruction field. And he cited the old U.N. inspectors' organizations reporting on weapons of mass destruction, for which Iraq had never accounted adequately.

And these judgments were based on intelligence that -- intelligence reports and intelligence analysis that not only went back years but predated this administration. In February 1998 President Clinton said, "Iraq continues to conceal chemical and biological weapons and the missiles that can deliver them, and Iraq has the capacity to quickly restart production of these weapons." Secretary of Defense Cohen, in -- also in 1998, said, "I believe that Iraq is developing them, because they've used them in the past. The acquisition of these types of weapons does make Saddam Hussein a major player in the region. He's concerned about the power, and the opportunity to have nuclear or biological or chemical weapons gives him the status and the ability to project that power to intimidate the neighbors in the region." And there are similar quotations from Vice President Gore and others.

The -- it -- from our perspective, it's pretty clear that the intelligence community's judgments concerning Iraqi weapons of mass destruction did not undergo a major change between the Clinton and Bush administrations. And that's -- without regard to the issue of whether the officials from the previous administration agree or disagree with the policies of this administration about how to deal with the problem, the basic intelligence reports did not undergo any kind of change from the previous administration to this one.

4.   On the third point that I raised, on this issue of reports about the department's attitude toward toppling the Iranian regime, there was a recent Financial Times article that grossly misrepresented Secretary Rumsfeld's views on Iran. It is true that the United States government wants Iran to turn over all al Qaeda members currently in Iran and to comply with its obligations under the Nuclear Nonproliferation Treaty. But as for the future of the Iranian government, that's a matter to be decided by the Iranian people. And our policy is what President Bush has said: that we see Iranian citizens risking intimidation and death as they speak out for liberty and human rights and democracy. Iranians, like all people, have a right to choose their government and determine their own destiny, and the United States supports their aspirations to live in freedom. And everything that we have done and that we support in this department is consistent with and captured in that statement by the president. And it's not good to be reading inaccurate descriptions of what our policy is on Iran.

A sub-point on that is the last point that I wanted to address in these opening remarks, and that is the issue of the policy toward the MEK, the Mujahedeen e Khalq. The United States has designated the MEK a foreign terrorist organization; it is on the State Department's list of such organizations. Accordingly, we demanded the surrender of MEK forces in Iraq. That demand is being complied with, and the MEK forces are being disarmed.

Now, earlier in the war, a U.S. commander on the ground reached a temporary cease-fire with the MEK which he justified on the grounds that it enabled our forces to contain the MEK forces in cantonment areas, while not having to fight against them or to actively disarm them. And it was also a way of making sure that these MEK forces were not going to get into a clash with the pro-Iranian forces. There were a number of different groups floating around in Iraq that were not under our control, and we didn't want them clashing in a way that could interfere with our operations.

Now, because of that local decision to work out this temporary arrangement, there were some people who believed that we were giving the MEK special treatment, and there were even news stories that said that the Defense Department planned to use the MEK as a Northern Alliance-type organization -- making the analogy to Afghanistan -- as a Northern Alliance-type organization against the government of Iran. There never was such a plan. We will not do that. We view the MEK as a terrorist organization and we are treating it as such.

And with that, I will be happy to take your questions.

Q: On Iran, you made the point that the administration supports the aspirations of the Iranian people. The question seems to be how far are you going -- that's important to what kind of support you're talking about, and people are speculating that you could go as far as supporting by either actively undermining the existing government or by taking military action. And can you define exactly how far you would go?

Feith: Our policy is to urge the Iranians, as the president has done publicly and as other top administration people have done, to urge them to stop their support for terrorism -- Iran is one of the world's leading supporters of terrorist organizations -- to comply with their obligations under the Nuclear Nonproliferation Treaty and stop the development of nuclear weapons. And we know that there is widespread unhappiness in the country about the failures of the clerical regime. And the president has expressed his sympathy with the aspirations of the Iranians to have a free country. And that's our policy. And that's what we're willing to say and do.

And there are a lot of countries in the world who are coming increasingly to understand the dangers that this state support for terrorism and the development of nuclear weapons by countries that are not supposed to be developing them -- that represents the international security. And so, we're getting increasing international support for this kind of an approach. And we hope that the Iranians will change their policies.

Q: [And now] to the intelligence, one of the more puzzling aspects of all of this for a lot of people is the Niger letter, and why U.S. officials seem so willing to accept and promulgate what appears to people who were knowledgeable about it to have clearly been a forgery. Can you explain -- and there's been a couple of congressional requests for information about that. Can you shed some light on that?

Feith: I mean, I'm aware of it in general. I don't know how much light I could shed on it.

Luti: No, no, I can't either. No. I believe that that is an issue between the source of the document and the analysts in the government in the intelligence community, and they're sorting that out. We're not particularly as policy people involved in that process.

Q: I want to challenge your assumption here that the intelligence has remained consistent throughout the '90s. This administration, starting in September, painted the picture of an imminent threat from weapons of mass destruction, yet the DIA -- this is -- and this is something that U.S. News and World broke [a past sentence of] of this week, said in September, there's no reliable information on whether Iraq is producing and stockpiling chemical weapons. Just square the circle. You say the intelligence has been consistent, but yet you painted a much more imminent threat than anybody in the Clinton administration did during the '90s.

5. Feith: I think what we -- what we have been stressing is that September 11th highlighted the special dangers that come from the connection of weapons of mass destruction to state sponsors of terrorism. The September 11th attack forced a lot of people to rethink the dangers of both terrorism and weapons of mass destruction in light of the possible connection between the two. And the willingness of terrorist organizations to do as much damage as they possibly can was something that was driven home, you know, powerfully, by the September 11th attack. And the recognition that if a terrorist organization, perfectly willing to do as much damage as it possibly can, could get its hands on weapons of mass destruction from one of the state sponsors that is otherwise providing support to it, then the possibility exists, the danger exists that you could have an attack that would kill many times the number of people that were killed on September 11th.

So that caused a reassessment of the nature of the threat and the risk. That's a different issue from the analysis of whether one believes that the Iraqis possessed the capability to use chemical weapons, biological weapons; whether they had a program that was aiming toward the development of nuclear weapons. On the basic question of whether the Iraqis had the capability, I don't think there was any kind of major discontinuity in the analysis over the years from the intelligence community.

Q: Well let me push back then, because Rumsfeld, starting in September, and the president talked about that they had a capability. They had -- they produced -- they have weapons; they have this; they have that. That was a lot stronger than the Clinton people or the intelligence community publicly talked about in the '90s, and your DIA is even saying this now in September of '02, raising questions about we don't have reliable information.

Feith: As I -- I mean, I quoted from -- President Clinton said, in 1998, Iraq continues to conceal chemical and biological weapons. And the U.N., in its report, I believe it was in January of '99, when UNSCOM [United Nations Special Commission] shut down its operations, said that there were large quantities of chemical and biological weapons materials that were unaccounted for. And this was precisely the point that President Bush stressed in -- and I don't remember whether it was in his U.N. speech or his State of the Union speech, but he made a major focus on what the UNSCOM report from 1999 said about chemical and biological weapons in Iraq.

So, I mean, this is -- this was not news. I mean, a number of the recent stories have suggested that the basic question of whether the Iraqis -- whether there was intelligence to support the conclusion that the Iraqis had these weapons, there have been a number of stories that have suggested that this whole issue arose in recent months, and it didn't, it went back years.

Q: I think the question is that the issue -- you put a finer point on it than in past years and you raised the bar in terms of what Iraq allegedly had, and now we're seeing that they might not have had what you allegedly said they did.

Feith: Well, we'll see. We'll see what they had.

But the main thing that I think was different in the way this administration talked about the issue from the past, were the conclusions, the strategic conclusions that we came to as a result of the September 11 attack, and the particular strategic problems that arise from a recognition that you can't rely to the extent that we did in the past, or that at least some people did in the past, you can't rely on deterrence to deal with the problem of weapons of mass destruction in the hands of state sponsors of terrorism because the possibility that those state sponsors might employ chemical weapons or biological weapons by means of a terrorist organization proxy means that they could use the weapons without leaving their fingerprints, as it were, on the attack. And that meant that the traditional deterrence approach was not adequate.

Q: If I could just go back, Mr. Secretary, and look at the relationship -- I think three key relationships you have tried to -- (inaudible) -- I think; the one between the intelligence team and the special plans office, the intelligence team the Iraqi exile project, and the intelligence team and the assessment on weapons of mass destruction. Let me make sure I understand this now. The team is going to put out a report that's going to become a part of a larger body of material that policymakers, including those in the special plans office, would look at, right? So it's not to say while they may not have been resident in the same office, I would -- it certainly sounds like special plans would be aware of and would -- and have available those reports that they make, right? I mean, they would --

Feith: If the -- yeah, I mean, if the connection is that a team that is analyzing a policy problem by looking through a lot of intelligence is going to generate a briefing that is going to come to the attention of various offices -- I mean, that's true. That connection exists. There were various offices that were informed by, you know, that briefing.

Q: And given the importance that this team had within your office, would it not also be logical that the special plans office would give its -- whatever reports came from the team special significance? And this is something you're looking at, you created especially to look at the intelligence in a different way --

Feith: No, no, you see, it was not created to look -- there is this idea -- again, there have been a number of press stories that have said that the reason this team was created was because we wanted the intelligence looked at in a different way. That's not true. It was -- what happened was, on September 11th we were attacked, and the president announced we are in a global war against terrorism. And the office that's responsible for strategy is my office. And we asked ourselves: What does it mean to be at war against terrorism? What -- and how is this different from previous wars conceptually? How does one develop a strategy for fighting an international network?

So it just was kind of an obvious thing to do. I asked for some people to review the existing intelligence on what do we know about the nature of these terrorist networks. This was not because we were dissatisfied with, as some of the news stories have suggested -- it's not because we were dissatisfied with the intelligence or the intelligence analysis. It was because we needed people looking at that intelligence, good intelligence produced by the CIA and other agencies -- we needed people looking at it from the point of view of what do we need to understand from this intelligence about these connections to allow us to develop a Defense Department strategy for the war on terrorism.

Q: That's looking at intelligence in a different way, with a different perspective.

Feith: Well -- but I mean, not as --

Q: (Off mike.)

Feith: -- but it's been portrayed as this was done --

Q: They did not find their own intelligence. They took existing intelligence, given this new perspective, given this new focus you've asked them to address, and said, "Here. Here's a new way of looking at it." Right? That's what you asked for.

Feith: You could say that, except the way it --

Q: All right. Let me move on to my second point, then.

Feith: Well, let me just say, the way it's been portrayed in a number of stories was that this was set up because there was dissatisfaction with what the intelligence community had done. That's not true. It was set up because we had a different function to be performed; we had a different mission to be performed. We had to develop a strategy to fight the global war on terrorism. And so, we needed to take this material and review it in that light.

Q: Point two, on the Iraqi exile project. While these guys didn't run, obviously, the interrogations or anything, they obviously took the information that was provided for them from those interviews, right? And they looked at it and they put it in a larger context, as well. That's part of the existing intelligence, no? Part of their definition?

Luti: No, Eric (sp), who took those reports and looked at them?

Q: The team.

Luti: No, no.

Q: They were ignorant of that when they did their analysis?

7. Luti: No, the information collection program was removed from the State Department and deposited into Defense HUMINT Service to ensure that proper tradecraft was used, accounting procedures. And it was a program to interview Iraqi defectors.

Q: Right.

Luti: The INC would remove them from Iraq to a different location. DHS [Defense HUMINT Service] teams would go to that location, debrief them according to the tradecraft -- all the professional tradecraft that's required -- and then they would write a report. Those reports would go into the intelligence system, writ large --

Q: Right. And that would be one of the many things that this team would look at, right, and draw upon for your -- for the tasks that they were assigned, correct?

Feith: There were lots [of customers] throughout the building --

Luti: Many customers, not only --

Q: Were those reports given any extra weight or significance by this team that you're aware of?

Luti: The information collection program was moved into the Defense HUMINT --

Q: That's a mechanical issue. I'm asking about the report that they produced, giving the fresh information that Iraqi exiles are providing. And that's now going into the system. Among all of the other things that they're going to look at, does the team hone in on these type of reports as a special source and give them that hint of added significance, that you're aware of? That's essentially what the accusation --

Luti: No more than -- in fact, I'm trying to remember when --

Q: (Inaudible.) -- you weigh it -- the intelligence that is coming from defectors was given unusual and disproportionate weight among all the other sources.

Luti: I don't know.

Q: Do you agree with that?

Luti: No. I don't know what the basis of that charge -- no, no, there's been no basis for that. None whatsoever.

Q: But the third point was you said there's no connection between this team and WMD. But you've just said that the relationship between terrorists and terrorist states and WMD has been -- is -- that was -- demonstrated how they --

8.   Feith: No, I didn't mean no connection between the team and WMD. If I said that, I misstated it. What I said is it was not the purpose or the special focus of this team to look at WMD. Its focus was to look at terrorist networks and the connection.

Q: (Inaudible.) -- terrorist networks, and you've just explained how what 9/11 demonstrates is that terrorist networks and WMD and their acquisition thereof are importantly intertwined. And so, how do you not look at WMD when you're looking at terrorist networks in the case of Iraq?

Feith: No, I didn't mean to suggest that they didn't look at WMD at all. I'm saying that the mission that this team was given was not: Look at WMD. The mission that they were given was: Help us understand how these different organizations relate to each other and to their state sponsors.

Q: That may not have been their stated mission, but certainly that's one of the things they found, right?

Feith: I imagine -- yes, I imagine that they looked at WMD along with other stuff. All I'm saying is it was not as it is portrayed in a number of erroneous press stories that we've read. It was not the purpose of this group to focus on the WMD issue.

Staff: Sir, I hate to bring this to a close, but I know you're at the end of your time here. Maybe you can take one or two more.

Q: Critics have raised the issue of the slanting of intelligence findings, the alleged slanting, basically to conform with the views of top policymakers. Can you say what pressure, if any, was put on intelligence analysts in the CIA, DIA, anywhere else, to endorse the view of Iraq possessing chemical and biological weapon stockpiles and reconstituting the nuclear weapons program as an imminent threat to U.S. interests? And can you rule out that intelligence analysts may have perceived that this pressure existed, whether it did or not?

9. Feith: I know of no pressure. I can't rule out what other people may have perceived. Who knows what people perceive? I know of nobody who pressured anybody. We have a -- we have a normal and, I think, useful interchange between the intelligence community and its customers, basically the policy community. It is not a one-way transmission. If people understand the way intelligence -- the intelligence agencies relate to their customers, they understand that it's -- there's a process of back and forth where we get reports, I get a briefing every morning. I know that Secretary Rumsfeld has talked about this too. I mean, we're all, I think, in the same boat, those of us who get daily briefings from the CIA. I get a briefing. As I'm being briefed, questions occur to me. I ask for clarification of items. I sometimes say, "Well, that's an interesting point. That suggests that it might be good to get a report on x, y, and **10.** z. And I'd like to learn more about that." And those questions go back and they produce additional work and reports. And the intelligence community prides itself on being responsive when its customers raise questions and make requests for additional information or clarification or tables or historical perspective on some topic. I mean, things go back and forth all the time. And, I mean, that is the way a good system works.

And in this particular case, we, as customers, were analyzing this information about terrorist networks, and when we happened to come up with some interesting observations, we took them back and gave them to the intelligence community. And I must say, I was very pleased with the response that we got. I mean, people over there said that's -- you know, that's worthy of looking at and study. And I think that, you know, that George Tenet received it very well and found it useful.

Q: Two questions. Are any of the people who were on the intelligence team, which you said is now no longer doing that work, are any of those people still paid by the department and perhaps in other parts of your organization basically doing that same work on other topics? That's my first question. Are any of those people still there doing that work, perhaps on Iraq or on WMD?

And my second question, I am really puzzled why you two gentlemen are exactly doing this briefing today. Neither of you are well known to come down here and talk about what you read in the news media. Were you asked to do this briefing by Secretary Rumsfeld, by the White House, by Torie Clarke? Do you have any sense that there's some article coming out somewhere in the news media that you're trying to respond to ahead of time?

Feith: On the latter question first, there have been enough articles that have come out already on these subjects that have been inaccurate that -- and it's quite clear that some of the articles that are inaccurate are getting reverberations in numerous other articles that clearly are derivative of the mother lode of inaccuracies here and there. And we just -- and since it directly relates to our office, we just thought it might be useful to straighten the record out. So --

Q: So this briefing was your idea?

Feith: This briefing was my idea. And -- I mean, I hope it is in the nature of a public service.

Now, the first question you asked was --

Q: Is anybody who was on that intelligence team doing that work still --

Feith: Well, as I mentioned before you arrived, the --

Q: No, I was here.

Feith: Oh. Okay. The team that has gotten so much attention was two people, full-time. (Chuckling.) I mean, this is much less than one would infer from a lot of the press coverage of it. And altogether, as I said, there might have been a half a dozen people who were in and out, working either on the team full-time, part-time.

Q: (Off mike.) --

Feith: And some of those people -- because some of them were Reserve officers, so I mean, I think they're -- they've moved on, but some of them are people who are still in the government.

Q: May -- what I'm not understanding is, are any of those half dozen people -- bluntly, what I'm trying to ask -- doing the same work, perhaps not in an assembled team --

Feith: No, this was a project.

Q: I understand that.

Feith: So the answer's no.

Q: But the question is, I want to make sure there's no bureaucratic misunderstanding. That team has been disbanded. That label is gone. But is that work, candidly, going on somewhere else?

Feith: "Disbanded" is a peculiar term to apply. They had a project. They finished their project.

Q: And the project -- fine. The project is done. Nonetheless, is that work of reviewing information still going on in your organization? Is that basic task --

Feith: I would say that there are hundreds and hundreds, perhaps thousands, of people in this building who review intelligence for policy purposes every day. So that work is ongoing by thousands of people in this department.

Q: So why did you need these special people?

Feith: As I explained, we had a particular requirement to review the existing intelligence, to help us develop the strategy for the Defense Department for the global war on terrorism.

(Cross talk.) I'll take one last question here. This lady has had her hand up.

Q: And couple of -- (Inaudible.) -- here. These two people you say you had managed to come up with a link, you say, between al Qaeda and Iraq -- using the same intelligence, because you didn't gather intelligence -- that the CIA hadn't really come up with, and then you present this to George Tenet. Is that just coincidental that these two -- was their analysis more intense?

Feith: I don't think it's all that unusual or hard to understand. If a large amount of material is reviewed by fresh eyes -- I mean, this -- I think this would apply to -- you know, any intelligent people sitting down with this pile of intelligence, looking it over, reading it over, has a chance of finding certain things in it. I mean, ask yourself why new history books get written about old events. I mean, people look over very often the very same material. But in light of experience or just because they see something that nobody had seen before, certain connections become clear or appear, and, you know, new hypotheses get developed and new facts surface. I mean, it's not that mysterious. It's just -- there was an enormous amount of intelligence about terrorist networks that had been developed for many years before September 11th. And the idea that we would look at it again in light of September 11th and maybe see some new things in it shouldn't be that surprising.

Q: But you act as if the other intelligence agencies weren't looking at it that way.

Feith: No, they were. I -- no, I'm not acting that way.

Q: Only in post-9/11. So why --

Feith: They were too, but, I mean, I don't know why it should surprise anybody that any given group of people looking at a mass of material might come up with a few interesting insights that other people didn't come up with.

Q: And in --

Q: Why not just hire the CIA to do it then? I mean, that's what they do full time.

Feith: Because, well --

Q: (Inaudible.) -- the DIA, and you have to get in your own people and say, "This is what we're looking for. Go find it."

Feith: No. Nobody -- nobody helped -- see, this suggestion that we said to them -- "This is what we're looking for. Go find it." -- is precisely the inaccuracy that we are here to rebut.

Q: Can I just do one final one. Can I just --

Q: Can you give us an example of information that they found that did not fit those scenarios; that did not say there was an imminent danger; that did not present the facts that there was a belief that they were -- had an active and ongoing weapons of mass destruction program? Was that a part of what they found --

Feith: No, as I told you, the main thing that the briefing of this team produced was not this Iraq-al Qaeda connection. That was incidental. The main thing that the team produced was it helped -- it helped educate a lot of people about the fact that there was more cooperation and interconnection among these terrorist organizations and state sponsors across ideological lines than many people had appreciated before. That was really -- I mean, to sum it up in a sentence, that's it

Q: Just one final point. What do think now of --

Feith: And this is her final point.

Q: (Laughs.) What do you think of the intelligence now? You said we'll see about the weapons of mass destruction, and yet some of the intelligence thus far that the United States was told about has been wrong. The Iraqis didn't use chemical weapons when American troops advanced. The first 200 sites you've checked that were suspected sites for weapons of mass destruction had nothing. You're backing away from some of the other sites, unless you get further intelligence. Can you assess the intelligence thus far?

Feith: The process of gathering information about the Iraqi programs is underway. I'm not going to come in and preempt the careful work that's being done. As you all know, there's a major new team going over to make systematic and comprehensive the work on studying what exists in Iraq and what became of this and that, about which we had information regarding the Iraqi weapons of mass destruction programs. They'll do their systematic and comprehensive work, and they'll come back and report.

Q: Can we talk about the last couple of months, though?

Feith: Thank you all.

Q: What about the last couple of months?

Feith: I'm not going to preempt what the team is -- (Off mike as he leaves the podium.)

Feith News Conference Comments

1. This description of the research aims of the project undersecretary Feith describes does indicate that discovering a connection between Saddam Hussein and Al Qaeda was a principal goal. In contrast to the 1980s, when the Soviet Union, Syria, Libya, and Iraq were identified as "state sponsors" of terrorism (for which role they are still identified on State Department lists), by 2001 the whole question of state sponsorship of terrorism had receded. Except for groups involved in the Palestinian conflict with Israel, with which the Bush administration was not concerning itself in the immediate aftermath of 9/11, there was no serious state sponsorship going on. The idea that the Shulsky unit was created to study the link between Al Qaeda and the Taliban in Afghanistan made some sense, except for the date–October 2001–by which time the U.S. campaign against Afghanistan had already begun. At that date, however, charges had already been made implicating Saddam in the 9/11 attacks, and it was at this same time that the Office of the Secretary of Defense sent former CIA director R. James Woolsey to Europe to seek evidence for such a connection. The Shulsky study would have amounted to the Pentagon inquiry, into which any evidence turned up by Woolsey could have been plugged.

2. The thesis of an alliance between Saddam and Bin Laden required overturning the whole logic of the Al Qaeda religious argument, which was that states should be forced to convert to the fundamentalist "way." Al Qaeda's goal was therefore the overthrow of a secular state like Saddam's Iraq, while Saddam's response, given that his branch of Islam was less numerous in Iraq than the (more fundamentalist) Shi'ite one, necessarily had to be preserving secularism. A conclusion from the Shulsky study that religious values had not prevented cooperation with secular states was a necessary precondition to postulating a Saddam–Al Qaeda alliance.

3. In this passage, undersecretary Feith mounts a direct attack on the article by Seymour Hersh in *The New Yorker* (May 12, 2003) that has already been quoted in the main narrative. Later during the question period Feith proved unable to show how the distinctions he is making here to refute the article make any substantial difference to Hersh's analysis.

4. An entire account similar to this one could be crafted on how the Bush administration handled intelligence and diplomacy on Iran (and a third on North Korea). That country and its weapons of mass destruction programs may be next

on the Bush strike list. North Korea, with its self-professed and widely accepted *real* weapons, is off the list. Contrary to Bush rhetoric, the signal this sends to potential proliferators is "hurry up and do it," because once the weapons are in hand the United States dares do nothing.

5. Here undersecretary Feith indulges in the mantra that has become the goal line defense for President Bush, Vice President Cheney, secretary Rumsfeld, and security adviser Rice, to name just some of the more important figures who have used it. September 11 was an attack by a nonstate actor, using *conventional* means, that inflicted large-scale damage and huge tragedy. In and of itself, 9/11 does not make alliances between terrorist groups and states any more likely than before. Nor does it make more likely a resort by terrorists to weapons of mass destruction. And 9/11 did not change in any way the *access* of terrorist groups to weapons of mass destruction. In the CIA letter of October 2002 and the national intelligence estimate on which it comments (Chapter 2), director Tenet is clear that in the considered judgment of U.S. intelligence, the calculus of access would be changed far more by an American invasion that threatened the existence of the Saddam Hussein government. *Those* are the conditions that *now* exist, brought about by the Bush people themselves. The constant use of the September 11 attacks in this way is an attempt to invoke the hysteria of their immediate aftermath, an effort to make political cover out of Americans' fears.

6. The Shulsky team was created to clear the way for a certain intelligence interpretation (the Saddam–Al Qaeda alliance) by undermining a traditional view of the situational attributes (Al Qaeda's attitude toward secular states). If undersecretary Feith means to say this goal did not involve attacking the intelligence reporting at large, he is correct. If Feith meant to say the goal had nothing to do with fitting the intelligence to an alternative conclusion ("because we wanted the intelligence looked at in a different way"), he is dead wrong. That had been the precise purpose of the study.

7. Dr. Luti refers here to the same defector program that the Defense Intelligence Agency reviewed in early 2003 and deemed almost completely useless. Note than in his remark, Luti acknowledges the defectors had been provided by the Iraqi National Congress.

8. Note how important it is for undersecretary Feith *not* to be seen as saying his study team had had nothing to do with weapons of mass destruction intelligence, that is that there was no connection between weapons and terrorism. Since a main pillar of the Bush case for war with Iraq was the contention that Saddam

might give his (actually nonexistent) weapons to terrorists, the Pentagon's special intelligence study needed to be seen as having weapons as part of their concern.

9. Imagine the scene of exultation in Luti's office, and Doug Feith's as well, when the Pentagon analysts returned from their climactic, August 2002, briefing on the Saddam–Al Qaeda connection, a meeting at which undersecretary Feith was present (as he acknowledges an instant later in this press conference). That presentation had been the essence of "pressure." This answer is, at a minimum, misleading.

10. The stock line of asking and answering questions would be used widely in the Bush administration to explain why outsiders might erroneously conclude that pressure was being put on analysts. Secretary Rumsfeld said the same thing, in virtually the same words, at his October 24, 2002 appearance, when he was first asked about the Shulsky study group. On a different front, we are told that it was a query of exactly this kind by Vice President Cheney, about allegations that Iraq was purchasing uranium ore in Niger, that led to the mission to that country by ambassador Joseph Wilson. Yet despite assertions like Feith's here about "back and forth," Cheney's office has maintained they heard nothing about Wilson's conclusions (though preparation of a two-page memorandum at CIA has been admitted). As Douglas Feith states here, "Those questions go back and they produce additional work and reports." It is simply not credible that Cheney heard nothing further after his question on Niger uranium.

Into the Abyss

While the Bush administration in Washington struggled to contain the stream of revelations that its case on the Iraqi threat had been contrived, finding actual weapons of mass destruction in Iraq steadily gained in importance. The case for war had turned so much on the weapons that finding them could rescue the president from a rising tide of criticism, while not finding them could lead to political disaster. The solution would be dispatch of a fresh team of searchers, the Iraq Survey Group, in June 2003. With more than 1,200 specialists and support staff, the Iraq Survey Group was created by the Defense Intelligence Agency to do the kind of detailed inspections that the 75th Exploitation Task Force had not had the time for. Headed by Major

General Keith Dayton, who had previously directed the DIA service that interrogated Iraqi defectors, the survey group was also supposed to make much more use of the growing number of Iraqi senior scientists and top leaders in U.S. custody.

Colonel McPhee's searchers with the 75th soon learned how their status in the pecking order had changed. At their compound, a former Iraqi intelligence service facility, they had had to make due with things begged and scrounged, from phone sets to intel data, to electricity. They were also largely taken out of the field—several of McPhee's seven site survey teams were stood down and told not to expect any mission orders for the next three weeks. Meanwhile, the new task force also spent three weeks executing no missions—this in an environment in which observers worried that looters were carting any remaining evidence away from sites by the minute—while refurbishing their base, one of Saddam's former presidential palaces, with computers, generators, air conditioners, fax machines—the full panoply of the modern executive suite. The men and women of the 75th, hauled in to brief their successors, can only have envied the task force's resources. The survey group called their base Camp Slayer.

The Iraqi lab truck and the one trailer that had not been shipped to the United States stood in the courtyard.

Sensitive site teams were led by an army colonel, John Connell. By mid-June, Connell, who had arrived expecting to find big warehouses stacked deep with containers of live agent, had become used to the idea that bits and pieces of former programs were the most they were going to uncover. The rocket science team, eighteen specialists led by Navy Captain Richard Weyrich, spent their early days working back through the same target list of Iraqi rocket manufacturers, field units, and test sites that had already been visited by the 75th and, before them, by the UN inspectors. A direct support team for things nuclear was headed by Navy Commander David Beckett. The leading nuclear investigators were from the national laboratories run by the Department of Energy: William Domke from Lawrence Livermore and Jeffrey Bedell from Los Alamos.

The United States also set up a unit to destroy such weapons as were

actually discovered, under Douglas M. England of the Defense Threat Reduction Agency. This would have up to a hundred personnel, with a team
each for rockets and nuclear weapons, and four that concentrated on chemical
and biological agents.

What to search and who to send were big questions. There would be
an Australian contingent with the Iraq Survey Group and some British experts. Australian Brigadier General Steven D. Meekin headed the Joint Captured Enemy Materiel Exploitation Center, which focused on conventional
weaponry but was in Dayton's command chain and tasked by the survey
group. For all the brass, neither Dayton nor Meekin was an expert on weapons of mass destruction. General Dayton was an espionage expert, Meekin
the chief of scientific and technical assessment for Australia's Defence Intelligence Organization. President Bush decided to buttress the credibility of the
weapons investigation by sending a third chief to Baghdad, styled as an adviser to the director of central intelligence, but who would personally direct
the search for weapons. The Iraq Survey Group's report on the search would
be put out in his name.

One man's name automatically came up for the choice of top inspector,
David A. Kay. The sixty-three-year old Dr. Kay had become a hero in the
early days of the UN's Iraq arms monitoring with his aggressive stance on
site visits and his willingness to challenge the Iraqis. On more than one
occasion in 1991, Kay and his teams had pulled off such finds that Iraqi
troops surrounded them to demand the return of documents, the handing
over of photos the inspectors had taken, or other sensitive items the Iraqis
thought they had found or taken. Kay became a sort of celebrity at the time,
and Iraq had blocked his return after 1992. Living in Vienna as a senior
inspector for the International Atomic Energy Agency, from which he had
received a distinguished service award, Kay had also acquired a patina of
objectivity. He had studied at the University of Texas and had a masters of
international affairs and Ph.D. from Columbia University.

At the same time, from the Bush people's point of view, Kay would be
a known quantity. He held a dim view of Saddam Hussein and believed
weapons were there to be found. Even some American scientists traced his

departure from the UN monitoring staff not so much to difficulties with Baghdad as to the closeness of his ties with American intelligence. After the IAEA, Kay held a top job at Science Applications International Corporation, a major defense think tank, and then at the Potomac Institute for Policy Studies, another. In 1998 when Secretary General Kofi Annan had renegotiated UN access in Iraq, Kay had gone on record saying Annan was taking a bum deal. In 2002, when the new UN inspections regime was established in Iraq, Kay had argued that this voluntary arms control "may fail to detect or prevent massive violations" and that—fitting nicely with Bush's attitude toward Saddam Hussein personally—it was the nature of the Iraqi regime that made its weapons programs dangerous. He seemed untroubled by Kofi Annan's characterization of aggressive inspectors like himself as "UNSCOM cowboys." In January 2003, after Hans Blix and Mohammed ElBaradei had actually begun reporting on Iraq, Kay had returned to the attack, writing: "The only evidence of Iraq's weapons program we need has been clear since early December [2002], when it filed yet another weapons declaration that was anything but full, final, and complete."

George Tenet announced Kay's appointment on June 11.

In late April, the Bush administration had decided to reorient the weapons search a first time, shifting the mission and personnel of the 75th Exploitation group. From that moment President Bush began changing his own emphasis—rather than speak of "weapons" he began to talk about "programs." Instead of focusing on searches he began to harp on information to come from interrogating captured Iraqi scientists and officials. (Bush's "Eureka!" comment at the end of May about the alleged mobile weapons plants had been an exception at a moment of exhuberance.) The Iraq Survey Group would be the concrete expression of the new approach, and a new reorientation of the weapons search.

By June, the Americans had custody of most of Iraq's senior weapons officials, as well as a number of other weapons scientists. These people included General Amer al-Saadi, Saddam's science adviser, head of the arms monitoring directorate that interfaced with the UN inspectors and an official on the committee in charge of Iraqi deception and avoidance decisions. For-

mer nuclear program chief Humam Abd al-Khaliq Abd al-Ghafar was another. Dr. Mahdi Obeidi had led Iraq's effort to enrich uranium with
centrifuges. Dr. Rihab Rashid Taha ("Dr. Germ") had run the principal Iraqi
biological weapons lab, and her boss, Dr. Huda Salih Mahdi Ammash ("Mrs.
Anthrax"), both were being held, as well as oil minister Amer Mohammed
Rashid, another of Saddam's science advisers. These and lesser prisoners
potentially held the keys to knowledge of Saddam's efforts. The searchers
also had huge quantities of Iraqi secret documents—enough paper to make a
stack seven and a half miles high—that could be exploited for data.

In early July all this was held up as progress. A congressional delegation
including several members of the Senate intelligence committee came through
Baghdad, and their briefing from General Dayton and Dr. Kay would be
distinctly upbeat. While conceding that no weapons had been found, Kay
and Dayton argued that the Survey Group faced the task of unraveling two
decades of Iraqi deception efforts, operated in the face of ongoing violence,
and had to cope with the dispersed infrastructure of the Iraqi programs. They
were nevertheless quite optimistic. The chairman of the Select Committee on
Intelligence, Republican Pat Roberts of Kansas, told reporters when the delegation reached home that the United States now had evidence of the weapons. Virginia Republican John Warner of the Armed Services Committee
added that any fair-minded person would have to conclude the weapons had
been there. Michigan Democrat Carl Levin expressed greater uncertainty.
Roberts and Warner may have been reflecting partisanship more than surety.

The true situation, however, remained exactly the same as before. By
September, the reluctance of the Iraq Survey Group to offer incentives to its
Iraqi detainees, whether release, remission of legal proceedings, money, or
anything else, had come under criticism as a reason for the continued lack
of evidence for the weapons. The unstated subtext is that what the scientists
were saying—and suspicious interrogators took it as clever coordination on a
cover story among all these people—was that Iraq had destroyed all its weapons of mass destruction (or given them up to UN inspectors) in the 1990s
and no longer had any.

The experience of Dr. Mahdi Shakur Obeidi is exemplary of the way the experts and their data were mishandled. Obeidi attempted to surrender to American forces in April, hoping to gain asylum in the United States and resident visas for his family. No one paid any attention. He then went to private scientist David Albright of the Institute for Science and International Security and asked help in making contact. That was on April 22. Exhausting other possibilities, at the beginning of May Albright called the Pentagon, which saw no use for the man, then the State Department, who had no idea whom Obeidi should talk to. On May 7, Albright learned Obeidi had actual centrifuge parts, and then he contacted the CIA. The agency, initially unresponsive, eventually took interest. By the 17th, Obeidi was speaking to CIA officials, but negotiations on immigration went nowhere. Albright went back to senior CIA officers to specify what the Iraqi scientist could offer. The CIA then sent several people over to Baghdad to question Obeidi more thoroughly over the first two days of June. The Iraqi scientist took the CIA analysts out to his backyard, where they dug up a metal container filled with a two-foot-high stack: 180 documents, 200 blueprints, and several pieces of hardware for a gas centrifuge machine. From this material, a real centrifuge could be prototyped and then manufactured. He explained that Qusay Hussein, Saddam's son, had instructed him to bury the materials in the summer of 1991. The design used maraged steel. One of Obeidi's CIA inquisitors was the WINPAC analyst "Joe T.," whose role in the aluminum tube debate had been so destructive, and whose theory that the tubes were for centrifuges was directly contradicted by Dr. Obeidi's materials. It is reported that Joe's messages to CIA headquarters accused Obeidi of lying.

While Obeidi was working with the CIA people, the U.S. military arrested him on June 3. The CIA secured Obeidi's release but refused to budge on asylum, until Obeidi spoke to television reporters. Then the agency swiftly spirited the scientist out of Iraq. The CIA issued an official statement on Obeidi's data on June 26, saying that he "told us that these items, blueprints and key centrifuge pieces, represented a complete template for what would be needed to rebuild a centrifuge enrichment program."

The Obeidi data showed three things. First, a senior-level scientist had been inactive and key enrichment equipment buried, indicating no current

Iraqi nuclear program. Second, the materials had been buried in 1991, which is when the Iraqi government had repeatedly said it had halted its nuclear weapons programs, suggesting that Baghdad's official statements, far from the tissue of lies they had been made out to be, had in fact been accurate. Third, the design materials contradicted the aluminum tube hypothesis that underlay Bush administration charges about Iraqi nuclear programs.

The White House nevertheless tried to claim the Obeidi information confirmed the existence of an Iraqi nuclear program. When the holes in that assertion became obvious, Ari Fleischer stated: "Nobody [in the White House] said it was operative. We expressed concerns about the development of a nuclear program, but nobody ever maintained that Iraq had nuclear weapons."

While conversations with Iraqis continued, so did site visits by Iraq Survey Group teams. On July 10, the group hit the Baghdad former head-quarters of the Revolutionary Command Council, which, among its other functions, made decisions on deception measures. The searchers found an archive of documents, but also evidence of systematic destruction of some records and computer hard drives. Laboratories were found to have been cleaned up (how cleaning for the purpose of deception is to be distinguished from the cleaning that would be done at the end of any laboratory use as a standard safety and quality control measure is nowhere defined). Documents had been destroyed in other places as well. As indicated by the seven-and-a-half-miles boast, Iraqi efforts at records destruction cannot have been all that systematic.

Survey Group teams were also impeded by military action, an unavoidable consequence of the coalition occupation of Iraq. In one instance, a vehicle on mission was surrounded by Iraqi insurgent gunmen, and the two Survey Group members on board had to shoot their way out of the situation. In September, the Group's post at Erbil was bombed, with four persons wounded. On September 24, Camp Slayer was itself mortared, not for the first time.

Military opposition remained a nuisance but not a real obstacle. The Iraq Survey Group had everything it needed to find the weapons—in fact, more than $300 million worth of support for its mission. But investigative teams on weapons of mass destruction had more downtime than active missions, and more horseplay than road play. The chief nuclear investigators went home, William Domke to Livermore and Jeffrey Bedell to Los Alamos. Domke and Bedell had been central to the DOE's rejection of the theory that Iraqi aluminum tubes had anything to do with nuclear enrichment, and it is reported that while with the survey group, they had confirmed their original views.

It was not due to any lack of resources, of captured documents, or of access to Iraqi scientists that reports began appearing around the middle of September that the Iraq Survey Group had found nothing. Kay was in Washington about that time, beginning preparation of an interim report. On September 16, Scott McClellan, who had succeeded Ari Fleischer as White House press spokesman, commenting on the Kay investigation declared, "We still stand by what we've previously said," which was that the Iraq Survey Group would find "weapons of mass destruction and weapons programs." Six days later, questioned about White House confidence that weapons would be found, security adviser Condoleezza Rice changed the subject, indulging in a bit of revisionist history of her own: "What we went in [to Iraq] with a view toward was a view that was shared by intelligence agencies around the world, by three American administrations, and by the United Nations. There was nobody who knew anything about Iraq who believed that Saddam Hussein had destroyed all of his weapons of mass destruction."

On September 24, Dr. Rice, now off-the-record masquerading as a "senior administration official," was asked directly about the Kay report, by then widely rumored to cite no discoveries of ongoing Iraqi efforts to produce weapons.

"I think it is premature for anybody to start saying what is or is not in that report," Condi Rice shot back.

Rice's comments did nothing to hold back the slew of media commentary over the next days speculating that the Kay report would not claim any success in finding arms, would not be conclusive, or would not confirm the presence of Iraqi weapons. By the eve of Kay's presentation of his interim report to the Senate Select Committee on Intelligence, tensions were running high. Speaking of Saddam's motives for leaving indications of weapons on the table when in reality he possessed no weapons of mass destruction, a Bush administration official was quoted as saying, "He might have been bluffing to his own people." After months of deliberately sabotaging UN inspection efforts, fighting a war at a significant cost in blood and a huge one in treasure, and spending $300 million on its own weapons search, the Bush administration here echoed comments made months earlier by its least favorite international inspector, Hans Blix.

David Kay testified at the Senate intelligence committee on Thursday, October 2, 2003. Underwhelming would be the best description for Kay's evidence, and he would be the first to agree, arguing his presentation was just a "snapshot," an interim effort. Kay's major theme was Iraqi deception measures—nothing new. He extracted a set of bullet points in which the only completely fresh material was the Iraq Survey Group's discovery of chemical and biological laboratories concealed within the Iraqi intelligence service, and its statement that one scientist's house had stored reference strains of biological organisms, including one canister of a culture that could have been refined sufficiently to lead to botulinum toxin. That Iraq had attempted to buy missile parts from North Korea was a novelty, but Kay's own evidence showed the deal had never been consummated. Points on SCUD fuel, the Obeidi data, unmanned aerial vehicles, design work on long-range missiles, and prison laboratories were all things known for months or years. Kay claimed the discovery of "dozens" of "program-related activities," glossing over the point that he was no longer even claiming Iraq had had weapons programs, only microscale components, "program-related activities."

By contrast, in the body of the report, admissions came one after another. On biological warfare, the word was that after 1996 Iraq had focused not on production but on "maintaining a capability for resuming BW production." There was no growth culture for anthrax. The reference strains in storage contained only one from which a biological agent could have been produced. That was of the same type (botox) routinely used in the United States to restore skin tones.

On the notorious mobile biological weapons plants, the Kay testimony reported: "We have not yet been able to confirm the existence of a mobile BW production effort." On the trailers specifically, the report turned a delicate phrase. Rather than saying the plants were suited for hydrogen production, missile fuel creation, or biological agents, Kay used contorted language: "technical limitations would prevent any of these processes from being ideally suited to these trailers." Kay would not rule out biological agent production, but by the same token he could not rule out the other possible functions. He promised future results based on identifying the scientists who had allegedly worked on the mobile production program.

Regarding chemical weapons, "Iraq explored the possibility" of production, an even weaker claim, though one Kay dates to as recently as 2003. Buried six paragraphs down in the text is the key admission: "Multiple sources with varied access and reliability have told ISG [the Iraq Study Group] that Iraq did not have a large, ongoing, centrally controlled CW program after 1991." The report cites an Iraqi expert who told Saddam the previous year that production of (unsophisticated) mustard gas could be possible within two months, but that a start-up for sarin nerve gas would require two years. The searchers had not "yet" found evidence that Iraqi troops in the field had been ready to employ chemicals against invading coalition forces.

On nuclear weapons, the best the Iraq Survey Group could come up with was "several small and relatively unsophisticated research initiatives that could be applied to nuclear weapons development." Those initiatives "*did not in-and-of themselves constitute a resumption of the nuclear weapons program*" (my italics) but they "could have been useful in developing a weapons-relevant science base for the long-term." In other words Saddam was nowhere near a nuclear weapon, or even reconstituting a nuclear program, Iraq stood at the far end of the six-to-nine-year interval projected in the intelligence estimates, the opposite of Bush administration claims.

The item that Kay recited first in his nuclear text gives the flavor of what he tried to achieve in this report. It was that testimony "should clear up any doubts about whether Saddam still wanted to obtain nuclear weapons." That point was purely rhetorical and had been since at least 1983, when the CIA did its initial National Intelligence Estimate purely on Iraqi nuclear weapons development.

Unmanned aerial vehicles were covered under the category "delivery systems" for weapons of mass destruction even though the Iraqi scientists interviewed mentioned only "surveillance and use as decoys." The report dragged out the hoary MIG tests from 1991 to justify the inclusion. Kay made lemonade with Iraqi missile systems too, including cruise missiles, long-range missile designs, and fuel. He managed to find *one* Iraqi "high-level detainee" who agreed that Saddam had kept a "covert" force of SCUD-type missiles, though that individual subsequently recanted his claim. Then there was a North Korean deal, the one new item in this area. At the time of the invasion, the $10 million arrangement (quite small at missile prices) "had not led to any missiles being transferred to Iraq." In fact the North Koreans had taken the money and never delivered anything at all.

The Iraq Survey Group turned up precious little in terms of a current threat. The net was that Kay had discovered a single container of growth culture for botulinum. In his State of the Union address, President Bush had contended that Saddam possessed sufficient materials to manufacture 38,000 liters of botulinum toxin.

The unit wanted an additional $600 million to continue its search.

"I'm not pleased by what I heard today," Senator Pat Roberts announced. Roberts had gone out on a limb for the administration a couple of months before, when his delegation visited Baghdad and he had come back citing secret evidence. Now the Bush people had neatly snipped that limb off behind him.

George Bush had his own take on the Kay report. It proved, Bush said on the South Lawn of the White House, that "Saddam Hussein was a danger to the world." Bush cited Iraqi expenditures of billions and employment in

nefarious tasks of thousands of people over decades—material from the classified annex to Kay's remarks—to reiterate, "Saddam Hussein was a threat,
a serious danger." A cynic might say the justification for the invasion of Iraq
had now become what Saddam had done in distant past decades.

The adage in bureaucratic politics is that where you stand depends on
where you sit. In November 2003, David Kay still claimed that the public
misunderstood the aluminum tubes issue, that the United States *knew* Iraq
used tubes for rockets but that increasingly precise specifications for tubes
ordered after 1999 (and never delivered) could have been for uranium enrichment. Kay also made the most of Iraqi negotiations with North Korea
on missile imports, about which more had been discovered (but still no de-
liveries), and research for alleged biological weapons at an agricultural facility.
On the other hand, Kay admitted Baghdad had had no plant that actually
could use aluminum tubes in a nuclear program, no evidence of chemical
weapons production, and evidence from prisoner interrogation that most
Iraqi troop units thought only other units, not their own, had chemical weapons. Kay insisted that Iraq Survey Group resources, particularly translators
and intelligence analysts, were not being diverted to cope with the continuing
guerrilla insurgency.

The Bush people have gone on the defensive because the stakes are
high and their manufactured version of Saddam's threat has come unglued.
Colin Powell appeared in the *Washington Post* on October 7 to reiterate Kay's
discoveries of dozens of "activities"—again those microentities, "program-
related activities"—that might add up to programs someday but in Powell's
view were already current threats to the United States. He brought back the
mobile biological weapons plants, and his finishing flourish recalled an assertion that had been troubling when Powell made it the first time, in Iraq in
September. There the secretary of state traveled to the village of Halabja,
sorely beset by Saddam's ethnic cleansing during the Iran-Iraq war. Powell
said that what Saddam had done at Halabja justified the American war on
Iraq, and after the Kay report, his mention of the village invoked that statement. This formula followed the logic Bush had used with the Kay report—

Saddam could be attacked for what he had done in the past. Powell went one better—actions taken in the past by the adversary against a third party could justify war in the present.

Almost immediately President Bush began one more of his coordinated message offensives. Condi Rice kicked it off with a speech in Chicago on October 8. George Bush followed up with a speech the following day. Vice President Cheney spoke on the 10th at the Heritage Foundation in Washington. Cheney's speech, designed as the roundhouse punch of the trio, amounted to an aggressive defense of the concept of preventive war. The vice president's rhetoric, hard-line on Iraq from almost the beginning, remained crusty through the summer and fall after the invasion. Just a few weeks before, in his first television appearance since March (when he charged Saddam with "reconstituting" nuclear weapons), Cheney had brought back the claim that there had been a terrorism meeting in Prague between Iraqi agents and a key Bin Laden operative. That was an assertion that had since become so threadbare that even Paul Wolfowitz had disowned it. President Bush felt obliged to refute it himself. At a photo opportunity prior to a lobbying session with congressmen, President Bush was asked about the Cheney remark and answered, "No, we've had no evidence that Saddam Hussein was involved with September the 11th." By then, Bush had gotten plenty of political mileage from the assertion. Similarly, on January 8, 2004, Secretary of State Colin Powell came to the same admission. Powell told a room full of reporters, "You know, I have not seen smoking gun, concrete evidence about the connection, but I think the possibility of such connections did exist." That a *possibility* existed was a far cry from Powell's declaration at the UN that Iraq's denials of ties with Al Qaeda were "simply not credible." The secretary's further assertion in January 2004 that it was "prudent" to take the Saddam–Al Qaeda alliance into account amounted to a declaration that suppositions can be used to justify war.

Driven to the brink of frustration by the evaporation of their case against Iraq, the Bush people cannot bring themselves to concede error. Powell's news conference was the occasion for questions on a new report from the Carnegie Endowment for International Peace, which systematically critiqued the Iraq NIE and the secretary's UN presentation. Powell responded by invoking the extensive preparation of his UN text as assurance of its accuracy, then worked up to the declaration that, "The fact of the matter is, Iraq did have weapons of mass destruction, and programs for weapons of mass destruction." The statement, of course, is true only for the period of the Gulf war and just afterwards, more than a decade earlier.

Vice President Richard Cheney, who continues wedded to his own agenda, is the paradigm example of refusal to admit any mistake. Although he has made similar statements since, Cheney's speech at the American Enterprise Institute (AEI) is a good illustration. The institute, where Lynne Cheney works, is another conservative Washington think tank where the vice president could get a friendly audience. While the AEI speech is a little bit of a throwback in terms of our chronology, in this talk Cheney employs many of the same points as in his later address to the Heritage Foundation, the vice president's most recent major presentation. In addition, at AEI Cheney chose to use the CIA's original National Intelligence Estimate to underpin his arguments. This affords an opportunity to comment directly on the estimate and how it looked a year out from the original predictions.

document 9. *Cheney's Remarks.*

For Immediate Release
Office of the Vice President
July 24, 2003

Vice President's Remarks on War on Terror at AEI

12:13 P.M. EDT

THE VICE PRESIDENT: Good morning. Please. Thank you very much, and good afternoon to all of you. It's a pleasure to be back at AEI, where I spent a considerable period of time, and among so many friends. AEI, of course, is home to some of our nation's most distinguished scholars - one of whom also serves as the scholar in residence at the Naval Observatory. (Laughter.) If you think Lynne gives good lectures here, you should stop over at our house sometime. (Laughter.)

But I do want to thank Danielle Pletka for her introduction this afternoon, and I want to thank all of you for being here. And I bring good wishes to all of you from President Bush, who spoke to your annual dinner in February. In his remarks that evening, the President said that the United States "must look at security in a new way, because our country is a battlefield in the first war of the 21st century". For the last 22 months, the United States has been fighting this war across the globe. We have seen many challenges, and many victories. Those victories have come exactly as President Bush said they would - sometimes in pitched battle; sometimes in the stealth of special operations; sometimes in sudden, decisive strikes -- like the one witnessed two days ago by the late Uday and Qusay Hussein.

1. This worldwide campaign began after the attacks of September 11th, 2001, a watershed event in the history of our nation. We lost more people that morning than were lost at Pearl Harbor. And this was the merest glimpse of the violence terrorists are willing to inflict on this country. They desire to kill as many Americans as possible, with the most destructive weapons they can obtain. They target the innocent as a means of spreading chaos and fear, and to shake our national resolve. This enemy holds no territory, defends no population, is unconstrained by rules of warfare, and respects no law of morality. Such an enemy cannot be deterred, contained, appeased, or negotiated with. It can only be destroyed, and that's the business at hand.

For decades, terrorists have attacked Americans - and we remember every act of murder, including 17 Americans killed in 1983 by a truck bomb at our embassy in Beirut; and 241 servicemen murdered in their sleep in Beirut; an elderly man in a wheelchair, shot and thrown into the Mediterranean; a sailor executed in a hijacking; two of our soldiers slain in Berlin; a Marine lieutenant colonel kidnapped and murdered in Lebanon; 189 Americans killed on a PanAm flight over Scotland; six people killed at the 1993 World Trade Center bombing; 19 military personnel killed at the Khobar Towers; 12 Americans killed at our embassies in East Africa; 17 sailors murdered on the USS Cole; and an American diplomat shot dead in Jordan last year.

2. All of these were terrible acts that still cause terrible grief. Yet September 11th signaled the arrival of an entirely different era. We suffered massive civilian casualties on our soil. We awakened to dangers even more lethal - the possibility that terrorists could gain weapons of mass destruction from outlaw regimes and inflict catastrophic harm. And something else is different about this new era: Our response to terrorism has changed, because George W. Bush is President of the United States. For decades, terrorists have waged war against this country. Now, under the leadership of President Bush, America is waging war against them.

3. Our strategy in the war on terror is based on a clear understanding of the enemy, and a clear assessment of our national interest. Having lost thousands of Americans on a single morning, we are not going to answer further danger by simply issuing diplomatic protests or sharply worded condemnations. We will not wait in false **4.** comfort while terrorists plot against innocent Americans. We will not permit outlaw states and terror groups to join forces in a deadly alliance that could threaten the lives of millions of Americans. We will act, and act decisively, before gathering threats can inflict catastrophic harm on the American people.

From the first hour, we've known that the war on terror would be long and difficult. It would test our resolve, demand many sacrifices - above all, from the fine young men and women who defend this country.

The skill and courage of our military have brought a series of major successes in this war. With the best of allies at our side, America took the battle directly to the terrorists hiding in Afghanistan. The Afghan people have reclaimed their country from a depraved regime, and the violent rule of the Taliban has been ended forever.

America and our allies have continued the relentless pursuit of the global terror network. Of those directly involved in organizing the September 11th attacks, many are now in custody or confirmed dead. The leadership of al Qaeda has sustained heavy losses. We must recognize, however, that terrorism is a long-term challenge, and fighting terrorism will require a long-term commitment. The loose and decentralized networks of terrorism are still finding recruits, still plotting attacks. A hateful ideology, which defiles a great religion, has taken root in many parts of the world. Terrorists have conducted attacks since September 11th in Bali, Mombassa, Casablanca, and Riyadh. The terrorists intend to strike America again. Yet no one should doubt the intentions of our nation: One by one, in every corner of the world, we will hunt the terrorists down and destroy them.

5. In Iraq, we took another essential step in the war on terror. The United States and our allies rid the Iraqi people of a murderous dictator, and rid the world of a menace to our future peace and security.

6. Events leading to the fall of Saddam Hussein are fresh in memory, and do not need recounting at length. Every measure was taken to avoid a war. But it was Saddam Hussein himself who made war unavoidable. He had a lengthy history of reckless and sudden aggression. He bore a deep and bitter hatred for the United States. He cultivated ties to terrorist groups. He built, possessed, and used weapons of mass destruction. He refused all international demands to account for those weapons.

Twelve years of diplomacy, more than a dozen Security Council resolutions, hundreds of UN weapons inspectors, and even strikes against military targets in Iraq - all of these measures were tried to compel Saddam Hussein's compliance with the terms of the 1991 Gulf War cease-fire. All of these measures failed. Last October, the United States Congress voted overwhelmingly to authorize the use of force in Iraq. Last November, the UN Security Council passed a unanimous resolution finding Iraq in material breach of its obligations, and vowing serious consequences in the event Saddam Hussein did not fully and immediately comply.

7. When Saddam Hussein failed even to comply then, President Bush, on March 17th, gave him and his sons 48 hours to leave Iraq. Saddam's decision to defy the world was among the last he made as the dictator of that country.

I have watched for more than a year now as President Bush kept the American people constantly informed of the dangers we face, and of his determination to confront those dangers. There was no need for anyone to speculate what the President was thinking; his words were clear, and straightforward, and understood by friend and enemy alike. When the moment arrived to make the tough call - when matters came to the point of choosing, and the safety of the American people was at stake - President Bush acted decisively, with resolve, and with courage.

8. Now the regime of Saddam Hussein is gone forever. And at a safe remove from the danger, some are now trying to cast doubt upon the decision to liberate Iraq. The ability to criticize is one of the great strengths of our democracy. But those who do so have an obligation to answer this question: How could any responsible leader have ignored the Iraqi threat?

Last October, the Director of Central Intelligence issued a National Intelligence Estimate on Iraq's Continuing Programs of Weapons of Mass Destruction. That document contained the consensus judgments of the intelligence community, based upon the best information available about the Iraqi threat. The NIE declared -- quote: "We judge that Iraq has continued its weapons of mass destruction program, in defiance of UN Resolutions and restrictions. Baghdad has chemical and biological weapons, as well as missiles with ranges in excess of UN restrictions. If left unchecked, it probably will have a nuclear weapon during this decade." End quote.

9. Those charged with the security of this nation could not read such an assessment and pretend that it did not exist. Ignoring such information, or trying to wish it away, would be irresponsible in the extreme. And our President did not ignore that information - he faced it. He sought to eliminate the threat by peaceful, diplomatic means and, when all else failed, he acted forcefully to remove the danger.

10. Consider another passage from last October's National Intelligence Estimate; it reported -- quote: "all key aspects - the R&D, production, and weaponization - of Iraq's offensive [biological weapons] program are active and that most elements are larger and more advanced than they were before the Gulf War." End quote.

Remember, we were dealing here with a regime that had already killed thousands of people with chemical weapons. Against this background, to disregard the NIE's warnings would have been irresponsible in the extreme. And our President did not ignore that information - he faced it, and acted to remove the danger.

11. Take a third example. The NIE cautioned that quote: "Since inspections ended in 1998, Iraq has maintained its chemical weapons effort, energized its missile program, and invested more heavily in biological weapons; in the view of most agencies, Baghdad is reconstituting its nuclear weapons program." End quote.

Here again, this warning could hardly be more blunt, or disturbing. To shrug off such a warning would have been irresponsible in the extreme. And so President Bush faced that information, and acted to remove the danger.

12. A fourth and final example. The National Intelligence Estimate contains a section that specifies the level of confidence that the intelligence community has in the various judgments included in the report. In the NIE on Iraq's weapons of mass destruction, the community had "high confidence" in the conclusion that "Iraq is continuing, and in some areas expanding, its chemical, biological, nuclear and missile programs contrary to U.N. Resolutions." The Intelligence Community also had high confidence in the judgment that - and I quote: "Iraq could make a nuclear weapon in months to a year once it acquires sufficient weapons-grade fissile material." End quote.

Ladies and gentlemen, this is some of what we knew. Knowing these things, how could we, I ask, have allowed that threat to stand?

13. These judgments were not lightly arrived at - and all who were aware of them bore a heavy responsibility for the security of America. When the decision fell to him, President Bush was not willing to place the future of our security, and the lives of our citizens, at the mercy of Saddam Hussein. And so the President acted. As he said in the announcement of military action: "We will meet that threat now, with our Army, Air Force, Navy, Coast Guard and Marines, so that we do not have to meet it later with armies of firefighters and police and doctors on the streets of our own cities."

Critics of the liberation of Iraq must also answer another question: what would that country look like today if we had failed to act? If we had not acted, Saddam Hussein and his sons would still be in power. If we had not acted, the torture chambers would still be in operation; the prison cells for children would still be filled; the mass graves would still be undiscovered; the terror network would still enjoy the support and protection of the regime; Iraq would still be making payments to the families of suicide bombers attacking Israel; and Saddam Hussein would still control vast wealth to spend on his chemical, biological, and nuclear ambitions.

All of these crimes and dangers were ended by decisive military action. Everyone, for many years, wished for these good outcomes. Finally, one man made the decision to achieve them: President George W. Bush. And

14. the Iraqi people, the people of the Middle East, and the American people have a safer future because Saddam Hussein's regime is history.

Having now liberated Iraq, the United States and our allies are determined to see all our commitments through. The leader of the Coalition Provisional Authority, Ambassador Paul Bremer, was at the White House yesterday and to brief us on the progress that the Coalition Provisional Authority is making. Nineteen nations now have provided more than 13,000 troops to help stabilize Iraq - and additional forces will soon arrive. In the relief and reconstruction effort we are renovating schools, and restoring basic services. Coalition authorities are training Iraqi police forces to help patrol Iraqi cities and villages, and will soon establish a new civilian defense force. Iraq will also have its own new army - a military force that defends the Iraqi people instead of bullying and terrorizing them. A governing council of Iraqis, recognized by the United Nations, is now operating, naming ministers, and drawing up a budget for the country. All major cities in Iraq now have municipal councils. The process of drafting a constitution will soon be underway, and this will prepare the way eventually for elections.

We still have many tasks to complete in Iraq, and many dangers remain. There are still some holdouts of the regime, joined by terrorists from outside the country, who are fighting desperately to prevent progress of any kind for the Iraqi people. These killers are being systematically dealt with, as we saw in Mosul on Tuesday. That action also showed the great skill and bravery of our men and women serving in Iraq today. America is proud of all the men and women serving and sacrificing in this cause - and they will have all the resources they need to complete the vital work that we've asked them to do.

Our ongoing mission is not easy, but it is essential for our security and for the peace of the world. We will help the Iraqi people to build a free, sovereign, and democratic nation. That free nation will stand as an example to the entire Middle East, proving that freedom and the hope of peace have far more power and appeal than ideologies of hate and terror. And a more peaceful, stable Middle East will contribute directly to the security of America and our friends.

The United States of America has been called to hard tasks before. Earlier generations of Americans defeated fascism and won the long twilight struggle against communism. Our generation has been given the task of defeating the purveyors of terrorism, who are a direct threat to our liberty and our lives. We will use every element of our national power to destroy those who seek to do us harm. But, as in the past, we will do far more than merely defeat our enemies. In Afghanistan and Iraq and in other places where tyranny has been a fertile breeding ground for terror, we will help those who seek to build free, more tolerant, and more prosperous societies.

America's commitment and generosity in rebuilding ravaged lands in Europe and Asia was a hallmark of our foreign policy in the 20th century. It was a good investment for America then -- it is just as wise now. We do this not only because it is right, but because it is essential to our own security, the security of our friends and allies, and to our eventual victory in the war against terrorism. Our soldiers serving so bravely in Iraq and Afghanistan today know they are ensuring a safer future for their own children and for all of us.

In the 22 months since that clear September morning when America was attacked, we have not lost focus, or been distracted, or wavered in the performance of our duties. We will not rest until we have overcome the threat of terror. We will not relent until we have assured the freedom and security of the American people.

Thank you. (Applause.)

END 12:30 P.M. EDT

26 Hoodwinked

Cheney Speech Comments

1. Vice President Cheney's mention of Pearl Harbor is certainly intended to evoke the first moments and days after the September 11 attacks, when these comparisons were widely bruited about in the media. But his remarks assume the linkage between terrorism and Saddam Hussein's Iraq, which has previously been shown to have been contrived from twisted intelligence and biased defector sources.

2. Cheney's specter of terrorists getting weapons of mass destruction from "outlaw regimes" joins together two very different issues. The general problem of terrorism is real enough, but "outlaw regimes" are an invented category. No international body or other authoritative source has established any list of nations on this globe that are generally accepted outlaws. George Bush himself designated an "Axis of Evil" and put Iraq on that list. By Cheney's logic, the Bush administration can unilaterally determine a list of outlaw countries that must then be overthrown in order to prevent a (hypothetical) transfer of weapons to terrorists. This logic would require an endless series of wars. The facts that Iraq in the end possessed no such weapons that could have gotten to terrorists, and that the coalition invasion created incentives for the type of transfers Cheney holds out as the danger here, only sharpen this point.

3. Whether Bush administration strategy has been based on a clear understanding of the enemy is debatable. Note that in the months *after* the success of the invasion, the Bush people have not even been able to identify the composition of the Iraqi resistance.

4. As many foresaw, the Bush strategy seems to have driven "outlaw states" and terror groups into a collusion that did not exist prior to the U.S. attack on Iraq.

5. That the invasion of Iraq was an "essential step in the war on terror" assumes the validity of the intelligence, which we have found flawed, plus the logic of the Bush strategy, which is debatable.

6. The stipulation that "every measure was taken to avoid a war" is necessary to forestall the charge that the Bush administration engineered this conflict, that is, mounted a deliberately aggressive war. It is quite plausible to argue that nothing Saddam Hussein could have done would have avoided this war, the opposite of what Cheney claims here.

7. The language of this sentence is crafted to suggest that the world was united in support of the American invasion, that there was some sort of a UN mandate. There was no international authority for this action.

8. Here the vice president attempts to evade responsibility for the Bush administration's calculations. There were a number of ways to have responded to the situation in Iraq, beginning with distinguishing accurately between long-term security problems and clear and present dangers. A responsible leader could have dealt with the Iraqi threat through the UN inspection regime, already in place, which would have made the development and production of actual Iraqi weapons almost impossible, and which the United States pushed out of the way in order to conduct its invasion.

9. The reference to the National Intelligence Estimate (NIE) on Iraq is highly disingenuous here. Vice President Cheney uses the very existence of the estimate to suggest a threat upon which the United States had to act, in spite of the fact that the NIE was created at the behest of Congress and of so little interest in the White House that, by the White House's own admission, the national security adviser did not bother to read it.

10. Vice President Cheney's lead point reverses the administration's prewar arguments, which led with the supposed nuclear threat. The specific reference, to a chemical and biological program "larger and more advanced" than before the Gulf War, was a mistake in the NIE. All the UN inspections and the postwar U.S. inspections as well, including the Iraq Survey Group, failed to uncover a program of any such dimension. Even the Kay report's mention of hidden documentation and small labs concealed within the Iraqi intelligence service is very far from the dimensions of the Iraqi programs in 1990, the time of the Gulf War. Worse, by July 2003, when Richard Cheney made these remarks, *the Bush White House knew* that the NIE had been in error. Having pressured the CIA and intelligence community to exaggerate in the direction the Bush people wanted, Cheney here is saying that President Bush may be excused from making this war because he did so based on an innocent reliance on the intelligence provided. The truth is that the administration's reliance on intelligence was for political purposes. Details of the intelligence had little importance save for operational military planning.

11. As already related, the NIE had explicitly acknowledged that its access to information had deteriorated since 1998, which ought to have raised an automatic red flag regarding observations for the interval since then. Cheney also cites the NIE assertions regarding Iraqi nuclear weapons *without* noting the dissent from the State Department, or the less-than-unanimous view of the U.S. nuclear experts at the Department of Energy.

12. Cheney continues his practice of telling only part of the story when he gets to the "confidence levels" in the NIE. He emphasizes the threat—Iraq could make a

nuclear weapon in less than a year *if* it had everything necessary to produce such a thing, *but* the NIE had moderate confidence that Iraq *did not have those things.* The actual consensus was that Iraq *might* attain a nuclear capability between 2007 and 2009. The NIE also admitted U.S. intelligence had little confidence as to when Saddam might actually use weapons of mass destruction, whether he might stage attacks on the U.S. homeland, or whether he might give weapons to terrorists. These parts of the NIE undercut the picture of threat the Bush administration wanted to present. The text of the NIE's discussion of Iraqi nuclear weapons remains classified at this time, but it should contain some language on the difference between obtaining sufficient fissile material for a nuclear device, constructing one, and actually creating a deliverable weapon. The latter is a lot more technically demanding as an application, and it is by no means clear that the "within one year" projection in the estimate's worst case actually took this difficulty into account.

13. As the entire story of the Iraqi threat makes clear, the lives of Americans and the future security of this country were never at stake in the troubles with Iraq.

14. It is also not clear that the American people have a safer future because Saddam Hussein is gone. The anti-American forces unleashed by the Bush administration's actions may be more damaging to American interests than anything contemplated by the Saddam regime.

Frying Pan or Fire

By the time Vice President Cheney gave his speech at the American Enterprise Institute, Americans were beginning to catch on to the Bush administration's game. The Cheney speech seems designed as a gambit to shore the situation up by cramming the Iraq debate back into the box of Bush's original rhetoric. But by July 2003, that rhetoric had lost its menace. Saddam, now overthrown, could be no impediment to searching out the proscribed weapons. On the day Cheney spoke, the searchers had had longer to look than the United States had permitted UN inspectors under Resolution 1441, and had found nothing. Worse, from the White House point of view, the American people were waking up to the costs of unilateral war: a messy, disorganized postwar occupation of Iraq, carried out and funded almost entirely by the United States. Casualties rose steadily, until American losses in the occupation exceeded those during the war.

In Great Britain, prime minister Tony Blair came under sustained criticism for following George Bush into the war. A major leak in the dike developed when the British began to question the evidence on which the war decision had been based. The British Parliament's foreign affairs committee conducted a formal inquiry into the decision, which focused on exactly how Blair's government had assembled the Iraq dossier it issued in September 2002. Parliament's intelligence and security committee proceeded with a separate investigation of the claims that had been made regarding Iraqi weapons of mass destruction. The most powerful charge in the dossier—alleging that Iraq could use its weapons of mass destruction within forty-five minutes—was shown to have been based on a single source, like much of the problematical intelligence the Bush people were using, and to have been taken out of its context (again as in the United States), which had applied only to battlefield control of (supposed) chemical and biological munitions. Like the Bush administration's pronouncements, the distorted claim had then been reiterated four times.

David Kelly, a British government scientist (and former UN weapons inspector) who was thought to be the source of television reports that the Iraq dossier had been "sexed up," died by his own hand in July 2003 even as Tony Blair was in the United States with President Bush defending their war decision to the public. Kelly had been brought before the foreign affairs committee and treated as a hostile witness once his name was revealed in the press. A judicial investigation of Kelly's death conducted by Lord Hutton became a further official inquiry into the creation of the Iraq dossier, as well as the way in which David Kelly was "outed," thus leading to Blair's being called for parliamentary testimony, and having Blair's role directly investigated.

Rendered on January 28, 2004, Lord Hutton's report could not have been more favorable to the Blair government. Aside from clearing Prime Minister Blair in the outing and subsequent death of David Kelly, the report simply took the government at its word on the intelligence dossier of September 2002. Lord Hutton found no excessive cabinet involvement in the creation of the dossier, and accepted the Secret Intelligence Service's assessment of the quality of its report on the forty-five minute claim, which is now said to have been based on a single source of unknown reliability but passed along by an intelligence service considered to be reliable. Hutton passed over the failure of dossier drafters to deal with the objections of the technical experts on the Defense Intelligence Staff. The Hutton report is widely seen by the British public as a whitewash and dismissed derisively in Western Europe. Tony Blair has admitted in Parliament that he was *not* aware of the forty-five minute claim pertained only to supposed Iraqi arrangements for tactical use of chemical weapons on a battlefield. Blair has created an independent panel to review British intelligence performance.

The chain of events in Britain had its own echoes in the United States, where developments eerily resembled the Blair controversy. Instead of the "Forty-five Minutes," in America the leading wedge would be the "Sixteen Words" in Bush's State of the Union address. Throughout the spring of 2003 a series of reports unraveled the Niger uranium claim and then others, including the aluminum tubes, the unmanned aerial vehicles, and more. On May 6 a column by Nicholas D. Kristof in the *New York Times* for the first time referred directly (though without using his name) to the Niger visit that ambassador Joseph Wilson had made in an effort to authenticate the charge that Saddam had sought uranium there. Other skeptical reports followed. The timing, on May 28, of the administration's release of the CIA/DIA paper on the Iraqi mobile biological weapons laboratory (p. 273) was intended to short-circuit the latest wave of criticism. Spokesman Ari Fleischer saw fit to argue, on May 29, that administration claims had been on the mark: "Rewind the tapes, and you'll see what the administration said before the war and you'll find a series of statements, all of which are valid." National security adviser Condoleezza Rice, appearing on the CBS television program *Face the Nation* on June 8, specifically denied having had knowledge of the forged documents: "We did not know at the time—maybe someone down in the bowels of the agency—but no one in high circles knew that there were doubts and suspicions that this might be a forgery." Rice did not say that she herself had been an addressee on a CIA memorandum that had helped get the Niger uranium story out of Bush's Cincinnati speech to the Veterans of Foreign Wars.

Observers questioned whether the president had been lying or merely exaggerating, and others raised the dangers of a Bush credibility gap. More leaks flowed. From undisclosed sources that must have been close to the White House came one leak that purported to show the CIA had never shared its doubts about the Niger uranium story. The counterleak from somewhere in the CIA promptly claimed the opposite. In the *New York Times* on June 13, Nicholas D. Kristof responded directly to Condi Rice's contention, reporting that CIA officers had reported their doubts both to Vice President Cheney's office, and to working levels on the National Security Council staff, which would have been Robert Joseph.

A number of the Democrats in Congress were not convinced by administration disclaimers and took the lead in pressing for clarification. On the Senate intelligence committee, vice-chairman Senator John D. Rockefeller IV of West Virginia called for a full-scale investigation. Later that month the committee agreed to an inquiry, with Democrats compromising by not terming the effort an investigation. California Democratic congressman Henry Waxman wrote to President Bush directly on June 2, and to security adviser Condi Rice on June 10, specifically questioning the forged documents and the claims in Bush's speech. Rather than answer, Bush used a White House photo opportunity that followed a Cabinet meeting to insist that attacking Iraq had been the "absolute right decision." Said the president, "Intelligence throughout the decade showed they had a weapons program. I am absolutely convinced that with time we'll find out they did have a weapons program."

The president then went on the offensive. Condi Rice supplied Bush the appealing phrase "revisionist history" to characterize critics' view of events. President Bush went ahead and sprinkled it liberally in his public appearances. In Elizabeth, New Jersey, on June 16: "This nation acted to a threat from the dictator of Iraq. . . . Now there are some who would like to rewrite history—revisionist historians is what I like to call them." Bush repeated the bulk of that speech in Annandale, Virginia, the next day, adding, "I know there's a lot of revisionist history now going on." A few days later he claimed that the intelligence services of many nations all agreed that Saddam had had weapons of mass destruction.

Within a couple of weeks, the rhetorical offensive collapsed. The agent of its demise was none other than Joseph Wilson. On July 6 the former ambassador went public with an article in the *New York Times* plus an interview in the *Washington Post*. In both he gave accounts of his trip to Niger and details regarding why he had been asked to look into the matter and what he had reported. The intelligence aspects of the Niger uranium story have already been presented (see pp. 186–98); what is important here is its political impact. As is classic in American political scandals, a whiff of hard information blows away a mountain of obfuscation. Almost immediately, new questions on the Bush administration's handling of the Iraqi intelligence arose widely.

At the time of the Wilson revelations, President Bush, about to leave for Africa on a state visit, initially treated the story as a minor one, leaving the issue to Ari Fleischer. On July 7, Fleischer took the line that the Wilson account was meaningless: "Well, there is zero, nada, nothing new here," except that Americans now knew who ambassador Wilson was. Fleischer was questioned on the relationship between the Niger of the story and the "Africa" of the State of the Union address, and the spokesman continued to maintain, using a double negative ("I see nothing that goes broader that would indicate that there was no basis to the President's broader statement"), that Bush's declaration had, in fact, been accurate. But Fleischer acknowledged that the Niger claim itself had been bogus, saying, "specifically on the yellow cake, the yellow cake for Niger, we've acknowledged that that information did turn out to be a forgery."

That night the White House provided a "senior Bush administration official" who made a statement in the name of the president that "knowing what we know now, the reference to Iraq's attempt to acquire uranium from Africa should not have been included in the State of the Union speech."

The following day Bush, by then in South Africa, inevitably faced questions about the latest developments but dismissed the reports as attempts to rewrite history. Colin Powell and Condi Rice also defended the State of the Union speech. Naturally, CIA sources insisted they had reported problems with the intelligence behind the "Sixteen Words" long in advance of the speech. On July 11, Dr. Rice insisted, "The CIA cleared the speech in its entirety," and maintained "there was even some discussion on that specific sentence." (Dr. Rice was actually talking about the Bush Cincinnati speech several months before the State of the Union, a fact admitted by the White House some days later, which raises real questions about revisionist history.) She continued, "If the CIA, the Director of Central Intelligence, had said, take this out of the speech, it would have been gone, without question." Rice went so far as to declare, "We have a higher standard for what we put in presidential speeches."

Dr. Rice referred directly to the now-notorious National Intelligence Estimate (NIE), saying that the dissenting footnote "is kind of 59 pages away from the bulk of the NIE." In fact, as seen earlier (p. 77) there was an abbreviated version of that dissent incorporated directly into the Key Judgments section of the paper. She also maintained that the CIA had been depending on British intelligence for statements on the uranium story in the U.S. estimate, a clear error since the CIA had itself asked the British to remove that material from their Iraq dossier.

Three times Rice insisted the White House had no knowledge of doubts about the uranium story. "If there were doubts about the underlying intelligence to that NIE," said the national security adviser in one of these sallies, "those doubts were not communicated to the President, to the Vice President, or to me."

Since Condoleezza Rice had been sent an explicit CIA memorandum expressing doubts regarding the presence of uranium claims in Bush's October Cincinnati speech, those assertions are demonstrably false. Further, because Rice herself alluded to the October speech in her presentation here, the assertion that doubts were never communicated is even more perplexing. The real question is whether the NSC staff ignored the doubts inadvertently or deliberately, not whether they were ever communicated.

Behind the scenes, furious activity was in progress, as the NSC staff insisted that George Tenet step up to the plate. At this point it must have seemed to the White House that if the CIA would take responsibility for the "Sixteen Words," George Bush would be off the hook. Director Tenet did what he was told. That same day the CIA issued a statement from Tenet that recognized "legitimate questions" over how the Africa uranium charge had gotten into the State of the Union address, acknowledged that the claim should never have gotten into the speech, proclaimed that "I am responsible for the approval process in my agency," and admitted that the CIA had approved the speech.

Damage control continued. Both Dr. Rice and Secretary Rumsfeld appeared on the Sunday morning talk shows on July 13. Rice must have been just off Air Force One returning from Africa. On the CBS show *Face the Nation*, she called the uranium charge a mistake about a single sentence: "And I frankly think it has been overblown." Rice went on to term as "ludicrous" the proposition that George Bush had taken the nation to war over the uranium error, conveniently omitting the role of that charge, and the similarly debatable one about the Iraqi aluminum tubes, as the central pillars of the administration's fear mongering that Saddam would have nuclear weapons within a year and would give them to terrorists. The rest of Rice's commentary—that the British had other evidence besides the bogus documents—has already been analyzed in the section above on the substance of the uranium charge. Donald Rumsfeld added a further extravagance: "There isn't anyone who's looked at all the intelligence that I know of who doesn't believe that the intelligence community is correct." At the White House, Ari Fleischer helpfully contributed: "There can be no doubt that Iraq pursued nuclear weaponry prior to the war."

During the same daily briefing where Fleischer made the statement just quoted, he was pressed on how President Bush felt about the CIA letting him down (in its supposed failure properly to consider the uranium charge text before Bush had actually delivered his State of the Union speech). Fleischer made it out that Bush, though not pleased, kept his eyes on the big picture. Not long afterwards, President Bush issued a statement in which he expressed full support for director Tenet and the CIA and considered the matter of the "Sixteen Words" closed.

But a wealth of unresolved issues kept the matter before the public, with the Bush people themselves adding fat to the fire. That same day, July 14, political columnist Robert D. Novak published a piece on the Joseph Wilson mission to Niger in which he exposed the ambassador's wife, CIA officer Valerie Plame, as "an agency operative on weapons of mass destruction."

Novak's article mentioned his sources had been two senior Bush officials. The timing of the article and the necessities of the writing cycle clearly suggest that Novak had to have come by his information in the period of intense questioning of the Bush people on the "Sixteen Words." The nature of Plame's outing—exactly analogous to the sudden outing of David Kelly in Great Britain—can only be read in the context of the war of leaks that had been going on among the White House, the CIA, and the Pentagon over the uranium charges in the Bush speech. The Plame outing certainly would have a chilling effect on CIA personnel wanting to defend their agency by putting out any more information that refuted White House efforts to shift blame onto them.

Under the Intelligence Identities Protection Act passed during the Reagan administration, it is a felony for a government official (and, under certain circumstances, others) to identify an intelligence officer working undercover, as Valerie Plame had done for the CIA. Thus the Plame outing attached a potential criminal charge to the whole matter of the Iraq intelligence.

Within days, the inspector general of the CIA contacted the Department of Justice with regard to the Plame leak. Attorney General John Ashcroft's agency attempted to handle the matter as routine, waiting a few weeks, then sending back to the CIA a questionnaire designed to show whether its interest in an inquiry was a serious one. The CIA responded affirmatively. Presidential press secretary Scott McClellan was asked about the leak on July 22 and again in mid-September, replying that no one in the White House had the authority to reveal such information.

In the meantime, besides assuming responsibility for the "Sixteen Words," George Tenet's CIA statement had raised additional questions, about the vetting of Bush's speech, about the NIE, and about the specific intelligence issues of the uranium charge. Tenet did not say specifically that *he* had approved Bush's draft speech, only that he held responsibility for a process that had vetted the text. Tenet's statement also did not say that the CIA had seen the speech, only "portions" of it. And on the NIE, director Tenet mentioned that the CIA had never briefed Congress on the uranium issue, even though senators knew that the CIA's Robert Walpole had been questioned about it after Tenet himself had departed one of the briefings. Walpole had reportedly responded that his agency indeed had doubts about the uranium story.

In response to all of these discrepancies, on July 6, the congressional intelligence committees scheduled hearings and called CIA Director Tenet and other officers to testify. The details of the testimony—and the answering series of White House admissions—have been examined above, in the substantive analysis of the Niger uranium claim. Here the important thing is that George Tenet's five-hour hearing and his presentation of analyst Alan Foley revealed a story that could hardly be construed as being simply about CIA processes. The White House and NSC staff were centrally involved in the speech vetting and, as has been shown, in the presence of the Niger claim in Bush's speech. The "Sixteen Words" were in his speech because President Bush wanted to say them, not because of some silly CIA error.

When accounts of the CIA testimony appeared the following day, the participation of ambassador Robert Joseph of the NSC staff in vetting the speech would be revealed. What followed was another White House effort to chill opposition in Congress and elsewhere, which suggests the Plame outing was part of a pattern, not an isolated excess. One of the senators present at the Tenet hearing who had spoken critically of the President to the press afterward was Democrat Richard Durbin of Illinois. He had said that as important as were Tenet's remarks was the question of what individual or group had been so adamant on including this language in the speech, essentially that all roads led to 1600 Pennsylvania Avenue. When the CIA testimony was reported, White House press secretary Scott McClellan denounced Durbin's comments to the press as attempts at self-justification by someone who had opposed the Iraq war. In fact, Durbin had had an intense interest in the Iraq intelligence and had been among those most actively pushing to get the CIA to produce a National Intelligence Estimate on Iraq. Durbin had subsequently voted against President Bush's resolution, but that had no place in the debate over the State of the Union speech and its "Sixteen Words." Reacting to his comments about the CIA testimony, according to

Durbin, the White House press office floated a rumor that other senators wanted Durbin removed from the intelligence committee because he had leaked classified information. What had been leaked? The name of Robert Joseph and the number 550 for sites in Iraq on the list for weapons of mass destruction inspection. In fact, the number of sites had been revealed officially weeks earlier, and the name of NSC staffer Joseph was hardly classified. Durbin denies having been the one to reveal it in any case.

The White House responded to the State of the Union testimony with public comment as well. President Bush took the podium with a statement while meeting with prime minister Tony Blair on July 18. There Bush said he took responsibility not for the "Sixteen Words," but for making war, "Because the intelligence—not only our intelligence but the intelligence of this great country [Great Britain] made a clear and compelling case that Saddam Hussein was a threat to security and peace."

This same day the "senior administration official" whose job included supervising the presidential speechwriters, whom we have reason to believe was Andrew Card, gave an extensive press conference in an effort to defuse the situation. Here the White House admitted that Robert Joseph had handled the White House side of the State of the Union speech under deputy security adviser Stephen Hadley, declassified the Key Judgments section of the actual Iraq NIE, and made other assertions regarding the drafting of the State of the Union speech and the "Sixteen Words" (see p. 165). It was not until after this press conference that speechwriter Michael Gerson and deputy security adviser Hadley, we are told, discovered CIA memos in their files confirming that the agency *had* faulted the Niger uranium claim months before the State of the Union. That and continuing controversy forced the White House to present Hadley at a press conference of his own on July 22.

Public reception of the Bush team's latest version of events proved less than enthusiastic despite all the new details and an effort by Stephen Hadley to become the latest person to "take responsibility" for the language in the State of the Union address. The *Washington Post* headlined its analysis of the situation, "WHY THE COMMANDER IN CHIEF IS LOSING THE WAR OF THE 16 WORDS." At a news conference on July 30, Bush was asked first whether the intelligence on Saddam's links with Al Qaeda had been exaggerated—he fudged on his answer—and later, since he speaks so frequently about accountability, "Why is Dr. Condoleezza Rice not being held accountable for the statement that your own White House has acknowledged was a mistake in your State of the Union?" The president was asked about his personal responsibility as well.

"I take personal responsibility for everything I say, of course. Absolutely. I also take responsibility for making decisions on war and peace. And I analyzed a thorough body of intelligence—good, solid, sound intelligence that led me to come to the conclusion that it was necessary to remove Saddam Hussein from power. . . . Dr. Condoleezza Rice is an honest, fabulous person, and America is lucky to have her service. Period."

But the continuing inability of the weapons searchers to produce any evidence of Baghdad's arsenal of mass destruction belied the increasingly shrill pronouncements. President Bush went from claiming (at the end of May) that the weapons had been found, to asserting (over the summer) that the weapons would be found, to maintaining (in October) that some evidence for weapons *programs* was the same as the weapons that had been claimed. All the while the administration pleaded for the time to look they had not been willing to give the UN inspectors, and talked about miles of captured documents that, at some point in the future, would prove their case.

The intelligence committees of the House and Senate continued their inquiries into the Iraq war intelligence. By September, information coming out of the committees would be critical of the Bush administration's version of the Saddam threat. Ambassador Joseph Wilson took his accounts of the Niger uranium story on the road and added charges about the outing of his wife by senior officials. Between August and September, opinion polls measuring public approval of Bush's handling of Iraq dropped eleven points, to a minority for the first time since before the war.

Through that same period, the Bush administration retreated on its throaty assertions that Saddam Hussein had been in league with Osama bin Laden. The first crack came on July 31, when a senior White House official was quoted saying, "I don't believe that the evidence was there to suggest that Iraq had played a direct role in 9/11." In early August, Paul Wolfowitz, asked in a radio interview when he began to believe that Saddam had been involved in the September 11 attacks, replied. "I'm not sure even now that I would say Iraq had something to do with it." Vice President Cheney tried to hold the line, as briefly mentioned previously. On September 14, during his first television appearance since the Iraq invasion, Cheney brought back the canard of the alleged meeting in Prague between Iraqi agents and bin Laden conspirators. While Cheney said that the United States had "never been able to develop anymore of that yet, either in terms of confirming it or discrediting it," the simple mention kept the charge live while openly ignoring the wealth of material that disproved it. Cheney had now become isolated on this issue. Don Rumsfeld on September 16 said of the Saddam-Osama link, "I've not seen any indication that would lead me to believe that." The following day President Bush delivered his own renunciation. Cheney's sally had been so blatant that his own boss had had to undercut him.

All of this happened before the Wilson affair went to white heat. In late September the Department of Justice initiated an investigation of the leak of the CIA officer Valerie Plame's name to the press. It quickly came into the open that Robert Novak had been only one of half a dozen journalists who had been offered this information before someone chose to print it. Ambassador Wilson also alleged that in the days *after* the original leak, high Bush officials—he named Karl Rove—had encouraged even more reporters to go after Wilson and Plame.

The way the investigation of the Wilson/Plame affair has been managed raises questions about the Justice Department's dedication in this matter. Attorney General John Ashcroft waited days to assign the task to his counterintelligence unit, headed by John Dion (the department's announcement of the probe, however, asserted that Dion had made the decision to investigate on his own authority, without consultation at higher levels). By contrast, Ashcroft almost immediately ruled out appointing a special counsel to handle the case outside routine channels. Confronted with a barrage of questions about that decision from reporters at an event on October 1, Ashcroft simply walked away. The decision effectively meant that Ashcroft himself, with close relations to the Bush White House, had the authority to issue (or deny) subpoenas in the case. Much less consequential legal inquiries into White House matters during the Clinton administration were consistently handed over to independent prosecutors. Though the statutory authorization for the prosecutors has since expired, the special counsels have some of the powers, including subpoena power, that formerly adhered to the prosecutors. Polls in the fall of 2003 showed that 80 percent of Americans wanted the leak investigation given to a special counsel.

One clear argument for a special counsel is urgency. In the Iran-Contra affair, NSC staffer Ollie North and his aide Fawn Hall took only a weekend to shred the key documents of a major conspiracy. In the Wilson affair, Justice Department interest in the leak became known on September 26. Justice delayed any formal notification of the White House for about seventy-two hours after the information became public, waited until the following morning to order White House staff to preserve all paper and electronic records involved in the inquiry, and ordered them turned over only on the evening of October 2. Ashcroft's department then went along when White House counsel Alberto R. Gonzales gave executive office employees until October 7 to produce the records. He held on to them himself for another two weeks for review purposes before turning over the documents. In other words, there was plenty of time to manipulate the records. Since obstruction-of-justice infractions turn on the moment when records are demanded or a matter becomes of issue, this lackadaisical performance at the very outset of the leak investigation probably made it impossible to sequester records that might identify suspects. Administration critics may suspect the procedure had been designed to attain exactly that goal.

Several individuals were suspects in the illegal leak of Valerie Plame's name. The most obvious was I. Lewis Libby on Vice President Cheney's staff. Libby was known to have been at the CIA on numerous occasions and to have met with Alan Foley's Weapons Intelligence, Nonproliferation, and Arms Control (WINPAC) center, which employed Plame. Since Cheney had initiated the inquiry that led WINPAC to ask ambassador Wilson to undertake the Niger mission, "Scooter" Libby was a logical recipient for the CIA's conclusions at the end of the exercise. When Wilson went public, too, it was Cheney's office he pointed to. Libby was a fierce defender, and he had both access to the information and motive. Karl Rove, mentioned by Wilson as a candidate to be frog-marched out of the White House, had somewhat less motive than Libby, and no obvious access to Plame's identity. Elliott Abrams has also been seen as a potential source for the leak. An NSC staffer for the Middle East and a Bush White House denizen with an Iran-Contra past, Abrams was a fierce partisan fighter but had little reason to know Plame. Pictured in press accounts as a possible culprit is Richard Perle, who may have had contact with Plame in his role with the Defense Policy Board. Certainly a fighter, Perle would not have hesitated to blow Plame's cover, but he is not known to have been directly concerned by the Niger uranium controversy.

The White House moved precipitately to declare itself innocent. On another of her Sunday talk show appearances, Condi Rice declared she knew nothing of any White House effort to scare Joe Wilson, essentially treating the matter as mere speculation. Scott McClellan told reporters he had spoken with Karl Rove, that it was ridiculous that Rove might be seen as the leaker, and later extended his denial to cover Elliott Abrams and Lewis Libby as well. George Bush's first understated comment came on September 30: "If there is a leak out of my administration I want to know who it is. And if the person has violated the law, the person will be taken care of." That morning Alberto Gonzales sent out his memo ordering cooperation with the investigators. On October 6, the president declared that he regarded the leak as a serious matter, but the next day took it back, commenting, "I have no idea whether we'll find out who the leaker is." Both Bush and McClellan sidestepped specific questions as to whether Karl Rove had told a certain reporter that Joseph Wilson's wife was fodder for public attack, and Scott McClellan went on to say that he had personally spoken not only to Rove but to Libby and Abrams, and it was "correct," as he answered the question of a reporter, that he was "saying categorically [they] were not the leakers or did not authorize the leak."

The Justice Department office conducting the leak investigation consists of about a dozen lawyers. Attorney General Ashcroft took extraordinary measures both to track this inquiry and prevent knowledge of it from reaching the public. He was briefed several times a week on progress, while ordering that the special agent in charge of the FBI's Washington field office, who supplies personnel for the investigators and is as a matter of course cognizant of all activities within his jurisdiction, was cut out of the proceedings. There were only a handful of FBI agents on the case through late October 2003, the number then swelling to a dozen. Officials working on the investigation were required to sign special nondisclosure agreements. From October to December the Justice Department's counterintelligence chief, John Dion, with thirty years at the agency (twenty-three in his current specialty) led the investigation and had three other prosecutors on staff. In December a fourth prosecutor came on board. By then interviews were in progress, several dozen by press accounts, and some key documents had surfaced, including one written at INR whose account of a key meeting prior to the Wilson mission was reportedly disputed at CIA. Suddenly, on December 30 John Ashcroft recused himself from the investigation, and the deputy attorney general appointed a special counsel to lead the inquiry. The new chief investigator, Patrick J. Fitzgerald, U.S. Attorney in Chicago, is reputed to be a bulldog, chasing down evidence and putting together clues with grim determination. Fitzgerald had previously had a key role in prosecuting terrorists connected with the Al Qaeda embassy bombings in Africa that took place in 1998.

McClellan's efforts to exclude Rove, Libby, and Abrams from the suspect list invited the investigators to examine how the White House had determined their innocence, according to John Podesta, a chief of staff under President Clinton who had faced similar investigations. Podesta also warned of the pitfalls in White House review of documents before handing them over to the investigation, and those of not taking the matter seriously. Podesta wrote: "The administration's handling of this incident is at best curious and at worst irresponsible." The Bush people hoped they had contained the damage, but a criminal investigation always contains dangers, and many actions invite charges of cover-up, where the administration's political vulnerability may be far more serious than its legal problems.

Attorney General Ashcroft's recusal suggests that the investigation of the leak designed to damage ambassador Joseph Wilson has entered a critical stage at which evidence is indeed implicating White House figures with whom Ashcroft has relationships. On the other hand the most recent reporting is that investigators have been circulating requests to individuals interviewed in the inquiry to release Robert Novak and other journalists from their pledges to protect sources for the stories that blew Valerie Plame's cover. This hints at a failed investigation, since the individuals involved can hardly be expected to give this permission.

The latest White House wriggle is that the leak, even if purposeful and if the revelation of Plame's name *is* a felony crime, may not have been culpable if the officials responsible were not aware of her status as a CIA undercover officer. However, the original Robert Novak article that named the CIA officer described her as an "operative." That term specifically connotes an agent or undercover officer, and Novak had it in his first mention, which suggests that the leakers were indeed fully aware of Plame's CIA status.

At this writing the investigation continues.

Just as the Wilson affair triggered a Justice Department investigation, David Kay came home with the Iraq Survey Group report finding no Iraqi weapons of mass destruction. With his rationale for making war in tatters, President Bush mounted one more full court press with the public. The White House Information Group had more work to do than ever. Papers claiming progress in the occupation after a hundred days, then following six months, contained extensive lists of accomplishments, while Bush, Cheney, Rice, and others hyped the progress much the same way they had once pushed their vision of the Iraqi threat. Paul Bremer, proconsul of the occupation, was pressed into service as a new voice acclaiming progress in Iraqi electricity generation, school openings, and more. George Bush devoted every one of his weekly radio speeches during October to the wonders of Iraq, supplementing the major speeches he and the others gave.

But the list of achievements pales next to those other lists, of dead Americans and coalition soldiers, of new bombings and attacks, and the estimates of uncounted, unlisted dead Iraqis. Good intentions expired in the car bombs detonated outside the Baghdad Hotel, where many of the senior U.S. commanders lived, the UN compound, the Jordanian embassy, mosques, police stations, and elsewhere. Promises of reconstruction money flowing from renewed oil shipments disappeared in the oil pipeline sabotage that broke the export chain. And appeals for foreign aid to finance Iraqi reconstruction floundered amid the global disunity created by the way Bush had gone to war.

The constant drumbeat of ambushes drove the occupation troops wild. The occupying army insisted it was equal to the task, while canceling withdrawal of troop units and sustaining unusually high rates of suicide and sickness, disturbing signs of disintegrating morale. Leaks continued—that the growing guerrilla resistance had been predicted by intelligence before the war, that economic experts had warned of difficulties in restarting the Iraqi oil industry, more. By the fall, President Bush would be forced to ask Congress for an additional $87 billion to pay occupation and reconstruction costs, on top of roughly $60 billion just for the war. Iraq suddenly did not seem so much of a success after all. In December it became known that chief weapons searcher David Kay planned to resign from his job with the Iraq Survey Group. Even by then no Iraqi weapons of mass destruction had been found.

Dr. Kay went ahead and resigned on January 23, 2004. Five days later he appeared before both the Senate Intelligence and Armed Services committees and gave testimony on the U.S. weapons search. "It turns out we were all wrong, probably, in my judgment," Kay related, in a complete retraction of both his own prewar writings and of the United States' claims about Saddam's weapons. Even under questioning by senators defending the Bush administration, Kay stuck to his statement that the Iraq Survey Group had found no evidence of any large Iraqi weapons stockpiles and precious little else. The alleged mobile weapons factories, claims about which Kay had earlier told BBC television interviewers were "premature and embarrassing" in an episode he saw as a "fiasco," the chief inspector now unequivocally declared had not been weapons plants at all. "It was like a death spiral," Kay separately told reporter James Risen of the *New York Times*, Iraqi weapons programs had degenerated into a "corrupted process." Before the Senate, Dr. Kay now accepted the Iraqi account that Baghdad had dismantled most of its programs in 1991 and 1995, destroying the stockpiles it could find, with the remaining infrastructure destroyed by bombing in 1998. The Iraqi nuclear program had not been resurgent. There was no evidence of any uranium purchase from Niger. Indications were that Iraq had rejected a sales pitch from another African country. Saddam had been much more concerned over the skills of the U.N. searchers than the U.S. had supposed. Kay advocated an investigation of the intelligence on Iraq by an independent commission.

Both Vice President Cheney and White House spokesmen initially reacted by once again demanding that no conclusions be drawn until weapons searchers had more time to complete their survey of Iraq, but the wind had now gone out of that sail. On February 2, Secretary of State Colin L. Powell offered a tepid defense of the war decision essentially based on his Gulf War experience and the impression that Saddam had had both the intention and capability to create the weapons, but conceded that "the absence of a stockpile changes the political calculus," in effect, "it changes the answer you get, the formula I laid out." On February 4, Donald Rumsfeld told Congress that Dr. Kay's conclusions had been simply a "hypothesis" and that Iraqi weapons might eventually be found.

George Tenet was driven to mount an extended defense of the intelligence in a speech at Georgetown University on February 6. After making the point that "in the intelligence business, you are almost never completely wrong or completely right," Tenet offered a commentary on the October 2002 Iraq national intelligence estimate. Leading with his strong suit—that the NIE's missile conclusions had been accurate—the CIA director proceeded to concede very little: the U.S. detected the development of unmanned aerial vehicles and "the jury is still out" on their purpose; that "we have additional data to collect and more sources to question" on Iraqi aluminum tubes; that although there was no consensus on the function of the alleged mobile biological agent plants, "everyone agrees they are not ideally configured . . . but could be made to work in either [that or a hydrogen gas production] mode," and that Saddam had the intention and capability to quickly convert civilian industry to chemical weapons production. Finessing the NIE's conclusion that Saddam had a chemical weapons stockpile of 100 to 500 tons, Tenet lowballed the intelligence projection by calling it "at least 100 tons," conceded

that no physical evidence for that stockpile had been found, and then, like
other Bush people, declared that "we need more time."

On the alleged Iraqi nuclear weapons program, where the Iraq NIE had
specified a half dozen reasons for its key judgment that the program was
resurgent, George Tenet now said "we do not know if any reconstitution
efforts had begun." Here, at least, the CIA director admitted, "we may have
overestimated the progress Saddam was making." But Tenet emphasized the
NIE's prediction of a 2007–09 timeframe for an Iraqi nuclear weapon, made
no mention of the "within one year" worst case projection (which is what
the Bush administration had emphasized), and further muddied the waters
by introducing new allegations that Iraqi scientists had told Saddam he could
have a nuke within 18 to 24 months once the fissile material was in hand
(still longer than the NIE's worst case). Director Tenet then proceeded to
minimize the whole issue of performance on Iraq by expanding the discussion
to encompass wider questions of proliferation and claims of progress in the
intelligence war against terrorism. He also left himself an out by terming his
conclusions about the intelligence "provisional."

President George W. Bush was no longer able to skirt the problems of
his administration's inflation of the intelligence in the wake of David Kay's
testimony. The report of the Senate Select Committee on Intelligence is expected to be made public within weeks. The House report will no doubt
follow. Shortly after Kay's appearance on Capitol Hill, President Bush let it
be known he would be amenable to an outside investigation of the Iraq
intelligence, which the administration had resisted fiercely for the better part
of a year. But Bush's solution involved a fresh effort to evade responsibility:
suddenly the failure was global by intelligence agencies the world over; the
focus would be a narrow technical one on the intelligence estimates rather
than Bush's use of them; and the inquiry, like George Tenet's speech, would
be extended to cover broad aspects of proliferation, limiting the effort it could
devote to the Iraq questions. On February 6, the same day White House
press spokesman Scott McClellan was summoned to appear before a federal
grand jury looking into the outing of Valerie Plame, President Bush signed
an executive order creating the independent commission and announced

most of its members. Even this carefully circumscribed inquiry was too much for some in the White House. While Bush stood to say that he wanted to know why "some prewar intelligence assessments by America and other nations . . . have not been confirmed," sitting at the side of the room were Condoleezza Rice, Andrew Card, and Alberto Gonzales. The video of the three advisers speaks volumes. Card looked up at the ceiling. Condi Rice, her face contorted into a grimace, stared at the floor. Gonzales stared straight ahead.

8

Iraq, Lies, and Videotape

George Bush's game of three-card monte has played out. Bush got his way in the short run, but we have hardly begun to pay the price. The occupation of Iraq has supplanted war against Baghdad as America's chief concern. In the wake of a guerrilla bombing offensive at Ramadan (a month of Muslim religious observance beginning in 2003 in late October), the co-alition occupation forces came under increased pressure to transfer their Arab language translators, area specialists, and others with the Iraq Survey Group to improve the intelligence support for the security effort. George Tenet has continued to plead with those congressional committees investigating the Iraq National Intelligence Estimate to wait and hear CIA's explanations upon com-pletion of its internal review led by Richard Kerr, but early in January 2004 Tenet broadened the scope of the Kerr panel's inquiry to include whether the CIA missed evidence that Iraq was dismantling its weapons programs. Not only is the intelligence in question, Bush's planning for the weapons search and especially for the postwar occupation has been revealed as pa-thetically inadequate. Bush's disputes with old allies have shaken the foun-dation of U.S. foreign policy and may threaten American ability to conduct a war on terrorism. The Bush NSC organization has flopped and has had to be revamped. The White House faces criminal investigation over the leak of a CIA clandestine officer's identity. The picture is hardly a success story, whatever George Bush would like to believe.

There are no winners from the Iraq mess. In what already seems like ancient history, Henry Kissinger had warned of the need for speed in his exhortations during Bush's year of war planning. "A military operation against Saddam Hussein cannot be long and drawn out," Kissinger wrote in January 2002, "If it is, the battle may turn into a struggle of Islam against the West." That July, as the debate heated up and political difficulty led George Bush to adopt his hoodwink strategy, Kissinger made his point again: "The longer military operations last, the greater the danger of upheavals in the region, dissociation by other nations, and American isolation." With the occupation of Iraq and guerrilla warfare there, the conditions Kissinger feared have come to pass.

The American people, subjected to a systematic effort to mislead, to frighten them into acquiescence, lost a measure of the checks and balances that hold back the dogs of war, and are still paying the price in blood and treasure for Bush's folly. We have been suckered into a Middle East maelstrom from which extrication may prove exceedingly difficult. The country has lost most of the global sympathy that sustained us in the days after the September 11 attacks. The Bush administration is no further along with its war on terrorism as a result of Iraq and is vulnerable for all the reasons noted above. The British government, Bush's main ally in the war, has emerged more vulnerable still. The coalition's military campaign in March-April 2003 was a victory, but diminished, perhaps negated, by the escape of Saddam and the ensuing guerrilla resistance. The eventual capture of Saddam Hussein on December 13, 2003, did not end the Iraqi resistance though it had some political impact in the United States. In Iraq the image of Americans as liberators never quite took root, then faded steadily, to be supplanted by one of U.S. troops as occupiers.

The Bush doctrine of preventive war also lost, for the nation will be doubly resistant to the next claim of near and present danger. The CIA and other intelligence agencies have been weakened through the corruption of their product by a White House intent on having its way. The Pentagon,

wanting to wipe away the "Vietnam Syndrome," is well on its way to confirming it.

The Iraqi people have suffered thousands of deaths, a summer of pri-
vation, and face an uncertain future with the occupation. The jury is out—
and will remain so for the foreseeable future—on whether political reform
and physical reconstruction will even be possible, much less generate the new
democracy the Bush people tout. Saddam Hussein, of course, has lost his
job, his sons, and may still lose his life, though that is of less concern. Those
who argued that the road to peace in the Middle East lay through Baghdad
are now in Baghdad, yet the Palestinian problem remains intractable as ever,
Saudi Arabia totters on the brink of revolution, and Syria (despite cooperation with the war on terror) is being inscribed on the White House enemies
list. The UN, whose authority was supposed to be strengthened (in the Bush
view) by a war fought to enforce its resolutions, has instead been weakened
by members initiating war without its sanction, and the flouting of a disarmament process those members had insisted be adopted.

Coalition governments will answer to their own peoples. In the United States
there is plenty of blame and responsibility to be shared. The hoodwinking
of America was no accident or coincidence. It was carefully orchestrated and
planned within the White House and National Security Council. President
George W. Bush is the culprit here, though he had powerful assistance. Bush
also bears responsibility for lumping together the issues of a complex world
in a simplistic vision of terrorism, accepting the myopic optimism of his lieutenants, not questioning their assumptions, not adequately overseeing the
formulation of national security policy, not devoting sufficient attention to
postwar planning, treating criticism as an obstacle rather than an invitation
to review policy, creating an atmosphere in which political retaliation against
critics was the preferred demonstration of loyalty, and playing politics with
national security. Worst of all, President Bush directly participated in the
deception, the effect of which was to initiate a war of aggression. Shortly
before the invasion took place, Bush's personal friend and ambassador to the
Czech Republic, Craig Stapleton, said of the president, "This is his Omaha

Beach." Perhaps Bush forgot—or never knew—how close Omaha Beach came to being a huge disaster.

Vice President Richard B. Cheney planned and carried out the hoodwinking of America. Cheney played a key role in getting Iraq to the top of the Bush agenda and keeping it there. The vice president made speeches and public statements that pressured those less dedicated to the enterprise to get on board, then participated actively in taking the enhanced message of threat to the American people. Cheney attacked UN weapons inspections in such fashion as to undercut their (less threatening) results, cast doubt on the possibility of disarmament, and falsely implicated Iraq in Al Qaeda terrorism. The vice president actively intervened with the CIA and U.S. intelligence to obtain data to further those purposes, and his staff worked to include the misleading intelligence at key stages of the deception, such as in the Colin Powell UN presentation in February 2003. Cheney also served as apostle for certain inaccurate allegations, most especially the claim of Iraqi–Al Qaeda contacts in Prague. The vice president, finally, attempted to prevent the hoodwinking from unraveling after the fact, continuing to allege major items in the bill of particulars of the deception long after they had been discredited.

Condoleezza Rice, national security adviser, helped plan the hoodwinking of America in her private conversations with the president, discussions at the National Security Council, and leadership role in the White House Information Group. She participated in the deception through speeches, in numerous television interviews, by putting her name to articles and papers to further the manipulation of political and public opinion, and by exerting direct pressure on a UN weapons inspection activity to ensure a preordained conclusion. Rice failed to ensure a flow of accurate intelligence to the president. Dr. Rice failed to manage the NSC staff and national security machinery, permitting allegations that could backfire on the president to make their way into a key presidential speech—*or* she made sure those allegations *would* make it into the speech. It is difficult to determine which of these interpretations is the more damaging. Rice also bears a measure of responsibility in the failures of the Iraq occupation, even prior to the fall of 2003 when President Bush gave her special responsibility in this area, in that the security adviser's deputy (Stephen Hadley) had charge of the interagency committee planning and implementing the effort, an effort Dr. Rice should have been monitoring all along.

Secretary of Defense Donald H. Rumsfeld contributed to the hoodwinking through his Pentagon press conferences, appearances before Congress, and public speeches. Rumsfeld also used subordinates such as Paul Wolfowitz and Douglas Feith to further the project, either through their remarks in public or, indirectly, by helping put pressure on the intelligence community. Rumsfeld bears responsibility for much of the current situation in Iraq. Intent on validating his concept for transformation of the U.S. military to a technology-centered, minimal human participation force, Rumsfeld insisted on plans for the Iraq invasion that, while sufficient to win the initial victory, were inadequate either to prevent the escape of major resistance forces to the underground or to enforce security in the aftermath that might have short-circuited resistance before it took hold. Rumsfeld also had the direct responsibility for U.S. occupation planning. The failures of the early months of the occupation go straight to him. Rumsfeld's insistence that he did not "do" guerrilla warfare, finally, contributed to a failure to recognize the resistance challenge during the interval necessary for that insurgency to become established.

Secretary of State Colin L. Powell furthered the hoodwinking of America most notably in his presentation before the UN Security Council in February 2003. But Powell, whose instincts were better than those of his colleagues, made a number of other contributions also. He reiterated on many occasions inaccurate items in the litany of charges against Iraq, working up to the December 2002 "fact sheet" that used the litany to discredit Baghdad's declaration to UN weapons inspectors. The Bureau of Intelligence and Research of Powell's State Department, one of the few entities in the U.S. government to emerge from the Iraq mess with an untarnished, even heroic, reputation, repeatedly cautioned the secretary against many of the scare items. Powell ignored those warnings so frequently that his actions can only have been deliberate.

Director of central intelligence George J. Tenet contributed to the hoodwinking of America by failing to preserve the integrity of the intelligence process. Tenet, who even claimed in one statement that he *had* maintained that very integrity, buckled in several key instances and also succumbed to the temptations of policy relevance. In the workup of the Iraq National Intelligence Estimate, Tenet presided over an interagency review that gave short shrift to dissenting opinions. In the specific case of the alleged Iraqi nuclear program, director Tenet positively pushed the views of a single, nonspecialist analyst whose opinion furthered the deception over the weight of specialist technical opinion, and he avoided conducting a competent technical review of the dispute. In the case of the alleged links between Iraq and Al Qaeda, Tenet relied upon novel (and questionable) analytical techniques to accept a fringe Pentagon hypothesis with obvious policy-driven implications as analytical truth. In the case of the "Sixteen Words," Tenet failed to follow through on the CIA's negative position on the Niger uranium story when White House staff inserted it into a second speech, after forcing its deletion in the first. It is hard to decide whether the worse possibility is that George Tenet did not pay attention when the issue came up again with the State of the Union, or if the director had decided to throw in his lot with the White House cabal. Director Tenet also forthrightly failed to retract allegations about the supposed Iraqi weapons programs as they proved inaccurate, helping perpetuate the hoodwinking. Finally, in the aftermath of Bush administration officials blowing the cover of a CIA undercover officer, George Tenet failed to exert leadership at his agency by taking the initiative immediately to demand investigation and follow up by needling the Justice Department to get started. Instead Tenet left it to subordinate officials to make the request, and to routine procedures to move it along. Politically vulnerable in his job as a result of CIA intelligence failures prior to the September 11 attacks, Tenet's actions can be understood as an attempt to retain President Bush's confidence, but they did little for the integrity of the intelligence process. A former chief of the State Department intelligence bureau, Morton Abramowitz, makes the point quite directly: "Our intelligence analysis system has been wounded, its integrity made suspect at home and abroad."

Talk about litanies, this is a lengthy list of charges. They are real, however, not made up. Thanks to the miracles of modern technology, where videotape cameras are everywhere, and so much is broadcast in full or part, the hoodwinking of America is all on film. The burden of proof is on those who wish today to deny that they said what they did, in fact, say.

Americans have not only been hoodwinked, they have been shamed. Iraq did not attack the United States. Strip away the cant about Iraqi intentions—which was speculation by *Americans* (or British or whomever else)—and the Bush administration justification for the war comes down to stockpiles of Saddam's weapons of mass destruction. Reveal those stocks to have been mythical, and nothing remains. Except the jokes. "Smoking gun," that *bon mot* helpfully applied at an early date by Condi "Mushroom Cloud" Rice, became a joke among the American weapons searchers in Iraq after the invasion. In its 4th of July parade, the Maryland town Takoma Park included a contingent that conducted a "weapons search" of the audience with marchers carrying magnifying glasses and binoculars. For a time that summer, the top result on the Internet search engine "Google," when typing "weapons of mass destruction" as the subject, was a British-created site showing a seemingly genuine error message, "These Weapons of Mass Destruction cannot be displayed," along with the text "The weapons you are looking for are currently unavailable. The country might be experiencing technical difficulties, or you may need to adjust your weapons inspectors [*sic*] mandate." The tabloid newspaper *Weekly World News* reported in its August 19, 2003, issue that the weapons had been found: Saddam had bred killer dinosaurs, 3,600 eggs for which he had smuggled into the United States just before the invasion. The eggs were secreted in thirty-nine states just waiting to hatch a horrendous new *Jurassic Park*.

Behind the insouciance lay acute embarrassment. Americans do not like to think of themselves as aggressors, but raw aggression is what took place in Iraq. The march to war with Baghdad did not meet the constitutional or legal requirements for initiating war in the American political system. There was no declaration of war. For those who deem declarations obsolete, the congressional resolution (Public Law 107-243) permitted war to defend against the threat from Iraq, now known to be nonexistent, or to enforce all relevant UN resolutions. The Bush administration got Security Council Resolution 1441 based on a notion of the Iraqi threat, but approval for war under 1441 required a further Security Council resolution that the Bush people failed to achieve. The mandate from the U.S. Congress therefore *did not authorize war under Resolution 1441*. Short of that, the UN resolutions of the 1990s have to be invoked as basic documents. All those resolutions were about separating Saddam from his weapons of mass destruction. If Iraq had none, the basis for the resolutions disappears, save only for the inability of the UN to verify and certify that disarmament. Saddam truly paid a high price for his own deception, his unwillingness to show his hand and admit to having no weapons. In essence, the fact situation and the legal situation then diverge, leaving the thin reed of failure of the UN to certify Iraqi compliance as the sole basis for George Bush's ability to wage war.

In the murky darkness between Iraq's true status and the U.S. intelligence estimates lay the entire legal authority for conflict. (Given the Bush administration's pressure on the intelligence community to produce the views it wanted, and the administration's further exaggeration of what it got, so as to fuel its march to war, the underlying basis—the UN's failure to certify—can no longer be considered definitive.) Consequently there is at least an arguable proposition that President George W. Bush went beyond his powers in waging war on Iraq.

As with the war power in the American political system, so too there is a problem with the U.S. war on Iraq in international law. The most central element here is the UN Charter, Article 1 of which establishes its lead purpose as maintaining international peace and security. Article 2 of the Charter obligates members to settle their disputes by peaceful means and to refrain from the threat or use of force, and also explicitly commits member states and the UN itself *not* to intervene in matters that are essentially within the domestic jurisdiction of any nation. Three other articles of the Charter (39, 41, 42) permit the Security Council to determine the existence of a threat to peace and to decide on such nonmilitary and military action as may be necessary to enforce its decisions (hence the importance to the Bush administration of securing a Security Council approval for its Iraq invasion).

The Security Council never approved the Iraq war. Other Bush justifications—such as that Saddam was a bad man, that Saddam oppressed his own people, that Saddam used chemical weapons against Kurdish rebels and villages—are matters internal to Iraq in which use of force by the UN or member states is prohibited. There was no Iraqi revolution or civil war underway that might be deemed a threat to peace and security and give the world community grounds for action on that account. Article 51 of the UN Charter recognizes that nations have an inherent right to individual or collective self-defense—the *only* opening for President Bush and the reason Washington's pronouncements so carefully referred to "preemptive self defense."

However, self-defense implies defending against something or someone, and Iraq was not attacking the United States. "Preemption" implies acting even as the adversary's attack is in motion, which was not the case with Iraq. It is not admissible that a country may attack another with which it is at peace on the basis that, at some unspecified future time, that other nation might launch an attack. That is not preemption. Those were the precise conditions that obtained between the United States and Iraq. President Bush's invasion of Iraq was not a legitimate act of self-defense.

For the most part, aggressors strive to make others believe they act in self-defense. When Germany opened World War I in August 1914 with an invasion of Belgium, it began by asserting that it was responding to a (false) French entry into that same country. Japanese conquests in Manchuria and China in the 1930s started with staged bombings or shooting incidents Japan attributed to the adversary. In 1939, when Germany attacked Poland, that invasion too began with a staged incident in which it was made to seem that Polish troops had attacked a radio station in Germany. These efforts at shifting blame, especially Germany's deception over Belgium in 1914, are not very different from what George Bush did with Iraq in 2002–03.

In the American experience one needs to go as far back as 1898, and the beginning of the Spanish-American War, to find a case where the prelude to conflict was marked by such jingoistic posturing, though in that case the president was not the primary instigator of the inflamed rhetoric. A closer parallel, where a president was effectively the prime mover in triggering conflict, requires a journey back to 1845–48, when James K. Polk, crusading under the banner of "Manifest Destiny," confirmed the annexation of Texas by making war on Mexico. George W. Bush's gambits about disarming Iraq have an odd resonance with Polk's concessionary final offers to buy out Mexico's interests in what it considered sovereign territory. Talk today of American empire echoes a past that hardly encourages the globe to a benign view of American power. President George W. Bush has sown a whirlwind, and shown America to the world in a most miserly fashion.

Index

References to documents are in **boldface** type.

CORRECTION–Note 7 on page 78 should read as follows:

7. The NIE observes that 25,000 centrifuges would be capable of producing this amount of fissile material annually by 2007–09. Evidence on Iraqi industrial planning from CIA reports declassified in the mid-1990s indicates the task of reaching such a production base would be considerably more difficult than implied here. A January 1991 CIA report projected Baghdad's goal as attaining full production with cascades totaling 5,000 centrifuges by the late 1990s, yielding enriched uranium sufficient for four or five bombs a year. At the time of the Gulf War, the CIA believed Iraq had created exactly *one* centrifuge, the prototype. Iraq had already had difficulty supplying electricity for other components of its nuclear program (calutrons), and how it intended to power this array remains an unanswered question. Available portions of the 2002 NIE provide no information on the rate at which Iraq might be capable of manufacturing centrifuges, but the rate necessary to attain 25,000 machines exceeded the CIA's 1991 expectations by a factor of five, at a time when the agency assessed Iraq's economy as in decline and with Baghdad still starting from scratch on its reconstitution of a weapons program. How analysts could project a nuclear weapons capability even by 2007–2009, given these factors, is a mystery. United Nations inspectors in 1991 found Iraq had plans to complete a factory for producing centrifuges by the end of that year and expected to reach a 100-machine cascade by mid-1993 and a level of 500 centrifuges by early 1996–that is, an average production rate of 125 centrifuges per year. At that rate two hundred years would be required to reach 25,000 centrifuges.